Computer Studies

A Practical Approach

G. M. Croft F.B.C.S.
formerly Head of Computing
Knutsford County High School

HODDER AND STOUGHTON

LONDON   SYDNEY   AUCKLAND   TORONTO

British Library Cataloguing in Publication Data

Croft, G. M.
  Computer studies (BBC edition).
  1. Electronic digital computers
  I. Title
  001.64   QA76.5

  ISBN 0 340 37013 0

RML Basic edition first printed 1983
BBC Basic edition first printed 1985

Copyright © 1983 G. M. Croft

All rights reserved. No part of this publication may be reproduced or transmitted in any form or by any means, electronic or mechanical, including photocopy, recording, or any information storage or retrieval system, without permission in writing from the publisher.

Typeset in 10/11 Times New Roman (Monophoto)
by Macmillan India Ltd, Bangalore.

Printed in Great Britain for
Hodder and Stoughton Educational,
a division of Hodder and Stoughton Ltd.,
Mill road, Dunton Green, Sevenoaks, Kent
by Butler & Tanner Ltd, Frome and London

Contents

PART 1 THE MATERIAL: DATA

1 Background to data processing   1
Data and information
Calculating aids
Clerical aids

2 Processing of data   6
Manual methods
Mechanical methods
Using a computer

3 Representation of data   12
Need to encode data
Representation of numbers and characters in digital form
Analogue representation

4 Data capture and checking   18
Data capture
Form design
Data transcription
Data verification
Data validation

PART 2 THE TOOL: THE COMPUTER

5 Inside the computer   29
Concept of a binary word
Representation of machine instructions
Other computer codes
Two-state devices
Analogue to digital conversion

6 Computer arithmetic   41
Binary representation of fractions
Representation of negative numbers
Fixed point number representation
Floating point number representation
Errors in computer arithmetic

7 The hardware   52
Peripheral devices
The central processing unit
Backing store
Microprocessors
Word processors

PART 3 BASIC SKILLS: USING THE TOOL

8 Communication with the computer   74
Levels of communication
Compilers and interpreters
Operating systems
Methods of operation
Applications programs

9 Problem solving techniques   81
Problem definition and specification
System description
Flow charting
Documentation
Errors and diagnostics
Test data

10 Programming techniques   103
Searching
Sorting
Simulation
Iteration
Sample programs

11 File handling   122
Introduction
What is a file?
Types of computer file
File storage media
Creating a file
Reading the file
Interrogating the file
File updating
Security of files
Data processing

PART 4 THE PRODUCT: THE APPLICATIONS OF COMPUTERS AND THEIR IMPORTANCE IN SOCIETY

12 The use of computers — 151
General uses in business
Banking
Garment design and manufacture
Airlines
Police
Supermarkets
Medical use
Small businesses
Computers in the home
Computers in education
Real-time computing
The future

13 The impact of computers on society — 167
Individual appreciation
Effect on employment
Effect on freedom
Effect on privacy

Appendixes — 170
1 Coursework
2 Computer staff
3 History of data processing
4 ISO 7-bit character set
5 File handling programs
6 Comparison between ENIAC and BBC Micro
7 Suggested reading material

Revision questions — 189

Multiple choice questions — 191

Answers — 194

Index — 213

Foreword

Few doubt that computers are bringing about fundamental changes in the way many things are done. On the one hand they enable us to hand over to machines many tasks which we are accustomed to performing in factory and office, in coalmine and aeroplane, in the home and while travelling, in fact wherever logical control of a process is possible. On the other hand they represent an extension to intellectual activity enabling us to assemble and marshal facts in a way which enables us to tackle problems of hitherto insurmountable complexity. The advent of the microprocessor at (almost) give-away prices brings the techniques employed in all this within the grasp of education, obliged as it is to ride pick-a-back on the mass production in commerce and industry.

This represents a huge challenge to teachers, few of whom will have previous knowledge or experience in this area. They will wish to enrich their teaching in many, possibly all, subjects with the techniques of information retrieval, automatic text processing and simulation, to utilise the potential of the computer for encouraging logical problem solving and some, to study the computer itself.

In a decade and a half Computer Studies has matured from a mathematically orientated subject to one where the central emphasis is on the processing of information of all kinds, including numerical. The lack of a traditional body of knowledge and approach to the teaching of the subject makes the role of a good text book more than usually important. This book, written by a man who has the necessary combination of practical experience (with ICL) and latterly, of effective teaching experience at Knutsford, and of examining with AEB, strikes what I believe to be the right balance. While it cannot supersede in-service training, it provides an effective crutch on which the new computer studies teacher can lean while building his or her own experience. At the same time it proffers a wealth of material for the use of those already past this stage. The book combines a detailed look inside the computer with a comprehensive account of the ways in which the machine may be used and an attempt to assess its effect on our lives. I commend it as an essential weapon in the armoury of every computer studies teacher.

D.M. Esterson, J.P., M.Sc., F.B.C.S.

July 1982

Acknowledgements

The publisher thanks the following for giving permission to reproduce photographs in this book:

Acorn Computers Ltd (7.2); Barclays Bank (12.4, 12.5); British Airways (12.10); British Leyland (2.7, 7.40); Ron Chetwood (4.6, 4.7, 4.8, 7.12, 7.38, 12.2); Gerber Scientific-UK Ltd (12.6, 12.7, 12.8, 12.9); The Home Office (2.5, 12.11); IBM UK Ltd (1.3, 7.4, 7.5, 7.9, 7.15, 7.18, 7.44); ICL (5.19, 5.23, 7.17, 7.19, 7.24, 7.33, 7.35, 7.37); ITT (7.3); Dave King (5.21, 7.11, 7.16, 8.3); The Medical Illustration Unit, N. Manchester Hospital (12.13, 12.14); J. Sainsbury Plc. (12.12); Science Museum, London—Crown Copyright (1.1, 2.2); Thorn EMI Central Research Labs. (7.41).

Fig. 1.4 is reproduced by kind permission of East Herts College.

The 'cartoons' have been drawn by Bob Newnes, Head of Art, Knutsford County High School.

Software

Chapters 9, 10 and 11 contain 41 programs written in BASIC. Listings of all of these programs written in BBC BASIC are given in the text and some from Chapter 11 written in RML BASICS; APPLE BASIC and PET BASIC are given in Appendix 5.

All the programs have been written in these four versions of BASIC and are available from the publishers on floppy disk or cassette tape, as shown below:

BBC	$5\frac{1}{4}$ inch disk	(0 340 33184 4)
BBC	C60 cassette	(0 340 33181 X)
RML	$5\frac{1}{4}$ inch disk	(0 340 33182 8)
APPLE	$5\frac{1}{4}$ inch disk	(0 340 33183 6)
PET	$5\frac{1}{4}$ inch disk	(0 340 33186 0)
PET	C60 cassette	(0 340 33185 2)

When ordering software please give details of the computer, whether disk or tape is required, and quote the reference number.

Preface

Computing is a practical subject and this book has been written with this philosophy very much in mind. Nevertheless, it is not a programming text, although many programs appear in the book. It has been written as a basic text to cover most of the existing O level and CSE syllabuses and, in particular, the newer syllabuses now being published.

Although computer studies has been taught in schools since the late 1960s, its popularity has increased considerably since the introduction of microcomputers over the past 5 years and many syllabuses are now being rewritten to reflect the change in emphasis from 'how a computer works' to, 'how to use a computer'. It may seem surprising, therefore, that Chapter 6 deals with computer arithmetic in such detail, or indeed, that such a chapter is included at all. It is included for two reasons: the topics discussed are in most current syllabuses and there are few texts which develop the topic in a systematic manner suitable for teaching fourth and fifth years in school.

There is a continuing development of the technology associated with computing which, at the time of writing this preface shows no sign of slowing; indeed, all the indications are that there will be continuing significant developments in the foreseeable future. Writing a textbook with such a subject, to fit ever-changing syllabuses, has proved a challenge! I hope the reader will find the present text steers an acceptable course between 'computer technology', 'computing' and 'using a computer'. I have attempted, where possible, to look ahead, particularly in hardware developments and, where facts and figures are quoted, to obtain the most up-to-date available just before publication. Any teacher, or student, of this subject will find that any textbook, however 'forward looking' it is, requires continual updating with current news and views obtained from a wide variety of reliable sources. Appendix 7 gives a list of selected reading material.

Many of the objectives of current, and probably future, computer studies syllabuses can only be met and assessed through practical work. In this book, this is called coursework and is discussed specifically in Appendix 1 as well as having supporting material in Chapters 9, 10 and 11. Chapter 9 deals with the problems of developing and documenting any piece of practical programming, whether it is exam coursework or a project to develop a 'package' to help teach another subject in school. Chapter 10 looks at both the theory and practice of some standard programming techniques which are all too often considered to be A level topics. Simulation is a fascinating topic and computer simulation can be practised at many levels from simple dice or coin throwing to complex scientific experiments. Sorting is included in Chapter 10 because some sort routine should be included in any self-respecting data processing project, (but often isn't!).

Chapter 11 is a detailed study on practical file handling which, again, is often considered to be beyond the understanding of students at this level. It is encouraging to see this topic beginning to appear in revised CSE and O level syllabuses. This chapter is offered in the hope that *every* student of this subject will learn to create and handle files containing data in which *they* are interested and get some feel for the most important aspect of any computer studies course—data processing.

Many years of marking O level and CSE exam scripts in computer studies have led me to the sad conclusion that many students of the subject have very muddled ideas and whilst they may understand a particular concept in isolation, they have little understanding of how this fits into the wider spectrum of the whole subject of computing. I hope that diligent study of this text will enable students to see how all the various topics 'dovetail' together to form the exciting study of computing.

Some of the (more amusing) muddled thinking appears by way of a quotation at the start of some of the chapters of this book. These quotations, which do not acknowledge a source, are all taken without any modification, from answers to O level questions and whilst they may amuse, they did not earn the original authors any exam marks!

One of the major problems facing students (and teachers!), in a new subject is that there is no experience of what constitutes a good answer to an exam question.

This book is unique in that many of the answers to the end-of-chapter questions are the actual answers provided by the Chief Examiner for the stated year's exam. I am most grateful to the Associated Examinining Board for giving me permission to use selected questions from past O level papers and for allowing me to reproduce model answers. (It should be pointed out, however, that these are my answers as Chief Examiner for the AEB and that they have not been formally approved by the Board for this publication.)

Worked answers are given at the end of the book to the questions marked with an asterisk (*).

No textbook on a subject as wide-ranging as computer studies could be written without help and I gratefully acknowledge the help given by many people in writing this book. In particular, my thanks to Bryan Weaver, ILEA Inspector for Computer Education, and Judith Jolly, Tavistock School, who read the original script and who made most helpful comments and suggestions; to friends in ICL who provided me with up-to-date facts and figures; to students from my 1980 A level classes for their help with some of the programming and, very specially, to my wife, Jean who typed the complete book from first draft to final text.

G.M.C.

Preface to the BBC Edition

During the summer and autumn of 1981 I was writing the final chapters of the manuscript for the RML edition of this book and, along with many other people, awaited the arrival of my BBC microcomputer. Even if my BEEB had arrived in time to enable me to re-write all 41 programs in BBC BASIC before typesetting commenced, I do not think I would have done it at that time. BEEB was a new, unproved and seemingly unavailable microcomputer; could it compete with Apples, PETs, 380Zs etc which had been around for some time? During 1982 the answer began to emerge and I was able to include 5 programs 'translated' into BBC BASIC in an appendix in time for the first impression in Jan 1983. By that time it was quite clear that the BEEB had come to stay!

By late 1984 the BEEB has become the most popular micro in schools, as well as becoming established in small businesses and used in the home for much more than just playing games! Hence the requirement for a BBC edition.

All the programs in this edition are written in BBC BASIC and will run equally well on a tape or disk-based micro. No attempt has been made to 'clutter up' the basic program with routines to improve screen layout, make the programs robust, minimise storage space or include graphics were applicable; it is left to the reader to add these desirable features at his or her own convenience.

G.M.C. Oct. 1984

1 Background to data processing

1.1 Data and information

If we are going to spend the next year or two learning about the processing of data, it is clear that we must establish what data is and where it is found before we can learn what to do with it.

Here is some data: 3, 8, 2, 15.

These are merely numbers and unless we specify what they are, they must remain as just numbers. This is called numeric data.

Data can also consist of letters, for example A, P, Z or APE, FQ, RD. This type is known as alpha data.

Data containing both letters and numerals is known as alphanumeric data, eg. AB34.

Data does not just consist of meaningless groups of numbers and/or letters. The following are all data:
1 apple, orange, pear   (fruits)
2 Smith, Brown, Jones   (surnames)
3 25, 84, 3, 51, 77   (a batsman's scores)
4 061–437 1234, 0467–2831   (telephone numbers)
5 TXJ 135R, ABC 123X   (car registration numbers)

Although no explanation is needed in examples 1 and 2 above to make it clear what the data is, the other three examples *do* require explanation to make the data meaningful. The numbers in 3 could represent the number of peas in five jars, or the height in millimetres of five bean shoots in an experiment, or the amount of money, in pence, in the pockets of five members of your form, and so on. Example 4 looks like telephone numbers but could equally be catalogue numbers or spare part numbers. Similarly with example 5 which could equally be book codes used in a library.

There is an almost limitless supply of data which can be found in a wide range of places. Try walking along your high street and noting different types of data; go into a supermarket and look for different data, then, as a class exercise, group it all together under different headings, such as house names, shop types, product names, prices etc. You will be amazed how long your lists are! Some of this data will be meaningful, such as a list of grocers, and some will not be, such as a list of house numbers.

'In the beginning, God made data and left it to man to process it.'

What you have done in this exercise is to collect and classify the data. Classification of data can provide us with *some* information. Consider this list of numbers:

18, 4, 90, 26, 55, 0, 15, 21, 34, 10, 17

What does it tell us? Not a lot! It tells us more if we add that these are "cricket scores". However, we don't know if it is one batsman's score in 11 matches or each batsman's score in one match. It could even be the seventh batsman's score in 11 different matches! If it is the latter, it doesn't tell us very much anyway (except that the batsman who scored 90 should be early in the batting order). If we say that it represents one batsman's scores in 11 matches, we have changed our data into information. We can further add together all the data, giving *total runs scored* = 290 and by dividing by 11 find the average (mean) runs scored per match—26.36. All this *processing* is providing us with more *information* about one batsman.

It is not easy to see what we can do with a list of names in order to provide information but we could find how many Smiths in the list, or how many names begin with a particular letter. Take a page of words from any novel: reading this one page, without at least the preceding pages, wouldn't make much sense, but the page could be analysed by counting the frequency of occurrence of particular words or the pattern of use of verbs, nouns, adjectives etc. If a page of another book by the same author was similarly analysed, similar results would be obtained. If a record was kept of the 'pattern' produced by many authors it would be possible to identify the author of a single sheet of writing, by comparing this pattern with the recorded ones.

A fascinating piece of research, using this simple technique was undertaken by Glasgow University some years ago. In order to try to prove that St. Paul really *did* write all the letters of Paul, which make up so many books in the New Testament, each letter was analysed word by word using a computer and the pattern of useage of nouns, adverbs etc. was produced. The pattern produced from each book analysis was remarkably similar and this showed that the same author had written all these books.

This information was produced as a result of manipulating (processing) single words or data. Data usually needs to be organised in order to provide effective and useful information. Imagine a telephone directory being in two sections, the first containing a random listing of the subscribers' names and addresses and the second a random listing of their telephone numbers. All the data is there but in that form it is quite useless, as there is no link between names and telephone numbers. Even if the correct telephone number is printed alongside each subscriber's name and address, if these are printed in random fashion, finding the name you require could be a very long and tedious job. As we all know, names in a telephone directory are listed alphabetically and therefore it is easy to find any name and number, and as easy to find a name beginning with T as it is to find one beginning with C or N. The data—name, address and telephone number—has been organised and it now provides meaningful information.

We will be looking at this problem again later on in Chapter 10 when we will be considering the structuring of this data for subsequent writing, not on paper, but into a computer file for storage or for processing; we will be processing data to provide information relating to the stock of fashion goods in our shop.

1.2 Calculating aids

Man has processed data since he came on Earth and, from earliest times, he has found it necessary to try to invent 'devices' to help him to process this data. Until the middle of the last century, almost the only data that required processing was numeric so all the devices were aids to calculating.

By the seventeenth century, there was a growing shipping trade and a need to provide ships' captains with more accurate navigation tables. These had to be calculated 'by hand' and not only took a long time to compile but were notoriously inaccurate. The invention of logarithms by John Napier followed by the Rev. W. Oughtred's 'practical logarithm machine' (the slide rule), enabled calculations to be performed much more quickly and accurately.

The need to manipulate moving figures, or changing data, is still a problem in calculating income tax, as it was in the middle of the seventeenth century when Blaise Pascal invented his 'Pascaline' to help his father with tax calculations. This machine was the first mechanical calculator, but it could only add and subtract. Gottfried Von Leibniz developed Pascal's idea and produced a calculator which could multiply and divide as well as add and subtract. These machines, and others developed from them, were used to produce new mathematical and scientific tables which were needed during the industrial revolution of the eighteenth and nineteenth centuries.

In 1822, Charles Babbage took some of the ideas from these earlier machines and built a very complicated machine, known as a 'difference engine', which computed very accurate mathematical tables once a single set of initial values had been input to the machine. Babbage's second machine, the 'analytical engine', was really the design for a digital computer, but unfortunately never worked because the engineering technology of the time could not make the mechanical parts with sufficient accuracy.

Exercises 1.1

1 In how many different ways could a telephone directory be organised? Discuss the advantages and disadvantages of each method.
2 Discuss how a small business selling, for example, fashion clothes, should organise a list (or inventory) of the stock. The following data is to be recorded for each item: garment name, colour, style, size, price. Is this the best order in which to record the data? Could any of colour, style, size and price be used as heading?
Would it be sensible to keep a complete list of all garments coloured red or costing less than £20?
What other items of data relating to each item of stock could usefully be added to the list given above?

The historical honour of being the first person to 'process' non-numeric data falls to a French weaver, Joseph Jacquard, in 1805, who hit on the idea of using a wooden 'card' with a pre-set pattern of holes in it to control the warp rods of his loom (Fig. 1.1). By using a series of such cards, Jacquard was able to 'program' his loom to repeat patterns. Babbage intended to use this idea of a 'card' punched with data to program his analytical engine but as the machine never worked, the idea was never tried in a calculating machine until (many) years later.

We have already seen that there was a need for a calculating aid to help in the compiling of astronomical, nautical and mathematical tables, as well as for straightforward numeric calculations. The 'calculator' was being used to produce more accurate information in much less time than by previous methods. Greater accuracy in tables was a continuing requirement for navigation, science and engineering and still is, particularly for astro-navigation, to the present time.

Although the USA had not figured in any of the development mentioned above, that situation changed dramatically at the turn of the century due to the inventive genius of Herman Hollerith. Hollerith worked for the US Bureau of Census, which took a census of all the people living in the USA every 10 years. The population of the USA had risen so much between 1880 and 1890 that it was clear to Hollerith that, using the existing method of counting by hand, the 1890 census would not be finished before the 1900 census was due! He had read of Babbage's work and of his intention to use Jacquard cards to hold the data for processing, so he simply took these ideas and developed them so that the data relating to the census was punched onto cards as a pattern of holes and 'read' by an electro-mechanical device invented by Hollerith which he called a tabulator. With this technique, the 1890 census was completed in about half the time taken previously. The age of data processing had arrived.

1.3 Clerical aids

If we go right back to the caveman and his use of tally sticks to record numbers or events, we also see his use of the most important clerical aid—*writing*.

The ability to present data or information visually in a semipermanent form so that people in another country, or living in another age, can know what other people were, or are, doing or thinking is absolutely fundamental in our lives. It is so common and so easy to use that we tend to lose sight of its importance and probably don't even think about it at all, let alone how important it is to us.

Try to imagine a society that does not have the written word as a form of communication. All data and information can only be passed on to others by speech and received through hearing. Is this possible? Yes: blind people 'read' and learn in this way, but even blind

Fig. 1.1 Jacquard's loom and a card

people have 'writing'—in Braille. Having recognised the need to communicate in writing, man has used various media such as stone, wood and vellum, but paper has been the accepted medium for writing on for nearly 2000 years. The use of ink to record information in writing in a permanent manner has been accepted for an equally long time but, despite the common use of ink on paper, one other very important feature was very variable—the writing itself! Many attempts have been made to produce common writing, and two notable examples still in use today are Gothic script and copper-plate writing (Fig. 1.2).

Fig. 1.2 Gothic script (*top*) and copper-plate writing (*bottom*)

All these different styles, whilst producing easily read writing, still had to be written by hand and therefore the reproduction of any document, whether it was an account or a legal document was laborious and slow. However, in 1760 the most useful invention, prior to the computer, made its appearance: the *printing press*. Man now had the ability not only to 'write' in a standard way but to reproduce, in quantity, any book or document that could be typeset. The introduction of printing had, of course, a dramatic effect on the number of books available for reading and study but there was no marked effect on business office practice until the general introduction of the typewriter in 1850. It was then possible for every office to produce, and reproduce, data and information in a standard printing format (called a font) a great deal more easily and quickly than Mr. Micawber with his quill pen!

A number of other clerical aids have had a lasting effect on office practice and data manipulation and these are described below.

The *Dictaphone* was introduced about 1900 and it enabled data and information to be recorded (as speech) for subsequent processing (typing or action). This is directly comparable with the way data can be prepared for processing in a computer, as we will see in Chapter 4.

From about 1890, various methods of copying many forms of document have been available. Modern *photocopiers* allow, for example, copies of a single page from an examination paper to be made available to a class of students, or copies of the minutes of a meeting to be reproduced cheaply, quickly and easily. Photocopying is cheap because no human copying is involved, a typical modern speed is 100 copies a minute and the machine does all the work automatically.

The newest clerical aids—*word processors*—take us straight into the realm of microcomputers, but from a use point of view they must be mentioned here. A typical desk-top information processing system is shown in Fig. 1.3. This has a built in dictionary of 50 000 commonly used words and space for 500 'user words' for a particular profession or industry, thus providing spelling verifications, as well as giving simple instructions to guide the typist in creating, revising and editing documents. A large amount of office work is

Fig. 1.3 Word processor (IBM Displaywriter)

routine and the word processor can produce 'standard' letters, invoices and accounts very quickly and easily from data which is stored in the word processor and used when required. Standard paragraphs, clauses and sentences can be called for from the store to make up a particular letter before the word processor is told to produce one, or many, copies of the final version. The impact of the word processor on office practice has yet to be fully realised.

Another new addition to the growing list of office electronic aids is *electronic mail*. Letters, or other documents can be prepared on a word processor and transmitted to their destination via the telephone network. At the receiving end, word-processor-like equipment receives the 'incoming mail' and either stores it for later off-line output, or produces hard copy on a fast printer for immediate attention. Such a system has many advantages, particularly in transmission of orders, which can be received within seconds of dispatch and not subject to the delays of ordinary mail, and for transmission of long legal or technical documents which require no further typing once they are stored in the word processor. They can be transmitted exactly as stored, or with suitable customer modifications, to any point in the world which has the necessary equipment (see Chapter 13).

The concept of the 'office of the future' goes far beyond word processors and electronic mail, and indeed, beyond technical innovations in general. It will affect the whole structure of business organisation, with the disciplines associated with routine tasks becoming totally automated. The more informal functions as represented by management and decision makers will become a union between man and machine. The 'terminal' will provide a means of drawing on the total knowledge of the organisation and of inputting new information which can be used by, and of benefit to, many other people. Fig. 1.4 shows a possible structure for a business organisation in the very near future.

Appendix 3 shows the important events and dates in the history of data processing and computing in the form of nomographs.

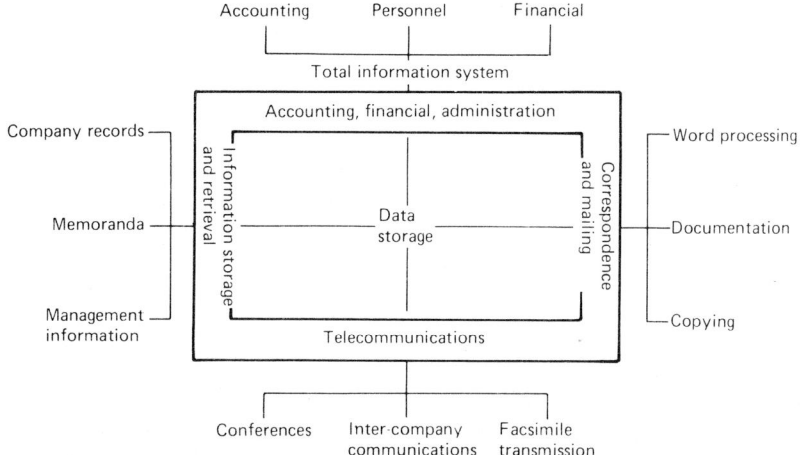

Fig. 1.4 Structure of business organisation

Summary

- Data can consist of letters, words, numbers and characters.
- Data which is defined, or has been processed to make it meaningful, is known as information.
- There have been many calculating aids invented over the centuries, usually to try to satisfy a particular demand.
- The impact of modern technology on office practices has not yet been realised. There will be far-reaching changes in the next few years.

2 Processing of data

2.1 Manual methods

Data has been handled manually for centuries. Bob Cratchet used a quill pen to enter details of Scrooge's customers' accounts in his ledger, and today this same method of book-keeping is still practised in many small firms—alas, using a ball point pen, instead of the shapely quill from a swan or duck! The data relating to an account is read by a person from some source document (such as an invoice) and written into the ledger. Totalling up columns of figures has, until the arrival of the calculator in the early part of this century, relied on the ability of a person to count and memorise and not to make mistakes!

Probably the most common feature of all offices is a filing system—manual of course! All data and information which needs to be kept for reference has to be filed. Most manual filing systems start off well organised but they tend to grow in a rather random fashion, and all too often there is only one person who knows how to find anything in the file! For *anybody* to be able to find a particular item in the file, it must be organised in some way. The manner in which it is organised will often depend on the data being kept. If, for instance, it is a doctor's file containing the name, address and medical history of all his patients, it is almost certain that the file will be organised alphabetically by name, because the doctor will want to refer to a named patient's record. On the other hand, a file containing records of various meetings will probably be organised under different subject or committee names. It is quite likely that such a file would have secondary organisation so that under each subject heading, the various papers are arranged in date order or meeting number order.

Reference has previously been made to a familiar organised file of data, a telephone directory. Its normal method of use is entirely manual: given a name and address, it is easy to look up a number. If only the name is known and it is Skyrunes, or some other unusual name, it will be much quicker to find that number than to find a Smith or Jones' number. It is worth realising that telephone directories are organised in another

'Data is dull and computer output is duller having no beauty like the script writing in Mr. Pepys diaries.'

way—that is, under a numeric listing of the numbers followed by the subscriber's name and address. The first number might be 01-123 1234 Smith P, 6, the Mews, Islington, London, followed by 01-123 1235 Carver R, 48, Hendon Way, NW1. (These directories are not available for public use.)

One other very familiar, organised file of data is a dictionary which, again, is always used manually. We look up the meaning of a word or find how to spell it correctly, but a dictionary cannot be used to find the meaning of a word if you do not know how it is spelt, except by a probable long search through all possible ways of spelling it. There are dictionaries organised in ways other than a straight-forward alphabetic listing: some under headings such as various sports, others under broad subject classification eg. law, classical mythology, music etc. Whatever the subject, a dictionary becomes almost valueless if it is not organised so that we can access the data we require easily and quickly.

2.2 Mechanical methods

We saw in Chapter 1, that many devices to aid calculations had been invented since the seventeenth century. By the year 1900, the 'adding machine' had been developed so that it could be used in the office to perform calculations. However, these were carried out, laboriously, by setting the numbers with wheels or pointers and turning a handle, possibly many times, to complete calculations. On such a machine a practised operator could only hope to complete the multiplication of two 10-digit numbers in about $1\frac{1}{2}$ minutes. On a similar electrically operated machine, this time could be reduced to about $\frac{1}{2}$ minute. The longest part of the whole operation was the setting-up of the machine to do the calculation and keying in the numbers. The last wholly electromechanical calculating machines (before the advent of the electronic calculator) had been developed to complete approximately 1000 counts per minute, but a division still took about 5 seconds to complete (Fig. 2.1).

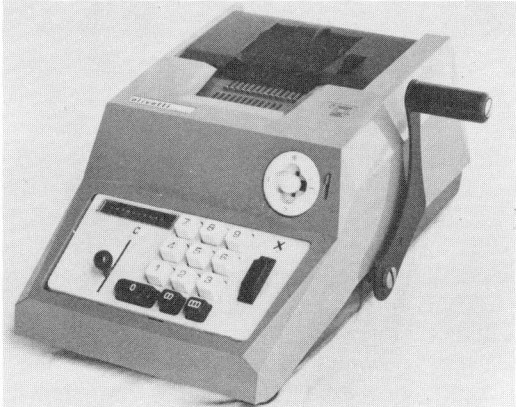

Fig. 2.1 Mechanical calculator

During the period 1900 to 1930 many types of 'adding machines' were developed for office and factory use. The most significant of these was the comptometer in which the key used to input a number also operated the counters at the same time, thereby speeding up the whole process so much that a column of figures could be added up faster than the numbers could be read aloud! Many forms of 'accounting machines' were developed for use in the preparation of bills and accounts. These usually had more than one register to enable sub-totals to be manipulated and were provided with a printing mechanism to output the results directly on paper, thereby avoiding the possibility of an error in copying the results from the machine's register.

Electronic calculators are widely used today and can store data as well as being capable of performing a wide range of mathematical functions at a very high speed.

In Chapter 1 we read, briefly, that the age of data processing was ushered in by Hollerith's invention of the tabulator (Fig. 2.2). This was an electromechanical machine which 'read' holes punched in cards and was the first of many similar machines developed between 1900 and 1940, which were all designed to manipulate data on cards. These machines could read punched cards, sort them, collate them and punch new data into new cards for reprocessing. As well as enabling large quantities of data to be processed faster than ever before, a new, and most significant feature was introduced. Data for processing was first punched into cards and these cards could be read over and over again. It was therefore most important to ensure that the punched cards were correct in the first place. This brought about the introduction of systematic data preparation and subsequent data checking before processing began. We will follow this process in more detail in Chapter 4 when we will see how data is prepared and checked before input to a computer.

Fig. 2.2 Tabulator and sorter

Card processing had another very desirable feature: the output from the processing was in printed form and also as a set of punched cards which, for example, may have represented the latest updating of the stock of a warehouse. The cards used as input could then be destroyed and the new cards used as input next time an updating run took place. A great many companies used punched card equipment from 1930 to 1950 for all their data processing and, indeed, many companies were quite resistant to changing from this tried and proven machinery and systems, which had been developed by such companies as ICT (International Computers and Tabulators) in the United Kingdom and IBM (International Business Machines) in the USA. Punched card systems were still widely used for many years after the introduction of electronic computers in 1950.

All the information recording and storage systems referred to in Section 2.1 have been, and still are being, used very successfully in offices, shops, factories and commercial businesses. Up to recent times, their operation has been almost entirely manual and therefore their use has been restricted by three important factors:
(a) the time taken to get at a particular item of data which may require searching of more than one file, ledger or book
(b) the amount of data that can conveniently be kept and can realistically be searched in an acceptable time
(c) the reliability of the data because of the slowness in updating files and ledgers.

For these and other reasons, most of the manual systems have been mechanised and it is now possible to store an enormous quantity of data in a ridiculously small space and be able to get at any item very quickly.

A particular example of this can be seen in most libraries where the entire catalogue of all the books available used to be housed in many cabinets. Each book was allocated one card and approximately 1000 cards filled one drawer. A medium sized local library had upwards of 200 drawers and the cabinets took up a lot of valuable book space. Each card was hand-written, or typed, and inserted in the correct place alphabetically or numerically. Large libraries have millions of such cards. These card systems are now being superseded by a system based on the use of microfilm. In one type of system the data is contained on a film wound on a cassette and, in more recent systems, the data is contained on a single sheet of film.

It is worth considering these two methods of searching for data at this stage as they are fundamental concepts in computing and we will discuss them on a number of occasions later in this book. The data held on a long film wound on a cassette can only be *accessed*, i.e. got at, *serially* by going through all the data, searching for the particular item required. All the data held on a flat film can be accessed *directly* independent of its position on the film. The flat film system is usually much quicker.

In both systems, the film is read through a viewer which magnifies the microfilm to a legible size for viewing on a screen. The details of the books are recorded photographically then reduced by a factor of approximately 50. A typical single book entry which previously was typed on a card measuring 13 cm × 7 cm (91 cm^2) now occupies a space of approximately 8 mm^2, and the details of approximately 5000 books are contained on a film measuring 15 cm × 10 cm (150 cm^2) (Fig. 2.3).

Fig. 2.3 Microfiche and viewer

This system of recording large quantities of data on to microfilm has also been used very successfully for keeping records of stock held in a factory or warehouse or spare parts in a garage. Microfilm viewers have replaced the common 'bin system' where many thousands of items of stock were recorded on large cards held in 'bins' or desks, sometimes occupying whole floors of an office block. Unfortunately, a system based on the use of microfilm, whilst excellent for storing very large quantities of 'fixed data', such as the item description, minimum stock level etc., cannot sensibly be used for recording changing numbers. A stock control system using microfilm would need a supplementary 'quantity recording system', which would probably be on manual cards!

The 'mechanisation' of our manual system brings its attendant problems and, using the library system mentioned previously, we will look at one of the main problems that is going to be even more important when we are considering using a computer. That is the problem of *systematic data preparation and checking*.

With a manual card system, when a new book is added to the catalogue, the card is hand written and inserted in the correct place in the correct drawer. If a mistake is made in writing the card, a new card is easily made. Inserting the card into the wrong place in the catalogue is easily put right, at any time, by moving the card. When the data is on microfilm, however, once the particular set of data has been photographed, it cannot be altered or its position changed until a new film is made. It is even difficult to remove data from the film, but with cards, the unwanted ones are merely destroyed without affecting the rest of the catalogue.

The need for the data to be 100% correct leads to the use of special pro-formas (pre-printed sheets), so that all the required data is written down and because the same type of data, eg. title, will be in the same place on each form, it makes the job of checking much easier. Pro-formas to do very different jobs, such as deleting a book, adding a book or amending the data, could be printed on different coloured paper so that, again, another check is made before, finally, the microfilm is made.

We will see, in Chapter 4, more of the need for form design when we come to input data to the computer. Whenever data is to be prepared for input to a 'mechanised system', it is easier to prepare, easier to check and easier to input if a prepared form is used instead of haphazardly using odd bits of paper (Fig. 2.4). Chapter 4 details how forms are designed.

```
Request for micro-film operation
Type of request: DELETION/ADDITION/AMENDMENT
Authorised by:              Date:

Name of book:
Author:
ISBN No:
Checked by:
Action authorised by:
Film number and issue number:
```

Fig. 2.4 Simple form for use in a library using microfilm for its catalogue

2.3 Using a computer

The introduction of the computer, in the 1950s, to process data has led to many changes in office practice in offices, shops and schools as well as in large industrial and commercial organisations. The advantages of using a computer can be summarised as: it can *automatically* process very large quantities of data in an *unbelievably short* time. These aspects of a computer have been exploited in many different ways and we will look at some examples of data processing by computer and see changes brought about by the introduction of the computer.

First let us look at the effect of the *speed* of the computer:

'The electronic computer can perform millions of calculations every second.'

Such statements, while true, are very difficult for a human mind even to imagine but to an electronic computer this speed is commonplace and it has to be recognised that this is simply the speed at which electronics operate. This incredible speed means two things:

(*a*) Calculations that previously took a long time to perform can now be done very much quicker.

(*b*) Calculations that simply could not have been done previously, because of the time involved in doing them, now can be done.

An example of the latter was the British Pavilion at the Montreal Exhibition of 1970. The engineering knowledge for the design of this building had been understood for many years but the calculations necessary to design a practical building using this principle would have taken far too long using normal methods. A computer completed these calculations in a matter of hours whereas it would have taken a team of human beings many hundreds of years to have done them.

A further important aspect of the speed of an electronic computer is that the data can be processed so quickly that the results of this processing can be used to influence the data being fed into the computer. Probably the best example of this use of the speed of computation, is in space flight. Data relating to the actual position of the space craft can be processed and compared with stored data which tells the computer where the space craft should be at that instant of time. The result of the processing would establish if there was an error and this error signal can be instantly fed back into the computer to correct the position of the space craft.

Coupled with the high speed of an electronic computer is the *power* of the computer to process large quantities of data. It goes almost without saying that if a computer can handle calculations and operations at very high speed, then, in a given time, very many more calculations and operations can be achieved. This enables some jobs to be undertaken which would have proved quite impossible to do before the introduction of the computer.

For example, the police use computers to help them in their battle against criminals (see Fig. 2.5 and Chapter 12.5). Imagine searching by hand through all the records of known criminals to try and match some details of some suspected bank robber. This would prove difficult and time consuming in any circumstance, but unless all the records were kept in one central place then it would be impossible to search through them all in a realistic time. With a computer, all the records can be held on computer files and the computer can search through these files in a matter of minutes.

One further example of the computer's ability to process large quantities of data is in the field of weather forecasting. Data relating to temperature, pressure, etc. over a wide geographical area is obtained from weather

10 COMPUTER STUDIES

Fig. 2.5 Communicating with the Police National Computer

balloons, satellites and weather ships and fed into the computer. Despite the use of a very powerful computer for this work, the processing of this data still takes many hours and processing started about 2 a.m. each day is completed just in time for the weather forecast at 6 a.m.

The third important feature of an electronic computer is its ability to *store* data. When the data has been processed, the result of the processing can be stored automatically so that it may be used again. One example of this feature could be making an alphabetically organised file of names and addresses which can subsequently be used over and over again, or it could be an airline booking system where the number of seats available on a particular flight is stored and immediately amended when any seat is taken. This booked seat would not then be offered to any subsequent inquirer for a seat on that flight.

In addition to offering the facilities of speed, power and storage, the computer can be used to *simulate* a situation or a set of conditions. This means that the computer can be used instead of mounting a very costly experiment or where a particular avenue of research may be extremely dangerous. Examples occur in atomic physics, or when it is required to carry out an experiment over an impossibly long time, such as looking at the growth of the population over the next 200 years.

The technique of simulation is by no means restricted to the fields of scientific research and it has been used very successfully and very widely in industry and commerce to forecast sales trends, predict work schedules, factory loadings and estimates of costings and profit based on the latest possible information available. Using the computer it is possible to vary all the parameters which influence a particular situation and see the effect of these variations on the problem which is being analysed. A common example of the use of this technique is in sales forecasting where every variable that might influence the sale of a product can be input to the computer simulation and the best course of action decided upon without any of the product actually having been made at that stage! Whatever example we take, the basic idea of processing data to give meaningful output can be illustrated simply as shown in Fig. 2.6.

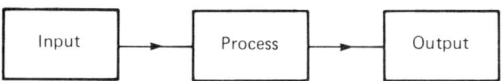

Fig. 2.6 The basic data processing concept

A computer system that is able to receive continuously changing data from outside sources, and that is able to process that data sufficiently rapidly to be capable of influencing the sources of data, is known as a *real time computing system*. One example of such a system has been quoted above, that of airline booking. A further example is in air traffic control where it is, of course, very important that the latest situation regarding the movement of an aircraft in a control zone is fed into the computer that will determine the flight paths of the aircraft under its control.

One further area where the computer is now widely used is that of *process control*. Many processes are now completely controlled by computers. One example of this is automatic train control where data relating to the movement of the trains is fed from track signals into the computer and if this matches the pre-programmed data, then the computer will allow normal operation. Any malfunction by any train will cause the computer to halt any further running until the fault is cleared.

Many machines are controlled using pre-programmed instructions to perform a particular job and one of the best known examples is the use of robots to assemble car bodies in a car assembly line (Fig. 2.7).

Process control computers are widely used in the chemical manufacturing industry where the performance of a complex plant is monitored by many sensors of differing types. The sensors might, for example, measure temperature, pressure and rate of flow, and these signals are fed into the computer to control the safe running of the plant. One particular sensor may measure the temperature of a particular liquid and if the temperature rises above a pre-set limit, a signal would be generated by the computer, which would turn down the system heating that particular container and possibly shut off the flow of all liquids and gases in the area until the temperature falls to within its preset limits (see Chapter 11).

PROCESSING OF DATA 11

Fig. 2.7 Robot welders on the Mini Metro line

Summary

- A computer can be used:
  (i) to solve problems much faster than could be done by hand
  (ii) to solve problems that were known to exist but that could not have been solved by mechanical methods in an acceptable time-scale
  (iii) to solve problems that have only been discovered by using computers to solve other problems
  (iv) to provide a response to continuously changing data fast enough to affect the source of the data.

- A computer works at very high speed and has the ability to store large amounts of data and process this data in a very short time.
- Whether data is to be processed manually, mechanically or by a computer, it should be organised for ease of processing. Computer processing will produce organised output very much more easily than manual methods.

3 Representation of data

3.1 The need to encode data

Ask your teacher to make up a secret message something like the following:

Agents Robinson I, Austin S, Ford T and Bond J are to meet at 273 Manobier Avenue, NW1, at 21.30 hr on Friday 23rd. Bring documents 21/h/482931/WW3 and P/4/79/52A3.

Now ask your teacher to read out the message once, not too fast and with no repetitions. You must write the message down as it is read out. When the message has been read, check what you have written down (received) against the message read out (transmitted). Did you make an accurate copy? If you had been one of the agents, would you know where to go and when? Perhaps even more important, would you have taken the correct documents with you? Can you suggest reasons why the message wasn't correctly received by everybody?

If we wanted to send such a message we would use a code system which would make for easier and quicker transmission. Of course, the code has to be known by both the person sending and the one receiving the message, then our secret message could look like this:

013, 004, 010 and 007 report location X at 213023.
Bring B3 and C5.

This message is much shorter and less complex than the first one. It can therefore be transmitted more quickly, read more easily and because it is shorter and uses short letter and letter/number combinations, its transmission and decoding will be much more accurate. Try a class example as before, but using a coded message and see how the accuracy improves.

Codes have been used as 'shorthand' to transmit information for centuries: the one that carries the most information for each item of coding is the Navy flag code where a single flag can mean: 'Get out of my way—and I am on a speed trial', and a series of flags can be strung together to send complex messages (Fig. 3.1). Of course, such a system relies on the signal flags being visible. It doesn't work very well at night or in fog!

Another visual code is the semaphore code which enables any message to be sent using hand flags by transmitting each letter separately, but the time taken to

'Data can be represented in many different ways.'

transmit a message varies exactly with the length of message.

A code that relies on sound, not sight, for its transmission is the well known Morse code where each letter or number is coded as a series of dots and/or dashes. Such a system is known as a two-state system. In this respect it has a major feature in common with the code used by computers—binary code—which similarly uses a two-state system, but consisting of 1s and 0s, instead of dots and dashes. *Computer Studies* encoded in Morse would be: –·–·/–––/–––/·–·–/·–·/–/·/·–·
···/–/·–·/–·/·/·/···

We will see how these words are encoded in a computer code later in this chapter.

From the above examples, we can summarise the advantages of encoding data as:

(*a*) It is easier and quicker to transmit.
(*b*) Accuracy of reading is improved.

REPRESENTATION OF DATA 13

'I am in distress and require immediate assistance: I have received serious damage in a collision'

Fig. 3.1 Signal flags and their interpretation

Fig. 3.2 A section of a page from a spare parts reference manual

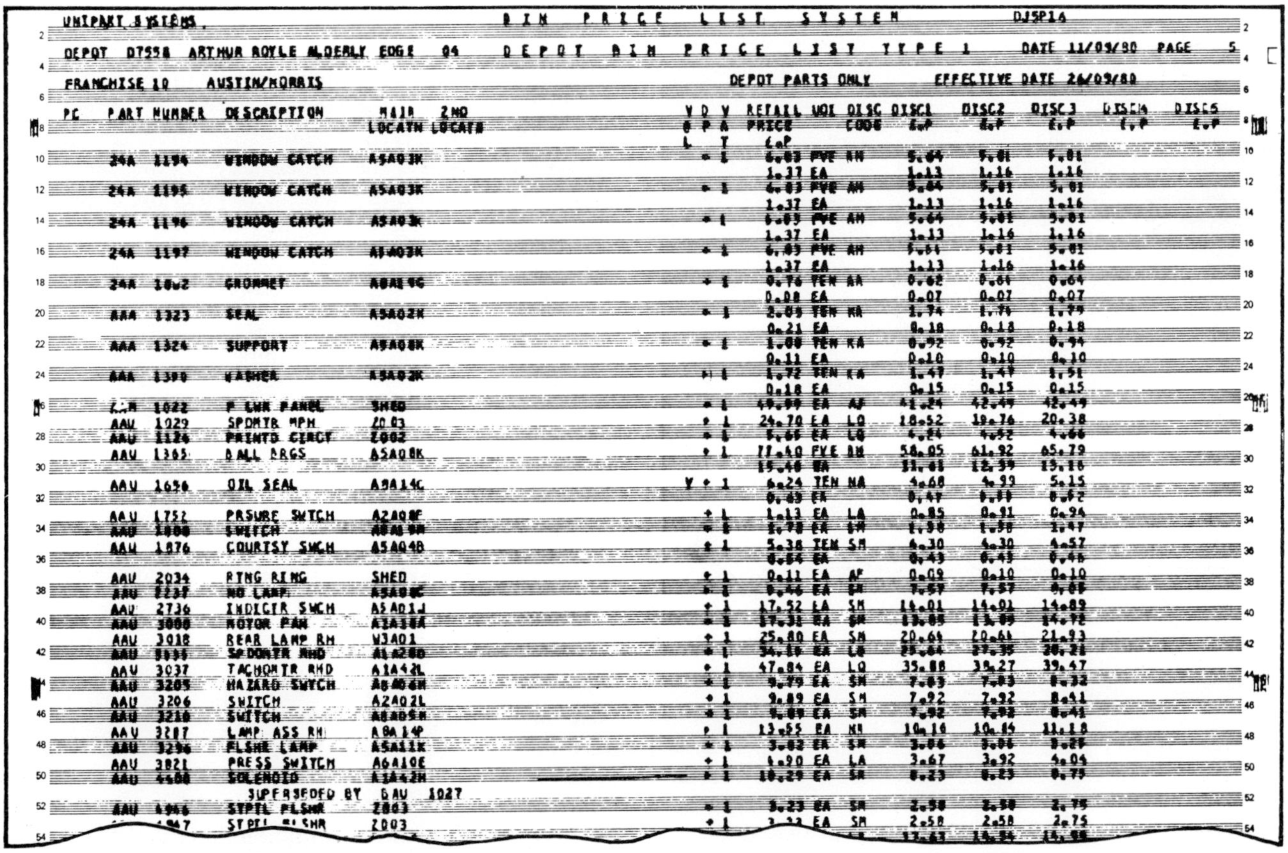

A third and most important reason, is that use of a coding system can save enormous amounts of space, particularly for data storage.

If we look again at a library cataloguing system, any book will have a title, and author and possibly other details. It also has an International Standard Book Number (ISBN). Every book has its own ISBN and if we quote this number on its own to a library, the library will be able to identify the book. One example of a long title becoming a short code number is: *In search of watermills: a light-hearted account in informative jingles of the vanishing water-mills in the county of Norfolk.*–ISBN 0 90309032 5.

Another familiar example can be found in catalogue shops where each item which can be purchased has its own catalogue number and this number is all that is needed to identify the item. For example, 200X0058 is the code number for a particular calculator in one catalogue.

A final example of the use of a coding system can be found in most large garages in the spare parts department. Such a garage may have thousands of different spare parts which are housed in hundreds of bins on many shelves in the stores. Each bin will have the part number of the spare part clearly marked on the outside so that once the part number has been obtained from the microfilm system described in Chapter 2, the actual spare can be obtained easily and quickly from the stores. The part number will appear on the invoice and will also be used when the garage re-orders from the manufacturer. Here is an example of a spare part which has a long description which is simplified into a simple part number: 'exhaust pipe clamp support bracket (rear); forward box; right-hand side' is coded as AEX 1007PB3. Fig. 3.2 shows a section of a computer print-out of a spare parts reference manual.

Class project: Find as many different codes as possible and try to group them into different types of coding, e.g. numeric, alpha, mixed. See if there is any pattern to the codes and suggest reasons why a particular code has been used. Is it an economical code and is it a good code to use with a computer? In groups, invent a code for use with, for example, different types of paper and exercise books used in your school. Discuss each code to see if it satisfies the requirements of a good computer code and modify where necessary.

3.2 Representation of data in digital form

Nowadays, most people are aware that a digital computer works using the binary system. This is correct, but it is only the start of the story. 'Binary' is a number system using base 2, just as denary is a number system using base 10, so we can clearly represent numbers, but we must be able to represent letters, words, mathematical symbols and other characters as well as numbers.

(a) Representation of numbers

The binary 'code' is a number system with base 2 and uses only the digits 0 and 1, so starting from zero in binary, the first eleven binary numbers are:

binary	equivalent to denary
0	0
1	1
10	2
11	3
100	4
101	5
110	6
111	7
1000	8
1001	9
1010	10

In any number system, the most right hand digit in a number *always* represents the units (i.e. x^0 where x is the base being used). The next digit on the left represents the number of (x^1)s; the next, the number of (x^2)s and so on.

In base 10 this gives us:

column heading	10^3	10^2	10^1	10^0
representing	1000	100	10	1

and in base 2:

column heading	2^5	2^4	2^3	2^2	2^1	2^0
representing	32	16	8	4	2	1

Each successive binary column, from the right, has the next power of 2 as its column heading, so to change a denary number into its binary equivalent, we need to know the highest power of 2 that will divide into the denary number and if there is any remainder then the highest that will divide into the remainder, and so on, until we have no remainder left.

To convert 25 to binary, divide it by 2, which gives 12 with a remainder of 1. This 1 is the lowest power of 2 in our answer, 2^0. Now divide 12 by 2, which gives 6 with a remainder of 0. This 0 is the number of (2^1)s in our answer i.e. the next highest power of 2. This is best set out as shown below to show the successive divisions and remainders:

```
2 | 25 | 1      this is the number to go in the 2⁰ column
2 | 12 | 0      this is the number to go in the 2¹ column
2 |  6 | 0      this is the number to go in the 2² column
2 |  3 | 1      this is the number to go in the 2³ column
    1→1         this is the number to go in the 2⁴ column
```

As these remainders represent ascending powers of 2 reading down the page, we must read the remainder column *upwards* to get the correct answer, which is 11001. Here are two more examples:

```
2 | 79 | 1                2 | 145 | 1
2 | 39 | 1                2 |  72 | 0
2 | 19 | 1                2 |  36 | 0
2 |  9 | 1                2 |  18 | 0
2 |  4 | 0                2 |   9 | 1
2 |  2 | 0                2 |   4 | 0
    1→1                   2 |   2 | 0
                              1→1
79 ≡ 1001111            145 ≡ 10010001
```

This method works for any denary number. Another technique is to use a powers of 2 table, and, if necessary, a calculator. It is well worth learning the first 10 powers of 2 or at least remember that $2^{10} \equiv 1024$. You will find this useful in later work with computer codes.

REPRESENTATION OF DATA

Powers of 2 table

Power of 2	Equivalent to
0th	1*
1st	2
2nd	4
3rd	8
4th	16
5th	32
6th	64
7th	128
8th	256
9th	512
10th	1024

* Remember that the 0th power of any number is 1.

To find the binary equivalent of 45, find the largest power of 2 below 45, i.e. $2^5 \equiv 32$, and write a 1 in the 2^5 position:

Power of 2   5 4 3 2 1 0
giving: 1 – – – – –

Subtract 32 from 45 giving 13. We cannot subtract the next highest power of 2 from 13 ($2^4 \equiv 16$), and therefore we must write a zero in the 2^4 position, giving:

1 0 – – – –

Can we subtract the next highest power of 2 from 13? $2^3 \equiv 8$. Yes, therefore write a 1 in the 2^3 position giving:

1 0 1 – – –

Continue this process: $13 - 8 = 5$. Can we subtract 2^2 ($\equiv 4$)? Yes: add a 1, giving:

1 0 1 1 – –

Subtract 4 from 5 giving 1. Can we subtract 2^1 ($= 2$)? No: add a 0, giving:

1 0 1 1 0 –

Can we subtract 2^0 ($= 1$)? Yes: add a 1, giving:

1 0 1 1 0 1

There is no remainder so the conversion is complete. This process looks lengthy when each step is written down but in practice it can be very quick and is a good mental exercise if a calculator is not used.

Fig 3.3 shows the conversion algorithm in flowchart form.

Try these: convert to binary 401, 225, 999.

It is easy to see then, that if we can generate zeros and ones inside a computer and join them together as we have just done to represent powers of 2, then we can 'make' a binary number. The maximum size of the binary number depends on the number of ones and zeros we can use. The ones and zeros are called *bits*. A number of bits joined together form a binary *word*. If we have a 1-bit word, this bit could either be 0 or 1 and we could therefore represent a total of two numbers. If we create a 2-bit word we can use it to represent 2^2 different numbers: 00,01,10,11, representing four denary numbers 0,1,2 and 3. Three bits will enable us to represent 2^3 different numbers, 0–7; four bits 2^4, 0–15; and so on.

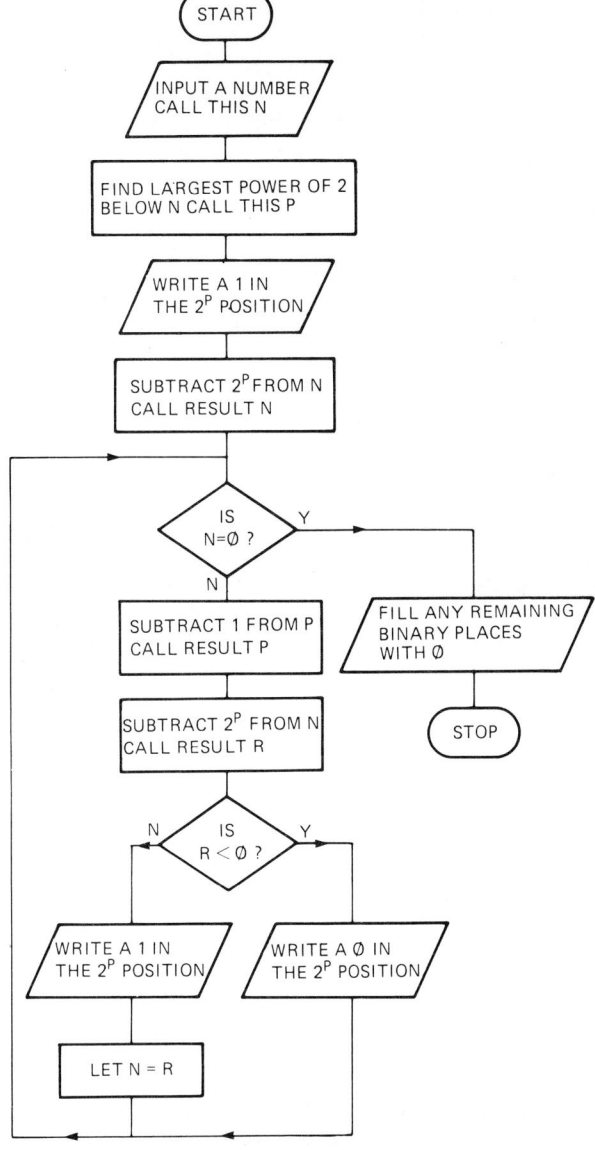

Fig. 3.3 Denary to binary conversion algorithm in flowchart form

In general, with *n* bits we can represent 2^n different numbers and the range of numbers is from 0 to $(2^n - 1)$. We can therefore see that an increase of one bit doubles the number of numbers we can represent. We will see, in Chapter 7, how many bits we need to use to make our word a 'useful' length.

Let us look at one more aspect of a digital binary word—accuracy of representation of a number. If we take, as an example, a 6-bit number, we know that the range of numbers that we can represent is 0–63. Using the upper limit, this would appear in our binary word as: 111111. We can change any of these ones to zero but only the most right-hand 1 really represents 1 (the others are all higher powers of 2), so that changing this 1 for a 0 changes 1 part in 63. Putting this another way, we can detect a change of 1 part in 63, which is just less than 1.6%. If our binary word has 10 bits, the smallest detectable change is 1 part in 1024 (0.1%). 16 bits gives an accuracy of 1 part in 65536 (0.0015%) and 32 bits gives an accuracy of 1 part in 4294967296 (0.000000024%).

(b) Representation of characters

In Chapter 1 we saw that data is not always just numbers. Data can be letters, words or symbols as well as numbers and data in this form must also be translated into 'binary' for processing in a digital computer.

This is done by converting each letter or character into 'binary' using a code which is itself based on binary. If we are going to code any sort of data, the minimum set of symbols we would need to encode would be all the capital letters (26) plus the numerals 0–9 (10). In order to code these in binary we would need 36 'binary combinations'. Five bits will only give 2^5 (i.e. 32) combinations so we need a minimum of 6 bits, which will give 64 combinations (2^6). We now have 28 unused codes but we have not coded any special characters from a normal typewriter keyboard, eg. ! " + (* etc. There are some 30 such symbols, depending on the type set in use and if we chose the 28 most useful, we have used up all the available codes.

Unfortunately, all computers need special characters to control the execution of the program or the operation of the computer, so more codes are needed. If we add one more bit, making 7, we can now have 128 codes which is quite sufficient for encoding most types of data. Many different codes were used in the early days of computing but (fortunately) in 1968 an international standard code was agreed. This code is known as the ASCII code (American Standard Code for Information Interchange) and is given in full in Appendix 4. We can see from a quick glance at the code that every letter, character and symbol is represented by a group of 7 bits.

There may now be some confusion regarding the binary representation of numbers. In section (*a*) we saw how numbers are represented in binary and 5_{10} (the number 5 to a base of 10) is converted into 101_2 (or 0101 in 4 bits), but in the ASCII code 5_{10} is converted to 0110101. The reason for this *apparent* difference is that the left hand 3 bits of the ASCII code are used to define the 'group' to which the right hand 4 bits belong.

We can see from the table that the 4-bit code for !, 1, A, a, Q, q and two control characters, is the same. The right hand 4 bits are 0001, but the left hand 3 bits change to indicate which group the character is in. This means that 000/001 are all control characters; 010/011 are the numerals and most of the normal keyboard characters; 100/101 are mainly capital letters; and 110/111 are mainly lower case characters. The eighth bit is used in two ways: in large mainframe computers it is usually designated as a parity bit (see Chapter 4) and in most microcomputers it is used to indicate that the remaining 7 bits are the code for a graphics character.

3.3 Analogue representation

Most 'natural' data occurs, not in digital form, but in analogue form. (The data is represented by a continuously variable physical quantity.)

Probably the most common example of analogue data is the speed of a car. This is usually measured by a speedometer with which we are all familiar. The needle of the speedometer does not move round the dial at 50 km/h, for example, but it moves slowly round as the vehicle gains speed and becomes stationary at a point on the dial where the figure 50 has been painted. Any change in speed is transformed into a change in position of the needle which moves to point to a new figure on the dial. The position of the needle on the scale represents an analogue of the actual speed, which is said to be *continuously variable*. The vehicle can go at any, and every, speed between say 30 and 50 km/h. For example it could go at 37 km/h, but it can also go at 37.5 km/h and 37.54325 km/h, but it is impossible to record speeds to this accuracy on a normal speedometer.

Many other physical quantities can only be measured using an analogue device to record their variations: pressure, temperature, voltage and current are probably

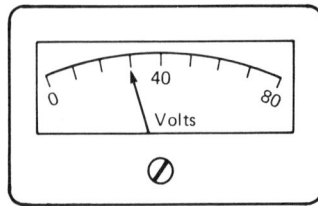

Fig. 3.4 A meter showing the analogue representation of voltage

the most easily appreciated. All of these quantities can vary continuously over some range and are measured, usually, on an instrument similar to a speedometer, i.e. a dial and a pointer needle (Fig. 3.4).

Whatever the quantity being measured, the accuracy of measurement depends on two factors:
(a) the accuracy of the dial
(b) the interpretation of a human reading.

We have seen that measurement using digital techniques can be very accurate, (if the binary word is big enough), but most physical quantities do not produce a digital output (normally called *discrete*), they produce one that is continuously variable. However, if these two techniques are combined we should have a method of recording a continuously variable quantity to a high degree of accuracy. This technique is widely used and is called *analogue to digital conversion*. It is discussed in detail in Chapter 5.

Exercises 3.1

1 Car registration numbers are made up in any of the following formats:
  (i) 1 to 3 letters followed by 1 to 3 digits followed by a single letter (e.g. ABC 123 X).
  (ii) 1 to 3 letters followed by 1 to 3 digits (e.g. ABC 123)
  (iii) 1 to 3 digits followed by 1 to 3 letters (e.g. 123 ABC)
  (iv) 1 or 2 letters followed by 4 digits (e.g. AB 1234)
  (v) 4 digits followed by 1 or 2 letters (e.g. 1234 AB)

(a) What is the least number of bits needed to represent an alphabetic character?
(b) What is the least number of bits needed to represent a 3-digit number?
(c) What is the least number of bits needed to represent a 4-digit number?
(d) Suggest a way of encoding registration numbers of the above types in an economical manner (i.e. using as few bits as possible). State the code which you have used.
(e) Fully encode, in binary, the following registration number:
$$\text{WNO 205 F} \quad (AEB, 1978)^*$$

2 (a) Explain the essential difference between the representation of data in digital form and in analogue form.
(b) Briefly explain how data in analogue form is modified for direct input to a digital computer.
(*AEB, 1978*)

Summary

- Data needs to be coded for ease and accuracy of transmission.
- In a digital computer, data is usually coded in binary form.
- All the letters, numerals and characters can be coded in 7 bits (ASCII or ISO7 code).
- Data in digital form is man-made.
- 'Natural data' is in analogue form.

4 Data capture and checking

4.1 Data capture

In Chapter 2 we learned that if we process data in a computer, we can get useful information as output, but if we are going to put data into the computer, we have got to get it from somewhere! What type of data? Where do we get it from? How do we obtain it? These are questions that we must answer every time we are preparing to input data to a computer.

What type of data?

We cannot answer the question 'What type of data?' properly unless we know *why* we want the data. If we want to make a file containing the names and addresses of pupils so that we can print address labels, then obviously we need to obtain the name and address of the pupils in whom we are interested.

If we want to find the top 10 records of the fourth form then we need to ask all the fourth form the name of their favourite record. If we want to find the average age of the cars in a particular road, we need to find the age of all the cars in the road. To find the average number of vehicles passing along a road, we need to count every vehicle going along the road over a long period. To work out who has come top in a particular exam, we need to know the marks of all the people who have taken the exam.

In these examples our data has varied from simple numbers, if we are counting vehicles, to names of pop groups to enable us to find the top 10 for our form.

Where do we get our data from?

Where we get our data from is very much linked to the type of data we require. In the first example above, where we want to make a file containing names and addresses, the most obvious 'place' from which to get the data is from the people themselves. However, if we cannot ask any of them directly at the time we want to make the file, we will have to obtain our data some other way. How? By asking someone else? They might not know. By looking in the telephone directory? They might not be on the telephone. By looking in the electoral register? They might have moved since the register was compiled. Somewhere, somebody has a record of the data we require, but we might have to search for it!

'We would not always use the same technique to collect the original data.'

How can we find the age of a car? We certainly can't ask the car! The number plate might tell us the answer, but only if we know the coding system used by the vehicle licensing department. The owner probably will know, but we might not be able to find him. If we do find him, and he doesn't know, he can look in the car's log book, which records the date the car was first licensed.

There is a very great amount of data which can be obtained from many different sources.

How do we obtain the data?

How we obtain the data again depends very much on what data we want. To find the top 10 records in our form we need to organise a survey and ask all participants to fill in a questionnaire. If we want to count the number of vehicles passing along a road, we must use some method of recording each time a vehicle passes. This might simply be by marking a tick on a sheet of paper. Alternatively, we might use a hand-held counter, operated by the observer when a vehicle passes, which adds to the total every time a lever is pressed. A more sophisticated method is often used by the transport department when the traffic density is high or the count has to be taken over a long period. This consists of a simple flexible tube fastened, temporarily, across the road and which is connected to a portable recorder on the footpath. When a vehicle passes over the tube, a small puff of air activates a counter in the recorder—it is simple, but very effective!

Although this is an automatic, (as distinct from manual), method of obtaining data, we would still need to input this data to a computer if we wish to process it. This involves a further stage of transcription or data preparation. In this case this would be simple as the data might be only one number representing the count per day (or hour) over the period of the survey. But imagine the problems involved in trying to record the number of different items sold in one week in a large store or supermarket. The job of recording what has been sold is itself difficult and tedious if the recording is done manually, even when special forms are used to capture the data. However, all this data has then to be read again whilst being prepared for input to a computer. This involves extra cost, longer time to complete the work and the very high probability of introducing errors.

Much development has taken place during recent years to enable this type of data to be recorded directly without the need for any human intervention. These techniques will be discussed fully later in this chapter but now let us look at how we can capture data by manual methods.

Manual methods of data capture

Probably the most widely used method of obtaining data is through a survey. These are carried out daily in many different ways to obtain a wide variety of data. You may have been stopped and invited to answer some questions regarding your television viewing habits or which toothpaste you use. Surveys are often taken at airports and railway stations to obtain information relating to the travelling public. Each week a list of the 'top 20' records is compiled and published from data obtained through a survey to find which records have sold most in record shops.

The quantity and variety of data that can be obtained through surveys is almost limitless but any survey about any subject requires a good, well designed form on which to capture data.

4.2 Form design

It is very easy to design a bad form!

The first, and most important thing to realise about a form for capturing data is that the use of the form does not finish when the data has been captured. The form must then be used, perhaps by another person, to enable them to process the data to obtain the required results. If the data is to be processed by a computer, it must be converted into a machine readable state, before it is fed into the computer. We do not want to waste time and money extracting the data from one form and entering in onto another form before it can be processed. We must, therefore, think ahead when we start designing a form to obtain data.

Secondly, the form should be as simple as possible, asking only the necessary questions in the most concise manner. It should not be cluttered up with a lot of unnecessary 'bumph'! Thirdly, the questions to be asked should be completely unambiguous. They should be written in such a manner that they can be answered without any further explanation necessary, and the questions must be worded in such a manner that only neat, precise answers can be given. Lastly, it should be quite clear where the answer is to be written—preferably in a designated place on the form.

Now, let us look at some examples of forms designed to capture data and see if they can be improved by considering the four 'rules' above. What is wrong with the form shown in Fig. 4.1? It is a poor form: the first three lines are quite clear but is the rest really necessary? It doesn't actually say what the project is, which might, at least, make it more interesting.

```
What is your age?     _____
Are you a boy or a girl?  _____
Which form are you in?  _____
This information is required for a computer studies project.
When you have completed the form, please return it to either
John Smith, Mary Evans, Peter Brown, Simon Wood or Fred Collins.
Thank you very much for completing this questionaire, the information
you have given will be treated in the strictest confidence and will
be very useful in our survey
```

Fig. 4.1 A form to capture data

What would be your answer to the first question on the form? Assume you are 15 years 3 months. Would you write that or 15.3 or 15 3/12 or just 15 or would you be one of those who would try and work it out exactly and write 15 years 3 months, 1 week, 4 days?

Although this is a very simple questionnaire requiring only three answers, the answers should be written in prepared areas or 'boxes', on the form. This makes it much easier for the person reading the form because the three answers will always appear in the same place on every form.

The version of the form shown in Fig. 4.2 statisfies the four 'rules' of form design given at the beginning of this section.

```
Questionaire to be used in computer studies survey

To find the average age in each fourth form class.
PLEASE WRITE YOUR REPLY ONLY IN THE SPACES PROVIDED
1   What is your age in years and months? (eg. 15.03)  _____
2   What is your sex? Write M or F                      _____
3   Which form are you in ?                             _____

Thank you. Please return completed form to Mr X.
```

Fig. 4.2 An improved form

For a second example let us design a questionnaire to enable us to find out about holidays. First, we must decide what we want to get out of the survey. We will choose:
(*a*) What is the most popular type of holiday?
(*b*) Where did most people go this year?
(*c*) Who did they go with?

Now, let us design our form in stages.

Stage 1: Write down the questions that you think will lead you to answers to the survey questions above. These could be:
(i) Where did you go for your holiday?
(ii) How did you travel?
(iii) Who did you go with?
(iv) How long did you go for?
(v) What did you do?

Now examine each question and decide if it *really* is going to contribute to what we are trying to find out.

Question (i) is clearly needed to answer part (*b*) of our survey. Does (ii) fit in with anything? No, so cross it out. Question (iii) matches (*c*) in our survey exactly so we keep this question, but can we say the same for (iv)? The length of holiday does not figure in (*a*), (*b*) or (*c*), although it could be implied in part (*a*). If we really want length of holiday to be part of our survey we must go back to the original aims and modify them to include length of holiday; e.g. (*a*) What is the most popular type/length of holiday? Alternatively we may include it as a completely separate aim; e.g. (*d*) What is the most popular length of holiday? Although question (v) is a very vague question in its present form, this question, or at least one something like it, must be asked to provide data for part (*a*) of the survey.

Stage 2: Rewrite the questions using stage 1 as a guide.
(i) Where did you go for your holiday?
(ii) What did you do?
(iii) Who did you go with?

Now we think we have asked the right questions, but are they worded so that only the replies we want can be given?

Stage 3: Ask yourself each question and write down possible replies.

To question (i) you might answer: Blackpool, France, cruising in the Mediterranean, Aunt Mary's, caravanning, my friend's cottage, Wash Lane Farm, Llwyndaffadd or New Orleans.

All the replies may well be correct but is this what we really want? You should realise that if 100 different people answered question (i) you could get 100 different replies! Clearly, we have got to stop replies like 'Aunt Mary's' and 'caravanning' and exact, but unhelpful, replies like 'Wash Lane Farm'. Also, do replies like France and New Orleans help or could they both be 'abroad'? If that is a better answer, how do we get 'abroad' as a reply instead of the actual country?

The answers to question (ii) could be even more varied and worse still, the question allows an individual to list *all* the things he did! Do we really want that or do we want to know, in broad categories, the *type* of activity he did?

Question (iii) seems less likely to produce the 'wrong' reply, but is: 'Mum, Dad, Billy, Frances, Alan, Uncle Joe, Auntie Jean and the twins, Spot and Paddy' a perfectly fair reply to the question?

It is, but is it the helpful reply we need to answer part (iii) of our survey? If we do not want this sort of reply we must ensure that we cannot get it and make it clear what we do want.

Obviously, the wording of the questions has to be altered to make them unambiguous and we must structure the questions to get the replies we want.

Stage 4: Rewrite the questions again!

Obviously questions (i) and (ii) allowed far too many answers, all of which were actually correct, so we must look again at the aims of the survey and decide on possible catagories for 'where' and 'what do' whilst still remembering the overall aim of the project is to find the most popular type of holiday and where this is. The answers to question (i) given above can clearly be split into two broad groups: abroad or UK, but are two categories of answer enough to satisfy the requirements of the survey? Probably not, so each of these categories can have sub-questions to make the replies more detailed but still structured. For question (ii) we will provide for a number of popular activities, but we must also allow for 'other activities'.

The questions for the survey form now look like this:
(i) Where did you go for your holiday this year? Abroad/UK Seaside/country/mountains.
(ii) What did you do on holiday? Walking/climbing/swimming/water-skiing/tennis/fishing/boating/horse riding/something else.
(iii) Who did you go with? Your family/friend/ friend's family/ alone.

Note that more than one answer is still possible in question (ii) and this should be made clear on the questionnaire.

Now we can move to the last stage which is to plan out the actual form in detail remembering the four rules.

Stage 5: Design the final form (Fig. 4.3). This form will certainly capture the data. but imagine you are the person who has to read perhaps hundreds of these forms for data input to a computer! Imagine trying to find the ticks! We haven't paid much attention to rule 1 and not considered rule 4 at all!

Holiday survey

Please tick the appropriate answer to each part of each question.
(Note: You may tick more than one activity in question 3)

1   Where did you go for your holiday this year? *UK / abroad*
2   Was your holiday in the *mountains / country / coast?*
3   What did you do on your holiday? *walking / climbing / swimming tennis / fishing / boating / horse riding / another activity*
4   Who did you go with? *your family / a friend your friend's family / alone*

Fig. 4.3 Holiday survey form

Also, by altering the method of answering question 2, we can find out more about the popularity of the listed activities than if we just use a tick. As question 2 is, in Fig. 4.3, any person who walked, played tennis and fished during their holiday, would tick these three activities. Another person might tick walking, swimming, tennis and a third person indicate walking, swimming and boating. If we now analyse just these three persons' activities, it would seem that walking is the most popular because it got three 'votes'; tennis and swimming equal with two 'votes' each, whilst fishing and boating only received one 'vote' each.

However, the first person might have played a lot of tennis, fished a fair amount and only walked once. The second person might be a keen swimmer, liked a bit of walking and play tennis only occasionally whilst the third only walked when he was forced to and spent almost all his holiday swimming and boating. Although all three people *have* walked, clearly this is not the most popular activity and from reading the above, it is not at all clear which activity really is the most popular. If we could get some detail of how each activity was rated by each person completing a questionnaire, without making the question too complex, then we could clearly make a much better analysis of activities than can be obtained from question 2 as it is in version 1.

This can be achieved by a system known as *weighting*. Instead of just ticking each activity which we have done on holiday, we rank them in order of preference by awarding each one a mark from (say) three to one. Three marks go to the most popular, two to the next and one to the least popular. If we now do this for our three people

above, they might be weighted as below:
Person 1: walking 1, tennis 3, fishing 2
Person 2: walking 2, tennis 1, swimming 3
Person 3: walking 1, boating 2, swimming 3

We can now see easily that, although walking does appear in each of the three people's activities, it was the least popular with two of them and only received a total of four 'votes' along with tennis. Whilst swimming, although only listed by two people, collected six votes, making it easily the most popular activity.

It is very easy to include a weighting system in a survey form but we must make it quite clear, on the form, how to use it.

We now need to structure question 2 in a different layout in order to provide space for the 'preference number' and, in doing this, we will see how to make all the answers easier to read when preparing the data for processing. This is done simply by allocating a defined space for each response which is well clear of the questions. This space is usually in the form of a box in which we can put one character, in this example, a tick or one number (Fig. 4.4).

In the example in Fig. 4.4, we have quantified our response to question 3 in order to get a more accurate result from the survey. It also means that the person reading the data for processing has only to read a single figure instead of a word. This is particularly important if the data is being prepared for input to a computer.

We should therefore try, wherever possible, to structure the questions to enable a single digit answer to be given. The question 'Can you drive?' can only be answered by 'yes' or 'no', but if we state that 'yes' = 1 and 'no' = 0 then 1 or 0 is the answer to the question. Multiple answer questions can be treated in the same manner.

e.g. Which house are you in?
    If Tatton, write 1
    If Durham, write 2
    If Egerton, write 3
    If Stanley, write 4

Even questions which can have different answers can be structured this way:

e.g. Do you go to the cinema?
    If regularly, write 1
    If sometimes, write 2
    If seldom, write 3
    If never, write 4

Remember, the aim of a questionnaire is:
To get only the data we require......
.. as accurately, as possible......
.. with the minimum amount of inconvenience to the participants...
.. in a form that can be read most easily when the data is being prepared for input to a computer.

22 COMPUTER STUDIES

```
Holiday survey

Please put a tick in the appropriate box for Question 1, 2 and 3
           (only tick one box per question)

1   Where did you go for your holiday this year?    UK          ☐
                                                    abroad      ☐

2   Was your holiday in the                         mountains   ☐
                                                    country     ☐
                                                    coast       ☐

3   Who did you go with?                            your family        ☐
                                                    a friend           ☐
                                                    your friend's family ☐
                                                    alone              ☐

For Question 4 only, please indicate which activity you did
most by putting a 5 in the appropriate box, then a 4 against
the one which came next, and so on, for a maximum of 5 activities.

4   What did you do on holiday?                     walking         ☐
                                                    climbing        ☐
                                                    swimming        ☐
                                                    water ski-ing   ☐
                                                    tennis          ☐
                                                    fishing         ☐
                                                    boating         ☐
                                                    horse riding    ☐
                                                    another activity ☐

Thank you. Please return the completed form to Mr. X.
```

Fig. 4.4 An improved version of the holiday survey form

Exercises 4.1

1 Get a class to answer question 4 of the holiday survey in two ways:
   (*a*) by ticking each activity each person did on holiday, and
   (*b*) by 'weighting', 5 to 1 in order of popularity of activity.
   Find 'the most popular activities' by each method. Discuss the differences.
2 Design a questionnaire
   (*a*) to find out how pupils come to school
   (*b*) to find out what pupils think of school uniform.

Forms are still used extensively in commerce and business as a prime source of data capture and some examples of typical forms are given in Fig. 4.5.

4.3 Data transcription

The data that we wish to process has now been captured and entered onto a special form which is, by definition, human readable, but which is probably not capable of being 'read' by a computer. Some of the methods by which this data can be input to the computer are given in this section. (Other methods, where the data is not on a human readable form, and details of the equipment used, are given in Chapter 7.)

Historically, the first technique for transcribing data into machine readable form used a *punched card* (invented by Hollerith in 1895), and for many years this was the main method used to input data to a computer. Most computer systems designed mainly for data processing between 1950 and 1975 included a card reader and card punch as part of their peripheral equipment (see Chapter 7).

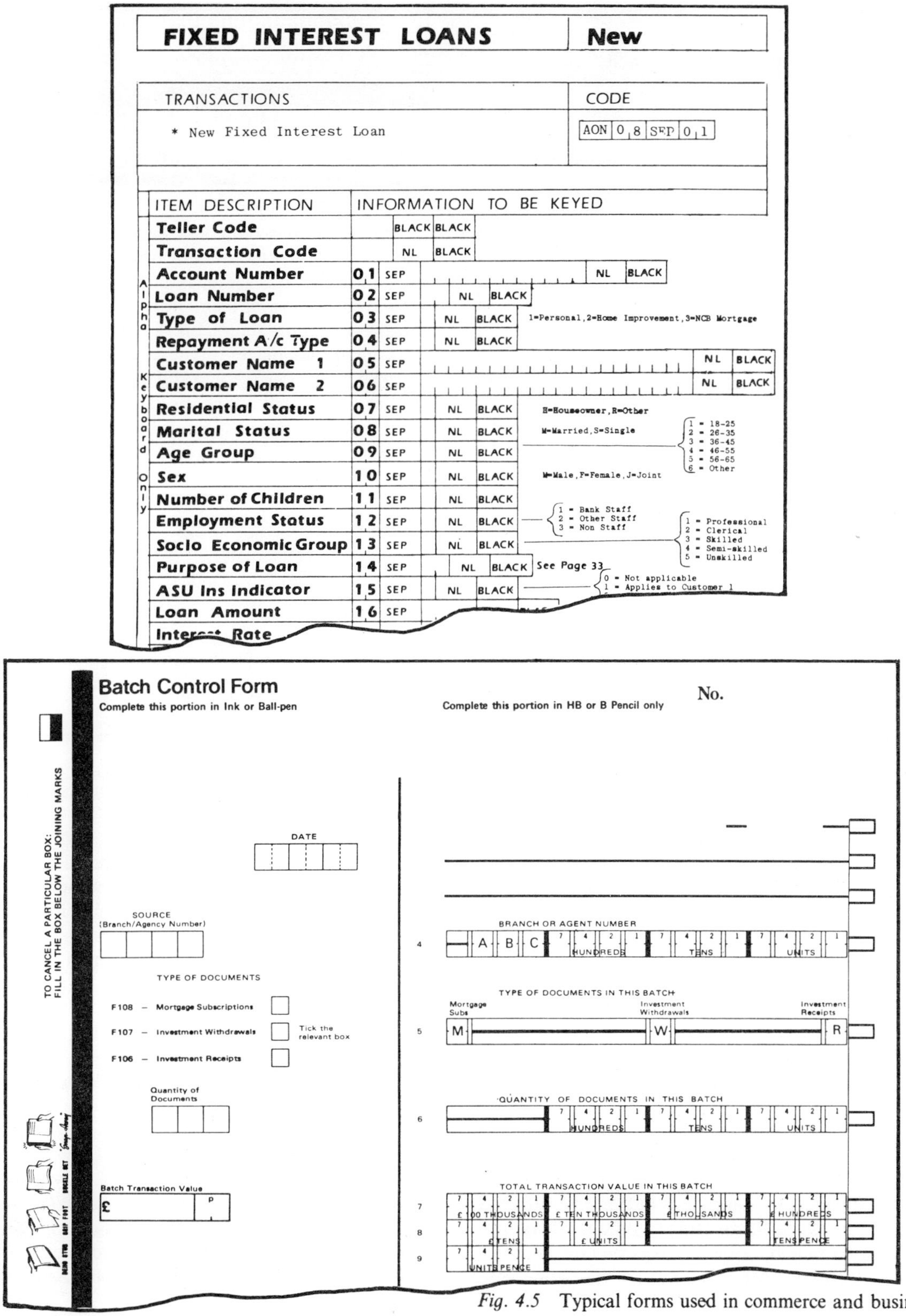

DATA CAPTURE AND CHECKING 23

Fig. 4.5 Typical forms used in commerce and business

24 COMPUTER STUDIES

Fig. 4.6 shows the most commonly used type of punched card. It is 80 columns wide and each column has up to 12 punching positions. Each letter of the alphabet, each symbol and the digits 0 to 9 have a code which uses one, two or three punching positions. When data is typed on a *card punch keyboard*, rectangular knives punch holes in the card in accordance with the code.

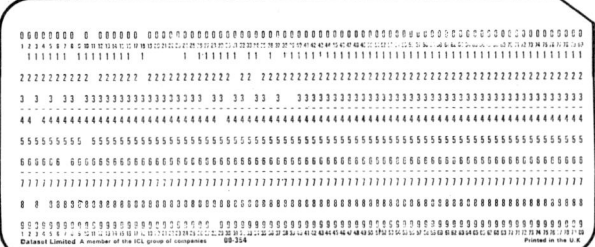

Fig. 4.6 Punched card

Barclaycard use a punched card in an interesting way, in that one card is used both to capture the data and to transcribe it into machine readable form. When details of the goods purchased are written on the top sheet of a 'pack' of stationery a carbon copy of these details is printed onto a blank (punched) card which forms the bottom sheet of the pack. This card is subsequently punched to record the transaction details in machine readable form, and subsequently 'read' the data using a *punched card reader* (see Chapter 7).

Although punched cards were the main form of machine readable data in most commercial data processing environments, *paper tape* was equally widely used in scientific and mathematical computing. The use of punched paper tape to hold coded data was well established by the early 1930s in telegraphic communication using the teletypewriter (see Chapter 7), and the early computers all used paper tape to input data or to control the operation of the computer.

As with punched cards, a special code is necessary to enable data to be punched into the tape. Although various codes have been devised using five, seven or eight holes, the seven-hole ASCII code (see Chapter 4) is most widely used. The eighth hole is usually used as a parity check bit. Each character is coded and when the data is keyed in using a tape punch or teletypewriter, round knives punch holes in the tape corresponding to the character code (Fig. 4.7).

Punched cards and paper tape have, until recently, been the most widely used methods of transcribing data into machine readable form. Unfortunately, the equipment needed to punch, or read, cards or tape, is slow, complex and costly, so much research has gone into finding alternative methods of data transcription.

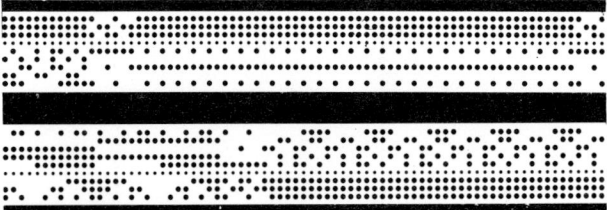

Fig. 4.7 Paper tape

One method which has been used widely in educational establishments, but not to any extent in commercial data processing, is based on the card system. However, instead of using punched holes in the card to represent the characters, black pencil marks are made in the appropriate places on the card. This card is known as *a mark sense card* (Fig. 4.8) and obviously does away with the need for a card punch, but as the person transcribing the data on to the cards needs to know the code for each character, the process is very slow compared with using punched cards.

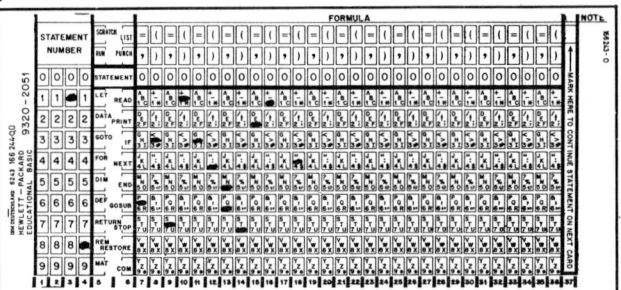

Fig. 4.8 Mark sense card

An extension of the mark sense card is the *mark sense document*. The documents are pre-printed and pencil marks are made in pre-defined areas on the form. The position of the marks determines the value of the data. The marks are read by optical methods. Mark sense forms are widely used as source documents for ordering goods for supermarkets where the quantity of any item to be ordered is marked on the printed form. Another popular use is in marking multiple-choice exam questions (Fig. 4.9). The student's answer to a question is selected from those given and a mark is made in the appropriate answer box.

The introduction, during the 1960s of the *visual display unit* (VDU), brought about a revolution in data transcription. It was now possible to type the data using a simple keyboard attached to a VDU and to display the data on the screen as it was typed. Any errors could easily be seen and corrected on the screen *before* the data was transmitted to the central processor. By the late 1970s, the VDU and keyboard had become the most widely accepted method of transcribing data for input to a computer.

DATA CAPTURE AND CHECKING 25

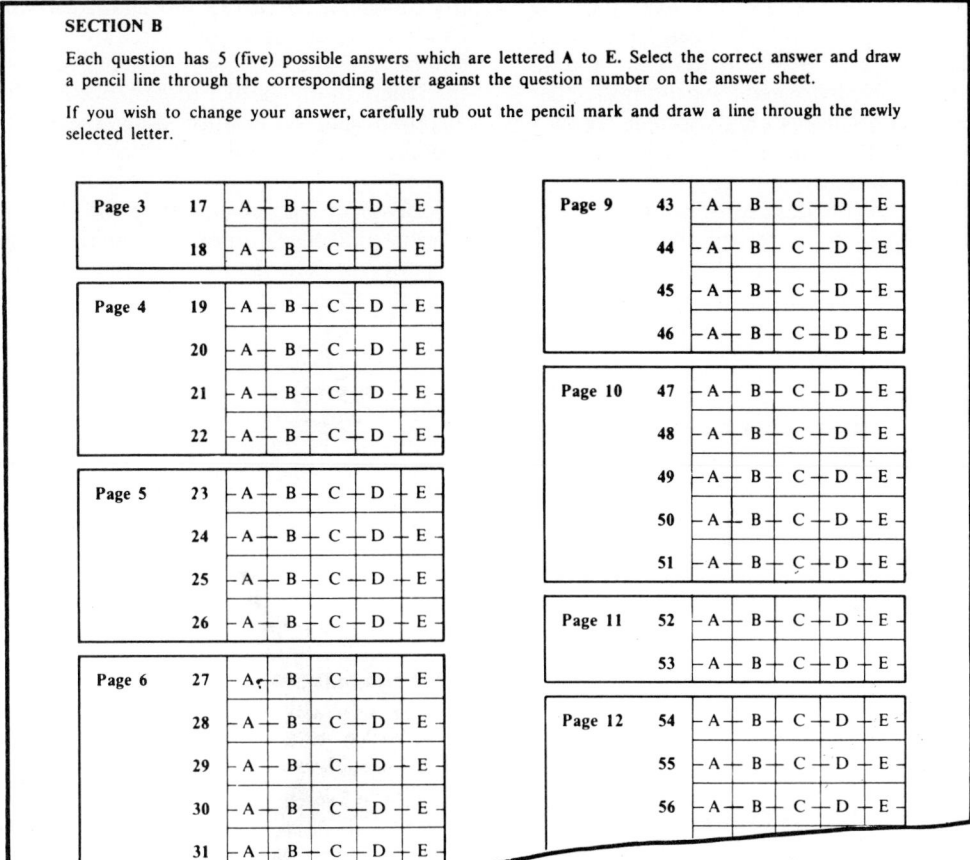

Fig. 4.9 Multiple choice exam answer sheet

4.4 Data verification

One of the oldest sayings in computing is 'Garbage in—garbage out' (GIGO). In other words, if the wrong data is input into the computer we must expect the wrong results to be output. It is therefore most important to ensure that the data input to the computer is (*a*) the data we want to put in and (*b*) the correct data. The process of checking data before input to the computer is known as *verification*. Data punched onto paper tape and cards can be verified by checking the punched media against a second keyed input of the same data. The machine used, a verifier, gives warning if the two sets of data do not match and the suspect card or tape is checked visually to detect the error.

Decline in the use of cards and tape as input media and increasing use of VDUs and 'intelligent terminals' for off-line data preparation has meant that more sophisticated methods of data checking have been introduced, which do not simply check the accuracy of data preparation but the accuracy of the data as well. Such checking is known as data validation.

4.5 Data validation

The actual type of validation checking performed varies considerably from system to system and depends largely on the type of data and the 'intelligence' of the VDU. An on-line, 'non-intelligent' VDU will simply display any data typed on its keyboard and, when instructed, transmit this data to the central processor. The only checking is visual and the only method of correction is by using the cursor to delete a previously typed character. An 'intelligent' VDU is one which uses some form of program to control its operation and use and is controlled by, probably, a microprocessor (see Chapter 7).

We will assume that an 'intelligent' VDU is to be used to transcribe the data and look at some types of data validation that can be achieved. All the checks which follow come under the general heading of *prompt* checks.

If the data to be input consists of name, address, age, telephone number etc. then the VDU would display these words as prompts and the actual data is then typed in, in the space alongside the prompt. The program controlling this would not allow, for example, the address to be typed in if the name had been omitted. As the data will almost certainly be read from a data capture form, it is possible to format the prompts so that they appear in the same places on the screen as they appear on the form, thus making it easier for the operator to read and check the data. This feature is used to great advantage when the data form is complex and 'nonesense data' (e.g. a part number such as A3XT4785Z/s) and only numerical data are being input. The form shown in Fig. 4.10 is typical.

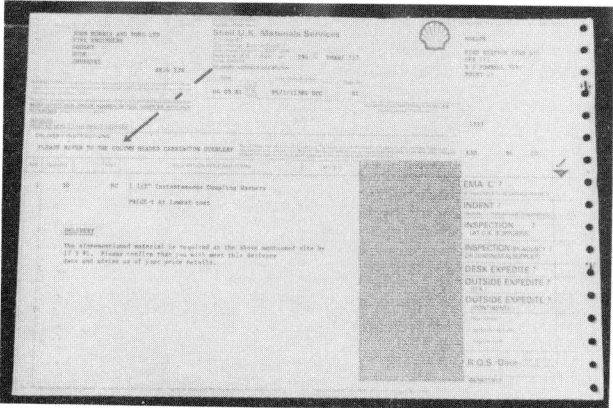

Fig. 4.10 A typical output document in which all the printed data has been validated through a prompt check before output

Many different checks can be done using this type of system. The number and type of check will depend on the type and complexity of the data and the amount of sophistication which has been built into the controlling program. Among these checks are:

(a) *Type of data.* Data can be of three different types: wholly alpha, wholly numeric or mixed. A name should always be alpha, an address could be either, and an age, only numeric. It is easy to check the data to see if it conforms to the right type.

(b) *Number of characters.* Most data can be stated as having a maximum or minimum or exact number of characters, e.g. any works number in company X is six characters; all part numbers used to make product Y have nine characters, a part number or a car registration number cannot be more than seven characters.

(c) *Data limits.* Some types of data will fall within certain pre-determinable limits which can easily be set. For example an insured person's age may have to be between 16 and 65; the maximum number of component Z which can be ordered at one time is 35; the range of works numbers in use at company X is between 1090 and 5280.

(d) *Restricted values* are particularly applicable to an ordering system. Some items may only be supplied in lots of 50 or 144 or some other fixed amount.

(e) *Combination checks* are again used mainly on an ordering system. If an item P requires 4 bolts to fasten it to a panel and a number N of item P have been ordered, then there should be an order for $4 \times N$ bolts. The cost of any item can be multiplied by the number of items ordered and often this must not exceed a pre-set cash limit.

(f) *Sense* checks ensure that the data makes sense. These would check for example that a gas meter reading was not *less* than the previous one; that a data of birth was not earlier than 1870; that a person's sex is given as either M or F!

Because of the complexity of the computer and its associated peripheral equipment, it is quite possible to input the correct data and get an incorrect result to the processing. To reduce such errors to a minimum, a number of further checks are carried out on the data *while it is being processed.*

Whatever the data which has been input to the computer—names, addresses, part numbers, quantities—inside the computer this data is represented in binary form. Many binary digits are required to hold data as above and if just one digit changes from 0 to 1 or vice versa, or is 'lost', during the processing, then the data changes and an incorrect result may occur or garbage may be output. Such faults can occur, although the introduction of complete microprocessors made as integrated circuits has reduced the likelihood of such errors dramatically.

To try to prevent any errors occurring during processing further validation checks are carried out. One of these checks—the parity check—is built into the computer system and takes place without the user doing anything to implement it, or even being aware that the check is taking place. Other validation checks may be built into the programs controlling the processing of the data. The most commonly used are outlined below.

Parity Check

From the table on page 176 we can see that the ASCII code for the letter B is 1000010; C has the code 1000011; N is 1001111 and V is represented as 1010110. If we examine these codes carefully we find two features:

(a) All the codes consist of 7 bits.

(b) The number of ones in each code varies from two to five, but the code for B and V has an even number of ones in it, and that for C and N has an odd number of ones in it.

An eighth bit is added to the left-hand end of the ASCII code to make the total number of ones even. The code for the above letters then becomes:

    B   01000010   (a zero added)
    C   11000011   (a one added)
    N   11001111   (a one added)
    V   01010110   (a zero added)

All the codes now have an even number of ones in the 8 bit code. This eighth bit is known as the parity check bit and a system using an even number of ones is known as even parity.

Most computer systems employ an even parity check as this makes the 8-bit code for null 00000000, and for delete 11111111, legal codes, i.e. the number of ones in each code is even. This parity check digit can easily be seen on the punched tape in Fig. 4.11.

Fig. 4.11 Punched paper tape showing the parity check digit

The parity check bit is 'added' to the 7 bit code as the data is transcribed and the 8 bits stay together throughout all the processing. At various times during the processing, particularly when the data is being sent to or from storage, the number of ones in each character code is counted (by the system). If the number is even, the processing continues. If it is now odd, a parity check error message is issued and processing stops. The parity bit is automatically removed when the data is output. It should readily be appreciated that if two ones were 'lost' from any code, the parity check would not spot the error as the number of bits would still be even. However, the chances of such an event occurring are very, very small indeed, and other data validation checks can be made to detect the error.

Longitudinal parity check
While the parity check digit described above is applicable only to a single character, a similar check may be done on a block of characters by counting the ones along *each row* and adding a one where necessary to make an even (or odd) number of ones. The length of the

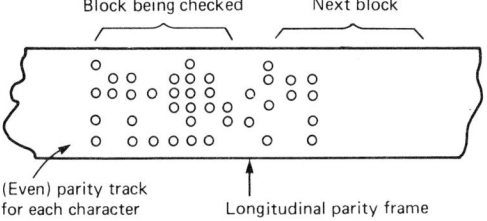

Fig. 4.12 Longitudinal parity check

block is fixed and has no significance other than being the point at which a check is made. This check is usually done on data being written to, or read from, magnetic storage media, particularly magnetic tape (Fig. 4.12).

It can now be seen that if two ones of any single character were lost or mis-read, the longitudinal parity check would fail and an error message would be generated.

The validation checks that follow are normally part of the program used to process the data and therefore as many checks as are considered necessary may be built into any program designed to manipulate data. (The reader is encouraged to include some validation check in any data processing undertaken as part of coursework.)

Check digits
A check digit is an extra digit attached to a number as a means of later checking the validity of the number. The check digit is derived from the number itself in one of a number of possible methods. We will consider some of these check digits as they would affect an account number: 508703127.

Digit sum check. The sum of the digits in the above number is 33 and the sum of these two digits is 6. This digit is calculated by the program and added to the right hand end of the original number at the commencement of processing (giving 5087031276). At various stages during the processing, particularly when data has been sent to, or from, the immediate access store, the check digit is re-calculated and the result compared with the previously calculated check digit. If they are the same, the processing continues. If they differ, an error message is generated and processing stops.

This check is also known as a Mod 9 check because the same check digit is obtained if the number is divided by 9 and the remainder is used as the check digit. One useful feature of a Mod 9 check is that the digit sum of the sum of the check digits will always equal the digit sum of the sum of the data. For example

$$\begin{array}{l} 5\,0\,8\,7\,0\,3\,1\,2\,7 \quad \text{digit sum} = 6 \\ 6\,1\,2\,3\,1\,0\,4\,3\,5 \quad \text{''} \quad \text{''} = 7 \\ 1\,0\,0\,7\,9\,3\,5\,0\,1 \quad \text{''} \quad \text{''} = 8 \\ 2\,7\,9\,3\,0\,4\,5\,1\,6 \quad \text{''} \quad \text{''} = 1 \end{array} \Bigg\} \begin{array}{l} \text{digit sum} \\ = 4 \end{array}$$

Total 1 5 0 1 1 1 1 5 7 9   ''   '' = 4

This is a relatively easy check to build into a data processing program.

It is worth pausing to realise that if the zeros are lost from the original account number, (giving 5873127), or any digits which add up to 9 are also lost (7 and 2 or 8 and 1, leaving 573), and these digits are mixed in any order then divided by 9, the remainder will ALWAYS be 6! Whilst it is highly improbable that all these errors would occur at the same time to any number being processed, transposition of digits when data is being keyed in is a fairly common error which must be detected as soon as possible in the processing.

The Mod 11 checks below are the most commonly used methods of generating a check digit and would detect all the errors which could escape detection using a Mod 9 check.

Modulus 11 check. The account number is divided by 11 and the remainder, 9 in our example, is added as the check digit to give 5087031279. Because 11 does not exhibit the rather magical properties of 9, any changed or missing digit in the original account number should give rise to a different check digit. If the last digit, 7, were lost and replaced by a 0, the check digit becomes 2 and does not equal the previously calculated one, 9. However, it is possible for a corrupted number to generate the 'correct' check digit by co-incidence. If two digits in our account number are swopped round, making the number 508703721, the remainder after division by 11 is still 9 and the number would therefore check as being correct.

Weighted Mod 11 check. This check is the one most commonly used in data processing as it should detect any change to the original data. The method of calculating the check digit is more complex and can best be described by an actual calculation.

1. Account number 508703127
2. Multiply each digit (from the right) by a factor: 7×2; 2×3; 1×4; 3×5; 0×6; 7×7; 8×8; 0×9; 5×10, giving: 50, 0, 64, 49, 0, 15, 4, 6, 14.
3. Add the products together giving 202
4. Divide 202 by 11, giving 18, remainder 4.
5. Subtract 4 from 11 giving 7
6. The check digit is 7 which, when added to the account number, has a weighting of 1.

When a check is performed on the data, the same arithmetic is done as above with the check digit included (again working from the right):

$(7 \times 1) + (7 \times 2) + (2 \times 3) + (1 \times 4) + (3 \times 5) + (0 \times 6) + (7 \times 7) + (8 \times 8) + (0 \times 9) + (5 \times 10) = 209$

This number, when divided by 11 should now give a remainder of zero:

$$209 \div 11 = 19, \text{ remainder } 0$$

It is very easy for a computer to test if a number is zero.

All the above checks have been concerned with a single item of numeric data. In data processing, large amounts of similar data are processed at the same time and can be used as the basis for a further check known as hash totals.

Hash totals

Hash totals are found by adding together similar numeric data items which have no arithmetic meaning but form a nonsense total, known as a hash total. This could be a total of all the customers' account numbers, employee numbers, ages or even telephone numbers. This hash total would be calculated (before processing) using (usually), a block of data and put into a temporary storage location. A similar calculation on the same data would be performed at least when the data is being transferred to permanent storage and before output, and the result compared with the previously stored total. If the totals are not the same, an error message is generated.

In commercial data processing, it is recognised that, despite all the checks that are performed, approximately 1% of all errors are undetected. This may appear to be a very small percentage, hardly worth bothering about, but it must be appreciated that in commercial data processing many thousands of data items are processed every hour and 1% undetected errors can represent a large number of data transactions. Happily, semiconductor technology is making computers much more reliable, but errors, human and machine, can still occur. Data verification and validation must be included in data processing in order to reduce the number of errors to an absolute minimum.

Exercises 4.2

1. Explain each of the following terms showing the distinction between them:
   (a) data capture
   (b) data verification
   (c) data validation (*AEB, 1980*)
2. Explain, with examples, the meaning of:
   (a) check-digit
   (b) hash total. (*AEB, 1979*)

Summary

- Consider, carefully, what the data is to be used for before capturing it, i.e. what output is required from the processing.
- A good data capture form will be **simple**, unambiguous, easy to complete and easy to use as an input document.
- A visual display unit with keyboard is the most widely used method of transcribing data for input to a computer.
- Data punched into cards or paper tape is usually *verified* before input.
- Data validation is a vital part of data processing. Many different validation checks can be performed: the number and type depend on the level of sophistication of the programs to be used, the type of data to be input and the required accuracy of the output.

5 Inside the computer

5.1 Concept of a binary word

We should now realise that any of the data we considered in Chapter 4 can be encoded in binary form for processing in the computer. This binary representation of a letter or number in a group of bits is known as a binary word. Inside the computer there are many storage locations, each location capable of holding one binary word. This word can often be divided into a number of smaller, equal units called *bytes*. A byte consists of 8 bits. In most microprocessors the word length itself is only 8 bits and a computer designed with this internal structure is known as a byte machine. Large mainframe computers of the 1960s and 1970s had word lengths of 16, 24, 32 or 48 bits. With, for example, a 32 bit word, four 8 bit ASCII characters (with parity) could be packed into such a word. In this chapter we shall at all times consider our word length to be 8 bits, i.e. one byte.

The internal storage and processing sections of the computer are made up of many thousands of storage locations and registers and each of these can contain an 8 bit word, so when our data has been encoded it is always contained within words (throughout its processing inside the computer).

Fig. 5.1(*a*) shows how the 8 bits may be used to store a letter or character.

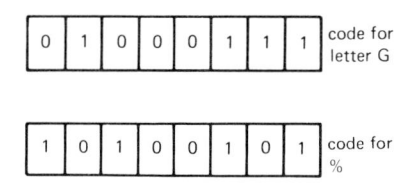

| 0 | 1 | 0 | 0 | 0 | 1 | 1 | 1 | code for letter G |

| 1 | 0 | 1 | 0 | 0 | 1 | 0 | 1 | code for % |

Fig. 5.1 (*a*) How eight bits store a letter or character

5.2 Representation of machine instructions

We have now seen that data is 'held' in binary words inside the computer, but before this data can be manipulated in any way the computer needs to 'be told' two important items of information:

'In the early computers, the correct gears had to be put in before anything would come out.'

(*a*) where the data is stored, i.e. which computer word, or words, it is held in
(*b*) what operation has to be performed on the data, e.g. print it out, add it to the data held in another binary word.

This information is given to the computer in the form of an instruction word.

When data is input to the computer, it is immediately put into a store location where it remains until it is required for processing. Each store location is, usually, one binary word and has a unique address.

As each data item is stored, the computer makes a note of the store address—the first item of data is usually stored in the first available empty store location and each successive item is put into the next adjacent location. Remember that the data being stored in each word is a letter, number or other character and many of these will go together to form a program or data to be processed. So when the central processor needs an item of data, it looks up the address where the data is stored in its 'address book'. This is a part of the immediate access store (IAS) of the computer and can be thought of as similar to an address book, but in a computer, the addresses remain the same and the contents (data) change. The address where the data is stored forms part of the instruction word and if we assume an 8 bit word and a maximum of 32 store locations, i.e. requiring 5 bits to represent all possible addresses, the instruction word can be depicted as shown in Fig. 5.1(b).

| | | | 0 | 1 | 1 | 0 | 1 |
address 13

Fig. 5.1(b) Instruction word

This 8 bit word is used only to illustrate the principle of the instruction word. Typically a microcomputer would have 32 K* store locations which would require a 14 bit address.

The three empty bit positions in Fig. 5.1(b) are used to tell the computer what to do with the data stored in the address. These bits are known as instruction bits and with 3 bits, eight binary codes can be generated (000 to 111). Each code represents one instruction, e.g. ADD, LOAD, OUTPUT etc., and all the instructions form the instruction set of the computer. The complete, 8 bit, instruction word is shown in Fig. 5.1(c).

| 0 | 1 | 1 | 0 | 1 | 1 | 0 | 1 |
instruction bits / address bits

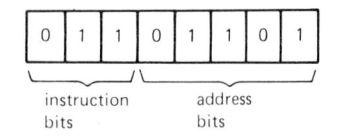

Fig. 5.1(c) Complete 8 bit instruction word

A sequence of instruction words to add two numbers together and store the result, could be shown as;

0 1 1 0 1 1 0 1 Fetch the number stored in location 13 and load it into the accumulator (operation code 011).

1 0 1 1 1 0 1 1 Add the number in location 27 to the number in the accumulator (operation code 101).

1 1 0 0 1 1 0 1 Copy the number in the accumulator into store location 13 (operation code 110).

The instruction word holds one operation code and one address and a computer using such a system is known as a single address machine. To improve the speed of processing and to use less storage space, modern computers use a multi-address system; this is often two addresses, but many computers use a three-address instruction word.

Using a two-address system the three separate instruction words in the above example would become a single word:

1 0 1   0 1 1 0 1   1 1 0 1 1
          13   27

The operation code 101 now means: 'Add together the numbers stored in locations 13 and 27 and write the result into location 13'. Note, that although the instruction word is bigger, storage is required for only one more address—in this example, 5 bits.

If we want to store the result of the addition somewhere else instead of overwriting the number in location 13, a further instruction word is required, but with a three-address system, this can be achieved in one instruction word:

1 0 1   0 1 1 0 1   1 1 0 1 1   1 0 0 0 1
          13   27   17

Operation code 101 now means: 'Add together the contents of locations 13 and 27 and store the result in location 17.'

Every computer has its own instruction set which is designed by the computer manufacturer and cannot be altered subsequently. The codes used above are for example only.

The number of bits used in the above examples are for illustration only. Typically a microcomputer would have about 100 instructions in its set which would require 6 bits to code them.

5.3 Other computer codes

Binary coded decimal

As its name implies, binary coded decimal (BCD) is a binary code which is normally used to encode the numerals 0–9 only into 4 bit groups. Leading zeros are always added to make up 4 bits. The complete code is:

0	0000
1	0001
2	0010
3	0011
4	0100
5	0101
6	0110
7	0111
8	1000
9	1001

These codes are all *legal* BCD codes. (It is possible to code the denary numbers 10, 11, 12, 13, 14 and 15 by using the remaining bit patterns of the 4 binary bits but

---

* In computer storage, the value of K is 1024 (2^{10}), so 32 K is actually 32768.

these have a special use and as far as numeric representation is concerned, these six codes are illegal.)

With this code, each denary digit is coded separately:

$$2 \quad 3 \quad\quad (23_{10})$$
$$\text{codes as} \quad 0010 \quad 0011 \quad \text{in BCD}$$

$$4 \quad 7 \quad 0 \quad 6 \quad\quad (4706_{10})$$
$$\text{codes as } 0100 \ 0111 \ 0000 \ 0110 \text{ in BCD}$$

Of course, this code also works in reverse, e.g. BCD to denary:

$$0111 \quad 0100 \quad 0001 \quad 1001 \quad \text{BCD}$$
$$7 \quad\quad 4 \quad\quad 1 \quad\quad 9 \quad\quad \text{denary}$$

If we look at the table of ASCII codes (p. 176), we can see that the BCD code for the 10 numerals is the same as the right hand 4 bits of the ASCII code for the numerals. The leading 3 bits are always 011, and therefore as soon as these 3 bits have been decoded we know that the 7 bits represent either a numeral or one of the six symbols which are also in the 011 group. If the remaining 4 bits form a legal BCD code, they must represent a numeral, in which case the leading 3 bits can be dropped.

This means that two BCD numerals can be packed into one 8 bit word:

$$0 \ 1 \ 1 \ 0 \ 1 \ 0 \ 0 \ 1 \quad \text{BCD}$$
$$6 \quad\quad\quad 9 \quad\quad\quad \text{denary}$$

and a four-digit number 8103 would be held in two 8 bit words as:

$$1 \ 0 \ 0 \ 0 \ 0 \ 0 \ 0 \ 1 \quad 0 \ 0 \ 0 \ 0 \ 0 \ 0 \ 1 \ 1$$
$$8 \quad\quad 1 \quad\quad\quad 0 \quad\quad 3$$

The main use of BCD is in *coding* denary numbers but it is possible to perform arithmetic operations using coding as shown above and some computers do their arithmetic in this way.

BCD can also be used as a form of shorthand when dealing with long 'bit strings'. If we wanted to communicate a great many 32 bit binary words to another person, it is very easy to make a mistake in copying only zeros and ones. To improve accuracy and reduce the time taken to copy and check long binary words, these can be coded into BCD and the denary equivalent is copied or transmitted. Using BCD in this manner means that the six 'illegal codes' may be used, but their use is limited to acting as a temporary code.

$$0110 \ 1001 \ 0111 \ 0000 \ 1101 \ 1000 \ 0101 \ 1110$$
$$\text{codes as:} \quad 6 \quad 9 \quad 7 \quad 0 \quad 13 \quad 8 \quad 5 \quad 14$$

and of course, the reverse procedure will give back the original binary word. This technique is used in software design (Chapter 8).

Two other number systems are widely used in computers: they are *octal* and hexadecimal. The latter is used much more widely than the former, particularly in microcomputers.

Octal

Octal is a number system which uses 8 as its base. (This is often referred to as the radix.) The numerals are 0–7 and the system finds its place in computers because these numerals can all be coded in 3 binary bits.

$$0 \equiv 000 \quad \text{to} \quad 7 \equiv 111$$

Conversion from pure binary to octal is therefore a matter of dividing the binary number into 3 bit groups, *starting from the right hand side*, and converting each group directly into denary. For example, convert 11010111101 to octal:

$$11 \mid 010 \mid 111 \mid 101 \mid$$
$$3 \mid 2 \mid 7 \mid 5 \mid \quad (2)$$
$$\quad\quad\quad\quad\quad\quad (8)$$

The process works in a similar manner in a conversion from octal to binary. The above conversion can be checked by first converting the binary number to denary, and then converting this to octal by successive division by the radix, 8:

$$8 \quad 1725 \quad 5$$
$$8 \quad 215 \quad 7$$
$$8 \quad 26 \quad 2$$
$$\quad\quad 3 \rightarrow 3$$

Hexadecimal

Hexadecimal (hex) is a number system using 16 as its radix. Its digits are 0–9, A, B, C, D, E, F. The six letters are used to represent the denary numbers 10, 11, 12, 13, 14 and 15 which, of course, cannot be used as they are two-digit groups of numerals previously used. Hexadecimal numbers tend to be a bit 'off-putting' when they are first encountered because of the letters that may appear in them, but, remember, they are only being used as a code. It is well worth becoming familiar with hexadecimal representation as this is widely used in microcomputers as a short-hand for 8 and 16 bit binary codes.

$2F_{hex}$ $\quad\quad (2 \times 16) + (15 \times 1) = \quad 47$
39_{hex} $\quad\quad (3 \times 16) + \ (9 \times 1) = \quad 57$
$3E_{hex}$ $\quad\quad (3 \times 16) + (14 \times 1) = \quad 62$
$13E_{hex}$ $\ (1 \times 256) + (3 \times 16) + (14 \times 1) = \ 318$
$2FF_{hex}$ $\ (2 \times 256) + (15 \times 16) + (15 \times 1) = \ 767$
ABC_{hex} $(10 \times 256) + (11 \times 16) + (12 \times 1) = 2748$

Conversion from denary to hex is accomplished by successive division by 16 and should present no problem if you know your 16 times table! It is advisable to use a

32 COMPUTER STUDIES

conversion table such as the one in Fig. 5.2 to help in converting both from hex to denary and vice-versa.

```
                      DIGIT IN:
DIGIT    COL4     COL3     COL2    COL1
0        0        0        0       0
1        4096     256      16      1
2        8192     512      32      2
3        12288    768      48      3
4        16384    1024     64      4
5        20480    1280     80      5
6        24576    1536     96      6
7        28672    1792     112     7
8        32768    2048     128     8
9        36864    2304     144     9
A        40960    2560     160     10
B        45056    2816     176     11
C        49152    3072     192     12
D        53248    3328     208     13
E        57344    3584     224     14
F        61440    3840     240     15
```

Fig. 5.2 A hexadecimal to denary conversion table

The following examples illustrate denary to hex conversion.

1 Convert 231 to hex.
  16 231   7
      14   E   Answer: E7$_{hex}$

2 Convert 4096 to hex.
  16 4096 0
  16 256   0
  16 16   0   Answer: 1000$_{hex}$
      1   1

3 Convert 51243 to hex.
  16 51243 (11) B
  16 3202   2
  16 200   8   Answer: C82B$_{hex}$
      12   C

Exercises 5.1*

1 Convert to denary:
(i) 3F (ii) BB (iii) 44 (iv) 100 (v) FFFF
Convert to hexadecimal:
(vi) 27 (vii) 99 (viii) 3135 (ix) 431 (x) 43788.

Conversion from binary to hex is similar to conversion to octal but this time the binary word is split up into 4 bit groups from the right hand side:

```
10   1110   0101   1010   base 2
2    D      5      A      hex
```

The conversion from hex to binary involves coding each hex digit into 4 bits (adding leading zeros where necessary). For example:

```
    2      4      0      9      hex
    0010   0100   0000   1001   binary
```
So 2409$_{hex}$ ≡ 0010010000001001$_2$.

```
    E      8      C      B      hex
    1110   1000   1100   1011   binary
```
So E8CB$_{hex}$ ≡ 1110100011001011$_2$

Exercises 5.2

1 Convert the following:
(a) 18.0625 to binary
(b) 92 to hexadecimal
(c) 901 to binary coded decimal. (*AEB, 1979*)*

2 (a) Convert the denary number 257 into binary and binary coded decimal.
(b) If the word length in a computer is only 8 bits, would you use binary or binary coded decimal to represent denary integers in the range 0 to 999? Explain your answer. (*AEB, 1980*)*

5.4 Two-state devices

In Chapter 3 we saw that all data is represented in a digital computer in binary form and that each bit of a binary word can only be either a 1 or a 0. Inside the computer there are many thousands of electronic devices, each of which can be set to one of two states, representing a 1 or a 0, and switched to the other state *very* quickly. These devices, known as bistables, may be connected together in different ways to form *logic circuits*. Some of these circuits *add* binary numbers together. Some *shift* binary words and others *store* them. Some control the flow of data between different parts of the computer and others are used to *decode* instructions. Whatever job the logic circuit is designed to do, it will, almost certainly, be made from a combination of simple logic elements. These elements are simply electronic switches (often referred to as *gates*), and they can operate at speeds quite beyond our comprehension: over 10 million operations every second!

The purpose of these gates is to perform the logical operations of AND, OR, NOT, NOT AND and NOT OR on the bits of the binary words which represent the data. By combining many gates into logic circuits to form a central processing unit, the data is processed.

The different logic gates can be shown by different symbols and their logical operation by means of a logic table known as a *truth table*.

Note that all the logic gates, except the NOT gate, can have many inputs, but in the diagrams here only two are shown.

AND gate
Definition. An AND gate will give an output of logic value 1, only if *all* the inputs are logic value 1 (if *A* and *B* and *C* and *D* ... are 1) (Fig. 5.3).

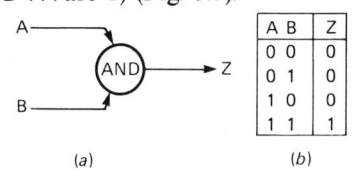

Fig. 5.3 AND gate (a) Logic symbol (b) Truth table

OR gate
Definition. An OR gate will give an output of logic value 1 if *any* of the inputs are logic value 1 (if *A* or *B* or *C* or *D* ... is 1) (Fig. 5.4).

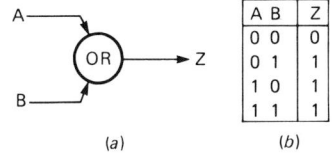

Fig. 5.4 OR gate (a) Logic symbol (b) Truth table

NOT gate
Definition. A NOT gate inverts a logic signal (*Z* is not *A*) (Fig. 5.5). Note that this gate can only have a single input.

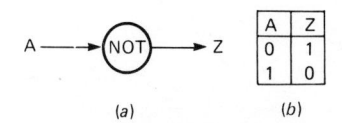

Fig. 5.5 NOT gate (a) Logic symbol (b) Truth table

A NOT AND gate is, logically, an AND gate followed by a NOT gate (Fig. 5.6). Similarly, a NOT OR gate is an OR gate followed by a NOT gate (Fig. 5.7). These gates are normally shown by a single symbol and are, respectively, called a NAND gate and a NOR gate.

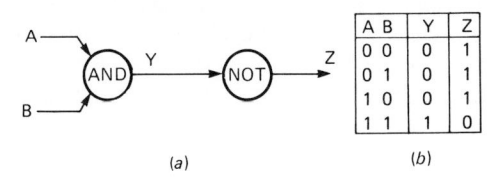

Fig. 5.6 NOT AND gate

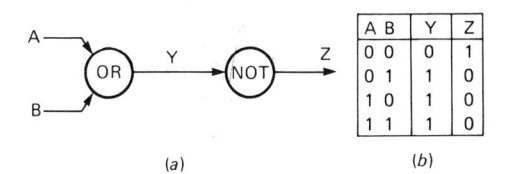

Fig. 5.7 NOT OR gate

NAND Gate
Definition. A NAND gate will give an output of logic value 0, if *all* the inputs are logic value 1; otherwise the output is logic value 1 (Fig. 5.8).

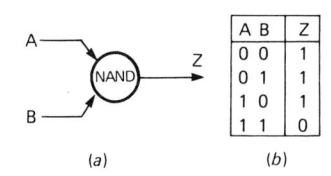

Fig. 5.8 NAND gate

NOR Gate
Definition. A NOR gate will give an output of logic value 1 only if all the inputs are 0 (Fig. 5.9).

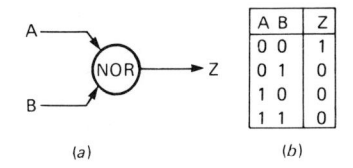

Fig. 5.9 NOR gate

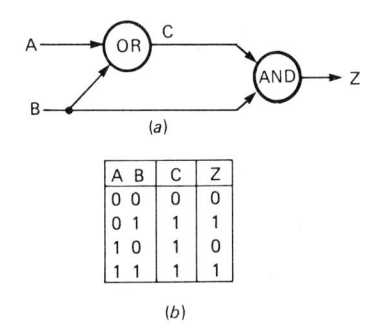

Fig. 5.10 A logic circuit

A B	C	Z
0 0	0	0
0 1	1	1
1 0	1	0
1 1	1	1

(b)

These logic elements are combined together in many different ways to form logic circuits and an example is shown in Fig. 5.10. Note the use of the partial output C to help in the compilation of the truth table. This technique can be very helpful when the truth table for a complex logic circuit is being compiled.

Fig. 5.11 shows a more complex circuit. Note that the first logic circuit has two inputs, A and B, which give rise to 2^2 entries in the truth table. The second circuit has three inputs, A, B and C, needing 2^3 (i.e. 8) entries in the table. When you are writing out all the input combinations, always start with all zeros and count in binary up to all ones. When you are completing the 'outputs section' of the table, always complete a *column* at a time—never a row—and identify the logic rule that will give an output of 1 at the point under consideration. Take the circuit in Fig. 5.11 as an example. For output D, ask the question: 'What combination of inputs at A and B will give a 1 at D?' Answer: 'A and B both have to be 1'. This input combination occurs only with the last two inputs, so in column D write a 1 against both these inputs. The remainder of column D *must* be zeros.

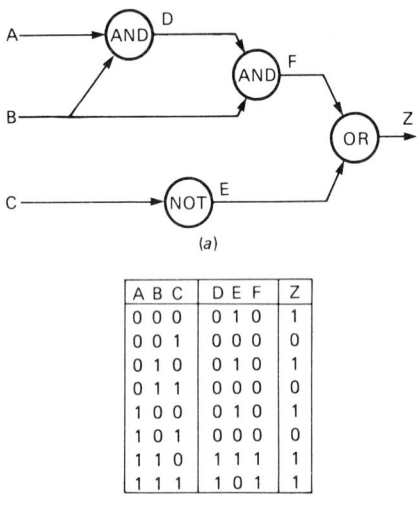

A B C	D E F	Z
0 0 0	0 1 0	1
0 0 1	0 0 0	0
0 1 0	0 1 0	1
0 1 1	0 0 0	0
1 0 0	0 1 0	1
1 0 1	0 0 0	0
1 1 0	1 1 1	1
1 1 1	1 0 1	1

(b)

Fig. 5.11 A more complex logic circuit

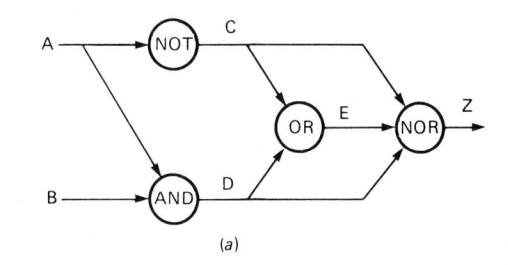

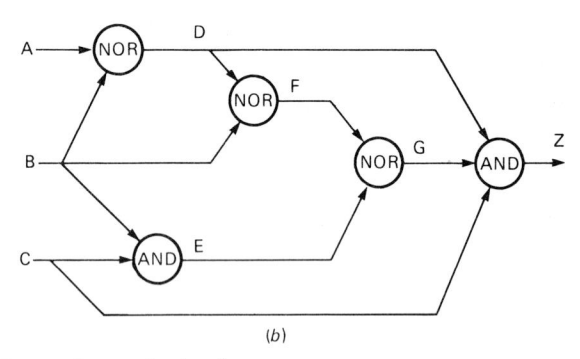

Fig. 5.12 Logic circuits

Look at the logic circuit in Fig. 5.12(a). The truth table for this could be completed as follows:
 (i) C is the opposite of A. Fill in column C.
(ii) D will be 1 *only* if A and B are both 1. Find the rows where A and B are both 1. Put a 1 in column D. Fill all the other spaces in column D with 0.
(iii) E will be a 1 if C or D is a 1. Put a 1 in column E against any row where C or D is 1 (and zeros in the rest of column E).
(iv) Z will be a 1 only if C, D and E are all 0. Find any row where C, D and E are 0. Put a 1 in column Z for that row and zeros for the rest of the rows.
This gives the table shown in Fig. 5.13(a).
The circuit in Fig. 5.12(b) could be analysed as follows:
  (i) D will be 1 only if A and B are *both* 0.
 (ii) E will only be 1 if B and C are 1.
(iii) F will be 1 only if D and B are *both* 0.
(iv) G will be 1 only if F and E are *both* 0.
 (v) Z will only be 1 if D *and* G *and* C are 1.
This gives the table shown in Fig. 5.13(b).

A B	C D E	Z
0 0	1 0 1	0
0 1	1 0 1	0
1 0	0 0 0	1
1 1	0 1 1	0

(a)

A B C	D E F G	Z
0 0 0	1 0 0 1	0
0 0 1	1 0 0 1	1
0 1 0	0 0 0 1	0
0 1 1	0 1 0 0	0
1 0 0	0 0 1 0	0
1 0 1	0 0 1 0	0
1 1 0	0 0 0 1	0
1 1 1	0 1 0 0	0

(b)

Fig. 5.13 Truth tables

Exercises 5.3

Compile a truth table for each of the logic circuits shown below.

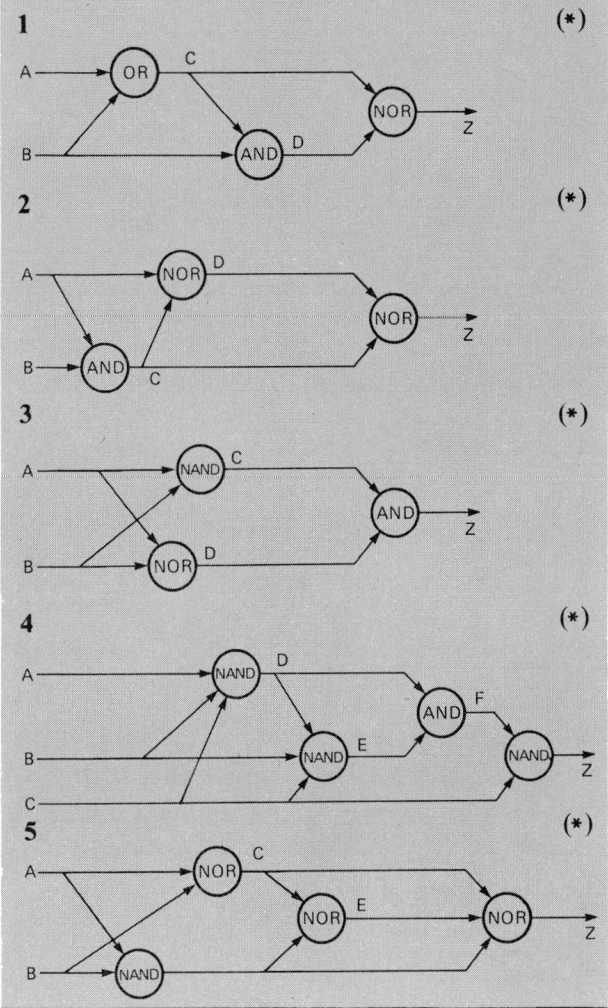

1 (*)

A → OR → C → NOR → Z
B → AND → D ↗

2 (*)

A → NOR → D → NOR → Z
B → AND → C ↗

3 (*)

A → NAND → C → AND → Z
B → NOR → D ↗

4 (*)

A → NAND → D → AND → F → NAND → Z
B → NAND → E ↗
C ↗

5 (*)

A → NOR → C → NOR → E → NOR → Z
B → NAND ↗

The circuits in the exercises above were contrived for the purpose of the exercises and would serve no useful function in a computer. One particular circuit, however, has a very important function and we will consider it in more detail. At a first glance, the circuit in Fig. 5.14 appears to do no more than any of the previous ones but a closer examination of the truth table will show us that this circuit is *adding* two binary bits together according to the rules for binary addition:

A:	0	0	1	1
+B:	0	1	0	1
=Z:	0	1	1	0
C:	0	0	0	1

We can see from the above that Z is the *sum* of the binary bits A and B, and that C is the *carry*. Therefore we can say that this circuit will add together two binary bits and produce a sum and a carry.

However, this *adder* is only doing part of the job. Consider this binary sum:

column	5	4	3	2	1	
	1	1	0	1	0	
	1	1	1	0	0	+
	1	1	0	1	1	0

The circuit in Fig. 5.14 could be used to add together the two bits in columns 1, 2, 3 and 4, but what happens in column 5? We have two 1-bits, as in column 4, but there is also a carry bit from column 4. The circuit above has no provision for accepting a carry bit as input. Therefore, as it is only doing half its job, it is known as a *half adder*. The circuit is normally drawn as shown in Fig. 5.15.

(a)

A → AND → C → NOT → E → AND → Z
B → OR → D ↗

A B	C D E	Z
0 0	0 0 1	0
0 1	0 1 1	1
1 0	0 1 1	1
1 1	1 1 0	0

(b)

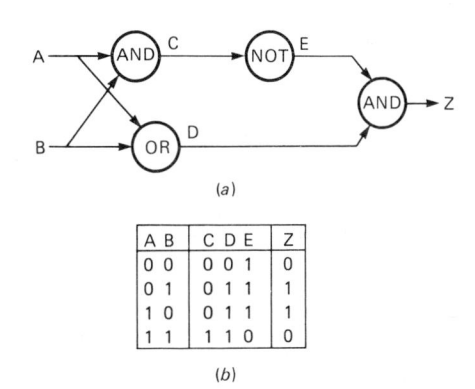

Fig. 5.14 Adding two binary bits

(a)

A → AND → CARRY
B → OR → NOT → AND → SUM

(b)

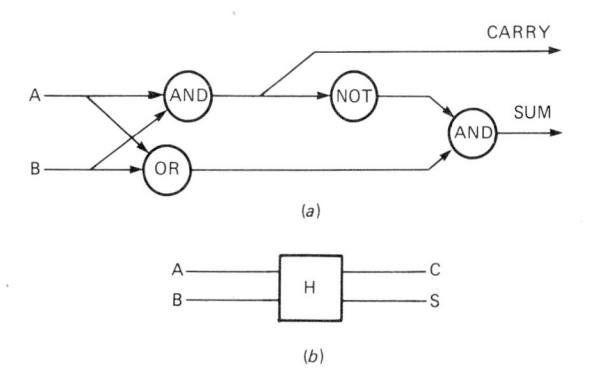

A, B → H → C, S

Fig. 5.15 The half adder
    (a) Complete circuit
    (b) Standard symbol

36 COMPUTER STUDIES

To overcome the problem of the carry bit, a second half adder is joined to the first, making a *full adder*, which is shown logically as in Fig. 5.16.

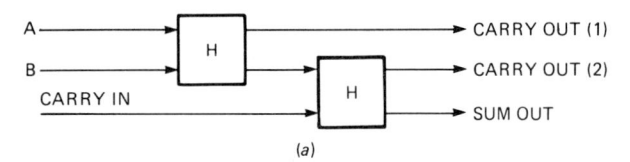

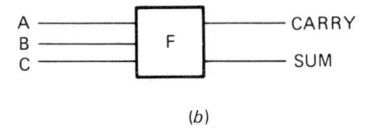

Fig. 5.16 The full adder
(*a*) Complete circuit
(*b*) Standard symbol

Notice that the two 'carry outs' have become one in Fig. 5.16. The reason for this can best be understood if we draw a simplified circuit of the full adder and a slightly modified truth table (Fig. 5.17). D is the carry from the first half adder and E the carry from the second half adder. F is the sum from the first half adder and Z the sum from the second half adder. A and B are the two bits to be added and C is a (possible) carry from a previous bit position.

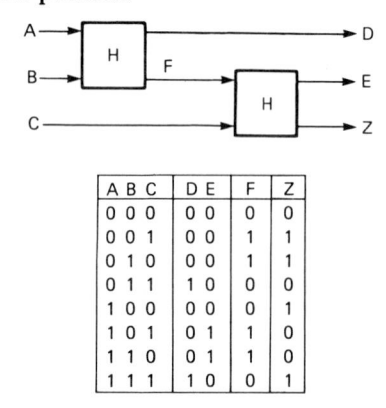

A B C	D E	F	Z
0 0 0	0 0	0	0
0 0 1	0 0	1	1
0 1 0	0 0	1	1
0 1 1	1 0	0	0
1 0 0	0 0	0	1
1 0 1	0 1	1	0
1 1 0	0 1	1	0
1 1 1	1 0	0	1

Fig. 5.17 Simplified circuit of the full adder

It can be seen from the table in Fig. 5.17 that there is a carry either from D or E but never at the same time. These two carry outputs are therefore fed into an OR gate and the single output used as a carry from the full adder; as shown in Fig. 5.18.

The use of the full adder to perform arithmetic operations is described in Chapter 7. With integrated-circuit technology, 64 full adder circuits can be put on to one chip measuring 5 mm square (Fig. 5.19).

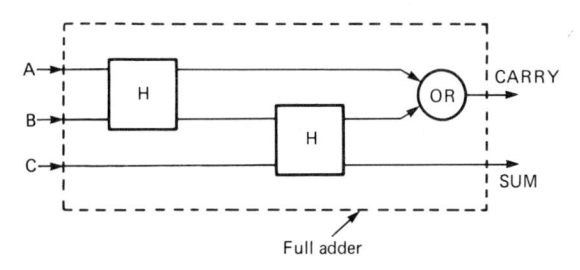

Fig. 5.18 Single carry from the full adder

Fig. 5.19 Adder chip

The logic diagram of the half-adder shown above uses mixed logic elements i.e. AND, OR, NOT. In actual practice, an adder is usually made from NOR gates only. The logic diagram for a half adder is shown in Fig. 5.20. Note that the single input NOR gate is acting as a NOT gate.

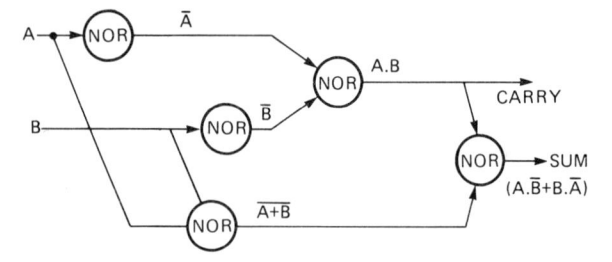

Fig. 5.20 NOR half adder

INSIDE THE COMPUTER 37

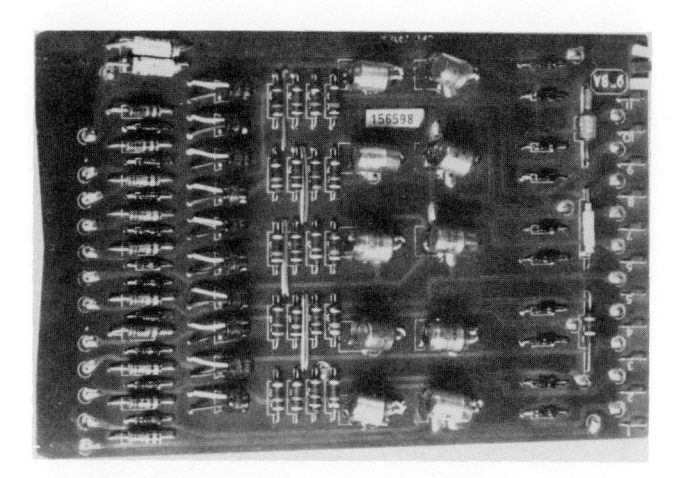

Fig 5.21 Atlas logic board (actual size: 20cm × 12.5cm)

In the early computers, the logic circuits were made from discrete components (valves, resistors, capacitors, transistors) and each logic gate could be identified by looking on the correct sub-chassis or printed circuit board. One such board might, for example, have contained all the logic elements to make a full adder or a fast register. A typical logic board from an Atlas computer is shown in Fig. 5.21. Many hundreds of such boards were required to make a central processor unit and logic and power interconnections between the many boards was achieved using many kilometres of ordinary wire—known as 'back-wiring'.

Modern design technology has allowed a dramatic change to take place in the practical implementation of computer logic. Parts of a computer which, up to the early 1970s, occupied many cubic metres of space, are now 'grown' into a single silicon chip 5 mm square. The design of integrated circuits or 'chips' is a fascinating and extremely complex process and any detailed study of the techniques involved is outside the scope of this book, Suffice to say that the design of complex integrated circuits would be quite impossible without the use of computers to aid the design (this is computer aided design or CAD).

In Fig. 5.22 we see the various operations which form a CAD system. In practice the *user* requirement of 'a computer with the following specification' is defined by the *system builder* in terms of 'black boxes'. (The term 'black box' is commonly used to describe a piece of electronics, usually designed to perform a specific func-

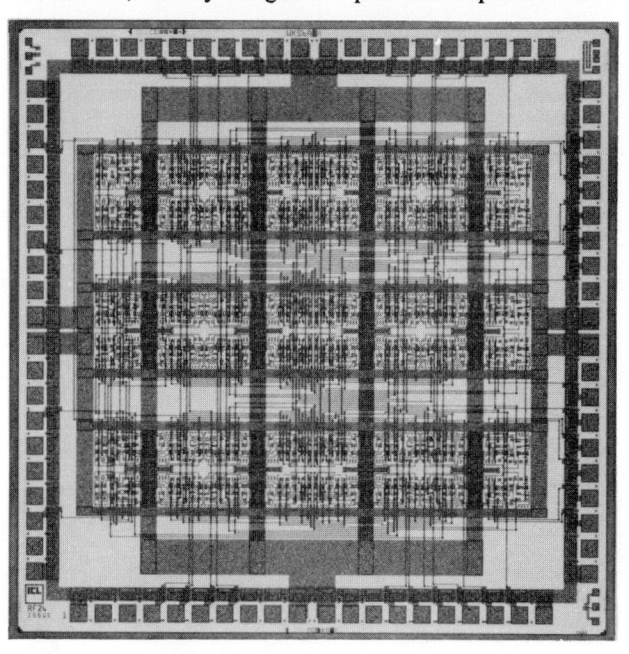

Fig. 5.23 A silicon chip (actual size: 5mm × 5mm)

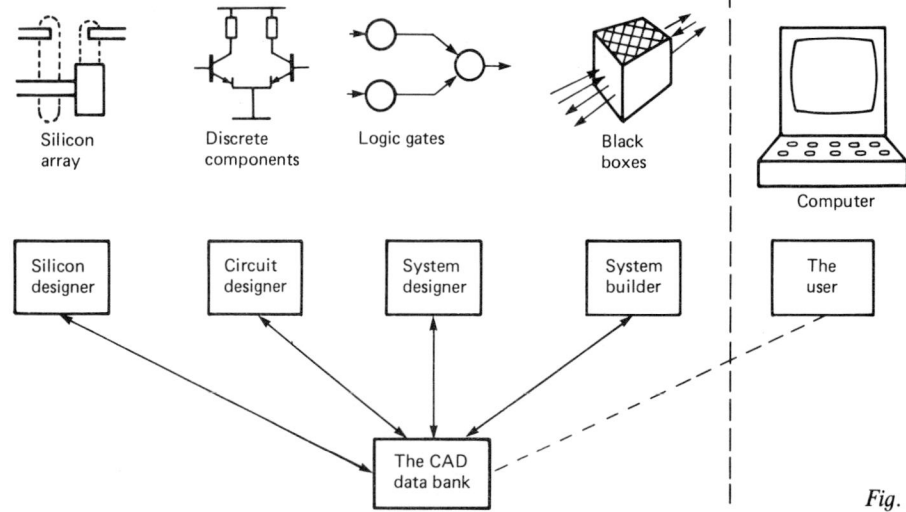

Fig. 5.22 Computer aided design system

tion.) These black boxes would be the registers, adders etc. and all the associated interconnections to enable them to perform as the user specification demands. All the different 'standard' logical units are stored in the CAD data bank and can be called for by the system builder as required. Each of these logical units has been designed in terms of logic gates by the *system designer* and these designs are again stored in the CAD data bank. The *circuit designer's* job is to define each gate in terms of discrete components (transistors and resistors) and, when complete, this data too is stored in the CAD data bank. The *silicon designer* has to define the individual circuits, for example a bistable, in terms of a design capable of being manufactured as a silicon chip. This data too is stored in the data bank. When the system builder requires an arithmetic logic unit, for example, the complex programs of the CAD system work their way through the various data banks selecting the appropriate designs and finally producing the complex layout diagram of the chip with all the necessary components and interconnections to be manufactured as a silicon chip (Fig. 5.23).

The advantages of producing complex electronic circuits as integrated circuits instead of as discrete component units are:

Exercises 5.4

1 (*a*) Draw a logic diagram showing how two half adders may be connected, along with any other necessary logic elements, to form a full adder.

(*b*) A bank uses a double security system based on key-operated switches. The manager, the chief cashier and his deputy each have a key. The door to the vaults can be opened by using two of the three keys, but the door to the strongroom can only be opened if the vault door is open and all three keys are used to operate the strongroom lock. Design and sketch a logic circuit to satisfy the above conditions, using standard logic elements. Ensure that your diagram is fully annotated. (*AEB, 1977*)*

2 A section of a model railway, controlled by a microprocessor, is shown in the diagram.

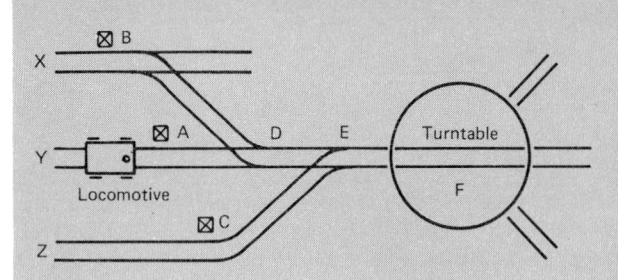

A, B and C are train signals which feed a logic signal of 1 to the micro processor when green and 0 when the signal is red. D and E are track points which each give a logic signal of 0 when set to routes X and Z respectively and 1 when set to route Y. The turntable gives a logic 1 when it is aligned with route Y.

Design and draw a logic circuit using only AND, OR and NOT logic gates to switch current to route Y given the following conditions: 'A is to be green and D and E are to be set to route Y and the turntable is to be aligned with route Y, or B is to be red and C is to be red and D and E are to be set to route Y and the turntable is to be aligned with route Y.'*

3 Your school is setting up a drama club. The secretary, a computing expert, is designing a machine to produce membership cards automatically. The machine will have five buttons labelled as follows:

A = Member of staff.
C = Fourth and fifth year pupils.
D = Pupil studying drama.
E = Pupil studying English.
F = Sixth form pupil.

Prospective members push the buttons which describe themselves and the machine will produce a membership ticket if they are in one of the following categories:

  (i) Member of staff.
  (ii) Fourth or fifth year pupil studying drama.
  (iii) Sixth form pupil studying English or drama.

Draw a diagram of the logic circuit required inside the machine. (*AEB, 1980*)*

4 Copy and complete the truth table for the logic circuit shown.*

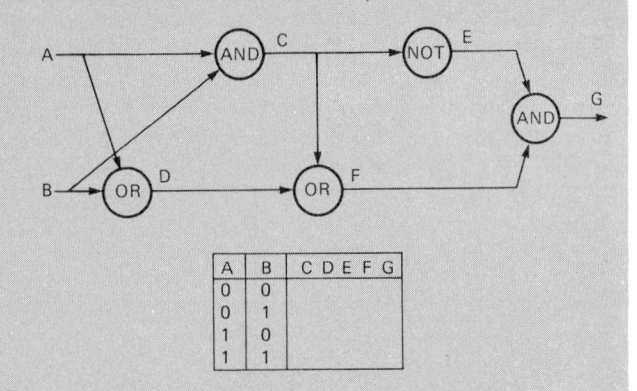

A	B	C D E F G
0	0	
0	1	
1	0	
1	1	

(i) They are much cheaper to produce (after the initial design). A CPU on a 1960 computer may have cost £50 000. An integrated circuit CPU costs less than £10.
(ii) They are easy to mass produce—it is a completely automated production process. '1960 type' units were all hand made.
(iii) Switching times are very much faster and transmission delay between components is very much reduced. Distances on an integrated circuit are measured in microns, (thousandths of a millimetre), compared with inches and feet in 1960 units.
(iv) They are very much smaller.
(v) They are much more reliable—there is no technical reason why an integrated circuit should ever fail (in correct useage).

5.5 Analogue to digital conversion

In Chapter 3 we saw that data can be represented either as a series of discrete pulses—digital—or as a continuously varying quantity—analogue. To enable data in analogue form to be processed in a digital computer, and to utilise the speed and accuracy of the computer, the analogue data has to be converted into digital form before input to a (general purpose) digital computer. This process is known as analogue to digital conversion. A physical quantity such as voltage may vary with respect to time and can be measured by either continuous recording on moving graph paper or by human, or mechanical, readings at regular intervals.

Graphs drawn from both methods would appear as shown in Fig. 5.24(a) and (b). If the interval between successive readings in Fig. 5.24(b) is too long, the plotted results might look like those in Fig. 5.24(c), or, with an even longer interval between readings like those in Fig. 5.24(d). Clearly, this graph bears very little resemblance to the correct curve at (a) although the graph at (b) almost reproduces the continuous curve at (a). The reason for this is the difference in the rate of reading the data; clearly, more readings taken in a given time will give a more accurate representation of the actual change in voltage. This technique is known as sampling and is the basis of converting an analogue signal to a digital output.

The analogue signal is sampled frequently—typically every 20 microseconds—and converted into an n bit binary word of a magnitude that is directly proportional

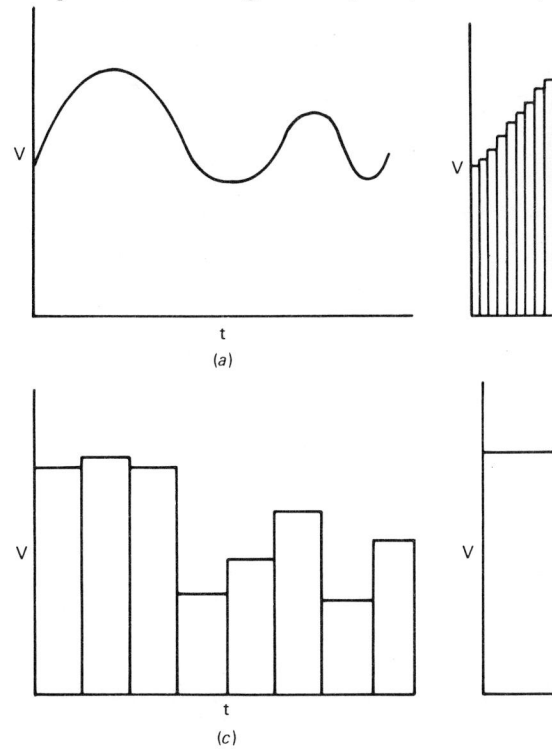

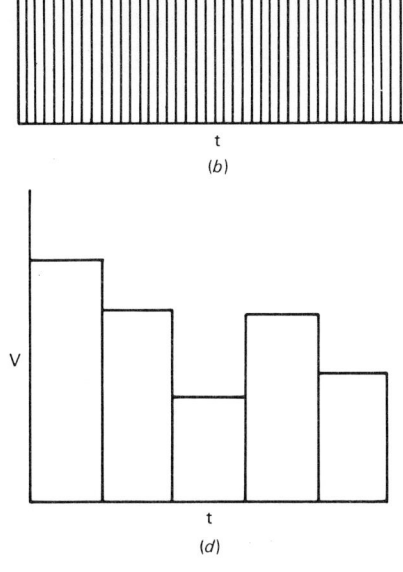

Fig. 5.24 Measurement of voltage with respect to time
(a) Continuous recording
(c) A longer interval between successive readings
(b) Readings taken at regular intervals
(d) An even longer interval

to the analogue signal. This digital signal is then input to a digital computer and 'processed' as required before being output either as printed information or to be converted back to an analogue signal.

The conversion of a digital signal to an analogue one is not simply the inverse of the sampling process described above. The heart of a digital to analogue convertor is a direct current amplifier, which is an electronic circuit with a very high gain (10^6). The digital signal is used to produce a very small voltage which is fed into the direct current amplifier to produce a voltage equivalent to the binary input. This output could be fed to a voltmeter or to a control circuit to control some process as described in Chapter 11.

Fig. 5.25 shows how an analogue to digital and a digital to analogue convertor would be used in conjunction with a digital computer to control the temperature of a furnace. Such a system is known as a hybrid computing system because it uses both analogue and digital techniques.

A pyrometer measures the temperature of the furnace and converts the reading into a small DC voltage. This is converted into a digital signal by the analogue to digital convertor and fed to the digital computer, where it is compared with the required temperature which is also input to the computer. If the furnace temperature is too low, an error signal is fed into the digital to analogue convertor and converted into an analogue signal, which is used to open the gas valve and allow more gas to heat up the furnace. As the temperature increases, the error signal will reduce and cause the gas valve to be closed gradually until the actual temperature is equal to the required temperature when the error signal will be zero and the gas at a minimum. As the furnace starts to cool down, an error signal will again be generated and cause the gas to be increased until the required temperature is again reached. This process continues and the furnace temperature will 'cycle' slightly either side of the required temperature. By using this technique, control of any process can be very accurate if the sampling rate is faster than any change in the parameter being controlled. Accuracy also depends on the length of the binary word, as discussed in Chapter 4.

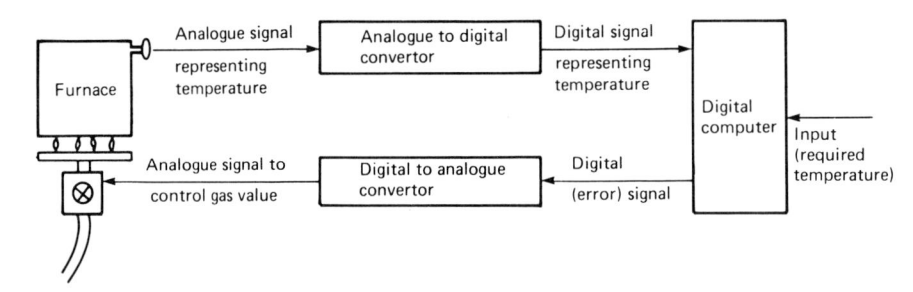

Fig. 5.25 Controlling the temperature of a furnace

Summary

- Inside a computer, data is held in binary words, usually known as *bytes*, with each byte usually consisting of 8 bits.
- A machine instruction word consists of instructions bits and address bits.
- Binary coded decimal (BCD) uses 4-bit groups to encode the digits 0–9.
- Octal (base 8) and hexadecimal (base 16) are numeric codes used in computers.
- A computer contains many thousands of logic elements, connected together to perform specific functions. In modern computers, the logic elements are formed on a slice of silicon and joined together on the slice to form a logic unit.
- Data in analogue form is converted into digital form, by means of an analogue to digital convertor, for subsequent processing in a digital computer and through a digital to analogue convertor back to an analogue signal to control, for example, the source of the original analogue data.
- Very accurate control over physical 'processes' can be achieved by using a hybrid computer system to control the operation.

6 Computer arithmetic

6.1 Binary representation of fractions

In Chapter 5 we saw that it is possible to represent any positive denary whole number greater than zero by using the binary code. Such numbers are called integers and, of course, there is an infinite number of them. In between 0 and 1, however, there are just as many fractions — $\frac{1}{2}$, $\frac{1}{8}$, $\frac{1}{3}$, $\frac{5}{7}$ etc.— and we must be able to represent these in binary as well.

We know that the binary scale is based on ascending powers of 2 (starting from 1) so if we write these down as below,

$$2^5 \quad 2^4 \quad 2^3 \quad 2^2 \quad 2^1 \quad 2^0$$

We see that, from right to left, the power, or radix, is increased by one for each move to the left. These powers go on indefinitely.

Now consider what happens when we start at the left hand side and move right: the power is decreased by one for each move right. We do not stop, however, when we reach 2^0 but continue subtracting 1 each step right. The sequence now becomes:

$$2^5 \quad 2^4 \quad 2^3 \quad 2^2 \quad 2^1 \quad 2^0 \quad 2^{-1} \quad 2^{-2} \quad 2^{-3}$$

2^{-1} is only an index method of representing $1/2^{+1}$ or $\frac{1}{2}$; $2^{-2} \equiv 1/2^2$ or $\frac{1}{4}$; and $2^{-3} \equiv 1/2^3$ or $\frac{1}{8}$ and so on. If you are not familiar with index representation, consider the sequence to be:

$$32 \quad 16 \quad 8 \quad 4 \quad 2 \quad 1 \quad \tfrac{1}{2} \quad \tfrac{1}{4} \quad \tfrac{1}{8} \quad \tfrac{1}{16} \quad \tfrac{1}{32}$$

Working from left to right, each column heading in the binary scale is divided by 2 to get the next one in the sequence.

The denary number 3.5 can therefore be considered as $3 + \frac{1}{2}$ which, in binary, is 11.1. Note the bicimal point is used to show where fractional parts commence in just the same way as the decimal point is used in denary representation.

Examples

$7\tfrac{3}{4} = 7 + \tfrac{1}{2} + \tfrac{1}{4} \equiv 111.11$

$9\tfrac{1}{8} = 9 + \tfrac{1}{8} \equiv 1001.001$

'Computers only understand binary. It is very useful nowadays as we have gone metric as it only goes in 10's however, it will take time getting used to it as it is very new and is in a bigger scale than fractions so it will be very confusing.'

$2\tfrac{3}{8} = 2 + \tfrac{1}{4} + \tfrac{1}{8} \equiv 10.011$

$4\tfrac{3}{16} = 4 + \tfrac{1}{8} + \tfrac{1}{16} \equiv 100.0011$

$5\tfrac{1}{64} = 5 + \tfrac{1}{64} \equiv 101.000001$

This system of splitting a denary fraction up into fractional powers of 2 works fine if we can recognise the way to split the fraction, but a more organised method is the exact opposite of the method shown in Chapter 5 for converting a denary number greater than 1 to binary.

The algorithm used is:
 (i) Multiply the decimal fraction by 2.
 (ii) Write down the carry, which will always be 1 or 0
(iii) Repeat from (i)—but only multiply the fractional part by 2; i.e. to the right of the decimal point until there is no decimal part left or the required number of bits is obtained.
(iv) Read the answer in the carry column, *downwards*.

Example: Convert 0.625 to binary

```
       |.625
       |   2 ×
       |─────
    1  |.250
       |   2 ×
       |─────
    0  |.500
       |   2 ×
       |─────
    1  |.000
```

Answer = 0.101

Example: Convert 0.078125 to binary

```
       |.078125
       |     2 ×
       |────────
    0  |.156250
       |     2 ×
       |────────
    0  |.312500
       |     2 ×
       |────────
    0  |.625000
       |     2 ×
       |────────
    1  |.250000
       |     2 ×
       |────────
    0  |.500000
       |     2 ×
       |────────
    1  |.000000
```

Answer = 0.000101

Of course, there is no need to keep writing the trailing zeros, as in the next example:
Convert 0.6875 to binary

```
       |.6875
       |   2 ×
       |─────
    1  |.3750
       |   2 ×
       |─────
    0  |.750
       |   2 ×
       |─────
    1  |.50
       |   2 ×
       |─────
    1  |.0
```

Answer = 0.1011

Now consider the next example:
Convert 0.4 to binary

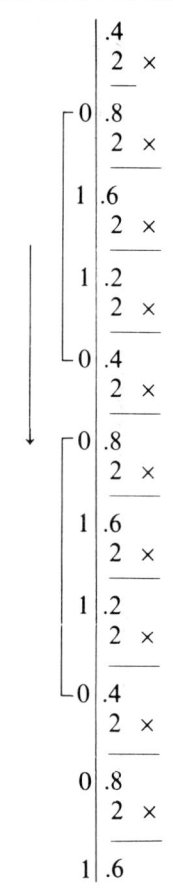

```
       |.4
       |  2 ×
       |────
    0  |.8
       |  2 ×
       |────
    1  |.6
       |  2 ×
       |────
    1  |.2
       |  2 ×
       |────
    0  |.4
       |  2 ×
       |────
    0  |.8
       |  2 ×
       |────
    1  |.6
       |  2 ×
       |────
    1  |.2
       |  2 ×
       |────
    0  |.4
       |  2 ×
       |────
    0  |.8
       |  2 ×
       |────
    1  |.6
```

and so on for ever!

Answer = 0.0̇110̇ . . . .

The group of binary digits 0110 repeats ad infinitum and is shown to be a repeating group by the dots at either end of the group.

The reason that the first three examples all terminated, and the last one did not is that 0.625, 0.078125 and 0.6875 can all be split into fractions which are themselves decimal powers of two. On the other hand, 0.4 represents $\frac{4}{10}$, or $\frac{2}{5}$ and these fractions cannot be split into 'powers of 2 fractions'. When it is necessary to represent a non-terminating decimal fraction, we need to be told how many bits to use; otherwise, go as far as the end of the first recurrance.

Example: Convert 0.6 to 9 binary places

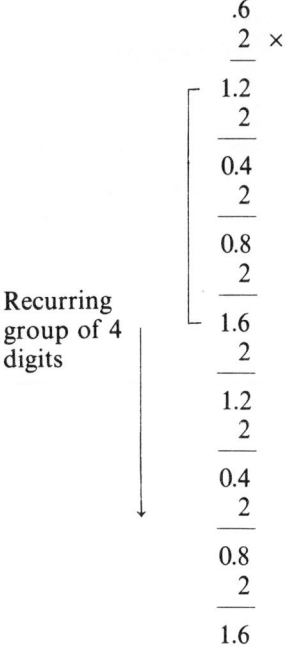

```
        .6
        2 ×
      ─────
        1.2
        2
      ─────
        0.4
        2
      ─────
        0.8
        2
      ─────
        1.6
        2
      ─────
        1.2
        2
      ─────
        0.4
        2
      ─────
        0.8
        2
      ─────
        1.6
```

Recurring group of 4 digits

Answer = 0.100110011.......

This answer could be written as $0.1\dot{0}0\dot{1}$ by showing the recurring group. It should now be obvious that it is quite impossible to hold the binary representation of some denary numbers to 100% accuracy even if the computer had a very, very long word length. This has to be accepted and gives rise to an error called a truncation error which is discussed in detail in Section 6.5.

More complex decimal fractions are dealt with in similar manner.

Example: Convert 0.234 to binary

```
        0.234 × 2
        0.468
        0.936
        1.872
        1.744
        1.488
        0.976
        1.952
        1.904
        1.808
        1.616
        1.232
```

At this point, we can see that the most recent product differs from the original figure by only 0.002 but it *is* different and suggests that any recurrence is unlikely. This binary fraction probably goes on for ever with a constantly changing pattern of zeros and ones.

COMPUTER ARITHMETIC 43

Exercises 6.1*

Convert to binary:
(i) 0.1   (ii) 0.9   (iii) 0.8   (iv) 0.15
(v) 0.265 (to 15 places)   (vi) 0.355 (don't give up!)

6.2 Representation of negative numbers

Here is a simple arithmetic problem: add together 149_{10} and 94_{10}, in binary.

First convert 149 and 94 into pure binary:

$$149 \equiv 1\ 0\ 0\ 1\ 0\ 1\ 0\ 1$$
$$94 \equiv 1\ 0\ 1\ 1\ 1\ 1\ 0$$

Now add: $\quad\quad\quad 1\ 1\ 1\ 1\ 0\ 0\ 1\ 1 \equiv 243_{10}$

If we look at the numbers used in the example above we will see that
(*a*) both numbers are positive
(*b*) one number needs 8 binary bits to represent it and the other one 7 (< 8)
(*c*) the result of the addition also fits into 8 bits—there is no carry from the left hand bit position (most significant bit—MSB).

We cannot, of course, have a system that will not accept negative numbers or allow carry so let us see how these constraints are overcome.

In denary arithmetic, a number is said to be negative if it has a 'minus sign' in front of it: -16; -85; -133.

The same technique can be applied to a binary number and the numbers shown above would become:
-10000; -1010101; -10000101.

If we show the second of these in an 8 bit word we have the representation:

| − | 1 | 0 | 1 | 0 | 1 | 0 | 1 |

But we know that a binary word can only 'hold' ones or zeros so the minus sign must itself be coded into a 'binary bit'. By convention, 1 is used to indicate a negative value and therefore the only other possible bit—zero—must be used to indicate a positive value. The above now becomes:

| 1 | 1 | 0 | 1 | 0 | 1 | 0 | 1 | $\equiv -85$

| 0 | 1 | 0 | 1 | 0 | 1 | 0 | 1 | $\equiv +85$

This method of representing negative numbers is known as the sign and modulus method. The most left hand bit is used only to indicate the sign of the number.

The range of numbers that can be 'held' in an 8 bit word is

from: 0 1 1 1 1 1 1 1 $\equiv +127$
to: 1 1 1 1 1 1 1 1 $\equiv -127$

In the middle of this range of numbers we find: 00000000, which clearly represents + zero, but the next 'binary pattern' is 10000000. This represents − zero, which is, of course, the same as + zero. Therefore, as zero is always taken as being positive, the second representation is redundant and we have wasted one binary representation. Instead of having 256 different representations (2^8), we only have 255: 127 positive numbers, 127 negative numbers, and zero.

A second method of representing negative numbers, known as two's complement form, overcomes the problem outlined above and is much more widely used in modern computers. The method of complementation to represent a negative number relies on the fact that any number, in any base, only takes on its true value if its reference point, or starting value, is known. Thus +8 is always taken as being 8 units *above zero* but what if the starting point was +10? Now, +8 represents 2 units *backwards* from 10 i.e. −2. Similarly +3 would be 7 units back from 10 i.e. −7, and so on. The second number in each case is called the true complement of the first number.

There are two types of number complement. They are:
(*a*) radix-minus-one complement—in denary known as the nine's complement and in binary as the one's complement
(*b*) radix complement—known in denary, as the ten's complement and in binary as the two's complement.

We will now consider only the use of complementation to represent negative binary numbers. An earlier example showed the representation of +85 to be

0 1 0 1 0 1 0 1

where, the first zero is the sign bit indicating a positive number. The one's complement of this is found by changing all the zeros to ones and vice versa: i.e.

1 0 1 0 1 0 1 0

By the convention of 1 for negative and 0 for positive (most left-hand bit only), this representation can now be shown as:

−128	64	32	16	8	4	2	1
1	0	1	0	1	0	1	0

which is, arithmetically: −128 + (32 + 8 + 2)
= 42 − 128 = −86

But we set out to represent −85. We have finished up with −86 because we have only obtained the one's complement. To obtain the true complement (two's complement in binary) we need to add 1 to the one's complement:

1 0 1 0 1 0 1 0   one's complement
1 +

| 1 | 0 | 1 | 0 | 1 | 0 | 1 | 1 | two's complement |

This now represents −128 + 43 = −85

Example: Represent −97 in 8 bits (using two's complement form).
Step 1—Convert 97 to pure binary

1 1 0 0 0 0 1

Step 2—Add leading zero to confirm the number is positive and to make up to 8 bits

0 1 1 0 0 0 0 1

Step 3—One's complement

1 0 0 1 1 1 1 0

Step 4—Add 1 to create two's complement

1 0 0 1 1 1 1 1

This represents, in 8 bits, −97 (Check: −128 + (31) = −97).

Example: Represent −11 in 8 bits
Step 1   0 1 0 1 1   +11
Step 2   0 0 0 0 1 0 1 1   +11 in 8 bits
Step 3   1 1 1 1 0 1 0 0   −12
Step 4   1 1 1 1 0 1 0 1   −11
(Check: −128 + (117) = −11)

Example: Represent −62 in 8 bits.
Step 1   0 1 1 1 1 1 0   +62
Step 2   0 0 1 1 1 1 1 0   +62 in 8 bits
Step 3   1 1 0 0 0 0 0 1   −63
Step 4   1 1 0 0 0 0 1 0   −62
(Check: −128 + (66) = −62)

Some more examples should make the use of two's complementation clear.

Example: Represent −13 in 5 bits.
+13   0 1 1 0 1
One's complement   1 0 0 1 0
Two's complement   1 0 0 1 1
This is equivalent to −16 + 3 = −13

Example: Represent −161 in 9 bits
+161   0 1 0 1 0 0 0 0 1
One's complement   1 0 1 0 1 1 1 1 0
Two's complement   1 0 1 0 1 1 1 1 1

This is equivalent to: −256+95 = −161

Example: Represent −512 in 12 bits
+512   0 0 1 0 0 0 0 0 0 0 0 0
One's complement 1 1 0 1 1 1 1 1 1 1 1 1
Two's complement 1 1 1 0 0 0 0 0 0 0 0 0

This is equivalent to: −2048+1536 = −512

Exercises 6.2

1 Convert the following denary numbers into two's complement binary representation in 8 bits.
(i) −81 (ii) −100 (iii) −15 (iv) −49
(v) −123

2 Represent the denary number shown in two's complement form in the binary word length stated.
(i) −91 in 8 bits (ii) −9 in 6 bits
(iii) −222 in 9 bits (iv) −120 in 10 bits
(v) −654 in 11 bits (vi) −1023 in 12 bits

It should be realised by now that for any fixed number of bits there is a limit to the size of the numbers that can be represented. In 8 bits this can be shown as:

largest positive number 0 1 1 1 1 1 1 1 ≡ +127
largest negative number 1 0 0 0 0 0 0 0 ≡ −128

and in 16 bits the range is from +32767 to −32768

Now we will see how the computer makes use of this representation of negative numbers to perform subtraction.

First let us look at a simple denary subtraction:

$$149 - 94 = 55$$

At the beginning of this section, the binary representations of these two numbers were added together. Now let us subtract one binary number from the other:

```
  1 0 0 1 0 1 0 1 ≡ 149
−     1 0 1 1 1 1 0 ≡  94
  ─────────────────
    1 1 0 1 1 1 ≡  55
```

A computer does not subtract in this way—instead, the electronic circuits that are used for addition can also be used for subtraction by forming the two's complement form of the number to be subtracted and adding. The computer, therefore, treats (149−94) as (149+(−94)) and can manipulate the two numbers exactly as it did for addition.

Take the figures above as an example. Add leading zeros to make the number of bits in the second number the same as in the first:

$$94 \equiv 01011110$$

Form the two's complement of this representation:

$$10100010$$

then add this to the binary representation of the first number:

```
    1 0 0 1 0 1 0 1 ≡ 149
+   1 0 1 0 0 0 1 0 ≡ −94
  ─────────────────
  1 0 0 1 1 0 1 1 1 ≡  55
```

In any subtraction performed by this method (giving a positive result), there will always be a leading 1—this can be ignored.

Subtraction using two's complement form can be stated as a series of steps as before.

Example: 156 − 104 (= 52)
Step 1—Convert 156 to
pure binary: 0 1 0 0 1 1 1 0 0
(the leading zero is added to
indicate a positive number)
Step 2—Convert 104 to
pure binary: 1 1 0 1 0 0 0
Step 3—Add leading
zero(s):   0 0 1 1 0 1 0 0 0
Step 4—Form one's
Complement: 1 1 0 0 1 0 1 1 1
Step 5—Form two's
complement: 1 1 0 0 1 1 0 0 0
Step 6—Add step 5 result to
step 1 result: 0 1 0 0 1 1 1 0 0
                  1 1 0 0 1 1 0 0 0 +
                  ─────────────────
                1 0 0 0 1 1 0 1 0 0

Step 7—Ignore leading 1
Result is 0 1 1 0 1 0 0 ≡ 52

With practices, steps 2 and 3, and 4 and 5 can be done together.

Example: Subtract 18 from 420

Step 1   420 ≡   0 1 1 0 1 0 0 1 0 0
Step 2 and 3   18 ≡   0 0 0 0 0 1 0 0 1 0
Step 4 and 5   −18 ≡   1 1 1 1 1 0 1 1 1 0
Step 6   1 0 1 1 0 0 1 0 0 1 0
Result is   0 1 1 0 0 1 0 0 1 0 ≡ 402

A similar technique to the above can be used if the result of the subtraction is itself negative, but it is left to the reader to experiment to discover the rules—which are based on those above.

Exercises 6.3*

Perform the subtractions below, using two's complement method. Check your answer in denary.
(i) 34 − 31 (ii) 107 − 69 (iii) 277 − 17
(iv) 514 − 512 (v) 1904 − 360

6.3 Fixed point number representation

In Section 2 we learned that the binary representation of a number is held in a computer word:

| 0 | 0 | 1 | 0 | 0 | 1 | 0 | 1 | ≡ 37_{10} |

| 0 | 1 | 0 | 0 | 1 | 0 | 0 | 1 | ≡ 73_{10} |

and from the work of the last section we know we can also represent negative numbers in a similar manner (using two's complement representation):

| 1 | 0 | 0 | 1 | 0 | 0 | 1 | 0 | ≡ −110 |

| 1 | 1 | 1 | 0 | 0 | 1 | 1 | 0 | ≡ −26 |

In all these examples we are assuming that the binary point is at the right hand end of the word. If we now represent a non-integer denary number we must include the bicimal point:

$$37.5 \equiv 0\ 1\ 0\ 0\ 1\ 0\ 1\ .\ 1$$

Representing this in an 8 bit word gives:

| 0 | 1 | 0 | 0 | 1 | 0 | 1 | 1 |

and we can see that the bicimal point has now taken a position 'in' the binary word. As the point cannot be 'in' the word, we say that its position is implied and usually show it with only the arrow. The position of the bicimal point varies depending on the value of the denary integer and fraction:

6.75 ≡ | 0 | 0 | 0 | 1 | 1 | 0↑1 | 1 | 1 |
14.625 ≡ | 0 | 1 | 1 | 1 | 0↑1 | 0 | 1 |
$7\frac{1}{16}$ ≡ | 0 | 1 | 1 | 1↑0 | 0 | 0 | 1 |
−62.5 ≡ | 1 | 0 | 0 | 0 | 0 | 0 | 1↑1 |

Exercises 6.4

1 A simple computer was built with the following specifications:
(i) a fixed length of 12 bits
(ii) capable of executing 8 different functions
(iii) 512 addressable storage locations
(iv) to work in fixed point arithmetic with positive and negative numbers with a precision of 2 binary places.
(a) Show diagrammatically the format of a binary machine code instruction.
(b) What range of numbers could the word hold?
(c) Draw a diagram to show how the denary number 7.25 would be stored. *(AEB, 1977)**

2 (a) Convert the number 133.125 to (i) binary (ii) octal.
(b) Convert the number (i) $6\frac{3}{4}$ (ii) 9.5 to a binary fraction (and a power of 2).
(c) 'The decimal number 2.4 can never be converted into binary.' Comment on this statement and calculate the error when 2.4 is converted to binary, held in a 6 bit word and then converted back to decimal.
*(AEB, 1974)**

3 (a) A binary word consists of 6 bits. Draw a diagram to show clearly what each bit would represent if the word is to 'hold':
(i) the largest possible positive integer
(ii) the largest possible negative integer
(Assume that the least significant bit holds the binary representation of the denary number, 1.)
State what the number is in each case.
(b) (i) Draw a diagram to show what each bit in the above word would represent if it was to 'hold' positive or negative mixed numbers, including fractions, up to $6\frac{3}{4}$.
(ii) Show how $-4\frac{3}{4}$ would be represented.
*(AEB, 1975)**

4 Convert 77_{10} and 145_{10} into binary. Subtract the first from the second in binary, using complementation and addition only.
Convert your answer into denary. *Show all working.* *(AEB, 1978)**

5 A certain computer uses a 6 bit word length to store positive and negative integers only, in fixed point notation. With diagrams, show how:
(a) +26 is stored
(b) −18 is stored *(AEB, 1978)**

6 In a computer using a 5 bit register to hold positive and negative, integers in binary, the arithmetic subtraction, 9 − 2 = 7, is represented by:

Register A 0 1 0 0 1

Register B 1 1 1 1 0 +

Register C 0 0 1 1 1   answer

Explain why the operation shown in *addition.*
*(AEB, 1979)**

but what happens if we want to represent 73.125?

$$73.125 \equiv 0\ 1\ 0\ 0\ 1\ 0\ 0\ 1\ .\ 0\ 0\ 1$$

Clearly, we cannot fit this into an 8 bit word as it requires 11 bits; if we do, there will be an error (see Section 5). We must realise, therefore, that for a given word length, there is a maximum and minimum binary number that can be represented. For an 8-bit word, these are:

Largest positive   0 1 1 1 1 1 1 1$_\uparrow$ ≡ +127
Largest negative   1 0 0 0 0 0 0 0$_\uparrow$ ≡ −128
Smallest positive 0$_\uparrow$0 0 0 0 0 0 1 ≡ +0.0078125
Smallest negative 1$_\uparrow$1 1 1 1 1 1 1 ≡ −0.0078125

Two important points emerge from the above:
(a) The maximum and minimum numbers that can be 'held' in an 8 bit word are very small and the range of numbers is very limited.
(b) We need to know where the bicimal point has been moved to in order to be able to interpret the binary representation correctly. Despite the fact that the bicimal point moves, this method of number representation is known as *fixed point representation*, because the point is fixed somewhere within the word.

Many computers have been built using such a system but, in order to be able to use larger numbers than ±127, either the computer word is considerably longer — 32 bits — or two or more 8 bit words are joined together to make the required word length. (This latter method is sometimes known as double-precision working.) However, when a computer with a fixed-point arithmetic unit is being used, the programmer must keep track of where the decimal point really is. This can be a very difficult job, particularly if the arithmetic is complex. To overcome this problem and to improve the range of numbers that can be represented within a fixed word length, a second method of number representation, known as floating point, is more commonly used in general purpose computers.

6.4 Floating point number representation

In mathematics, it is common practice to write very large, or very small, numbers in standard form:

$$1234567.89 = 1.23456789 \times 10^6$$

Mean distance from earth to moon = 382185.6 km
$$\approx 3.82 \times 10^5 \text{ km}$$

The 'number' part of the representation is called the *mantissa* and the 'power of' part is known as the *exponent*. Floating point representation uses a similar system, but as a computer only holds binary numbers (i.e. number in base 2) the mantissa is in binary form and the exponent is a power of 2. The bicimal point is 'floated out' to the left-hand end of the binary word. The number of places the bicimal point moves is counted (x) and the new number has to be multiplied by 2 raised to the power x to make the floating point representation equivalent to the fixed point value. Look at these examples:

fixed point   *floating point*
10101101   ≡$_\uparrow$10101101 × 2^{1000} (2^8)
110101101 ≡$_\uparrow$110101101 × 2^{1001} (2^9)
00010111   ≡$_\uparrow$10111 × 2^{-11} (2^{-3})

In the last example above, the left-hand end of the word is taken as the left-hand end of the most significant bit.
Example: Convert to binary floating point representation:

37$_{10}$ 100101.   ≡$_\uparrow$100101 × 2^{110}
37.25$_{10}$ 100101.01 ≡$_\uparrow$10010101 × 2^{110}
7.0625   111.0001 ≡$_\uparrow$1110001 × 2^{11}

Note: all these examples are in pure binary. The leading 0, to represent positive, has been omitted for clarity.

Exercises 6.5*

Convert to binary floating point representation:
(i) 67 (ii) 19$\frac{1}{4}$ (iii) 7$\frac{1}{16}$ (iv) 154.5 (v) 603$\frac{1}{32}$
(vi) 127$\frac{3}{4}$ (vii) 0.5 (viii) $\frac{1}{16}$ (ix) $\frac{15}{16}$ (x) 15$\frac{7}{8}$

Now let us see what happens when we represent a denary number in floating point in a fixed-length binary word.
Example: Represent 14 in an 8 bit word.

$$14_{10} \equiv 1\ 1\ 1\ 0$$
$$\equiv 1\ 1\ 1\ 0 \times 2^{100}\ (2^4)$$

As the exponent will always be a power of 2, it is common practice to omit the 2 and show the representation as:

0	1	1	1	0	1	0	0

sign bit : mantissa : exponent

Note that in this example the exponent is unsigned.
Example: Represent 37 in 10 bits.

37$_{10}$ ≡   1 0 0 1 0 1.
        ≡   1 0 0 1 0 1 × 1 1 0
add leading zero ≡ 0$_\uparrow$1 0 0 1 0 1 × 1 1 0

which can be shown as:

0	1	0	0	1	0	1	1	1	0

sign : mantissa : exponent

Note that the 'floating point' is always assumed to be to the right of the sign bit.
Example: Represent 271 in 14 bits.

48 COMPUTER STUDIES

$271_{10} \equiv 1\ 0\ 0\ 0\ 0\ 1\ 1\ 1\ 1.$
$\equiv 0_\uparrow 1\ 0\ 0\ 0\ 0\ 1\ 1\ 1\ 1 \times 1\ 0\ 0\ 1$

which can be shown as:

| 0 | 1 | 0 | 0 | 0 | 0 | 1 | 1 | 1 | 1 | 0 | 0 | 1 |

Example: Represent $15\frac{7}{8}$ in 12 bits.

$15\frac{7}{8} = 15.875 \equiv 1\ 1\ 1\ 1.1\ 1\ 1$
$\equiv 0\ 1\ 1\ 1\ 1\ 1\ 1\ 1 \times 0\ 1\ 0\ 0$

represented as:

| 0 | 1 | 1 | 1 | 1 | 1 | 1 | 1 | 0 | 1 | 0 | 0 |

In this example, the sign bit has been added to the exponent as well as to the mantissa. *Both* sign bits will be included in all further examples and should always be included in the representation of numbers in floating point format.

Example: Represent $\frac{1}{8}$ in 4 bits.

$\frac{1}{8} \equiv .0\ 0\ 1$
$\equiv 0_\uparrow 1\ \ \times 2^{-2}$

Note that the exponent is negative because the bicimal point has moved to the right.

This is represented as: | 0 | 1 | 1 | 0 |

Where, starting from the left, the first 0 is a sign bit and the first 1 is the mantissa. The second 1 is the sign bit for the exponent, and the second 0 is the exponent itself. Note that the exponent is the two's complementary representation of -2 and the bit positions can be shown as: $+\frac{1}{4} +\frac{1}{8} -2\ \ 1$

| 0 | 1 | 1 | 0 |

Example: Represent $\frac{5}{32}$ in 5 bits.

$\frac{5}{32} \equiv .0\ 0\ 1\ 0\ 1$
$\equiv 0_\uparrow 1\ 0\ 1 \times 2^{-2}$
$+\frac{1}{8}\ \frac{1}{16}\ \frac{1}{32} -2\ 1$

| 1 | 0 | 1 | 1 | 0 |

Example: Represent -67 in 12 bits.

$+67 \equiv 0\ 1\ 0\ 0\ 0\ 0\ 1\ 1.$
$-67 \equiv 1\ 0\ 1\ 1\ 1\ 1\ 0\ 1.$ (two's complement)
$\equiv 1_\uparrow 0\ 1\ 1\ 1\ 1\ 0\ 1 \times 2^7$ (Remember *not* to go to the left of the sign bit)

$\equiv 1_\uparrow 0\ 1\ 1\ 1\ 1\ 0\ 1 \times 0\ 1\ 1\ 1$

shown as:

| 1 | 0 | 1 | 1 | 1 | 1 | 0 | 1 | 0 | 1 | 1 | 1 |

       mantissa   exponent

In all the above examples, the number of bits has varied and has been selected so that there are just enough bits to represent the number exactly. In practice, the number of bits in a computer word is fixed and the number of bits within the word allocated to the mantissa and to the exponent are also fixed—typically, in a 32 bit word, 23 bits for the mantissa and 9 to the exponent.

Using the last example above we can represent -67 in 16 bits, using 10 for the mantissa and 6 for the exponent:

$+67 \equiv 0\ 1\ 0\ 0\ 0\ 0\ 1\ 1.$
$\equiv 0\ 0\ 0\ 1\ 0\ 0\ 0\ 0\ 1\ 1.$ (in 10 bits)
$\equiv 1\ 1\ 1\ 0\ 1\ 1\ 1\ 1\ 0\ 1.$ (two's complement)
$\equiv 1_\uparrow 1\ 1\ 0\ 1\ 1\ 1\ 1\ 0\ 1 \times 2^9$
$+9 \equiv 1\ 0\ 0\ 1.$
$\equiv 0\ 0\ 1\ 0\ 0\ 1.$ (in 6 bits)

so the full representation becomes:

| 1 | 1 | 1 | 0 | 1 | 1 | 1 | 1 | 0 | 1 | 0 | 0 | 1 | 0 | 0 | 1 |

Similarly, for $\frac{5}{32}$ in 16 bits:

$\frac{5}{32} \equiv .0\ 0\ 1\ 0\ 1$
$\equiv 0.0\ 0\ 1\ 0\ 1\ 0\ 0\ 0\ 0$ (in 10 bits)
$\equiv 0_\uparrow 1\ 0\ 1\ 0\ 0\ 0\ 0\ 0\ 0 \times 2^{-2}$
$+2 \equiv 0\ 0\ 0\ 0\ 1\ 0.$ (in 6 bits)
$-2 \equiv 1_\uparrow 1\ 1\ 1\ 1\ 0$ (two's complement form)

represented as:

| 0 | 1 | 0 | 1 | 0 | 0 | 0 | 0 | 0 | 0 | 1 | 1 | 1 | 1 | 1 | 0 |

Just as there is a limit to the size of numbers that can be held in fixed point representation, there is a limit to the size of number that can be held in a fixed length word in floating point form. Let us examine the possibilities by considering an 8 bit word. Clearly, the exponent has the greatest effect in determining the maximum size of number that can be held:

11×111111 ($3 \times 2^{63} = 9\ 223\ 372\ 000\ 000\ 000\ 000$)   is greater than 111111×11 ($63 \times 2^3 = 504$)

The largest positive integer that can be held is therefore represented as:

| 0 | 1 | 0 | 1 | 1 | 1 | 1 | 1 | $+1 \times 2^{31}$

                             $= +2\ 147\ 483\ 600$

The largest negative integer is:

| 1 | 0 | 1 | 1 | 1 | 1 | 1 | 1 | -1×2^{63}

                             $= -9\ 223\ 372\ 000\ 000\ 000$

The smallest positive number (fraction) is:

| 0 | 1 | 1 | 0 | 0 | 0 | 0 | 0 | $+1 \times 2^{-32}$

                             $= +0.000\ 000\ 000\ 023\ 3$

The smallest negative number is:

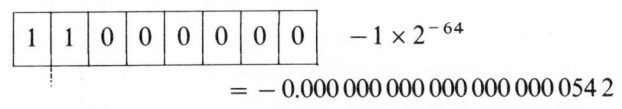

| 1 | 1 | 0 | 0 | 0 | 0 | 0 | 0 |

-1×2^{-64}
$= -0.000\,000\,000\,000\,000\,000\,054\,2$

If we compare these maximum and minimum representations with the similar ones for fixed point, we can see that using floating point gives a much wider range of numbers that can be represented, particularly fractional numbers.

	Advantages	Disadvantages
Fixed point	Much faster. More accurate.	Programmer needs to note position of point. Limited range for given word length.
Floating point	Looks after bicimal point automatically. Much increased range of possible representations for given word length.	Slower, less accurate. If done by hardware (to gain speed)—extra cost.

Fig. 6.1 Comparison of fixed and floating point representations

Exercises 6.6

1 (*a*) What is meant by floating-point representation? Give two ways of writing the number 4.5 in floating-point form. (The first way is purely arithmetic and the second way is for use in computer arithmetic.)
(*b*) In computer arithmetic, floating-point representation of numbers is usually held in two or more *n* bit words. A certain computer uses two 6 bit words to hold such numbers. If the most significant bit of one word represents −1 (denary), state what each word is intended to hold in floating-point arithmetic working.
(*AEB, 1975*)*

2 (*a*) (i) Explain how a number is represented in a computer.
(ii) How does its representation limit the size of a number that can be handled by the computer?
(iii) What provision is made to distinguish between positive and negative numbers?
(iv) How are fractional parts of 1 represented?
(v) What effect does word length have on accuracy of arithmetic calculations?
(*b*) Convert the following numbers to a binary, floating point representation. Using a 6 bit word for both the mantissa and the exponent:
(i) $3\frac{3}{4}$
(ii) $-7\frac{1}{2}$
(*AEB, 1976*)*

6.5 Errors in computer arithmetic

Perform the following simple arithmetic sum on a hand calculator: $1 \div 250 \times 250$. The answer, not surprisingly, is 1!

Now do another equally simple sum: $1 \div 111 \times 111$. Did you expect the answer to be 1? Of course, it should be, but you probably have to be content with 0.9999999. Why? In the previous section, we saw, that an error can occur in representing a denary number in binary in a digital computer. In this section, we will examine all the types of arithmetic error and how they occur.

(a) Errors in representation

The floating point, binary representation of 37_{10} is:

0 1 0 0 1 0 1 × 0 1 1 0
sign bit   mantissa   sign bit   exponent

This representation clearly requires 12 bits to hold it, but if we only have 8, what happens? The most important part of a floating point representation is the exponent, so this must be fitted in first:

| 0 | 1 | 1 | 0 |

leaving only 4 bits for the mantissa.

We must now fill the remainder of the word with the *most left hand 4 bits* of the mantissa, i.e. the most significant bits,

| 0 | 1 | 0 | 0 | 0 | 1 | 1 | 0 |

We can see that we have 'lost' the right hand 3 bits from the mantissa (101), and therefore we have an error. To find this error, we must now interpret the binary pattern above to find what we have actually stored.

This is (dropping the sign bits which are both positive):

$$.1\,0\,0 \times 2^{110}$$

We therefore have to right shift the bicimal point six places, giving: 1 0 0 0 0 0. This is equivalent to 32_{10}, but we started off with 37_{10}. The error therefore is $37 - 32 = 5$. This is a 13.5% error, which is quite unacceptable and would not occur in a 'real computer'. All the examples and exercises in this section use much smaller word lengths than would be encountered in a computer and therefore produce, seemingly, large errors. In Chapter 3 we saw that a change in the least significant bit of a 32 bit word represented a change of one part in 4294967296. When a 24 bit word is used, the loss of a significant 25th bit (1) represents an error of approximately $3 \times 10^{-6}\%$.

Examples

1 Find the actual error when $+37.25$ is held in binary floating point in 10 bits, allowing 4 bits for the exponent.

$37.25 \equiv 1\ 0\ 0\ 1\ 0\ 1\ .\ 0\ 1$ (pure binary)

Move the bicimal point to the left-hand end and count number of places moved:

$.1\ 0\ 0\ 1\ 0\ 1\ 0\ 1 \times 2^6$
$.1\ 0\ 0\ 1\ 0\ 1\ 0\ 1 \times 1\ 1\ 0$

Add leading zeros as both numbers are positive:

$0.1\ 0\ 0\ 1\ 0\ 1\ 0\ 1 \times 0\ 1\ 1\ 0$

giving a total of 13 binary bits to be 'fitted' into 10.

Always start with the exponent at the right-hand end,

					0	1	1	0

then fill up the remainder of the word from the left:

0	1	0	0	1	0	0	1	1	0

This representation is actually:

$.1\ 0\ 0\ 1\ 0 \times 2^6 = 1\ 0\ 0\ 1\ 0\ 0 \equiv 36_{10}$

Therefore error $= 37.25 - 36 = 1.25$

2. Find the percentage error when 14.625 is held in binary floating point in a 10-bit word, allowing 4 bits for the exponent.

$14.625 = 1\ 1\ 1\ 0\ .\ 1\ 0\ 1$
$\quad\quad\quad 0\ .\ 1\ 1\ 1\ 0\ 1\ 0\ 1 \times 2^4$
$\quad\quad\quad 0\ 1\ 1\ 1\ 0\ 1\ 0\ 1 \times 0\ 1\ 0\ 0$

| 0 | 1 | 1 | 1 | 0 | 1 | 0 | 1 | 0 | 0 | in 10 bits
|---|---|---|---|---|---|---|---|---|---|

$= .1\ 1\ 1\ 0\ 1 \times 2^4 = 1\ 1\ 1\ 0.1 \equiv 14.5$

Therefore percentage error $= \dfrac{0.125}{14.625} \times 100 = 0.86\%$

3 The denary number -71 is to be held in a 9 bit word in binary floating point form using 4 bits for the exponent. Calculate the error when this representation is read back.

$+71 \equiv 0\ 1\ 0\ 0\ 0\ 1\ 1\ 1$
$-71 \equiv 1\ 0\ 1\ 1\ 1\ 0\ 0\ 1$ (two's complement)
$\quad\ \equiv 1.0\ 1\ 1\ 1\ 0\ 0\ 1 \times 2^7$
$\quad\ \equiv 1.0\ 1\ 1\ 1\ 0\ 0\ 1 \times 0\ 1\ 1\ 1$ (12 bits)

| 1 | 0 | 1 | 1 | 1 | 0 | 1 | 1 | 1 | in 9 bits
|---|---|---|---|---|---|---|---|---|

$= 1{\scriptstyle\uparrow}0\ 1\ 1\ 1 \times 2^7$
$= 1{\scriptstyle\uparrow}0\ 1\ 1\ 1\ 0\ 0\ 0$ (in two's complement form)
$\equiv -72$

Error $= -1$

4 Calculate the actual error when the denary number 7.9 is held in binary floating point form in:
(*a*) a 9-bit word. (*b*) a 14-bit word.
(3 bits for the exponent in both cases).

$7.9 \quad 1\ 1\ 1\ .\ 1\ \dot{1}\ 1\ 0\ \dot{0}\ldots..$
$\quad\quad 0.1\ 1\ 1\ 1\ \dot{1}\ 1\ 0.\dot{0}\ldots\ldots \times 2^3$
$\quad\quad 0\ 1\ 1\ 1\ 1\ \dot{1}\ 1\ 0\ \dot{0}\ldots\ldots \times 0\ 1\ 1$

(*a*) | 0 | 1 | 1 | 1 | 1 | 1 | 0 | 1 | 1 | in 9 bits
|---|---|---|---|---|---|---|---|---|

$= 1\ 1\ 1\ 1\ 1\ \times 2^3$
$= 1\ 1\ 1.1\ 1$
$\ 7.75 \quad\quad\quad$ Error $= 7.9 - 7.75 = 0.15$

(*b*) | 0 | 1 | 1 | 1 | 1 | 1 | 1 | 0 | 0 | 1 | 1 | 0 | 1 | 1 |
|---|---|---|---|---|---|---|---|---|---|---|---|---|---|

$= 0.1\ 1\ 1\ 1\ 1\ 1\ 0\ 0\ 1\ 1 \times 2^3$ in 14 bits
$= {\scriptstyle\uparrow}1\ 1\ 1.1\ 1\ 1\ 0\ 0\ 1\ 1$
$\equiv 7 + \tfrac{1}{2} + \tfrac{1}{4} + \tfrac{1}{8} + \tfrac{1}{64} + \tfrac{1}{128}$
$= 7.8984375$

Error $= 0.0015625$

5 Calculate the error when the denary number $+0.04$ is held in binary floating point in an 8 bit word to the greatest possible accuracy, i.e. the exponent is to be given as many bits as necessary to be represented accurately.

$+0.04 \equiv .0\ 0\ 0\ 0\ 1\ 0\ 1\ 0\ 0\ 0\ 1\ 1\ldots\ldots$
$\quad\quad\ \equiv\ 1\ 0\ 1\ 0\ 0\ 0\ 1\ 1 \times 2^{-4}$
$\quad\quad\ \equiv\ 0\ 1\ 0.1\ 0\ 0\ 0\ 1\ 1 \times 1\ 1\ 0\ 0$
(two's complement exponent)

The exponent requires 4 bits, leaving 4 for the mantissa.

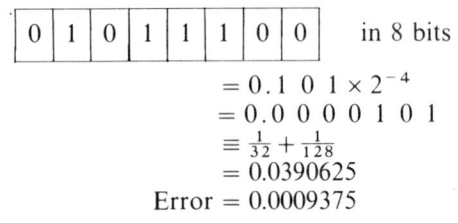

| 0 | 1 | 0 | 1 | 1 | 1 | 0 | 0 | in 8 bits
|---|---|---|---|---|---|---|---|

$= 0.1\ 0\ 1 \times 2^{-4}$
$= 0.0\ 0\ 0\ 0\ 1\ 0\ 1$
$\equiv \tfrac{1}{32} + \tfrac{1}{128}$
$= 0.0390625$

Error $= 0.0009375$

6 Find the error when the denary number $-\tfrac{1}{16}$ is held in binary floating point form in a 6 bit word to the greatest possible accuracy.

$+\tfrac{1}{16} \equiv 0.0\ 0\ 0\ 1$
$-\tfrac{1}{16} \equiv 1.1\ 1\ 1\ 1$
$\quad\quad\ =\ 1.1\ 1\ 1\ 1 \times 2^0$
$\quad\quad\ =\ 1.1\ 1\ 1\ 1 \times 0\ 0$

The exponent must still be provided even though it is zero.

| 1 | 1 | 1 | 1 | 0 | 0 | in 6 bits
|---|---|---|---|---|---|

$= -1 + \tfrac{1}{2} + \tfrac{1}{4} + \tfrac{1}{8} \times 1$
$= -\tfrac{1}{8}$

Error $= -\tfrac{1}{16}$

COMPUTER ARITHMETIC

Exercises 6.7*

Calculate the error when each denary number below is held in the word length given to the greatest possible accuracy.

(i)   +123 in 10 bits   (v)   +56.75 in 8 bits
(ii) −27.5 in 10 bits   (vi)   +9.9 in 16 bits
(iii) −74.3 in 15 bits   (vii) +0.05 in 8 bits
(iv) +192.875 in 16 bits (viii) −192.875 in 14 bits

(b) Errors due to rounding

Rounding errors—rounding up, down and off—are not caused by the computer but by the program, although rounding down can occur due to truncation (see below). All computers have a set, and known, system of rounding, (most microcomputers use rounding up), and therefore the programmer must write his program to suit this, depending on the required accuracy or possibly on the mathematical formulae being used.

Rounding up: 12.3456 becomes 12.35 or 12.4

Rounding down: 12.3456 becomes 12.34 or 12.3

Rounding off can be either rounding up or down depending on which makes the least change to the original number:

12.3456 becomes 12.3 to one decimal place
12.35 to two decimal places
12.346 to three decimal places.

(c) Errors due to arithmetic operations

(i) *Truncation* occurs when a binary number is too long to fit into the available word. We have seen this occur on p. 50 when an approximation to the original number is made, by the computer, by dropping off least significant digits as necessary:

1 0 1 0 1 1 0 1 1 1 in 8 bits = 1 0 1 0 1 1 0 1

(ii) *Overflow* occurs when the result of an arithmetical operation produces a result that is too large to hold in the receiving word:

```
  0 1 0 1 0 0 1 0    ≡ + 82
  0 1 1 0 1 1 1 1 +  ≡ +111
  1 1 0 0 0 0 0 1    ≡ − 63!
```

This binary result *is* correct if we add a leading zero—giving +193—but all 8 bits in the location holding the result have been used. Special arrangements are made in the computer hardware to handle this situation—often a right shift, which would lose the least significant bit only, giving an error of 1, not 256.

(iii) *Underflow* occurs when the result of an arithmetical operation is too small to be held in the computer word. If you have done Example 6 on p. 50, you will have encountered underflow already. The result of a division may be .0 0 0 0 0 0 0 1. In 8 bits this is .0 0 0 0 0 0 0 0. Special hardware arrangements again look after this situation as for overflow.

You should, by now, realise that almost every arithmetical operation performed by a computer *may* produce an error. Some cannot be avoided but can be minimised by using 'good' hardware and software. Others can be controlled by writing suitable routines into object programs. Since *all* digital computers have a finite word length, there is an absolute limit to the size of number that can be handled and the degree of accuracy that can be obtained in arithmetical operations.

Exercise 6.8

1 Briefly explain, by giving examples in binary, what is meant by:
(*a*) overflow
(*b*) truncation error
(*c*) rounding error.

Summary

- Fractions are represented in binary by descending powers of 2 (to the right of the bicimal point).
- Many decimal fractions do not have accurate representations in binary.
- Negative numbers are represented in binary in two's complement form.
- Binary subtraction is performed by *adding* the two's complement representation of the subtrahend (number to be subtracted) to the first number.
- Floating point representation enables the range of a fixed length word to be greatly extended (over a fixed point representation).
- The inaccuracy of binary representation of fractions, plus the limitations of a fixed length word, may give rise to errors in arithmetic which can only be minimised, never avoided completely.

7 The hardware

The simple concept of input → process → output from Chapter 3 must now be elaborated on and can be shown diagramatically as in Fig. 7.1.

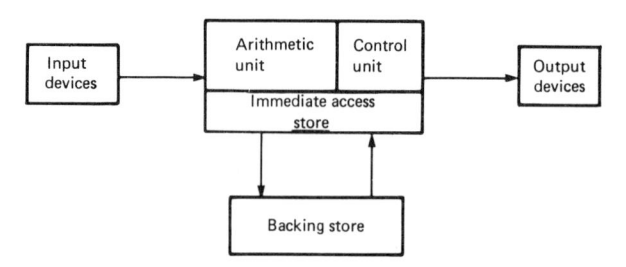

Fig. 7.1 The basic concept in more detail

7.1 Peripheral devices

A peripheral device is the term used to describe any input, output or backing storage device that can be connected to the central processor.

(a) Input devices
(i) Keyboard. The keyboard is probably the simplest method of data input and is rapidly becoming the most widely used. A keyboard may be used on its own, as in many microprocessors, or in conjunction with a visual display unit (see below). A typical keyboard is shown in Fig. 7.2. The layout of the keys is almost the same as on a

Fig. 7.2 The keyboard of a BBC Micro

'In the computer room we visited, all the units had been made to look like tape decks for security reasons.'

standard typewriter, but extra keys are required to enable control signals to be sent to the computer. An encoder unit, usually situated inside the keyboard, generates the ASCII code of the character represented by any key when depressed.
(ii) Visual display unit (VDU). A VDU consists of a keyboard attached, usually permanently, to a television-like display screen (Fig. 7.3). The ASCII codes from the keyboard are fed into a character generator and, after decoding, the appropriate character is displayed on the screen. A VDU is not capable of displaying television pictures!
(iii) Key to disk/tape unit. For off-line data preparation, a VDU is connected to a magnetic disk unit, or possibly to a magnetic tape unit. (Fig. 7.4). The operation of typing data on the keyboard, verifying it on the screen and recording it on the disk is controlled by a microprocessor built into the unit. The disk is sub-

THE HARDWARE 53

Fig. 7.3 Visual display unit

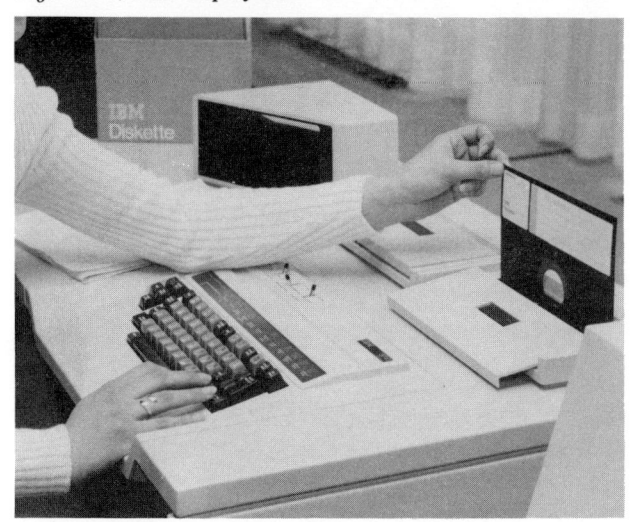

Fig. 7.4 Key-to-disk unit. This is an IBM 3740 data entry system. The operator is shown inserting a floppy disk prior to inputting data from the keyboard

Fig. 7.5 Graphical display unit with light pen

sequently used to input the data at very high speed to the central processor.

(iv) Graphical display unit (GDU). The GDU is similar in appearance to a VDU but has the facility to display lines on the screen as well as characters. It usually has a light pen attached to it. (Fig. 7.5). With this light-sensitive pen, lines can be drawn on the screen and data can be 'read' from the screen as pulses of light. These are transformed to electronic digital signals before being sent to the central processor unit.

(v) Document reader. Since the start of data processing there has been much development to make possible the machine 'reading' of data capture documents, thereby avoiding the necessity of transcribing the data into machine readable form. This development has had limited success, in that it is possible for a machine to recognise *printed* characters but only numerals if the data is hand-written. Because of the wide variations in hand writing, even numerals have to be of a prescribed size and style. Document readers usually are classified according to the method of character reading used— optical or magnetic. Some general purpose document readers have been developed combining both techniques but single system readers are the most common.

In an *optical character reader*, the printed characters are 'scanned' by a beam of light which is reflected off the paper on to light-sensitive cells. Much less light is reflected from the black character than from the white paper and this change in light falling onto the light-sensitive cells produces a varying electrical signal from the cells which, in turn, is decoded and interpreted as a numeral, letter or other character. The early OCRs required a special set of characters—known as a fount— in order to ensure the character was correctly read (Fig. 7.6(*a*)), but improved reading techniques have made it possible to read ordinary printed characters (Fig. 7.6(*b*)).

```
ABCDEFGHIJKLM
NOPQRSTUVWXYZ
0123456789
   ABCDEFGH abcdefgh
   IJKLMNOP ijklmnop
   QRSTUVWX qrstuvwx
   YZ*+,-./ yz m åøæ
   01234567 £$:;<%>?
   89       [@!#&,]
```

Fig. 7.6 OCR founts
A special character set (*top*)
Ordinary characters can now be read (*bottom*)

For a *magnetic ink character reader*, characters are printed with a special ink containing ferric oxide in one of two founts, E13B or CMC7. Some of the characters from each set are shown in Fig. 7.7. Note that the E13B fount contains only numerals plus four special characters, and can usually be seen on most cheques. (Fig. 7.8).

When it is necessary for the magnetic ink characters to be read, they are first magnetised by putting the whole document into a weak magnetic field then passing it under an electromagnetic detection coil. The magnetic characters induce a small current in the coil which is amplified and decoded to represent the character being cread. The E13B fount is scanned to determine the shape of the character but the CMC7 fount is, in fact, a 7 bit binary code and it is the relative spacing of the vertical bars that is decoded to determine the character being read.

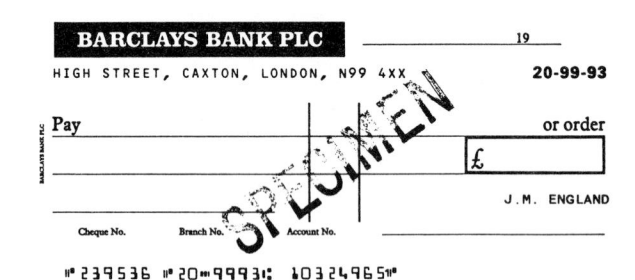

Fig. 7.8 E13B characters on a cheque

Both systems require a mechanism to transport the document from the input hopper, through the reading station and into the output hopper. The electronic signals resulting from reading the characters are sent as binary words to the central processing unit (Fig. 7.9).

With an *optical mark reader*, black pencil marks made in predefined positions on a special form can easily be detected by measuring the amount of light reflected

Fig. 7.7 Characters printed with magnetic ink
　　　　E13B fount (*top*)
　　　　CMC7 fount (*bottom*)

Fig. 7.9 Document reader (IBM 3890)

from a small area of the document (Fig. 7.10). If a mark is present, the amount of light reflected will be less than a blank area of form. This change in light level is detected by a photo diode and the resulting signal fed to the central processor. There is usually one detector for each predefined position on the form and, as each position has a 'value'—e.g. 10, 50 or 100 on an ordering form or 'yes' or 'no' on an exam form. The presence, or absence of a mark can be directly interpreted as data.

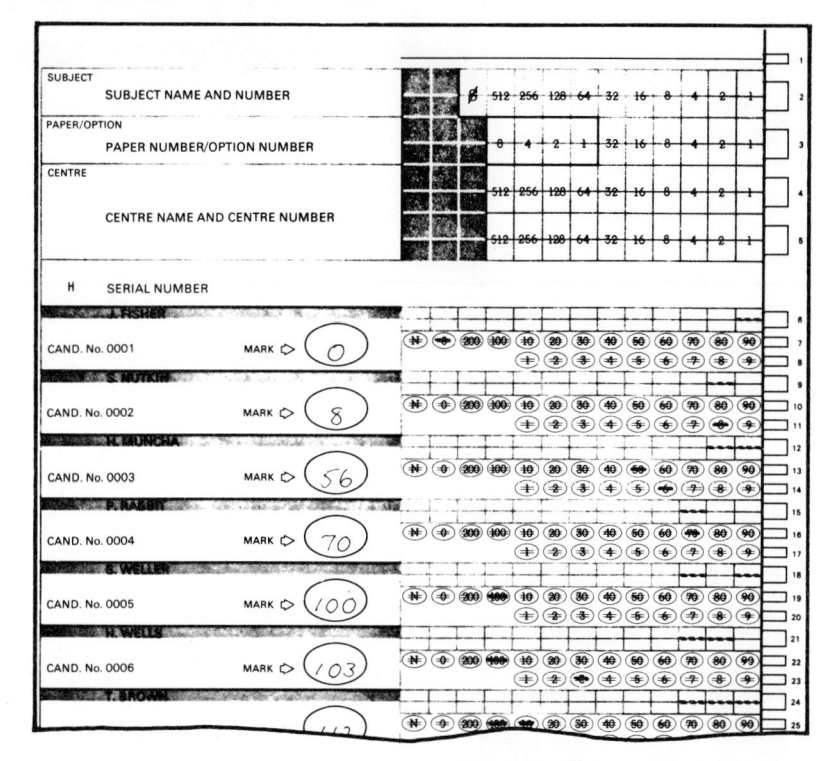

Fig. 7.10 Exam results input document showing 'marks' to be read

Fig. 7.11 Optical mark card reader

A particular optical mark reader that is used widely in education is the *optical mark card reader*. The cards used are usually the same size as an 80-column punched card, but, because of the extra space required for the 'marks' (compared with a small punched hole), there are, typically, only 40 columns per card. The reading speed is slow—typically 240 cards per minute (Fig. 7.11).

(vi) Badge reader. 'Badge' is a general term and usually means a small plastic card which may be, for example, a bankers card, a factory clock card, a security identification card or a credit card. The card contains details in some coded form—usually magnetic but it could also be optical—relating to the card owner and its use. A security identification card may have all the data coded onto a small piece of magnetic material firmly attached to the card and this card would be put into a small badge reader situated, for example, outside a laboratory. If the card owner is authorised to enter the laboratory, the card will match similar details stored on a computer file and will automatically open the laboratory door.

At least one bank has a system where the credit balance of a customer's account is recorded onto the magnetic part of the bank card along with other relevant data. This card is used to obtain cash from an automatic dispensing unit and when the card is inserted in the appropriate slot the details relating to the customer are read by a magnetic scanner and transmitted directly to the bank's computer. If the customer is in credit, the computer will allow the transaction and dispense the required cash and, before returning the card, will update the balance by writing new data to the magnetic media on the card. If the customer is already in the 'red' the dispensing unit keeps the card!

(vii) Point-of-sale devices. With the increasing use of computers by the retail trade, particularly supermarkets, during the 1970s, it became necessary to develop some technique that could record automatically the details of a sales transaction at the point-of-sale. The earliest of these was the *Kimball tag* which is used extensively in retail selling of garments. A small punched card (Fig. 7.12) is attached to the garment after manufacture. This card records details of the particular garment, e.g. style, colour, size and is detached from the garment at the retailer's cash desk.

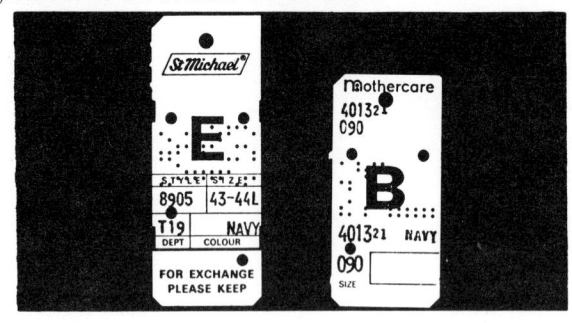

Fig. 7.12 Kimball tags

In some places the cards are simply collected and batched together each day or week, and sent to the computer department where they are read by a special card reader. Other systems have a miniature card reader at the point of sale which is directly connected to a microprocessor and a magnetic disk (or tape) unit. As each card is fed into the reader the details are recorded on the disk which is sent to the computer department for direct input for processing. The details of all sales transactions will be used to update the computer files and to produce a detailed record of all sales, stock levels, payments etc.

A second system of recording sales details, particularly in supermarkets, has now become widely accepted and *bar codes* can be seen on almost every item of food as well as on a great many other retail items. Typical bar codes are shown in Fig. 7.13.

Fig. 7.13 Typical bar codes

Unfortunately, there are many bar codes currently being used. One of these is known as the universal product code (UPC) and is being widely accepted as the standard. Whatever the actual code used, each product is allocated a code number that uniquely describes the product and its manufacturer. For example the code 1730426991 may decode as: Beans Baked; 8 oz; Heinz; factory code; date. Notice that the price is not included in the bar code—why not?

The bar code labels are 'read' by a light pen (commonly referred to as a 'wand'), which, when passed across the bars, produces a series of electronic pulses proportional to the light and dark pattern of the bar code. These pulses are then decoded to give numeric data as in the example above. The wand may be hand-held to read the bar code at the point of sale; such a system is in common use in lending libraries to record details of book loans. It may be built into the checkout point in a supermarket where the wand may be hand-held or fixed to scan each item as it is passed in front of the scanning position. Laser scanning is the most recent development and with this system the bar code is read correctly even if the product is upside down! (See also Chapter 12.6)

(viii) Card Reader. A device to 'read' punched cards has been the 'workhorse' of data processing since the early 1900s. The equipment is designed to detect the presence or absence of holes in the card (see Chapter 5.2) using a technique known as light-sensing. This technique utilises the fact that certain electronic devices known as photo-electric diodes or cells, or phototransistors, have the ability to generate a small electric signal when light is shone onto the cell (Fig. 7.14).

A card reader normally reads one column of a card, i.e. one character, at a time. As there are 12 possible punching positions in each column, 12 photocells are required to detect light from 12 light emitting diodes (LEDs) or lamps. The card is passed between the light source and the detectors and stopped when column 1 is in line with the lamps. Light will now pass to the detectors *only* where there is a hole in the card. When the resulting electric signal(s) have been sent to the central processor for decoding, the card is moved onto **column 2** and this pattern of holes is detected and decoded and

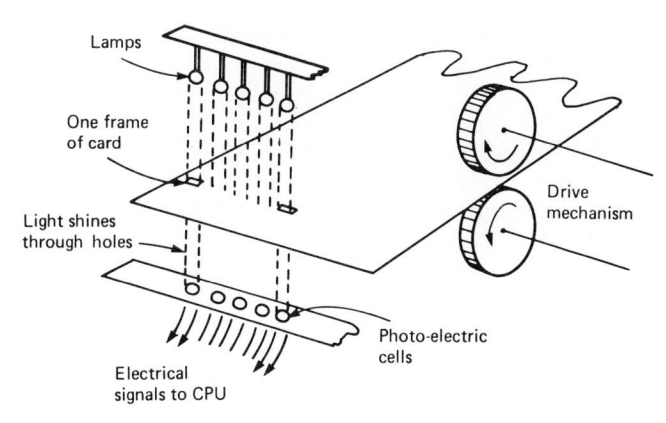

Fig. 7.14 Card being read using opto-electronic techniques

so on across all the columns of the card. Although this process sounds slow, the movement of the card is very fast and a reading speed of 1000 cards/min is typical in a modern card reader. If we assume that each card is about three-quarters punched, giving an average useage of 60 columns, a reading speed of 1000 cards/min gives an input to the central processor of 1000 characters per second. As the reader has to 'read' a whole card, we can see that cards which are punched in only the first 5–15 columns (typical Basic program statements) give a much lower data input to the central processor. Ten columns per card will give approximately 150 characters per second.

The cards are stacked in a hopper and transported across the reading station by means of rollers, although some very high speed readers (up to 5000 cards/min) use a vacuum system to move the cards very quickly; the cards are stacked in a receiving hopper after being read (Fig. 7.15).

Fig. 7.15 Punched card reader (IBM 3505)

Early card readers used wire brushes to sense the presence of holes in the card but these readers were much slower, typically 300 cards/min.

(ix) Punched tape reader. Two types of punched tape reader are in current use, low speed and high speed.

The low speed reader uses an electromechanical principle and is capable of reading 600 characters per minute. Eight small spring-loaded 'plungers' are pressed against one frame of paper tape. Any hole in the frame allows the 'plunger' to go through the tape and in doing so make an electrical contact which sends a corresponding pulse to the central processor. After the 'plungers' are withdrawn, the tape is pulled on one frame using the sprocket holes and stopped before a cam lifts the plungers again. This type of tape reader is to be found on most teletypewriters.

The high speed reader uses the same light-sensing principle as the card reader but, because of space restrictions, a single light source is used and spread out to cover the eight light-sensitive detectors by means of a prism. As there is no need to stop the tape to read each frame, much higher speeds can be obtained, typically 2000 to 3000 characters per minute (Fig. 7.16).

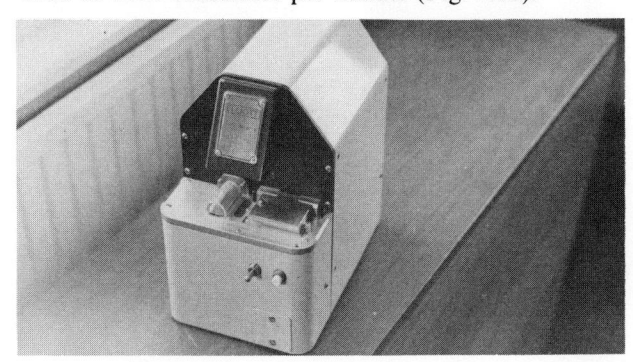

Fig. 7.16 High speed paper tape reader

(x) Teletypewriter. The teletypewriter has, until recently, been the most popular input, (and output) device used in educational computing. It consists of an electromechanical keyboard, which produces the ASCII code of the character represented when a key is depressed, and a print head which reproduces the character on continuous roll paper as the key is depressed (Fig. (7.17). Most teletypewriters also have a paper tape reader and punch attached to them. The signals from the teletypewriters can be fed directly into the central processor or via a telephone link to a remote computer.

(xi) Graphics tablet. A graphics tablet consists of a flat board on which paper or drawings can easily be held. A cursor or stylus, like a light pen, can be freely positioned anywhere on the board and this position interpreted as x and y co-ordinates from a fixed point on the board.

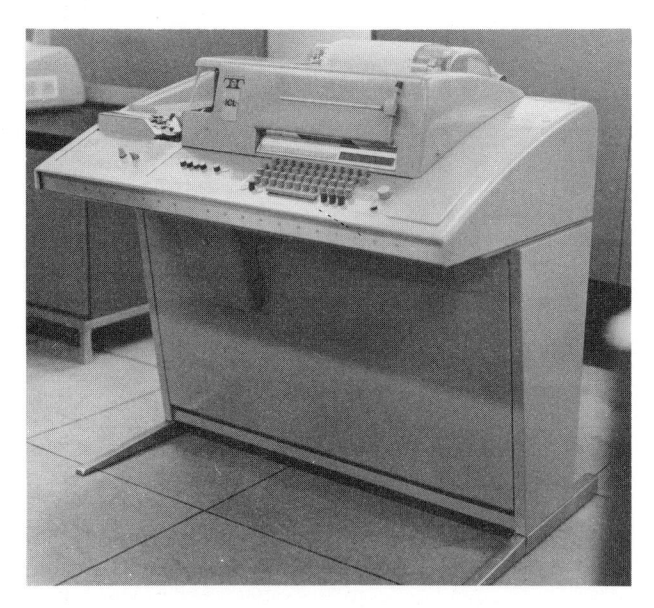

Fig. 7.17 Teletypewriter

The cursor is normally used for 'reading' from a drawing. The cross-wires are positioned over each point to be read and the co-ordinates of each point are fed to the central processor to be stored. This data can then be used to produce, for example, a scaled version of the drawing on paper or to display it on a GDU (Fig. 7.18).

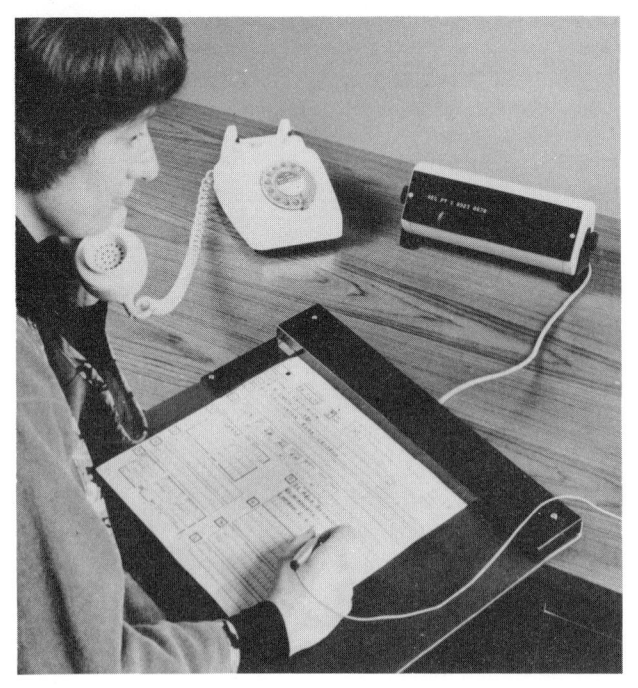

Fig. 7.18 Graphics tablet

The stylus is hand-held and can be used in a similar way to the cursor to read drawings but it can also be used to trace the outline of writing. If the co-ordinates of three or four points of a letter or number are fed to the central processor and compared with a set of stored data for every character, it is possible to 'recognise' the character being scanned. Such a system could be used to 'write' data directly into the central processor.

The most common system for detecting the position of the stylus or cursor uses a matrix of fine wires embedded under the surface of the board. Typically the wires may be 0.5 mm apart and the x-wires separated from the y-wires by a thin sheet of insulating material. Electronic pulses are sent down all the x-wires and all the y-wires simultaneously and a capacitive method of detection senses where the stylus is at any instant.

Many new forms of input are being developed based on the graphics tablet and it is likely that some of these will become important input devices in the 1980s.

(xii) Voice input. Direct input of data, using the human voice has been a 'pipe-dream' and a technical challenge to electronic engineers over many years. Recently, some of these dreams have become a reality and some limited voice input systems are being used.

As yet, these work on a restricted vocabulary and only recognise a limited number of words, for example operating system instructions, programming commands or numbers. Even with a small vocabulary, they have great difficulty in interpreting the same word spoken by two people with different accents! The latest developments in this field suggest that within a few years vocabularies will have increased to enable a complete programming language to be recognised word by word, enabling programs to be 'written' by reading the commands, variables etc. into a microphone, but alpha data will probably still need to be input letter by letter!

(xiii) A universal device. The use of a standard television camera along with a micro-processor and VDU is claimed as the forerunner of a 'universal input device'. Such a device can be used to 'read' printed documents or drawings but the same problems face this device, in attempting to read handwriting, as the document reader mentioned previously.

(b) Output devices

Output devices fall into two categories: those that produce human readable output and those that do not. In the first group are the most widely used output devices.

(i) Printers. Many different types of printer are now in daily use producing 'hard copy' output from computers. These can be classified into three types: character printers, matrix printers and non-impact printers.

The first type of printer uses embossed characters to do the printing in much the same way as junior printing outfits do but the material used is steel or plastic, instead of rubber. There are no actual characters used in the second group of printers—each character is formed from a matrix of dots.

The character printer most commonly used in data processing is the *drum line printer*, so called because the character set is embossed on a drum and one line of characters is printed at a time (Fig. 7.19). One complete character set is embossed round the drum and this set is repeated along the length of the drum, usually 132 times. When a line of characters is to be printed, the paper is stopped and the drum rotates once. As the appropriate characters are in the correct position along the line for printing, electromagnetic hammers hit the paper against the embossed character and, through carbon, the character is printed on the paper. 'A' will be printed first, then 'B', 'C' and so on through the complete character set. After one revolution of the drum, the paper is moved on to the next line and the process started again. A drum printer can print at a very high speed—typically 2000 lines per minute; i.e. 33 lines per second. A page of printer paper can have 64 lines of print and therefore the output of two pages per second creates the impression of continuous paper flow. Unfortunately, drum line printers can be very noisy and are very expensive.

Another much cheaper, much slower, but almost as noisy, character printer is the *chain line printer* where the characters are embossed into 'tabs' fastened to a chain which rotates at right angles to the direction of the paper flow (Fig. 7.20). When the required letter is in the correct position, across the line of print, a hammer strikes the paper and carbon against the character tab. The paper moves on one line space when the complete character set has passed across the paper. Typically a chain printer prints 1000 lines per minute.

A third character printer which, because of its relative cheapness and small size, is being used extensively with microcomputers, is the *daisy-wheel printer* (Fig. 7.21). Each character—there are usually 96—is embossed at the end of a small plastic or metal spoke and all the spokes radiate from a central hub rather like petals of a flower, (hence the name daisy-wheel). In operation, the wheel is rotated until the required character is in the printing position, when a single hammer strikes the character against an ink ribbon and on to the paper. As the carriage carrying the printing mechanism moves to the next position, the wheel is rotated to have the next character to be printed available as the printing position is reached. A big

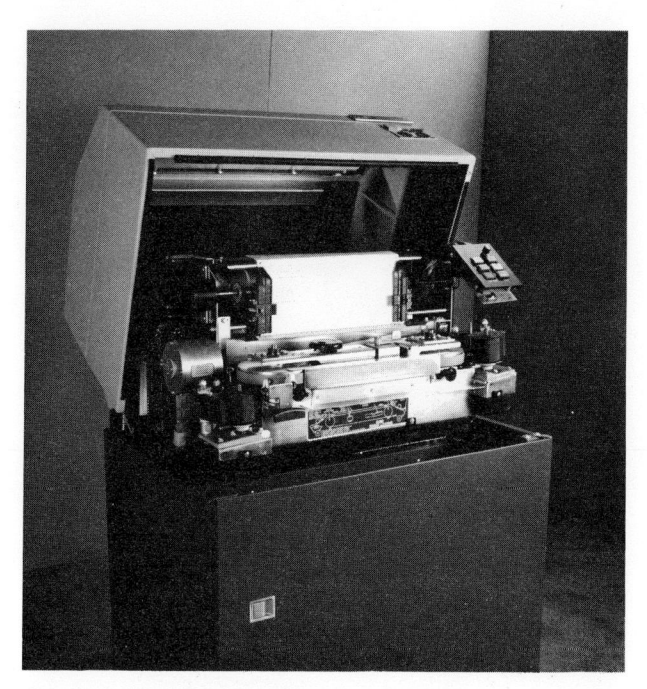

Fig. 7.19 Drum line printer

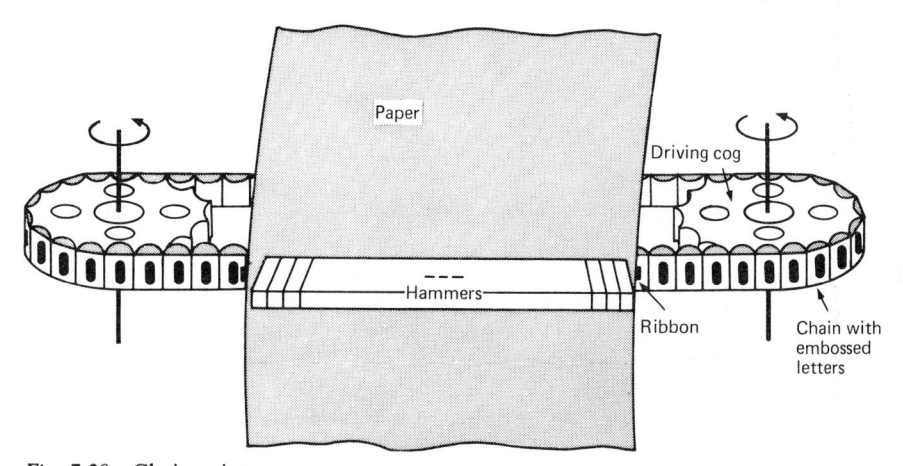

Fig. 7.20 Chain printer

60 COMPUTER STUDIES

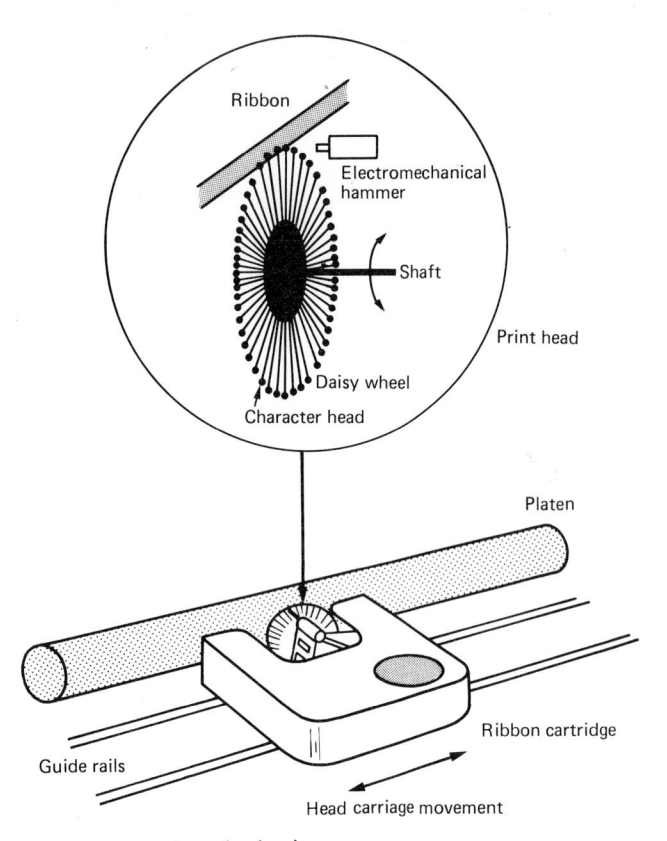

Fig. 7.21 Daisy wheel printer

E ɜ   E g

Fig. 7.22 Printing the letters E and g
With a 9 × 7 matrix printer *(left)*
With an 11 × 7 matrix printer *(right)*

advantage of this printer is that the daisy-wheel can easily be changed to provide a new character set, e.g. for a mathematical set or a larger type face. Printing speeds of about 150 characters per second can be obtained. The number of lines printed per minute depends on the number of characters printed per line but with a full line of 80 characters, this type of printer can print 75 lines per min.

There are a number of types of *matrix printer* but, generally, they all use the same principle of a number of very fine 'needles' impacting against an ink ribbon and on to the paper. The number of needles used depends on the matrix size, but typically this will be 9 × 7, which requires nine needles. These are arranged to impact against the paper in a single column, although the electromagnets which 'fire' the needles are usually mounted in a circular pattern. The operation of a matrix printer is simple but ingenious. Each character is formed by firing the appropriate needles from the column of nine, moving the print head *one column* across the paper and firing selected needles again, and repeating this a total of seven times. One character will then have been printed. The print head then moves on to the next printing position and repeats the process. Fig. 7.22 shows how the letters E and g would be printed by a 9 × 7 matrix printer. Note that a 9 × 7 matrix does not normally permit descenders on lower case letters. Fig. 7.22 also shows the same letters printed using an 11 × 7 matrix (with descenders).

Most matrix printers are bi-directional, that is, they print as the print head is 'returning' from right to left as well as left to right. On the return cycle, the characters have to be formed by printing the right-hand column first. The pattern of dots required to make up each character is stored in read only memory (ROM), within the printer and any characters that can be represented within a defined matrix can be printed by changing the necessary ROM to the printer. This feature is particularly useful when it is required to output in languages like Chinese or Sanskrit.

Matrix printers are generally much slower than character printers because of the time required to form each character, but a printing speed of 100 characters per second is typical and, taking 50 characters as an average line, an output of 120 lines per minute can be achieved, which is quite adequate for the average, non-commercial, data-processing computer department (Fig. 7.23).

A variety of techniques has been developed to produce high-quality printed output without using a mechanical device to transfer the character to the paper. The non-impact type of printer tends to be large and complex and therefore expensive, but it is generally silent in operation and can operate at very high speed. Therefore these printers will become widely used in business and commerce rather than in education. Some of these printers are listed below.

With an *electrostatic printer*, the characters are printed on special paper using an electrostatic charge.

With an *electrosensitive printer*, characters are formed by 'burning' an aluminium coating off the surface of the paper with an electric spark, thus exposing the paper underneath. This is usually black, but other colours can be used. A small, slow version of this printer is available but its output of black letters on silver is not always as acceptable or useful as ordinary paper.

In an *ink-jet printer*, as its name implies, characters are written on plain paper using a very fine jet of ink. The jet is deflected by electronics according to the shape of the character to be printed; this data to control the deflection is stored in ROM. The method is a somewhat refined version of writing on glass using Christmas Snow! The jet is approximately $\frac{1}{20}$ mm in diameter and consists of droplets of ink. Approximately 1000 drops are required to write one character and a typical printing speed is 200 characters per second.

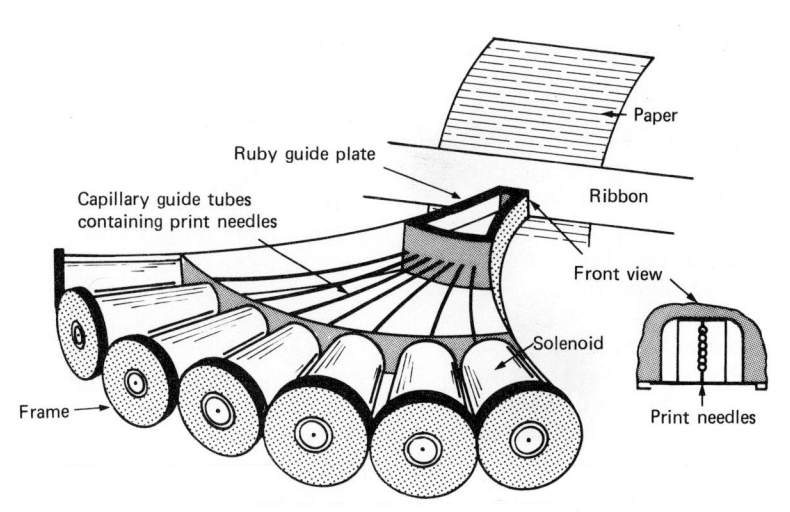

Fig. 7.23 Print head of a matrix printer

At the time of writing the *laser printer* is capable of the fastest output of all the printers—approximately 25 000 lines per minute. The method of operation is complex but the principle is that of printing data transmitted over a laser beam by an electro photographic method. (This latter is the same technique as used in photocopying). The current price of a laser printer is approximately £200 000 but, as yet, not many computer users need an output speed of 33 000 characters per second!

(ii) Graph plotters. Early graph plotters were, generally, very large and capable of drawing lines only. Many different types of graph plotter are now available, some very large (see Chapter 12.3 for the use of a large plotter), but small plotters which can draw characters as well as complex line drawings, are being attached to microcomputers to provide a hard copy of a pattern or drawing appearing on a VDU. The basic principle of all types of plotter is mark a sheet of paper with a pen. The pen can be brought into contact with the paper and moved from side to side, thereby drawing a straight line (continuous or broken). Most plotters move the paper, and keep the pen stationary, in order to draw lines along the length of the paper and move both the pen and the paper to draw lines at an angle or curved lines. In one type of plotter, the paper is fixed to a flat bed and the pen is moved over the paper in both *x* and *y* directions (Fig. 7.24).

Fig. 7.24 Graph plotter

Very good quality output can be obtained from a good plotter which can easily be reproduced to provide multiple copies. Output speeds vary considerably, but a medium size plotter will draw a complex diagram, complete with letters, words, numbers etc. in approximately 5 minutes (Fig. 7.25).

Fig. 7.25 Typical output from a graph plotter

(iii) Punches. Two output devices which were widely used but which do not produce human-readable output are the card punch and paper-tape punch. When used as a direct output device, attached to the

central processor, both will produce output which is in a form that can be directly input to a computer via a card, or paper tape reader.

Both devices punch one character into one frame; the card punch uses rectangular knives and the tape punch, round knives, then the card or tape is moved on and the next frame punched. The speed of card punching depends on how many frames are punched on each card but this would typically be 300 cards per minute. As each character is punched one after the other on paper tape, the speed can be measured in characters per second. Typically this would be 300 characters per second.

Both cards and tape can be punched by hand using small portable hand punches. Such devices cannot be connected to a computer and are classified as off-line, or data preparation equipment.

(iv) Voice output. At the time of writing, 'voice output' is limited to a few experimental kits and, because the use of spoken output in data processing has little to offer, it is unlikely that much development will take place in this field (see Chapter 13).

Music synthesisers, to produce polyphonic output from digitised signals, are in wide use, however, and the latest developments in this field allow sheet music to be 'read' and the digitised signals stored and output with the sound of 'real instruments'.

7.2 The Central Processor

The diagram below shows that the central processor (usually abbreviated to CPU for central processing unit) consists of three sections.

Immediate access store	Arithmetic logic unit
Control unit	

Fig. 7.26 The three sections of a central processor

Unlike peripheral devices, none of these 'units' is readily visible or easily recognisable inside the CPU. All three units are wholly electronic and, in a microcomputer, may consist of 20 or 30 integrated circuits, depending on the amount of main store in the CPU.

(a) Immediate access storage
The main requirements of immediate access storage (IAS) are:
 (i) very fast access time to any bit of data
 (ii) as cheap as possible per bit so that,
 (iii) the 'largest' possible IAS can be built into the CPU.
From the late 1950s until the middle 1970s, these requirements were satisfied by using *core storage*. Typical specifications are given below.

Exercises 7.1

1 A supermarket has introduced *point of sale* terminals
(*a*) Give *two* advantages that these terminals offer to the supermarket chain.
(*b*) Give *one* advantage and *one* disadvantage that the use of these terminals give to the customer.
(*AEB, 1980*)*

2 (*a*) Give two examples of the use of point-of-sale machines. State clearly how the data is input to the machine in each case.
(*b*) Choose one of the above examples and describe, in detail, how the system works. You must include details of how the data is encoded, how this data is read at the point-of-sale and what happens to it when it has been read. (*AEB, 1979*)

3 The following are examples of source information which contain data in machine-readable form:
(*a*) cheque, (*b*) credit card, (*c*) mark sense card (*d*) Kimball tag.
Select two of the above and explain the principles of operation, how the data is encoded, how it is read and what advantages this method has over more traditional methods of capturing same data. (*AEB, 1978*)*

4 (*a*) Describe, briefly, with the aid of sketches where appropriate, the essential features of *each* of the following forms of input:
 (i) mark sense cards
 (ii) magnetic ink characters
 (iii) optical characters.
(*b*) Give one example of the use of each of the above forms of input in computing applications. Clearly state why the particular form of input is used in each case. (*AEB, 1977*)

5 From the following list of peripheral devices choose *three*:
 (i) exchangeable disc store, (ii) visual display unit, (iii) teletypewriter, (iv) graphical plotter, (v) paper tape reader.
For each of those chosen, describe, with the aid of sketches:
(*a*) its function, (*b*) its operation, (*c*) an example of its use in a computing system. (*AEB, 1975*)*

	Access time	cost per bit	typical unit size
1960	12 ns	10p	8 K
1975	5 ns	5p	16 K

Note: 1 ns = 1/1 000 000 000 s; 1 K = 1024

Because of the high cost, most computers had a maximum of 32 K of IAS. Many 'medium sized' computers managed with 16 K.

THE HARDWARE

Use of *semiconductor storage* has dramatically changed the situation and now, even most microcomputers have a minimum of 16 K of IAS. The access time and cost of semiconductor storage have improved as the figures below show.

	Access time	cost per bit
1975	300ns	10p
1981	50ns	0.007p

(*i*) *Semiconductor store.* Many types of semiconductor store now exist and are known by such acronyms as RAM, ROM, PROM and EPROM. The type used for IAS is RAM, or random access memory. This is made entirely from integrated circuits and, depending on the size of the store (i.e. number of bits), may physically be one or more 'chips'.

(*ii*) *Core Store.* The term core store is used because the basic storage element is a tiny circular core of magnetic material which can be magnetised in either of two directions; one direction represents 1 and the opposite, 0. Cores are threaded together with wires to form a matrix—usually 64 × 64—which is known as a core plane (Fig. 7.27). Any single core in the plane can be made to represent 1 or 0. Core planes are mounted vertically above each other. The number of planes is equal to the number of bits in the computer word, often 16 (Fig. 7.28).

Cores are set to 1 by passing small currents in one direction through selected write wires on each plane. In order to read the data, *all* the write wires are pulsed in the

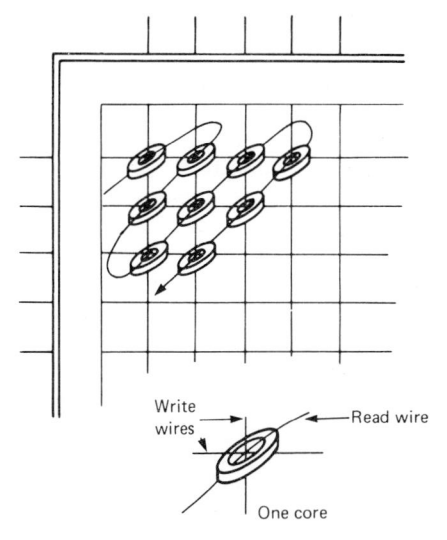

Fig. 7.27 Core matrix
Section of a matrix showing read and write wires (*top*)
How wires are threaded through a single core (*bottom*)

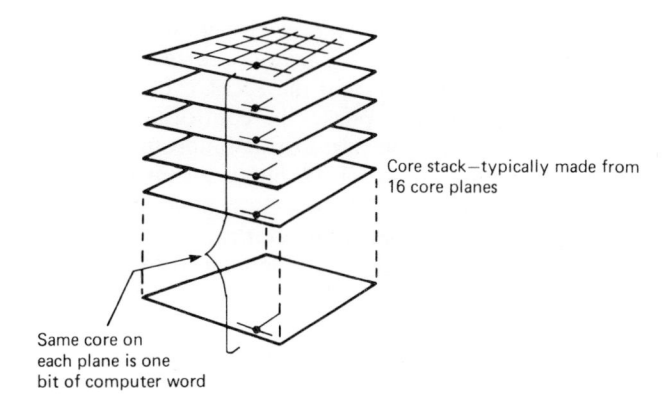

Fig. 7.28 Core stack showing position of bits to represent one word

opposite direction, thereby setting all the cores to 0. Any which were representing a 1 will have changed polarity and this change is detected by a read wire on each plane. Immediately the data has been read, it is written back to the same cores so that it can be read again, as often as required.

In operation, the state of any, or all, of the cores can be changed approximately one million times in every second. This rapid change of state generates so much energy that it is necessary to mount the core planes in an oil-filled tank to absorb the heat and prevent the cores melting!

(b) The control unit

We have learned that data is input to the central processor from one of many input devices. Whilst in the CPU it is stored, moved, checked, manipulated, checked, moved and stored again before it is finally output. The correct movement and manipulation of the data is the responsibility of the control unit, whose functions are based on logical operations, and therefore it is made from two-state devices (Chapter 6), plus one other unlikely item—an electronic clock. The computer's clock is literally the heartbeat of the CPU and all operations of the CPU are controlled by the control unit, which is itself controlled by the clock.

The clock, being electronic, produces a series of electronic pulses (Fig. 7.29).

We can see that the pulse is ON for half of the 'one pulse' time period and OFF for the other half. These two periods are often referred to as 'tick' and 'tock' but,

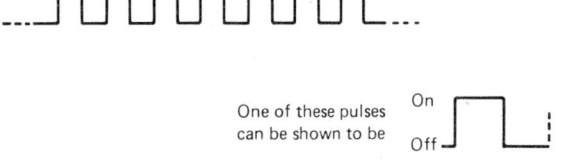

Fig. 7.29 The series of electronic pulses produced by the computer clock

because the control unit has special functions to perform in each period, or phase, they are more correctly referred to as the FETCH phase and the EXECUTE phase.

During the FETCH phase, the control unit is concerned with fetching the next instruction from store and decoding it. On the EXECUTE phase, the instruction is carried out. Movement of the data is along 'highways' connecting the various units of the CPU and it is controlled by 'gates' which can be opened or closed to allow data onto a selected highway (Fig. 7.30).

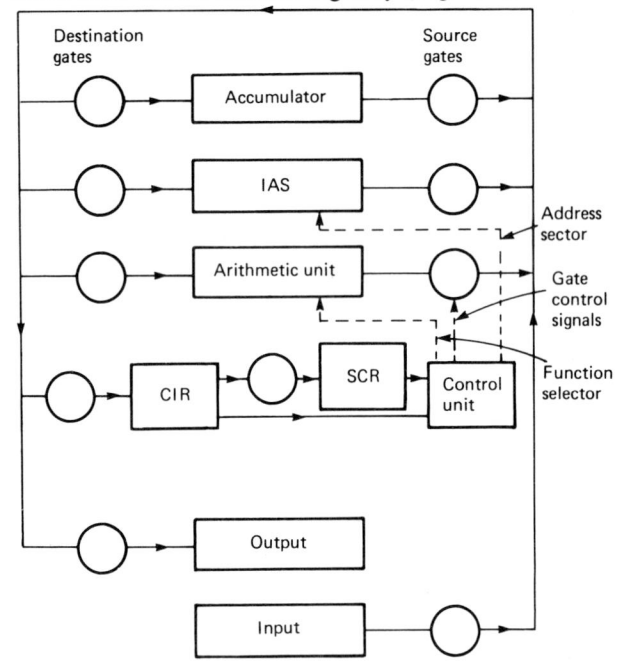

Fig. 7.30 Highways and connections to central processor system

In Chapter 5 we learned that the instructions which the control unit has to carry out are stored in 'instruction words' in the immediate access store of the central processor. The instructions have been 'generated' by the program (see Chapter 8) and are stored in the IAS in the order in which they are to be executed. Each instruction is put into the next store location to the previous one in an area of store which is reserved for (program) instructions. The instructions are usually executed sequentially.

On being told to RUN, the control unit starts a sequence of operations which can best be understood by referring to an example. We will use the one previously given in Chapter 6: 'Add together the numbers stored in locations 13 and 27 and store the result in location 13'.

The three instruction words are:
   0 1 1 0 1 1 0 1
   1 0 1 1 1 0 1 1
   1 1 0 0 1 1 0 1

1. At the start of the FETCH phase, the control unit sends a signal to the store location which holds the first instruction—we will use 203 as the first location. This *address* is copied into a special store called the sequence control register (SCR)
2. The *instruction word* is copied into a temporary store, called the next instruction register (NIR)— 0 1 1 0 1 1 0 1 to NIR
3. 1 is added to the number in the SCR (making it 204)
4. The instruction word is now split and the operation code bits are sent to a special temporary store known as the current instruction register (CIR)—0 1 1 to CIR

This is the end of the FETCH phase. Actions 5 and 6 occur during the EXECUTE phase.

5. The instruction bits are decoded—in our example, 0 1 1 means 'load the number (in store 0 1 1 0 1) into the accumulator'.
6. The control unit now acts on the instruction and sends a signal to location 13 (0 1 1 0 1), which allows the number stored there to be copied and sent to the accumulator.

One cycle of the clock is now complete and the sequence restarts by reading the SCR to find the location of the next instruction. The SCR tells us this is in location 204 and the instruction word is 101 11011, which is now copied to the NIR and the first three bits sent to the CIR for decoding. The SCR is again incremented by 1, becoming 205, and the start of the EXECUTE phase begins.

1 0 1 decodes as 'Add the contents (of store 1 1 0 1 1) to the number in the accumulator' and this instruction makes the control unit open the correct gates to allow the number in location 27 (1 1 0 1 1) to be copied into the accumulator and added to the number already there. In order to complete the processing, the result still has to be copied back into location 13, and therefore a further clock cycle is necessary: the operation code 1 1 0 causes the control unit to set the necessary gates to enable this action to be completed.

Reading this, it appears that even such a simple operation as adding two numbers together is very complex and appears to take a long time to complete. The first assumption is true: a computer *does* have to perform very many operations in order to complete even the simplest of processes, but it makes up for this with the speed of doing such operations. A typical clock frequency is 1 MHz which means that in *one second* the computer can obey *one million* instructions! Therefore it would have taken three millionths of a second, or three microseconds to complete the three instructions in the example above.

Instruction decoding. The instruction bits are sent from the instruction word along 'highways' to a decoding unit which consists of as many single logical decoding units as

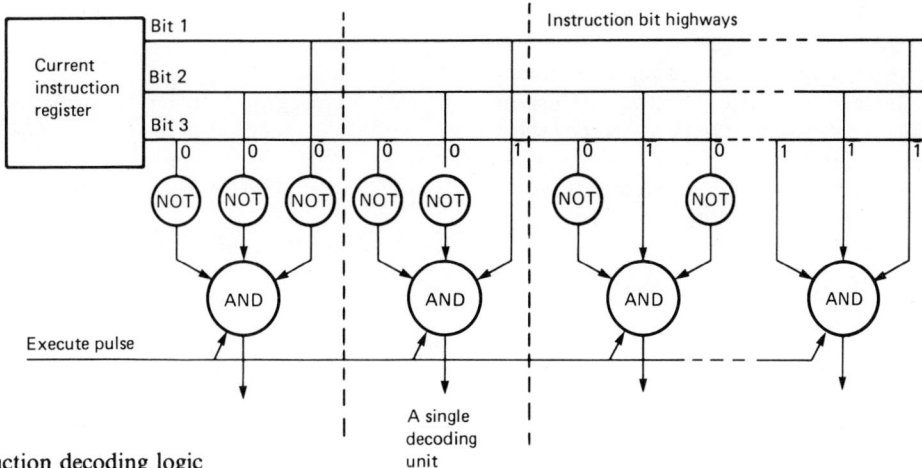

Fig. 7.31 Instruction decoding logic

there are instructions in the instruction set. (For illustration purposes only we are considering a set with eight instructions) (Fig. 7.31).

At the beginning of the FETCH phase, the 'next instruction bits' are sent along the highways and go to each decode unit. Each decoder will respond to *one bit pattern only* and when it receives that pattern, will respond by giving out a signal (pulse) of logic value 1. Note from Fig. 7.31 that each AND gate has four inputs: three from the instruction bit highways and one from an 'execute pulse highway'. Because of complex timing in the control unit, the three instruction bits may be present at the decode logic units before execute phase begins, so a fourth input pulse is generated at the start of the execute phase and provides the missing 'key' to 'unlock' the selected decode unit. This pulse is then used to open the correct gates to enable the instruction to be carried out. Fig. 7.32 shows the necessary logical paths to implement the first instruction in the example above:

0 1 1 0 1 1 0 1—'load the data in store location 0 1 1 0 1 (13) into the accumulator'

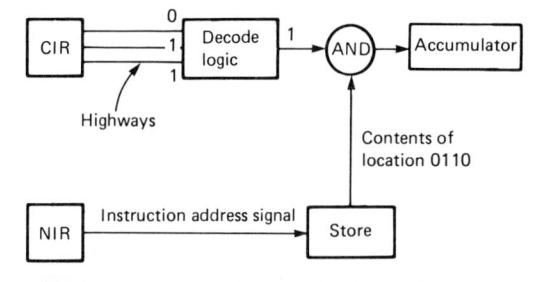

Fig. 7.32 Logic paths to implement instruction

The decode logic opens the logic gate to the accumulator thereby allowing the contents of the address 0 1 1 0 to be sent to the accumulator.

At the end of the EXECUTE phase, all gates are reset ready for the next instruction.

(c) **Arithmetic unit**

Part of the CPU is the arithmetic unit, often called the arithmetic logic unit (ALU) because it carries out some logical operations as well as performing all the arithmetic.

The 'heart' of the ALU is the accumulator. This is a set of very fast registers through which all data enters and leaves the ALU. It also contains the registers in which the arithmetic actually takes place. In Chapter 6, we saw how two binary bits are added together using a logic circuit called a full adder. Therefore, in order to add together two 8 bit words, eight full adders are required.

Most computers add all the corresponding bits of two binary numbers together at the same time—this is known as parallel operation and is the quickest mode of performing arithmetic operations. If more than two numbers are to be added together, the ALU adds the first two together and stores the result in the accumulator. The third number is then added to the partial result in the accumulator and the result written back to the accumulator which always holds the partial result until all the numbers have been added, when the accumulator holds the final total ready for output.

The following example shows these steps in adding together four 8 bit binary numbers:

First number   0 0 1 1 0 1 1 0 +
Second number 0 1 0 1 1 0 1 0
                         ─────────────
                         1 0 0 1 0 0 0 0 +   (partial result 1)
Third number   0 0 0 1 0 1 0 1
                         ─────────────
                         1 0 1 0 0 1 0 1 +   (partial result 2)
Fourth number   0 1 1 1 0 1 1 1
                         ─────────────
                      1 0 0 0 1 1 0 1 0   (final result)

Fig. 7.32 shows the necessary connections within the ALU to perform addition as above.

The ALU has another special type of register known as a *shift register* and in order to appreciate its use in performing arithmetic we will first look at a very useful property of a binary number.

Consider the denary number 14 in a 5 bit binary word:

0	1	1	1	0

Now shift the binary digits one place to the right, and, as each bit position must be either a 1 or a 0, write a zero in the 'empty' bit position:

0	0	1	1	1

This binary representation is clearly equivalent to the denary number 7.

In other words, we have *divided* the original number by 2. A further right shift of one place gives:

0	0	0	1	1

which is the rounded-down result of dividing 7 by 2 or:

0	0	0	1	1	.	1

which is the accurate result 3.5, but to achieve this result, the 'lost' right-hand bit has to be preserved in another binary word. This is, in fact, what happens in the arithmetic processes in the ALU.

A left shift has the opposite effect, i.e. each shift of one binary place *multiplies* the previous binary number by 2:

0	0	1	1	1	0	becomes	0	1	1	1	0	0

(14)   (28)

but a further left shift gives 1 1 1 0 0 0, which is equivalent to −8, so again, special measures need to be taken within the ALU to prevent arithmetic disasters occurring.

The only actual arithmetic operation which a digital computer can perform is that of addition. Subtraction is achieved by complementary addition (Chapter 6.2), multiplication by repeated addition ($7 \times 3 \equiv 7 + 7 + 7$) and division, by repeated subtraction ($21 \div 3 \equiv 21 - 3 - 3 - 3 - 3 - 3 - 3$).

Both multiplication and division could be very slow if performed only as shown above and they can be speeded up greatly by introducing shifting as well as addition into the process, which can best be understood by looking at some examples:

$$3 \times 9 \equiv 3 + 3 + 3 + 3 + 3 + 3 + 3 + 3 + 3 = 27$$

But, in binary, $9 \equiv 2^3 + 1$ so a left shift of 3 places will effectively multiply by 8 and then one 3 has to be added

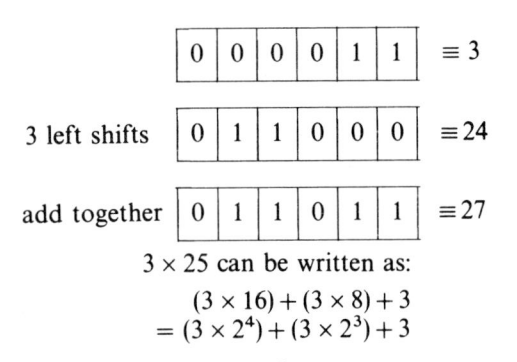

0	0	0	0	1	1	≡ 3

3 left shifts

0	1	1	0	0	0	≡ 24

add together

0	1	1	0	1	1	≡ 27

3×25 can be written as:
$$(3 \times 16) + (3 \times 8) + 3$$
$$= (3 \times 2^4) + (3 \times 2^3) + 3$$

Left shift 11 four times : 0 0 0 1 1 0 0 0 0
Left shift 11 three times : 0 0 0 0 1 1 0 0 0
plus 11 : 0 0 0 0 0 0 1 1
                      0 0 1 0 0 1 0 1 1 ≡ 75

3×31 can be written as:
$$(3 \times 32) - 3$$
$$= (3 \times 2^5) - 3$$

Left shift 11 five times : 0 0 1 1 0 0 0 0 0
Add two's complement
of 11   : 1 1 1 1 1 1 1 0 1
                      0 0 1 0 1 1 1 0 1 ≡ 93

The enormous improvement in speed can be seen by realising that, without shifting, multiplying a number by 1025 would require 1025 clock cycles. With shifting, the same result would be achieved in 11 clock cycles:

$$1025 \equiv 2^{10} + 1$$

i.e. 10 left shifts and one addition.

Exercises 7.2

1 Describe what takes place in each part of the fetch–execute cycle

2 (*a*) Briefly define the following terms:
 (i) decoder
 (ii) clock cycle
 (iii) fetch phase
 (iv) execute phase.
 (*b*) A certain computer uses a 4 bit function code. The code for the instruction ADD is 1001. By means of a logic diagram, show how this instruction is decoded to provide an output of 1 from the decoder.
 (*AEB*, 1977)

7.3 Backing store

Backing store, or secondary storage as it is sometimes called, is used to supplement the immediate access, or primary, storage during processing and to provide permanent storage for programs and data using a medium which can be accessed very quickly by the CPU.

From the early days of computing to the late 1970s, this medium has always been magnetic. (Punched cards have been used extensively as backing store but the method of using cards is different, and speed of access is many factors slower than magnetic backing store) Four types of magnetic backing store have been developed: drum, card, tape and disk. Although both drum and card storage have been used successfully in the past, their use has declined with the development of disk storage systems.

All magnetic systems are based on the principle of magnetising a very small part of a magnetic material using an electromagnet. The material is usually ferric oxide and each of the minute particles of 'iron' is capable of being magnetised in either of two directions, North–South or South–North. Particles arranged in one direction represent an 0 and in the other, a 1.

(a) Magnetic tape systems

Two types of magnetic tape systems are in common use: large open reel-to-reel and cassette. Large reel-to-reel tape transports are a common form of backing store in data-processing and scientific organisations where they provide a large, low-cost, 'reasonably quick to access', storage system. Typically a reel of tape holds 750 M of 13 mm wide tape, which can hold as much as 6×10^9 bits of data, depending on the packing density.

Fig. 7.33 Magnetic tape transport

Fig. 7.33 shows a typical large tape transport in which it is usual to employ separate write and read heads so that the data can be read immediately after it has been written for checking purposes. Usually, nine separate heads write one coded character across the tape at once.

Fig. 7.34 shows how the nine tracks are recorded on the tape.

The writing and reading speeds for large reel tape system are fast, typically 250 cm/s. Even at this speed it would take 5 min to write data to a complete tape and, of course, equally long to read through a tape. This inescapable feature of magnetic tape is its only real

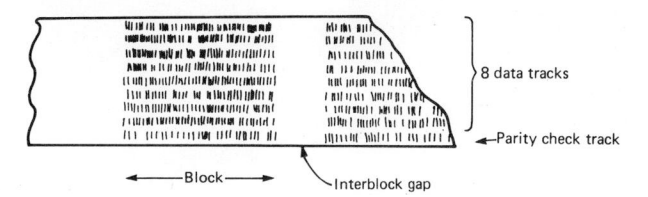

Fig. 7.34 How data is written on magnetic tape

disadvantage—if the data required is at the other end of the tape, the only way to get at it is to read through the whole tape.

This same problem is encountered when cassette tape is used and, as the writing/reading speed is much slower (usually 5 cm/s) even with much smaller tapes (135 m for a C 90 cassette) the time taken to read a tape can be 45 min! For this reason, cassette tapes for use as computer backing store need to be much shorter and tapes with an end-to-end reading time of 5 min are now being used widely as it is much quicker to load a new short tape than read through a long one.

Limitations of cassette tape are that most recorders have a single record/playback, (write/read), head which precludes any checking after writing and only writes/reads one track at a time. Therefore characters have to be written along the tape, reducing the packing density to 300–700 bits/cm. Nevertheless, cassette tape recorders are now widely used with microcomputers as a cheap and effective, but not very efficient, backing store.

(b) Magnetic disk systems.

Two types of magnetic disk are in common use, rigid and floppy disks.

(i) *Rigid disks.* Some older rigid disk systems used one large disk and a large number of fixed read/write heads, with one head per track, but the most common rigid disk systems use exchangeable disk packs which can be attached to the drive mechanism as and when required (Fig. 7.35). Data is written to a disk in concentric tracks by a read/write head which is able to move radially across the disk. When one track is full of data, the head moves to the next track, under the control of an actuator, and writes data to that one. The complex electronics of the disk drive 'make a note' of which tracks the data is written on. The head does not touch the disk surface but is specially designed to 'fly' *just* above the surface thereby eliminating surface wear. The head 'flys' on the wind

68 COMPUTER STUDIES

Fig. 7.35 Exchangeable magnetic disk pack

created by the fast rotation of the disk—typically 3000 rev/min.

Some disk packs contain only one disk but packs containing six disks are in common use. The disks are coated with magnetic oxide on both sides, thereby doubling their capacity, but as the top and bottom surfaces of the pack are not used, each pack has 10 useable surfaces and 10 heads read or write to identical tracks on each disk surface at the same time under control from a common actuator (Figs. 7.36 and 7.37).

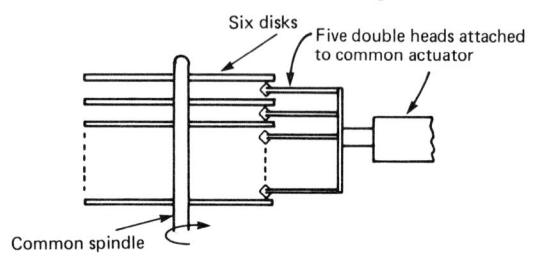

Fig. 7.36 Side view of magnetic disk pack and read/write arms

The high storage capacity (approximately 8×10^6 bits per disk) and fast access time (average 10 ms) combine to make this type of mass storage system ideal for data processing. The maximum distance the 'data has to move' is one revolution of the disk, and the head, from the outermost track to the innermost one, which is approximately 20 cm. Therefore it is almost true to say that the access time to any item of data is the same. On magnetic tape, this time is directly proportional to where the data is stored on the tape.

(ii) Floppy disks. During the late 1970s floppy disks came into prominence as cheap backing store to microcomputer systems (Fig. 7.38). The principle of operation is similar to that used with rigid disks above, but, in practice there are significant differences. The disks, (or diskettes), are small and flexible and are permanently mounted in a protective sleeve which has a slot cut into it

Fig. 7.37 Disk unit showing exchangeable pack in position

Fig. 7.38 Floppy disk

to allow the read/write head access to the disk surface. The disk rotates slowly, at approximately 300 rev/min, and, in operation, the head is in close contact with the disk. However, because of the slow speed and the flexibility of the disk, wear is reduced to a minimum. The disk is rotated only when reading or writing is taking place and this is the only time when the head is brought into contact with the disk surface. The head is moved across the disk by means of a helical drive driven by a stepper motor (Fig. 7.39).

Fig. 7.39 CUMANA disk drive

Floppy disks are currently available in two sizes, 20 cm diameter and 13 cm diameter. Their storage capacity is approximately 2 000 000 bits on each side of the larger disk and approximately 500 000 on a 'mini-floppy' (13 cm diameter). The average access time for either size disk is approx. 250 ms.

Floppy disk backing store is ideal for school and small business use, combining the advantages of disk storage with cheapness. Developments in this field to improve the storage capacity, using double density recording, and the access time, by using a higher drive speed and 'flying heads', should bring the specification of a floppy disk system closer to that of a rigid disk system, during the next few years.

(iii) Other mass storage devices. Use of a laser beam in a high speed printing device has previously been mentioned (p. 61). It seems probable that many other laser-based devices will be developed for use with computers. Some of these are already being used experimentally. The fascinating principle of holography has been used to produce a store with a very high storage capacity (6×10^{12} bits), but with an access time that is dependent on the size of the store: it would be minutes, for the capacity suggested here.

An optical disk store, similar in principle to video disks, combines the advantage of a high storage capacity (10^{12} bits on a 30 cm diameter disk) with fast access time (an average of 150 ms). This type of store, however, can only be used once. The laser 'burns' the data into the disk surface, thereby making it into a read only memory.

Bubble storage is the most recent development in fast, random access storage. The principle of operation is that of magnetising a piece of material with special magnetic properties so that it becomes full of 'magnetic bubbles', each bubble exhibiting the properties of a magnet. In use, the presence, or absence, of a bubble in the material represents a 0 or a 1. The access speed is relatively slow (approximately 20 ms), but this is likely to improve considerably with further development. The big advantages of bubble storage are first the small size per bit (currently, 256 K bits can be stored in a 'chip' measuring approximately 2 cm square by 1 cm deep) and secondly that it has no moving parts. Further development of this store could make it a replacement for disk storage but it is unlikely, in the foreseeable future, that the access time will be improved sufficiently to make it useable as IAS.

7.4 Microprocessors

Before considering the 'youngest member' of the computer family let us look at its family tree:

Mainframe computers	Large commercial/scientific system: ICL 2903 IBM 370
Minicomputers	Small business/education system: PDP 11
Microcomputers	Physically very small CPU; may use standard peripherals: Acorn/BBC, RML 380Z, Apple, PET
Microprocessor	Chip. Z80, 6502

A common misinterpretation of the above 'tree' is to describe a microcomputer as a microprocessor. A microcomputer *uses* a microprocessor as one of its basic parts—the CPU—but microprocessors are used in many applications other than computing.

A microprocessor is made using large scale integration (LSI) techniques and is formed on a single chip of silicon. For use in a microcomputer, the microprocessor would consist of the control unit, accumulators, fast registers and clock, i.e. the CPU without IAS.

Computer microprocessors are now commercially cheap and with the addition of IAS, power supply, keyboard and screen, they can be made into microcomputers.

Microprocessors are, however, used in many other ways, but each application is different. A 'standard' chip is not usually available and a special microprocessor is designed and made for each individual use. One of the most well known uses of microprocessors is to control machines in a car body assembly line (Fig. 7.40). Each robot is controlled by a microprocessor which has been programmed to perform a specific task. In order to perform another task, the robot will require a new

Fig. 7.40 Robots welding car bodies on the Mini Metro production line at BL Longbridge

microprocessor. This is a good example of the use of a microprocessor outside computing and is typical of the ability of a microprocessor to control a complex process or operation.

A highly sophisticated use of microprocessors is in the control of the EMI body scanner used to detect tumors in the human body (Fig. 7.41). The microprocessors are programmed to control the movement of the scanner and of the patient, to take the required electronic photographs, analyse the recorded data and display the results.

A job that could be described as 'made for the microprocessor', is that of lift control. Microprocessors can be programmed to optimise the use of two or more lifts serving a building, to reduce the waiting time to a minimum. One microprocessor could, for example, be completely responsible for deciding which lift to use to answer any call from any floor, whilst other microprocessors are used in each lift to control the speed, braking, floor line-up and door operation. Each processor can be 'given' a look-up table of speed/distance and sensors can measure the actual speed at a known distance from a reference and compare it with the stored data. Corrections can be made at electronic speed.

Whatever job the microprocessor is designed to do, it will have a CPU, some fast storage (small compared to computer IAS), and a control unit, all 'grown' on a silicon chip measuring approximately 5 mm square.

The technology required to manufacture 'chips' is complex and the cost of designing the logic circuits and making the necessary photographic masks to produce a

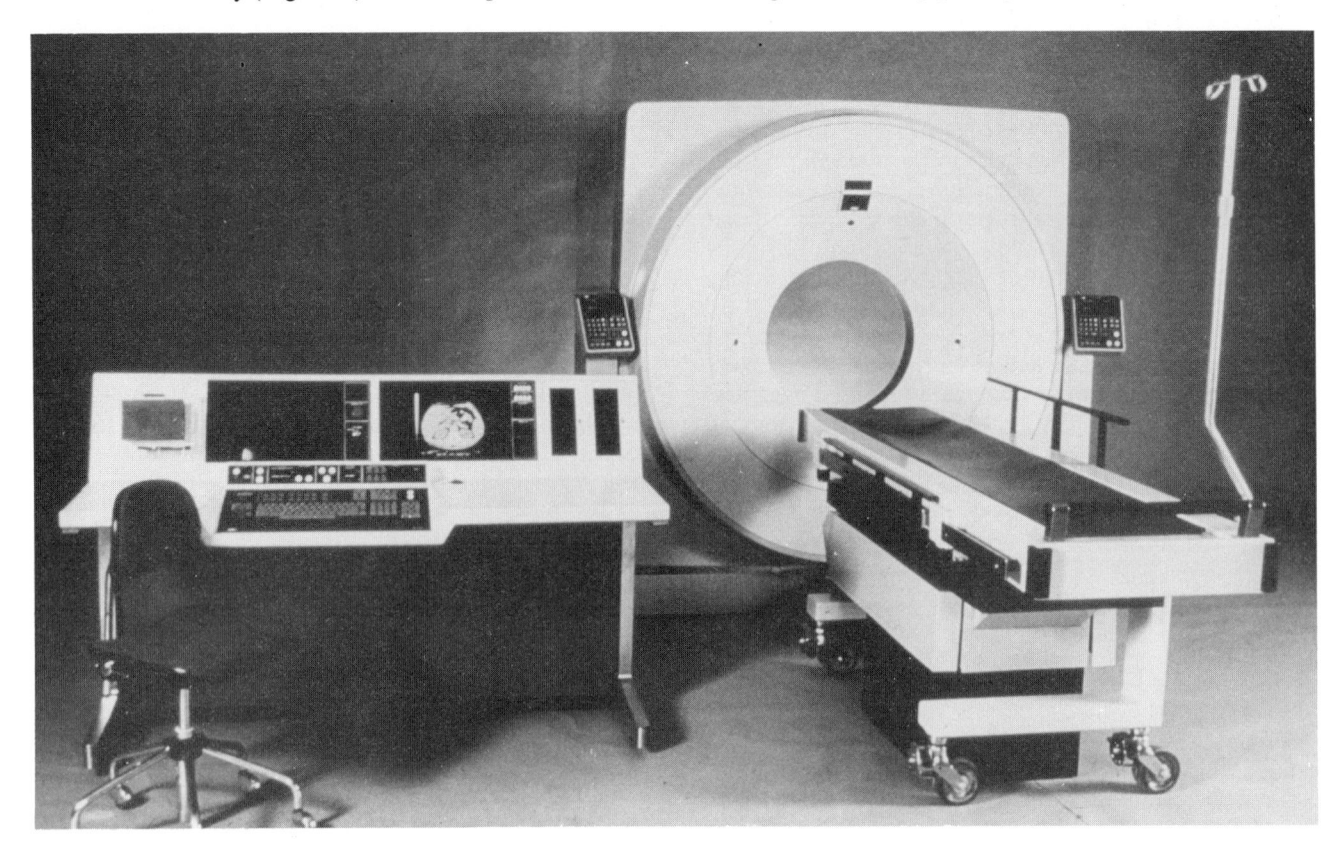

Fig. 7.41 EMI body scanner

specific design of micro processor is very high. Therefore only applications for which a large number of microprocessors can be manufactured, will benefit at present. The state of this technology is advancing so rapidly that soon the microprocessor will be found in use almost everywhere, from automatic air-traffic control to highly sophisticated television games. It is probable that a microprocessor with the equivalent power to an ICL 1904 mainframe computer will be contained on a single chip.

This rapid advance in microprocessor technology, making tomorrow into today, was shown in April 1981 when Commodore announced a 'Micro Mainframe'. This computer is the physical size of an ordinary PET microcomputer but contains 230 K of fast semiconductor store and is reputed to have the power of a mainframe computer system.

Microprocessors are being given many different uses, most of which are far less glamorous and less 'headline catching' than these quoted above. Washing machines and dishwashers are controlled by microprocessors. Many cars have microprocessors built into them to control speed, petrol consumption, exhaust fumes, lights and sophisticated automatic data logging with digital read-out of distance travelled, average speed, petrol consumption etc. Houses have been designed in which microprocessors are in complete control of the heating, lighting, air-conditioning, cooking, entertainment, burglar alarms etc. This is not too far removed from the idea of a robot to do the washing-up!

7.5 Word processors

During the late 1970s a new type of computer, called a word processor, was developed. As its name implies, this computer is designed to process text in the form of letters, documents, manuscripts, legal documents, insurance policies etc. All word processors use a keyboard for input and a VDU to display the text. A typical word processing system would consist of a CPU with large, fast backing store, one or more fast, high quality printers for output of documents and a number of VDUs, all connected directly to the central processor. Word processors are already being used for a wide variety of office applications: two 'popular' uses are to produce purchase orders and to compose 'standard' documents.

All manufacturing companies need to purchase materials and components from outside suppliers by placing orders for the required items when new stock is required. The supplier's name, address and technical descriptions of items supplied by that company are recorded onto magnetic disk and can be called for from a VDU by typing a special code number. The order form appears on the VDU as a series of prompts and data is keyed in in the correct position using a cursor, which is controlled by the operator and the central processor. Any errors can readily be corrected on the VDU screen before the purchase document is printed. As well as containing details of the actual order, many purchase orders require standard clauses relating to delivery,

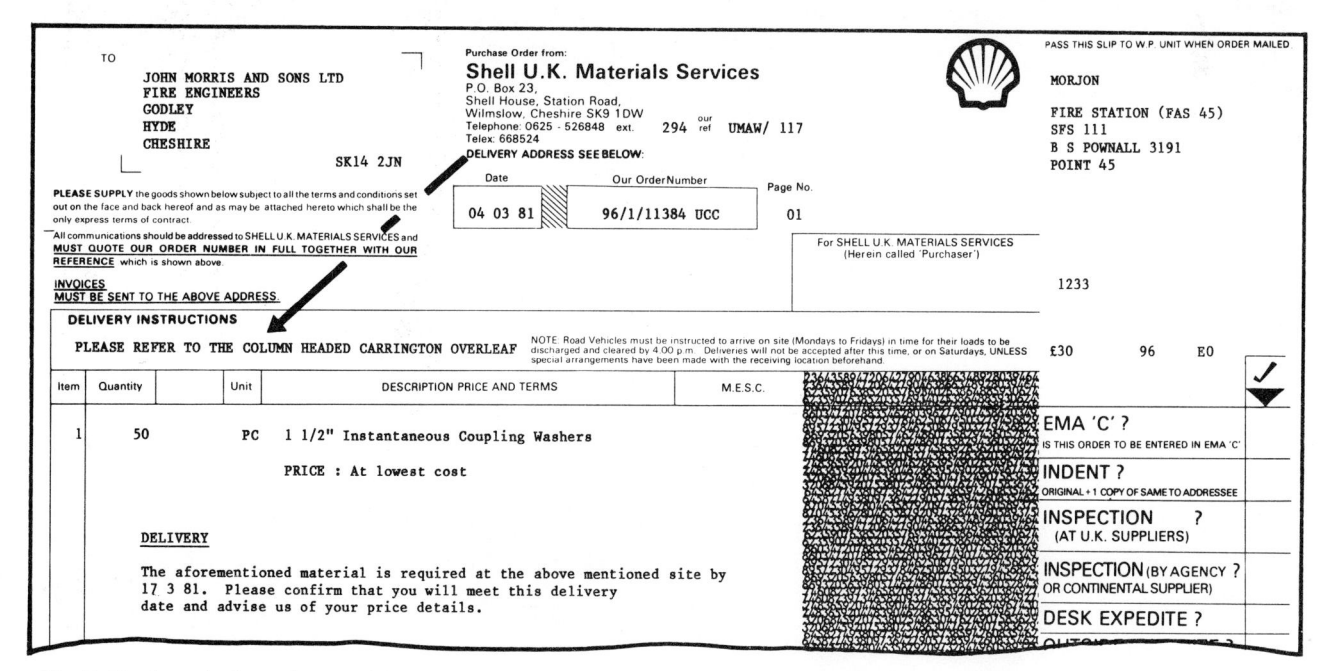

Fig. 7.42 A typical purchase order

inspection, rate of exchange, price variations, method of payment, discount etc., to be printed on the order form. These are also stored and again called by inputting a special code number. Fig. 7.42 shows a typical purchase order with a delivery clause added to the order.

The prompts for any order form—called a format—are held on disk, so a wide variety of different forms can be displayed on the VDU for different purchase orders. For security reasons, all orders are retained on disk for typically, 1–2 weeks, when they are automatically erased. A complete day's work may be stored on magnetic tape for many weeks before it too is erased.

Many offices produce standard letters, such as invitation to interview or offer of a job; a solicitor's office will produce many legal documents, such as contracts and deeds of covenant; the prosecutions departments of the police send out many summonses and notifications of court hearings. All such 'standard' letters and documents can be produced quickly and easily using a word processor. Each letter or document is typed into the work processor from the keyboard with any necessary blanks left for data, such as name and address, to be inserted at a later stage, and stored on disk. A code number is typed in to call up the required text from store and data is added from the keyboard as requested by the prompts. Legal documents may be made up of a number of paragraphs. These can be called for and edited on screen if necessary to produce the final document.

The letter shown in Fig. 7.43 was produced by a word processor by requesting document 19A. The words underlined were input from the keyboard to complete this particular letter.

Some microcomputers have on-screen text editing facilities which allow them to be used as a word processor, but as the central processor is designed as a general purpose computer, and not specifically as a word processor, text editing is software dependent and can be difficult to use. The Research Machines Text Editor is particularly powerful, with comprehensive text formatting facilities, but it is controlled by more than 110 editing commands!

A number of word processing software packages, each for use with one particular microcomputer, have been developed. Using one of these, a microcomputer can perform many of the simpler standard word processing functions, but even these packages require many instructions and commands for their operation.

Another approach to providing word processing power is being developed by at least one company. All offices use typewriters and many of these are modern electronic machines. With the addition of a screen and disk storage, an electronic typewriter can be converted into a powerful word processor, but can still be used as a typewriter if the need arises. Such a system is capable of development by replacing the typewriter with a number of keyboards with screens, all having access to the disk system and sharing a fast, daisy-wheel type of printer.

Word processing systems are still in their comparative infancy and will be subject to much development during the next few years to produce both dedicated systems, designed for a specific application, and general purpose text processors which will find their way into almost every office and many homes in the near future (Fig. 7.44).

```
5th June, 1982


Miss P. Sutcliffe,
4 Orchard Street,
WORCESTER.
W15 6AZ

Dear Miss Sutcliffe,

I am writing to offer you the position of
Office Junior in the Advertising Department.

Your salary will be £3 500 per annum and your
duties will commence on 1st July 1982.

Please write and confirm your acceptance of
the above post.

Yours sincerely,




Personnel Officer
```

Fig. 7.43 A letter produced by a word processor

Fig. 7.44 A desk-top business computer (IBM System 23)

Summary

- Many different input devices are currently in use. Of these, the VDU with keyboard and the bar code reader are probably the most widely used.
- The most popular output device, apart from a VDU screen, is a printer to produce 'hard copy output'. Many types of printer exist and, generally, the more you pay for a printer, the 'better' the printer.
- Semiconductor store has superseded core store as the main store of the CPU. Its cost per byte will continue to fall while the number of bytes on a single chip will continue to grow.
- The control unit is wholly electronic and is the 'control centre' for the computer.
- The ALU is also wholly electronic and performs all arithmetic functions and certain logical operations.
- Magnetic disks and tape are widely used as backing store on most computer systems. Most microcomputers use floppy disks and cassette tape.
- Microprocessors have many applications outside digital computers.
- Word processors have many uses in the office and in the home and will become the 'CPU' of the automated office in the very near future.

8 Communication with the computer

8.1 Levels of communication

We have learned that, inside a computer, all data and instructions are represented by ones and zeros. The (binary) code used in Chapter 7 for 'load the contents of store location x into the accumulator' was given as 011 and was contained in the left hand 3 bits of an instruction word, but where do the instruction words come from?

In any of the computers in use today, the binary instructions are produced automatically by 'software' within the computer itself. If we wished, we could 'talk to' a computer in binary and give it all its instructions and data in binary form, but it would be a *very* long winded operation. This was the only method of communicating with the early computers and not only had the input to be in binary but this was also the form of the output!

Happily, such a state of affairs did not last long and by the middle 1950s it was possible to communicate with a computer without the need to code everything into binary, by using a mnemonic, or symbolic assembly code (language). This was so successful in speeding up input to the computer that within a few years it was possible to communicate with a computer using 'ordinary' English words. High-level languages, as they are called, have since become the standard method of communication with a computer.

(a) Machine code
Machine code is a code, or language, given to the computer by its designers. Each type of computer has its own code which is the only language the computer really understands. Therefore, every communication with a computer which is not in machine code must be translated into machine code before the computer can do anything with it.

Here is an example of a set of machine code instructions to add together the numbers 51 and 16. The code is that used in a small computer called SHERLE designed in 1966 for use in schools.

'By the year 2000, computers will rule the world.'

000 000	0	0	00000000000	write zero to P side of adder
111 000	A	0	00000110011	write 51_{10} to register A (accumulator)
111 000	B	0	00000010000	write 16_{10} to register B
001 001	C	0		Add B to A and leave result in A
100 000	0	Z		output contents of accumulator to neon lights

A set of computer instructions, as above, is called a *program*.

(b) Assembly language
The break away from the use of binary came by designing a further code which enabled instructions to be written in a symbolic language instead of binary, e.g. LDA x was the code for 'Load the number in store x into the accumulator'. This symbolic instruction was translated by a special program known as an assembler, into 011 (continuing the code used previously).

A typical, eight instruction assembly code would contain: ADD, SUBtract, RETurn, JUMp, LDA,

STOre, INput, OUTput. The use of mnemonics greatly speeded up the process of program writing as the instructions could be more easily remembered. Despite this speeding-up, it was still necessary to write one mnemonic for each instruction and include addresses for instructions and data. A single letter mnemonic assembly code devised by the Associated Examining Board solely for teaching and exam purposes is given below.

A (*n*) Add the contents of stated location (*n*) to the accumulator
B (*n*) Copy the contents of location (*n*) to the accumulator
C (*n*) Copy the contents of the accumulator to location (*n*)
D (*n*) Subtract 1 from the contents of location (*n*)
G (*n*) If the contents of the accumulator are greater than 0 go to location(*n*) for the next instruction
I (*n*) Input a data value into location (*n*)
J (*n*) If the contents of the accumulator are equal to 0 go to location (*n*) for the next instruction
K (*n*) If the contents of the accumulator are less than 0 go to location (*n*) for the next instruction
L (*n*) Increase the contents of location (*n*) by +1
O (*n*) Output the contents of location (*n*)
P (*n*) Go to location (*n*) for the next instruction
S (*n*) Subtract the contents of location (*n*) from the accumulator leaving the result in accumulator
T   Halt
Z (*n*) Load zero into location (*n*)

A program written in the above assembly code, to leave the sum of the integers 20–50 inclusive in location 600 is shown below. The first instruction is stored in location 100 and location 500 and 501 contain +20 and +25, respectively.

Work through the program line by line, setting down the value of each store location in a table, as shown below:

Location	500	501	502	600	
	20	25	50	0	first pass

After about three passes through the program, it should be clear how it is solving the problem. Note that there is no output from this program. The final total is stored in location 600 and it will stay there unless the instruction to output is added into the program. What modification is required to this program in order to output the result?

The program to effect the translation from the assembly language to machine code, the assembler, was 'permanently' housed in the IAS in the early computers. Nowadays, it is usually supplied on backing store and loaded into the IAS only if it is required for assembly language programming.

Another 'assembly type' language is CESIL (Computer Education in Schools Instruction Language). This has two major advantages over a purely symbolic assembly language in that complete English words may be used for instructions and store locations can be labelled with a name instead of just a number. An example of a CESIL program is shown below:

Instruction location	Code	Data location	Comment
100	B	501	Copy +25 to accumulator
101	A	501	Add +25 to accumulator
102	C	502	Store contents of accumulator (+50) in 502
103	B	500	Copy +20 to accumulator
104	S	502	Subtract 50 from accumulator
105	K	108	Jump to 108 if accumulator < 0
106	J	108	Jump to 108 if accumulator = 0
107	T		Halt
108	B	500	Copy +20 to accumulator
109	A	600	Add contents of 600 to accumulator
110	C	600	Store in location 600
111	L	500	Add +1 to number in 500
112	P	103	Jump to instruction 103

76 COMPUTER STUDIES

```
              IN
              STORE      FIRST
              IN
              STORE      SECOND
              ADD        SECOND
              STORE      THIRD
PETER         LOAD       FIRST
              SUBTRACT   THIRD
              JINEG      JOHN
              JIZERO     JOHN
              HALT
              LOAD       FIRST
JOHN          ADD        FOURTH
              STORE      FOURTH
              LOAD       FIRST
              ADD        +1
              JUMP       PETER
```

Compare this with the program written in AEB code.

A segment of a program written in 6502 assembly code is shown in Fig. 8.1.

A programming language such as CESIL is often known as a low-level language, rather than an assembly language, because of the use of words instead of mnemonics or symbols.

Because a program written in an assembly language has to contain every instruction that the CPU requires in order to solve the problem, such programs can be very long and, because of the number of machine instructions that may need to be used (up to 150 in some computers) can be very slow to write. However, as one program instruction generates one machine instruction only, the execution time is very fast (compared with a high level

```
1CA4             OPT I%
1CA4             .BEGIN
1CA4 A2 00       LDX £0
1CA6             \ LOAD REGISTER X WITH 0
1CA6 86 70       STX F
1CA8             \ LOAD CONTENTS OF REGISTER X INTO F
1CA8             .LOOP
1CA8 BD 34 1C    LDA R,X
1CAB             \ LOAD THE ACC WITH THE CONTENTS OF R,INDEXED BY THE CURRENT VALUE
1CAB DD 35 1C    CMP R+1,X
1CAE             \ .. COMPARE   ITS VALUE WITH (R+1,X)
1CAE 90 13       BCC OVER
1CB0             \ BRANCH TO ´OVER´ IF THE CONTENTS OF (R+1,X) IS LESS THAN..
1CB0 F0 11       BEQ OVER
1CB2             \ ..OR EQUAL TO (R,X)
1CB2 85 71       STA T
1CB4 BD 35 1C    LDA R+1,X
1CB7 9D 34 1C    STA R,X
1CBA A5 71       LDA T
1CBC 9D 35 1C    STA R+1,X
1CBF A9 01       LDA £1
1CC1 85 70       STA F
1CC3             .OVER
1CC3 E8          INX
1CC4 E0 63       CPX £99
1CC6 D0 E0       BNE LOOP
1CC8 A5 70       LDA F
1CCA D0 D8       BNE BEGIN
1CCC 60          RTS
1CA4             OPT I%
1CA4             .BEGIN
1CA4 A2 00       LDX £0
1CA6             \ LOAD REGISTER X WITH 0
1CA6 86 70       STX F
1CA8             \ LOAD CONTENTS OF REGISTER X INTO F
1CA8             .LOOP
1CA8 BD 34 1C    LDA R,X
```

Fig. 8.1 Program segment

language). Also, because the assembly code used relates directly to the way the CPU has been designed (commonly referred to as 'machine architecture'), the assembly language is used to write programs concerned with controlling the operation of the computer, (see page 78), rather than programs to solve programs.

The advent of the microcomputer has brought about a 'revival' in the use of assembly language programming, partly to speed up the execution of some programs and partly because it is the only way to program some microprocessors.

(c) High-level language

By the late 1950s the use of computers had reached a stage where it was desirable to write programs in a language that used single word instructions to make the CPU perform complex procedures. Take, for example, the operation ADD (two numbers together), which would require at least five machine instructions in a low-level language, but could be accomplished by a single instruction like ADD *A* to *B* if the computer could be made to perform the necessary machine instructions on its own. This was made possible by using a compiler (see next section), to translate the single high-level instruction into many machine instructions.

The first high-level languages to be developed were for special purposes: FORTRAN (formula translation) which is mainly used for scientific programming, and ALGOL (algorithmic language) with its powerful mathematical facilities. As the use of computers for data processing increased, COBOL (common business orientated language) was developed, followed, soon after, by BASIC (beginners all-purpose symbolic instruction code). BASIC has since become an accepted language for educational purposes and far from being only a 'beginners language', it has been developed to be a powerful language capable of being used in almost every application.

The features of these high-level languages vary according to their use. Both FORTRAN and ALGOL have the facility to handle complex mathematical expressions in arrays and ALGOL has many 'built-in' mathematics functions. COBOL uses English sentences and has extensive file-handling facilities. BASIC uses a very simple syntax and program layout, and, being general-purpose, has mathematical functions, array handling and some file manipulation facilities.

There are other high-level languages such as PL1 (general purpose language), CORAL (for process control applications) and PASCAL. This last language is a new, general purpose language which is gaining wide acceptance and could be a replacement for BASIC in the future.

8.2 Compilers and interpreters

Whatever high-level language is used for program writing, it must be translated into machine code before it can be executed. This is the job of the compiler. Each high-level language requires a separate compiler for each computer on which it is to be used e.g. the BASIC compiler for an ICL 2904 computer is quite different to the BASIC compiler for an IBM 370 computer (because the instruction codes of the two computers are different).

A compiler is usually held on backing store and is loaded into the IAS when it is required to run a batch of programs written in the same high-level language. The original program is often referred to as the source program and the machine code instructions produced by the compiler are known as the object program.

The compiler has a number of jobs to do, two only of which will be discussed here:

(*a*) It has to check the source program for errors (see Chapter 9.5), by checking the validity of every word against the correct syntax stored in a 'look-up table' (rather like a dictionary).

(*b*) It has to translate each source program statement into machine code instructions: the compiler holds a table containing all the source code 'keywords' and their meaning or interpretation in machine code.

Any errors are printed out *at the end of the compilation* and execution of the program is halted. If the errors are removed and the program re-run, the process of compilation starts all over again, but this time the compiled program will be executed.

Compilers have two disadvantages. First, they can use up a large amount of IAS, as a complete program has to be compiled before it is run. Secondly, they are not suitable for interactive operation (see the next section). Almost by definition, a microcomputer does not usually have IAS to spare and its main mode of operation is interactive. Therefore the process of translation in a microcomputer is usually achieved by using an interpreter.

An interpreter translates one line of program and then attempts to execute it. If there is an error in that line, an error message is generated and execution stops. When the error is corrected and the program re-run, execution starts at the first line again and continues until a line is either unsuccessfully interpreted (syntax error), or impossible to execute (logical, or execution, error) (see Chapter 9.5).

Of all the high-level languages, only BASIC has an instruction format which lends itself to easy interpretation and this is one of the reasons why many microcomputers handle only BASIC programs. The BASIC interpreter is often held in ROM and is automatically available as soon as the computer is switched on. On some microcomputers like the RML 380Z, interpreters for BASIC, FORTRAN and COBOL are available on disk and are loaded into RAM as and when required.

Typical sizes for some compilers and interpreters are:

	BASIC	COBOL
ICL 2900 compiler	15K	150K
RML 380Z interpreter	9–12K	24K
BBC micro interpreter	16K	—

8.3 Operating systems

There are a number of different ways in which we can communicate with a computer in order to run a program:

(*a*) Batch processing, where a number of programs, written in the same language, are input to the computer and run one, or more, at a time. When, for example, a batch of BASIC programs has been run, the compiler can be changed and a batch of FORTRAN programs run. The computer will compile each program and execute only those that are error free. Programs containing mistakes are usually listed along with a list of the errors.

(*b*) Remote job entry is a form of batch processing where programs and data are transmitted to the computer from a remote terminal, usually a card or paper tape reader with printer, instead of being sent on coding sheets.

(*c*) Interactive computing is a mode of operation which allows the user and the computer to communicate directly with each other. This may be using a terminal which is permanently connected to a mainframe computer system or remotely connected via a telephone link and a modem, or acoustic coupler. Most microcomputers only operate in interactive mode.

The CPU of any computer has always been purely electronic, and capable of processing in the order of 10^6 instructions per second. However, the input and output devices are, in the main, electro-mechanical and are capable only of much slower operating speeds. It is easy to realise then, that whilst the peripherals are working 'flat out', the CPU is only operating in short bursts. In order to make more efficient use of the CPU, *multiprogramming* is a feature of most mainframe computer systems. This is achieved by allowing several programs to be processed by the CPU at, apparently, the same time. In actual fact, each program is allocated a short burst of processing time. Each program, or job as it is normally called, is given a priority rating and this, and the job requirements in terms of peripherals, determine how quickly a job will be completely processed. It is not uncommon for a low priority job to be in processing for hours whilst other higher priority jobs are processed almost immediately.

Many mainframe computers have a facility known as *multi-access* which allows more than one user to have interactive computing facilities at apparently the same time. In this case, each user is given access to the whole computer system for a very brief period called a time slice. Although this period is very short (around 75 ms) it is repeated as soon as all other users have had their 'slice' and each user is quite unaware of any interruptions or that the system is being shared with other users.

It is the responsibility of the computer's *operating system* to implement any one, or all, of the facilities mentioned above. An operating system is a very sophisticated piece of 'software' written in machine code and is loaded from disk after the computer is switched on. The operating system is responsible for the overall running of the computer system. Basically it is required to schedule jobs and the use of peripherals and main store to give maximum efficient use of all parts of the computer system. It is also able to communicate with the operator by printing out messages which can inform of a malfunction somewhere in the system, or simply that the line printer is running out of paper!

8.4 Methods of operation

On-line processing is processing performed on equipment that is directly under the control of the CPU and includes all the methods listed in Section 8.3 except batch processing and remote job entry. During on-line working, the user remains in contact with the computer.

The terminal may be situated in the same room, or building, as the computer and connected directly by cable or can be remote from the computer, and connected via a telephone line. The telephone line may be a special 'dedicated' line serving only the one user or may be any normal exchange line.

The data from a terminal, or from a CPU, is ones and zeros in the form of 'pulse trains' of high frequency and low voltage. It can be transmitted without loss of signal along a suitable cable (up to approximately 200 m in length) inside a building such as a school, hospital or factory. This allows more than one terminal to be connected to the CPU without the need for special data transmission equipment. If, however, it is necessary to use a telephone line to make this connection, a device called a *modem*, (modulator demodulator) is required.

A modem is an electronic device which converts the data bits into electrical impulses suitable for transmission over a telephone line and vice-versa (electrical signals back to data bits). Transmission rates of 10 000 bits per second can be achieved, although the standard rate over exchange lines is much lower, around 1000 bits per second. One bit per second is often referred to as 1 baud. If the terminal equipment used is a teletype then the slowest speed of 110 baud must be used, not because the data cannot be transmitted faster but because the terminal cannot receive it any faster. A good miniprinter, on the other hand, can receive data at 1000 baud or, if it is fitted with a buffer store, at up to 10 000 baud, either directly from a microcomputer or via a very fast modem.

Modems are expensive and have to be installed by British Telecom, but are extensively used in data transmission throughout the United Kingdom where fast transmission is required. They are used, for example by the Open University network and the Regional Universities Network (Fig. 8.2).

A much cheaper type of modem, widely used in education, is the acoustic coupler, which can be used to connect a terminal to the telephone network by using an ordinary telephone hand-set (Fig. 8.3). The acoustic coupler is connected to the terminal and produces tones which are analogous to the data to be transmitted, (or vice-versa if the signal is coming from the computer). However, because the signals are acoustically coupled instead of electrically, the transfer rate is much slower, only up to 400 baud.

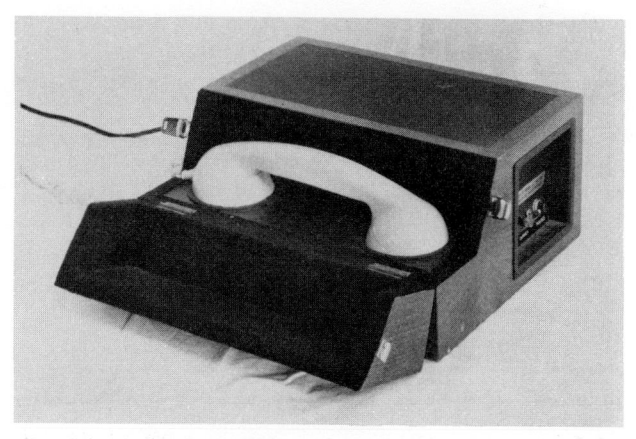

Fig. 8.3 Acoustic coupler

Key:
1 Stirling
2 Edinburgh
3 Glasgow
4 Coleraine
5 Belfast
6 Lancaster
7 York
8 Bradford
9 Leeds
10 Hull
11 Liverpool
12 Keele
13 Sheffield
14 Nottingham
15 Loughborough
16 Leicester
17 Birmingham
18 Aston
19 Warwick
20 Bangor
21 Aberwystwyth
22 Swansea
23 Southampton
24 Oxford
25 Reading
26 Surrey
27 Sussex
28 East Anglia

Fig. 8.2 Regional Universities Network

With all types of modem, there are three ways in which data can be transmitted:
(*a*) simplex, where data can only be transmitted in one direction
(*b*) half-duplex, where data can be transmitted in both directions but not at the same time; i.e. input can only be *followed* by response and no further input can be sent until the response has finished
(*c*) duplex, where data can be transmitted in *both* directions at the same time. For example, it would be possible to send a signal to interrupt a long output before the output has been fully transmitted.

8.5 Applications programs

Applications programs are often referred to as applications packages.

Most user programs are written to solve a problem. This might be to produce a payroll for a factory or to design the best aerodynamic shape for a new car; to forecast the work schedules for a new building project or calculate the stresses in a new design of bridge. Programs to solve this type of problem are referred to as standard programs or applications programs. A payroll program which is written to run, for example, on one 2904 computer will run on any 2904 using the same operating system. Once the program has been written, it is copied and made available to anyone with a similar system. In order to run the program, it is only necessary to supply the data (in the form required by the program).

Applications packages to solve most 'standard' problems are available for most mainframe computers and there is a rapid growth in the demand for similar packages for microcomputers. Applications packages are often written by a software producer in response to the demand from business and industrial users and therefore they are only available for purchase. Apart from timetabling and option packages, there are few which would be of benefit to a school.

Exercises 8.1

1 Using the code given on page 75 answer the following problems. Each line of program should have the format:

Instruction location Instruction code Location address
    x A y

(*a*) Given that x and y are positive integers, that x is in location 2000, Y in location 2001 and the first computer instruction is in location 1000, write machine code instructions to determine if x is a factor of y. If x is a factor of y, jump to location 1200 for the next instruction. If not jump, to location 1500.
(*AEB, 1974*)*

(*b*) Draw a flowchart and write machine code instructions to leave the sum of the integers 1–50 inclusive in location 302, given that:
 (i) The first instruction will be stored in location 123.
 (ii) Location 300 contains zero.
 (iii) Location 301 contains 50.
 (iv) All other store locations contain zero.
(*AEB, 1975*)*

(*c*) Given that storage locations 100 and 101 initially contain the first two terms of the Fibonnacci series; that the first computer instruction is to be stored in location 1000, and that all other store locations will initially contain zero, draw a flowchart and write machine code instructions to leave the sum of the first 20 numbers in the Fibonnacci series in location 102. (The Fibonnacci series is a series of numbers where the next number in the series is found by adding together the previous two numbers, for example, 1, 1, 2, 3, 5, 8, 13 . . . .)   (*AEB, 1977*)*

2 Explain the difference between machine code and assembly language.

Summary

- A computer's 'native language' is machine code.
- Human communication with a computer must be either:
  (a) machine code, which is very slow and long-winded to use, but very fast in execution, or
  (b) an assembly language which is easier to use because of use of mnemonics, or
  (c) a high-level language which is written in English, with different languages to suit different applications, such as business or engineering.
- All high-level languages require a compiler or interpreter to effect the translation into machine language.
- Most mainframe computers use compilers and most microcomputers use interpreters.
- All computers require an operating system to organise and run the computer system in an efficient manner.
- A computer can operate in a number of different ways. The two main methods of operation are batch processing and interactive processing.

9 Problem solving techniques

9.1 Problem definition and specification

Everybody knows that there is more than one way to solve most problems and that it is not always the obvious way that is the best. If we start to solve a problem by method A we may realise while we are only part way to achieving a correct solution that this method either will not work at all, or it is going to take too long, or even that we simply do not have the data we need to solve the problem by that method. Then we change our method of solution and start again. We might do this a few times and each time get part way towards a solution before finding that further progress is impossible. How often would most of us be prepared to do this before going back to the original problem and asking three fundamental questions:

(a) Have we understood the problem correctly?
(b) Have we defined the problem accurately?
(c) Does our method of solution require more data than we have available?

Most of the problems that we solve by 'human methods' are relatively small and are solveable by 'trial and error' methods so loved by humans. However, we are going to use a computer to solve larger problems and, as computers are nowhere near as clever as humans, they are not capable of assessing the 'goodness' or 'correctness' of what they are doing—they just do what they are told to do—by humans.

It is therefore, of great importance to ensure that:
(a) The problem is *capable* of solution by computing techniques.
(b) It is clearly and unambiguously defined.
(c) All the data required for a complete solution is available before an attempt is made to write a program!!

Let us see how this would be realised in terms of a real problem. The problem is to 'computerise' the school sports day so that if the results of each race are fed into it the computer will total the points obtained by each competing team, and calculate the winning team. On the face of it, this seems a straightforward problem which can certainly be solved using a computer, but is the problem clearly defined? Well, let us ask some other

'If you use a tree to store the data, the problem is to work out how to get at the data which is stored right at the top.'

questions first, and then see what our answer to that would be.

When is the result required? After each race? After the last race only? Or the next day? We don't know.

How are points awarded? (They are needed for calculations). We don't know.

What will the data input be and what form will it be in? Again, we do not know.

These questions, at least, must be answered before the problem can be defined clearly and could result in the problem being re-written as: The program is to provide the up-to-date points total of each team and their relative positions in a 'league table', as soon as possible after each event and a final total and position table at the end of the sports day.

The specification should then include such detail as:
(a) The first three in each event will be awarded 5, 3 and 1 points, respectively.
(b) The result of each event will be written on a special

form which will contain the competitors' names and team numbers in order of finishing.

(c) As up-to-date team positions are required after each event, the mode of operation must be interactive.

Notice that the problem does not require the competitor's name to be included in the output, but we are told that this data will be available. This is a bonus which we can include if it does not complicate matters too much.

9.2 System description

This is *how* we are going to solve the problem defined above. The problem must be considered in terms of input, process and output, but *not* in this order.

Any system *must* be designed by considering the output *first*, then the input and finally, the processing.

In other words,
(a) What do we want to get out of the program?
(b) What have we got to put in in order to get this output?
(c) What processing is necessary in order to achieve this?

Therefore, the correct sequence of the three main events above, in designing a system, is: output, input, processing.

The first attempts at a solution need be no more than ideas jotted down on 'the back of an envelope'. Have your ideas on paper, be prepared to cross out, re-write, scribble etc., until you are satisfied with your solution.

Continuing the example of the sports day program, the first attempt at a system description could be:

Output: The team numbers and their individual points totals, sorted into a 'league table'

Input: The names and team numbers of the first three in each event (only one competitor per team allowed in each event).

Processing: Add points to correct team points counters and re-sort so that the team with the greatest total is at the top of the list

There is a greatest temptation at this point to rush off and write a program. *Don't*! With a simple problem like this, it probably could be done quite easily, but it is *bad practice*. It is very difficult to write programs at this stage and even more difficult and very time consuming, to trace errors.

Consider the rough system description above and see if any of the sections can be redefined in more detail, but *not* programming detail. Programming is only the computer's method of solving a problem; at this stage in the solution of a problem, it should be capable of being understood and solved by 'human methods'. It is important to check the system description against the problem specification at all times, remembering that this specification defines the problem we wish to solve. It is good practice to jot down notes at this stage which may be helpful later on. These are included below:

Output: Updated league table showing team numbers and total points gained by each team (formatted output with headings).

Input: Name and team number of first three in each event. (What happens if there are fewer than three teams competing in any event? Can we allow for this in the program?)

Processing: Requires one counter per team (counter and team number to be linked). The correct counters are to be incremented by points input after each race then sorted so that the team with highest points total is at top of list. (Suggests use of an array?)

At this point, check to see if the problem could be solved by 'human methods' using only the description above and assuming nothing. It is a good test to ask someone who has not been involved in the system design, preferably someone who knows nothing about programming! Remember that the vital question to be answered is 'Will it solve the problem?' If the answer is 'yes' we are ready to go on to the next stage which is to 'draw' the system description in a more organised and standard manner in the form of a flowchart.

Exercise 9.1

A residents' association intends to investigate a demand for a controlled pedestrian crossing over a busy road by collecting data at the site of the proposed crossing, relating to the number of pedestrians wishing to cross the road and the number of vehicles using the road. This data will be procesed by a computer. Describe, fully, a system necessary to implement this job with particular reference to what data is needed; how it is to be obtained; any special forms necessary; how the data is to be input into the computer; the type of program needed in the computer to process the data; and the form of the output for analysis. Sketches and flowcharts should be given where appropriate. (*AEB, 1976*)*

9.3 Flowcharting

A flowchart is the graphical representation of the operations involved in the solution of a problem. Symbols are used to represent particular operations or data, and flow lines indicate the sequence of operations and the flow of data.

Many people, when they are describing something, sketch it in mid-air with a lot of hand waving or, if paper is available, actually try and draw the 'something'. This is because it is usually much easier to describe 'something' using diagrams rather than words, although it is

PROBLEM SOLVING TECHNIQUES

probable that we will need to use some words to supplement the diagram.

So it is with solving a problem using a computer. The computer will use a program designed to solve the problem set out in the systems description and in order to make the job of writing the program much easier, we need to draw the 'system' as a flowchart. This enables us to think out our problem in a logical manner, to set down our ideas precisely, to show the steps in the process of solution and to have a diagrammatic solution to the problem which can be followed and understood by someone with *no* knowledge of program writing. As well as the above, flowcharting teaches us some important computer concepts which will arise in most of our program writing. For example, if there are two possible answers to any question and if the correct answer is not the first, then it *must* be the second. We will see some of these ideas in the example flowcharts that follow.

Standard symbols are used to indicate the different operations. The more common ones are shown in Fig. 9.1. Every flowchart must show its beginning and ending. There may be more than one stop symbol. Data is input to a process and output from it using the input and output symbol. Any process such as calculating, sorting, initialising etc. is shown in the process symbol. The decision symbol always asks a question, usually with two possible answers. The connector symbol is used to continue a flow line off one page on to another or to show the connection between two parts of a flow line on the same page rather than crossing other parts of the flowchart.

Lines joining the symbols together indicate the flow of operations or data. Arrows should only be used to indicate the flow when they are necessary to avoid ambiguity.

We will draw a flowchart for the sports day project later in this section, but before that, let us look at a very simple problem and define it in a flowchart form:

'Find who is the tallest of two people—Mary and John'. In its simplest form this could be shown as in Fig. 9.2, but this does not show the three sections of input, process, and output. Based on these, the flowchart becomes as shown in Fig. 9.3. Fig. 9.4 shows this in more detail.

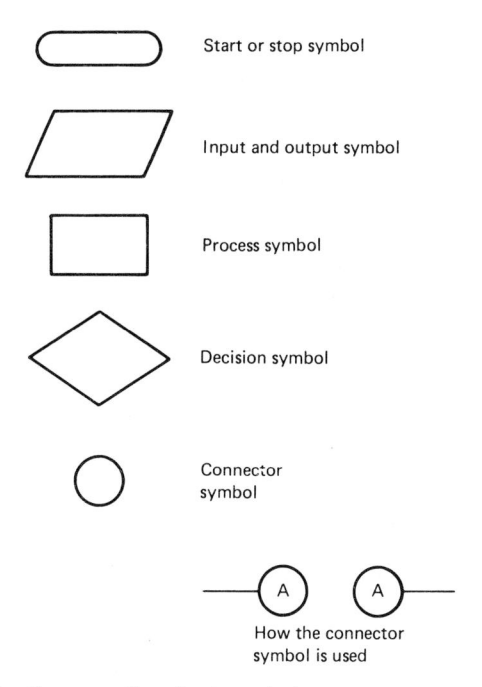

Fig. 9.1 Common flowchart symbols

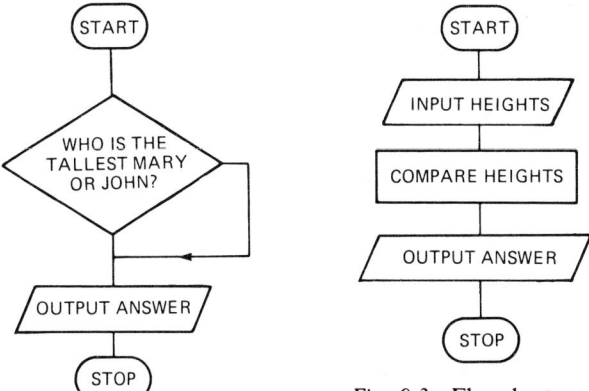

Fig. 9.2 Who is the tallest?

Fig. 9.3 Flowchart structured to basic input–process–output concept

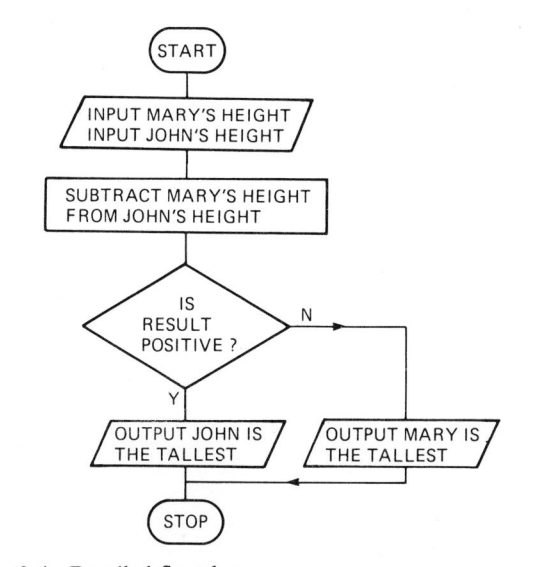

Fig. 9.4 Detailed flowchart

84 COMPUTER STUDIES

Note that these flowcharts show three stages in the solution to the problem which are directly comparable with the 'back of the envelope' approach to producing a systems description. Normally only the third flowchart would be drawn from the latest systems description. Note also that this flowchart is written in English and does *not* contain any programming terms or signs. For this reason, it is sometimes referred to as a system flowchart.

We could extend this problem and re-write it as: 'Find who is the tallest of three people—Mary, John and Peter'. Then, the first two flowcharts above are still correct but the detailed one clearly is not. Before drawing the detailed flowchart to solve the new problem, we will draw another one with more detail than in Fig. 9.3 but less than in Fig. 9.4. This new flowchart is shown in Fig. 9.5.

It is good practice to try to make the bottom exit from a decision box the 'yes' exit but *not* at the expense of flowlines crossing each other! The more detailed version of the above flowchart is shown in Fig. 9.6.

Although this problem was to find the tallest of three people, the same flowchart can be used to find the largest of any three numbers.

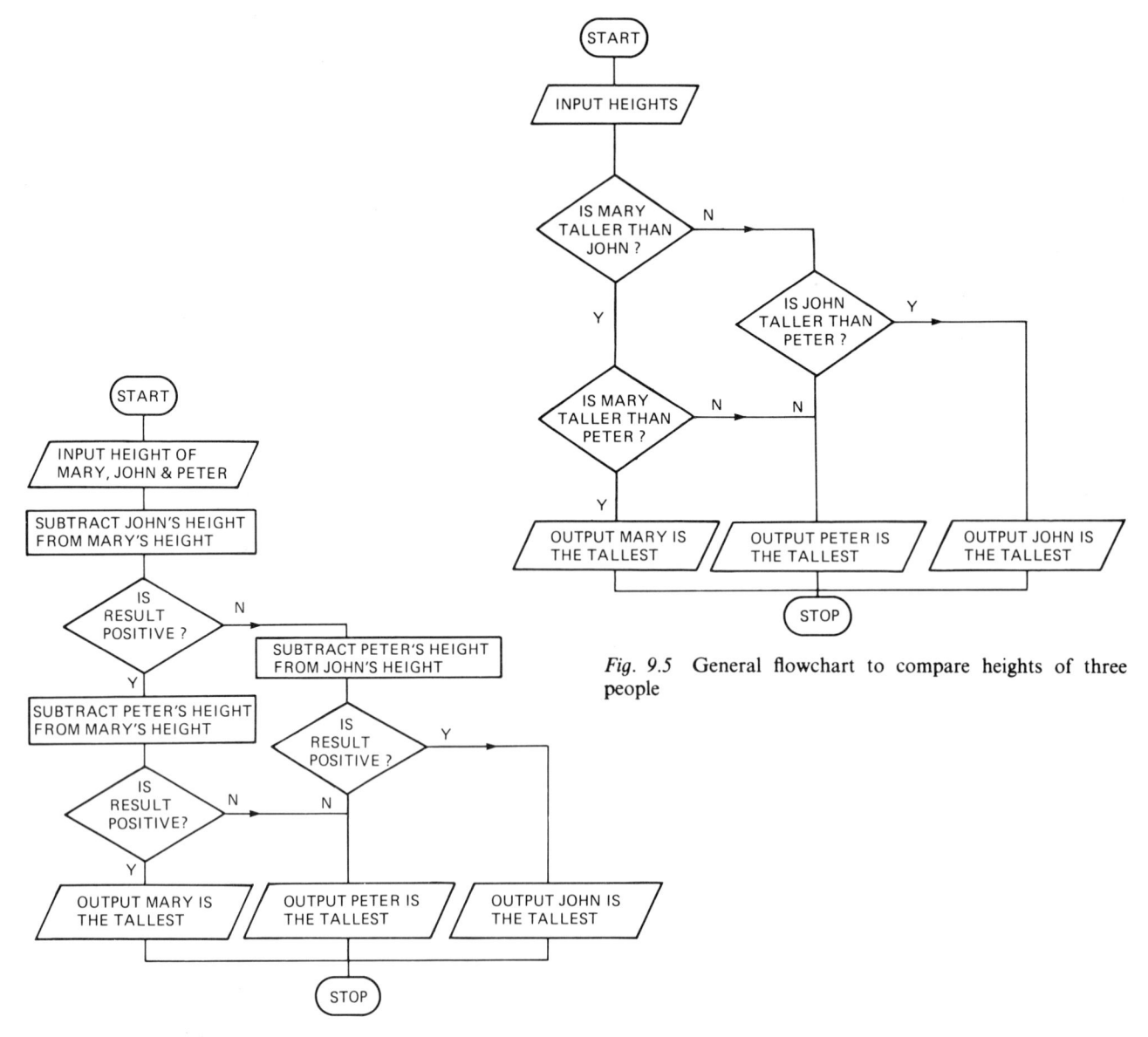

Fig. 9.5 General flowchart to compare heights of three people

Fig. 9.6 Detailed flowchart

Exercise 9.2

Modify the flowchart to output the shortest of the three people.

Example

A survey is taken of television viewing habits. Those who watch BBC 1 most are recorded as 1; those who watch BBC 2 most are recorded as 2; and those who watch ITV most as 3; those with no preference as 4 and those who do not watch television as 5. Draw a flowchart to count the number of people preferring each choice and output the totals.

Fig. 9.7 shows such a flowchart. Note that there is no need to test if the 'vote' is 5—if it is not 1,2,3 or 4 it must be 5 (assuming no other data has been input). If we wish

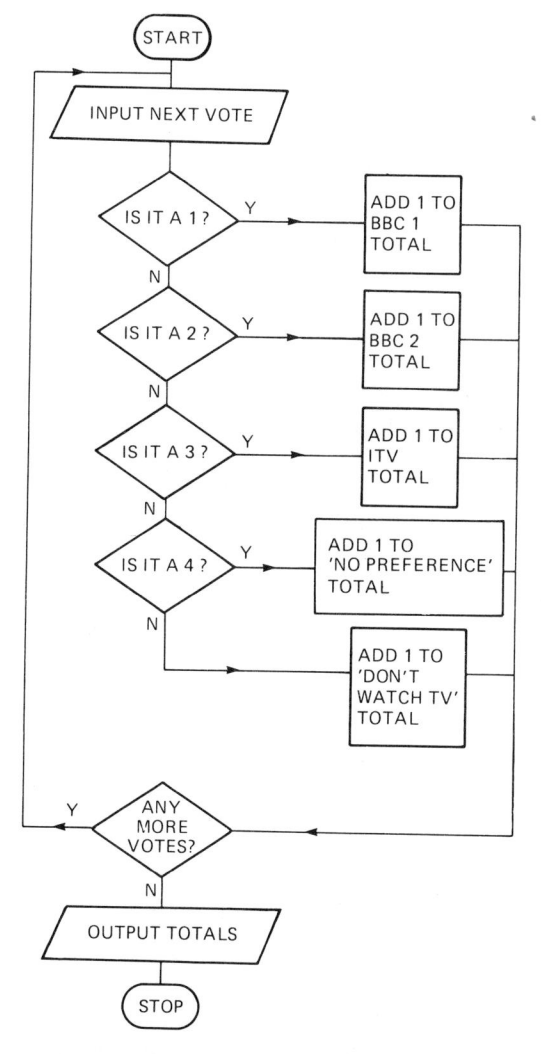

Fig. 9.7 Survey of television viewing habits

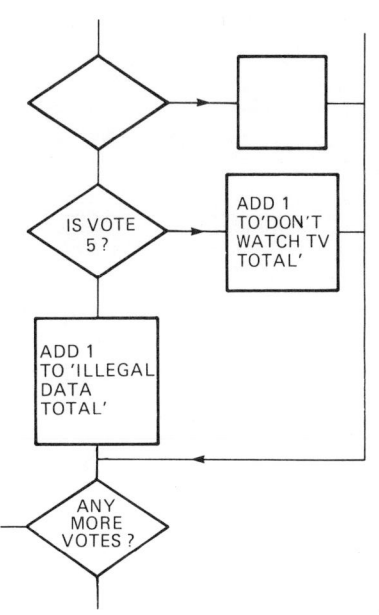

Fig. 9.8 Allowing for 'illegal data'

to allow for the situation where 'illegal data' might be input, the flowchart would be modified to the form shown in Fig. 9.8.

Exercise 9.3

Modify the flowchart above also to output each total as a percentage of the total number of 'votes' input.

Example
Draw a flowchart to find the average of any number of numbers.

The flowchart in Fig. 9.9 would be easier to read if we used only the letters shown in brackets (variables), but still used English words, like divide, and not program symbols, like /. If we do this, we must provide a listing of what the variables stand for, as shown in Fig. 9.10.

Let us now produce a flowchart directly from the system description of the Sports day on page 82.

Fig. 9.11 shows this chart. Note the use of the word 'next' in the input box. This is a commonly used word which enables *any* event to be referred to even if it is the first event. It should be appreciated that, although the input and output boxes are defining single operations, the process boxes are describing operations which may require many other actions in order to complete the stated operation. This is quite normal, and expansion of the process boxes is the next step toward the final flowchart.

Sorting is a standard procedure and can be considered as a routine to be executed every time new results are

86 COMPUTER STUDIES

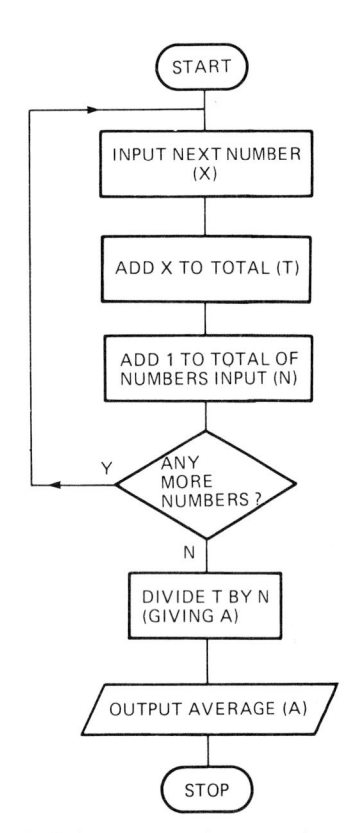

Fig. 9.9 To find the average of any number of numbers

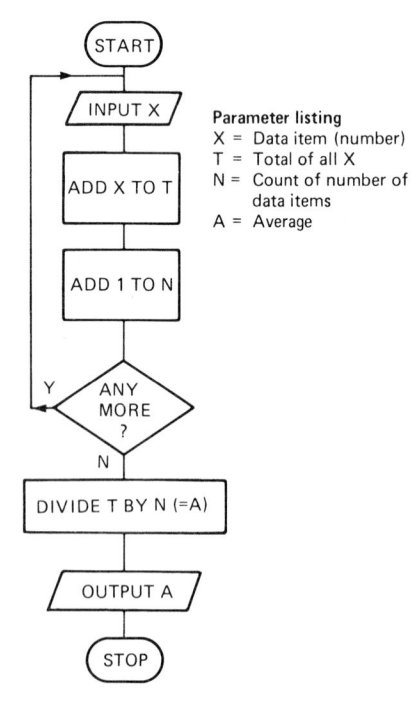

Fig. 9.10 Pre-programming flowchart

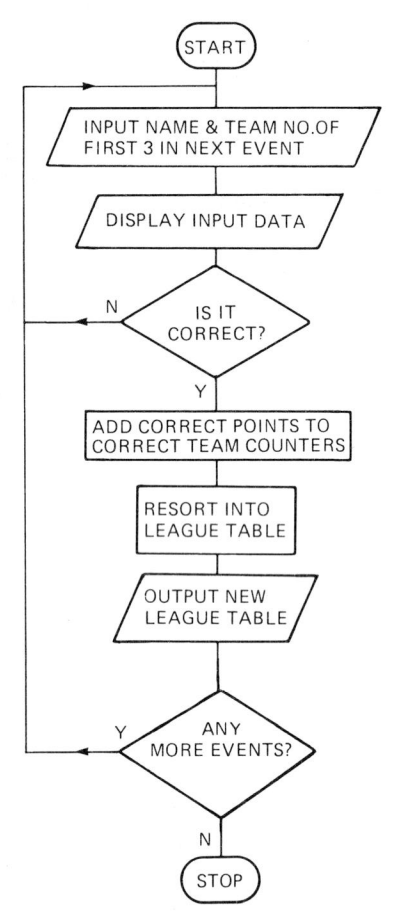

Parameter listing
X = Data item (number)
T = Total of all X
N = Count of number of data items
A = Average

Fig. 9.11 Flowchart from system description of sports day

input. Thinking ahead to writing the program, we can clearly make the sorting procedure into a subroutine and show this on the program flowchart thus:

| sort sub-routine |

When we come to the main process box—'add correct points to correct team counters'—we need to decide how the correct points are to be 'attached' to the teams placed first, second and third. We know that 5, 3 and 1 points are to be awarded for first, second and third places in every event, so one way of achieving this is simply to add 5 points to the winning team's total, 3 to the team coming second and 1 to the third team, for every event. The teams are identified by numbers and the first process box can then be shown as:

| Add 5 to total of team coming first
Add 3 to total of team coming second
Add 1 to total of team coming third |

Notice that the flowchart is still a 'systems flowchart' and, as yet, has nothing to do with programming.

The next flowchart to be drawn is called a programming flowchart and the program is written, almost directly, from this flowchart. We can now use signs and terms from the programming language that we are going to use but the full meaning of any abbreviations and variables must be given in a suitable table, preferably on the same page as the flowchart. The flowchart on page 84 to find the tallest of three people would then be drawn in more detail as shown in Fig. 9.12 (assuming BASIC is to be used to write the program).

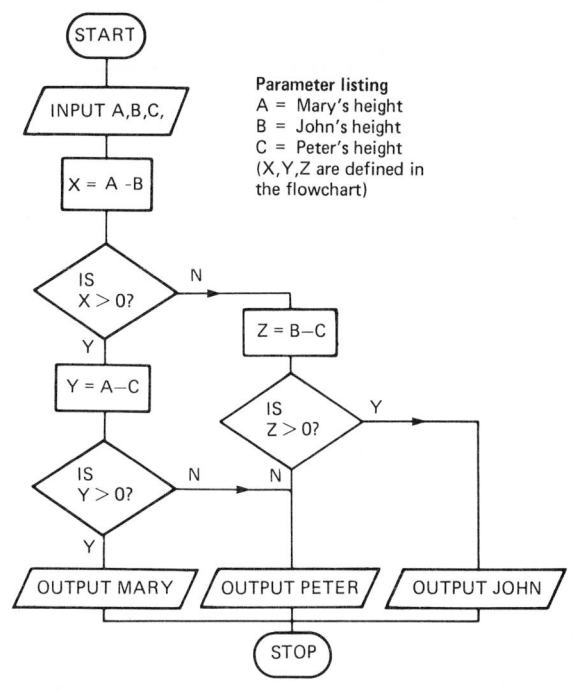

Fig. 9.12 Program flowchart

Flowcharts are essential to good program writing. *Never* try to write a program without having drawn a flowchart to solve the problem first!

Some do's and don'ts for flowcharting
(i) Be prepared to sketch a few flowcharts in order to get a satisfactory solution. Do not make any flowchart too complicated; remember, a flowchart should show the method of problem solution. Flowcharts which try to say everything say nothing!
(ii) Try a number of different layouts to produce a balanced diagram for the final version.
(iii) Always use a flowchart template and ruler!
(iv) *Never* produce a flowchart by writing program statements then drawing boxes round them!
(v) Dry-run the flowchart to check that it is correct. It is *much* easier to dry-run a flowchart than a program!

Exercises 9.4

1 Your school introduces a new assessment scheme. For each subject studied, the procedure is:
(a) Three assessments per term are given and a mark out of 10 is awarded for each assessment.
(b) Each term the three assessments are averaged.
(c) At the end of the year the best average over the three terms is printed on the pupil's report.

Consider a class of 20 pupils, studying several subjects. During one year each pupil will have nine assessment marks for each subject. Draw that part of a flowchart (which must be language independent) that will read in the nine marks for each pupil for one subject and will output:
(i) the three termly averages for each pupil
(ii) the best average for each pupil in this subject.
(*AEB, 1980*)*

2 Draw a flowchart to simulate the deal of a pack of 52 playing cards equally to four persons. (The flowchart should be programming language independent.)
(*AEB, 1979*)*

3 Draw a flowchart to illustrate the process necessary to input 100 numbers into the computer and to output the numbers in reverse order. (*AEB, 1978*)*

4 Three numbers are to be input as data to a program which is to be developed in stages as follows:
Stage 1. Check to see if the three numbers could be the lengths of the three sides of a triangle, that is, the sum of any two sides must be greater than the third side.
Stage 2. Calculate the length of the perimeter of the triangle and print out the answer in a suitable message.
Stage 3. Calculate the area of the triangle using the formula
Area $= [s(s-a)(s-b)(s-c)]$
Where a, b and c are the lengths of the three sides of the triangle and s is half the perimeter.
Stage 4. Allow for the input of many sets of three numbers, this data to be terminated in a suitable manner.

By following through each stage, build up in stages a flow chart for the total program. Indicate clearly the development of the flowchart necessary at each stage.
(*AEB, 1978*)*

5 A survey is being made of passengers using a particular train route. On each train using the route during the survey period, each passenger is asked his ticket type: first or second class; single, day or period return. This data is encoded for input to a computer. Draw a flowchart for the analysis of the above data to give:
(a) the total number of passengers using the route

during the survey period,
(b) the number of passengers with each ticket type,
(c) the average number of passengers, per day, with day return tickets.

(The flowchart should *not* contain any terms, signs, symbols, etc. which are part of the syntax of any programming language. All abbreviations, terms and conventions should be defined.) *(AEB, 1977)**

6 A new hymn book, containing 460 sequentially numbered hymns, is being compiled. The index is to list all the hymns in alphabetical order of their first line, against the hymn number. Draw a detailed flowchart showing how such an index could be produced as output from a computer. *(AEB, 1976)**

7 (a) Draw a system flowchart which will test whether a number is odd or even. (The flowchart should not contain any terms or signs which are part of the syntax of any programming language).
(b) Write a program, *in any high level language*, from the flowchart in (a), to input any six numbers less than 100 and to print out the number, followed by the words '*is odd*', if the number is odd, or to print out the number followed by the words '*is even*', if the number is even. *(AEB, 1976)**

8 Dry run the flow chart shown here showing the value of the variables, any output and the result of any tests at each stage of the flowchart, in a suitable table. *

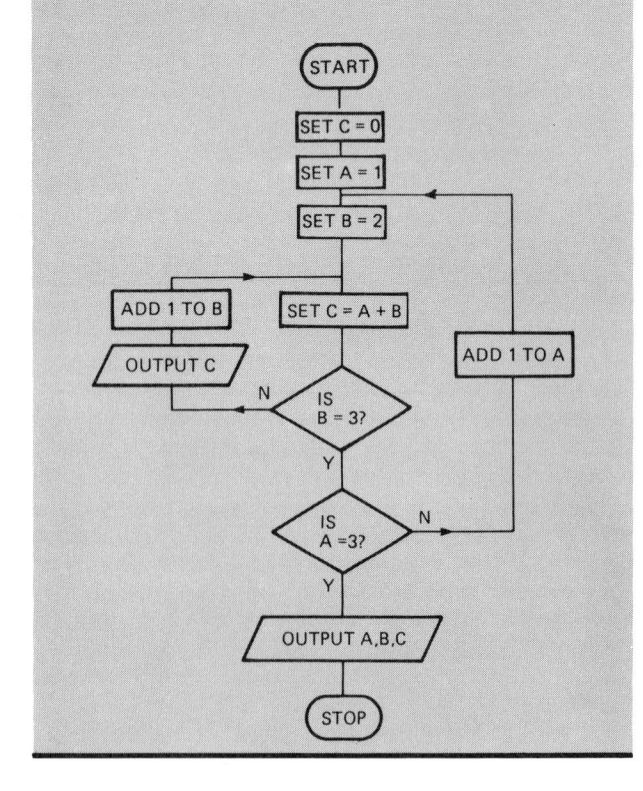

```
START
SET C = 0
SET A = 1
SET B = 2
SET C = A + B
ADD 1 TO B
OUTPUT C
IS B = 3?
IS A = 3?
ADD 1 TO A
OUTPUT A,B,C
STOP
```

9.4 Documentation

Documentation is the complete description of a program and should include helpful notes, flowcharts, a program listing, test data and expected results. More than that, documentation is the complete record of the development, testing and use of a program. No program can be complete without suitable documentation. It is common bad practice to write the documentation after the program has been written and run, but documentation should be started at the outset of any program or project.

Program documentation has five main objectives:
(a) to enable the program writer(s) to keep track of where they are up to in the development of the program
(b) to ensure continuity of development even if there is a change in the design team
(c) to ensure that maintenance of the program can be effectively carried out
(d) to allow for program development at a later stage
(e) to enable the program to be used by anybody with minimal computing knowledge.

Note that the documentation discussed in this section is that which should accompany *any* program and should not be confused with the documentation required for examination project work. (This is discussed fully in Appendix 1 coursework.)

Program documentation can be considered under eight main headings as listed below.

Section 1   Identification
1.1 Name or title of the program.
1.2 Name of programmer.
1.3 Date(s) written.
1.4 Programming language used.

Section 2   Description
2.1 Purpose of the program: statement of the problem to be solved.
2.2 Method of solution.
2.3 Outline flowchart(s): detailed one(s) only if absolutely necessary.
2.4 Program listing, including annotations.
2.5 List of all variables used in the program stating the purpose of each variable.

Notes
2.2 The method of solution should describe, in broad terms, the program techniques to be used, e.g. read data from file 1 into an array and after manipulation write to file 2.
2.4 Even medium-sized programs can contain dozens of variables. It is important that they are listed, stating

clearly what each one does and where it is used in the program. This is best done in table form as the example below:

Variable	Purpose	Where used	Line number	changed by
A$	Array for names	Input Sort routine	50 300–340	— X$
I	Names counter	Input Calculating	65 90 140	C if T = 0

'quantity limit' sets a maximum on the amount of data which can be input, for example 25 names and addresses.

Section 4 Output
4.1 Statement of the normal output from the program. Graphic or printer or user option.
4.2 Quantity of output expected.
Notes
4.2 There is nothing worse than running out of printer paper 90% of the way through a long output! Also, give some indication of the time for the output—some programs can take a long time in processing to produce

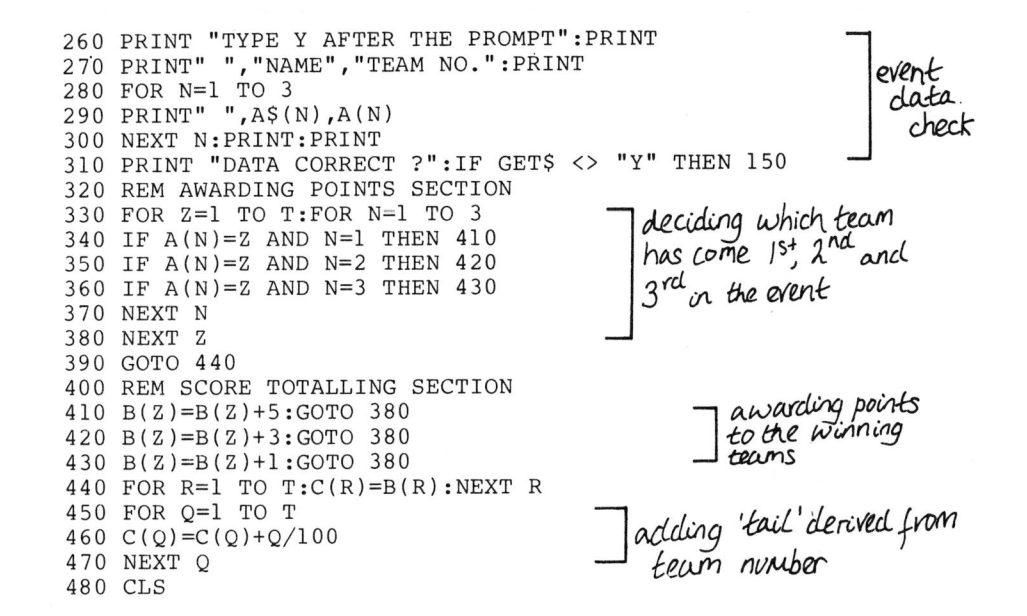

```
260 PRINT "TYPE Y AFTER THE PROMPT":PRINT
270 PRINT" ","NAME","TEAM NO.":PRINT        ] event
280 FOR N=1 TO 3                              data
290 PRINT" ",A$(N),A(N)                       check
300 NEXT N:PRINT:PRINT
310 PRINT "DATA CORRECT ?":IF GET$ <> "Y" THEN 150
320 REM AWARDING POINTS SECTION
330 FOR Z=1 TO T:FOR N=1 TO 3               ] deciding which team
340 IF A(N)=Z AND N=1 THEN 410                has come 1st, 2nd and
350 IF A(N)=Z AND N=2 THEN 420                3rd in the event
360 IF A(N)=Z AND N=3 THEN 430
370 NEXT N
380 NEXT Z
390 GOTO 440
400 REM SCORE TOTALLING SECTION
410 B(Z)=B(Z)+5:GOTO 380                    ] awarding points
420 B(Z)=B(Z)+3:GOTO 380                      to the winning
430 B(Z)=B(Z)+1:GOTO 380                      teams
440 FOR R=1 TO T:C(R)=B(R):NEXT R
450 FOR Q=1 TO T                            ] adding 'tail' derived from
460 C(Q)=C(Q)+Q/100                           team number
470 NEXT Q
480 CLS
```

Fig. 9.13 Hand annotated program segment

2.5 Annotation should be handwritten, (in colour), on the program to indicate the purpose of the various sections of the program (Fig. 9.13). This method is preferable to using REM statements, which take up storage space and do not always readily identify some features of a program, such as loops.

Section 3 Input
3.1 Description of the data required for input to the program and any special format.
3.2 Any limits to the value of the data and the quantity to be input.
3.3 Details of any validation checks carried out by the program.
Notes
3.2 A 'value limit' may be necessary if the program only accepts, for example, positive numbers less than 100. A

a small quantity of output—and what indication is given to signal the end of the output.

Section 5 Processing
5.1 Description of main processing tasks.
5.2 Approximate time for processing.
5.3 Formulae used, if any.
5.4 Any unusual programming techniques.
Notes
5.1 For example in the calculation of mean and standard deviation—hold the results in an array until they are required for output.
5.2 Some processing tasks can take a long time (e.g. a sort routine) and warning should be given that 'nothing happening for 3 minutes' is normal.

Section 6 Computer environment
6.1 Mode of operation—batch or interactive.

6.2 Type of computer for which program is written.
6.3 Compiler or other software needed.
Section 7 Testing evidence
7.1 Include test results with a sample run using dummy data.
Section 8 User instructions
8.1 Clear, 'idiot proof', instructions on how to load and use the program.
8.2 Any limitations on the use of the program.
8.3 A clear list of error messages and default routines.

Notes
8.1 Always assume that a 'user' is intelligent enough to understand clear, precise, instructions but incapable of making any technical (computing) decision. For example, don't say 'when you have loaded the operating system. . . . . .'
8.2 Never assume that a program written on one type of computer will work on another type—it is almost a certainty that it will not. Does your computer use disks for program and data storage? Very many do not.
8.3 Even the best operators have been known to hit the wrong key. In most systems, this won't matter too much but it is probable that an error message will be generated, and these are sometimes not very clear. (Would you know what 'CAN'T/O' means?) Even more important is for the user to be able to get the program going again without having to ask for outside assistance.

The remainder of this section is devoted to specimen documentation of the sports day problem presented in Section 2. Some of the detail has been written previously in Sections 2 and 3 of this chapter and will therefore be presented here in shortened form and marked with an asterisk.

1 Identification
1.1 Sports day results program.
1.2 G. M. Croft.
1.3 26th February 1984.
1.4 Basic—BBC Basic, Version 1.
2 Description
2.1 To find which team gains most points.*
2.2 Use of matrix (array) to store each teams points which are sorted into a 'league' after each event.*
2.3 See Fig. 9.11 on page 86.
2.4 See Fig. 9.15.
2.5 See Fig. 9.14.
3 Input
3.1 Name and team number of first three in event.

Variable	Purpose	Where used	Line number
T	Hold number of teams	Input and control of counter Z	60
E	Hold number of events	Input and control of counter V	90
V	Main event counter	Main program control	110
N$	Name of competitor	Input	170
P	Team number	Input	170
A$	Array to hold names	Input	200
N	Counter to control first 3 to finish	Input Validation	150 280
	To identify 1st, 2nd or 3rd in event	Process	'330
A	Array to hold team number of first 3	Input Validation Process	200 290 340–360
B	Array to hold scores of all teams	Process	410–430
R$	Hold answer to question	Validation	310
Z	Used as counter and to identify team numbers	Process	330
R	Counter to control copying of data from B to C	Process	470
C	Array to hold scores plus team identifier	Process	450 470 510
K	Counter to control sort routine	Process	500
W	Spare location used during sorting	Process	520
S	Team identifier	Output	640

Fig. 9.14 Table of variables used in sports day program

PROBLEM SOLVING TECHNIQUES

```
 10 REM SPORTS DAY PROGRAM.BKRACE(BBC BASIC)
 20 MODE 7
 30 DIM A$(20),A(20),B(20),C(20):PRINT
 40 PRINT"           SPORTS DAY"
 50 PRINT"           ----------"
 60 REM INPUT SECTION
 70 INPUT"HOW MANY TEAMS ARE COMPETING ?(MAX 20) "T:PRINT
 80 IF T<21 THEN 100
 90 PRINT"MAX. OF 20 TEAMS PLEASE!":GOTO 70
100 INPUT"HOW MANY EVENTS ARE THERE ? "E
110 CLS
120 FOR V=1 TO E
130 PRINT"              EVENT NO.";V:PRINT
140 GOTO 160
150 PRINT"PLEASE INPUT THE RESULT OF EVENT NO. ";V;"  AGAIN":PRINT
160 FOR N=1 TO 3
170 PRINT"NAME & TEAM NUMBER OF ";N;" TO FINISH       ";
180 INPUT N$,P
190 IF P<=T THEN 210
200 PRINT"YOU SAID THERE WERE ONLY ";T;" TEAMS         COMPETING!":GOTO 170
210 A$(N)=N$:A(N)=P
220 NEXT N
230 REM VERIFICATION SECTION
240 CLS:PRINT:PRINT
250 PRINT "PLEASE CHECK THE DATA YOU HAVE JUST ENTERED, IF IT IS CORRECT,"
260 PRINT "TYPE Y AFTER THE PROMPT":PRINT
270 PRINT" ","NAME","TEAM NO.":PRINT
280 FOR N=1 TO 3
290 PRINT" ",A$(N),A(N)
300 NEXT N:PRINT:PRINT
310 PRINT "DATA CORRECT ?":IF GET$ <> "Y" THEN 150
320 REM AWARDING POINTS SECTION
330 FOR Z=1 TO T:FOR N=1 TO 3
340 IF A(N)=Z AND N=1 THEN 410
350 IF A(N)=Z AND N=2 THEN 420
360 IF A(N)=Z AND N=3 THEN 430
370 NEXT N
380 NEXT Z
390 GOTO 440
400 REM SCORE TOTALLING SECTION
410 B(Z)=B(Z)+5:GOTO 380
420 B(Z)=B(Z)+3:GOTO 380
430 B(Z)=B(Z)+1:GOTO 380
440 FOR R=1 TO T:C(R)=B(R):NEXT R
450 FOR Q=1 TO T
460 C(Q)=C(Q)+Q/100
470 NEXT Q
480 CLS
490 IF V<>E THEN 510 ELSE PRINT"      FINAL TEAM POSITIONS":PRINT"      --------------------":PRINT:PRINT:GOTO 530
500 PRINT"----------------------"
510 IF V<>1 THEN 520 ELSE PRINT"      TEAM POSITIONS AFTER ";V;" EVENT":PRINT:PRINT:GOTO 530
520 PRINT"       TEAM POSITION AFTER ";V;" EVENTS":PRINT:PRINT
530 PRINT ,"TEAM NO.","TOTAL POINTS"
540 PRINT;"---------------------"
550 FOR N=1 TO T-1:FOR K=N+1 TO T
560 IF C(N)>=C(K) THEN 580
570 W=C(N):C(N)=C(K):C(K)=W
580 NEXT K
590 NEXT N
600 FOR J=1 TO T
610 S=INT((C(J)-INT(C(J)))*100+.1)
620 PRINT;S,INT(C(J))
630 NEXT J
640 PRINT:PRINT:NEXT V
650 PRINT:PRINT:PRINT"END OF COMPETITION"
```

Fig. 9.15 Sports day results program

3.2 Program can be used for up to 20 teams.

3.3 Immediately following data input, a formatted display of the input data will be presented on the VDU. Follow program prompts.

4 Output

4.1 An up-to-date league table will be displayed on the VDU after each event. An option of hard copy output is offered in the program. The time for printer output varies with the number of teams competing.

5 Processing

5.1 The first three teams are awarded 5, 3 and 1 point respectively and these points are added to the appropriate team counters after the team numbers have been identified. After each event the counters are sorted into descending order of total points.

5.2 Approximately 4 seconds with 20 teams.

5.3 No formulae have been used.

5.4 The team identifier (Q), is derived from the team number in line 460 and decoded to form S in line 640. Boolean operators are used in lines 340, 350 and 360.

6 Computer environment

6.1 Interactive

6.2 BBC Micro

6.3 BBC BASIC interpreter. Extended Basic version 5)

7 Testing evidence

See Fig 9.16.

8 User instructions

8.1 The program is stored on disk number 23 under the file name BKRACES. If the computer is up and running (if not, contact the computer department), load the program into the computer by typing: LOAD "BKRACE". After a few seconds, the system will respond with >. Now type RUN. All further instructions will be given on the VDU.

8.2 There is a maximum of 20 teams. If less than three teams finish in any event, input any letter for a dummy name and zero for the team number, for any unfilled places.

8.3 As the input data is validated before processing and the program has built-in checks and error messages, no other error messages should be displayed.

```
          RUN


                    SPORTS DAY
                    ---------


          HOW MANY TEAMS ARE COMPETING ?(MAX 20) 4


          HOW MANY EVENTS ARE THERE ? 2

                    EVENT NO.1

          NAME & TEAM NUMBER OF 1 TO FINISH       ?JONES,3
          NAME & TEAM NUMBER OF 2 TO FINISH       ?SMITH,2
          NAME & TEAM NUMBER OF 3 TO FINISH       ?BROWN,4



          PLEASE CHECK THE DATA YOU HAVE JUST ENTERED, IF IT IS CORRECT,
          TYPE Y AFTER THE PROMPT



                    NAME        TEAM NO.

                    JONES            3
                    SMITH            2
                    BROWN            4


          DATA CORRECT ?
```

Fig. 9.16 Output from run of sports day program

Fig. 9.16 (*Continued*)

```
          TEAM POSITIONS AFTER 1 EVENT

TEAM NO.   TOTAL POINTS
--------------------
3              5
2              3
4              1
1              0



               EVENT NO.2

NAME & TEAM NUMBER OF 1 TO FINISH    ?PETERS,3
NAME & TEAM NUMBER OF 2 TO FINISH    ?JAMES,1
NAME & TEAM NUMBER OF 3 TO FINISH    ?GREEN,4

PLEASE CHECK THE DATA YOU HAVE JUST ENTERED, IF IT IS CORRECT,
TYPE Y AFTER THE PROMPT

          NAME      TEAM NO.

          PETERS        3
          JAMES         1
          GREEN         4


DATA CORRECT ?

          FINAL TEAM POSITIONS
          --------------------

TEAM NO.   TOTAL POINTS
--------------------
3             10
2              3
1              3
4              2



END OF COMPETITION
```

9.5 Errors and diagnostics

Not every program you write will run correctly first time! The more complex the program, the more likely it is to have errors in it. Let us look first at the types of error that can occur.

(a) Types of error
(i) Compilation errors are errors detected during compilation or interpretation of the program. They can be either a syntax error or a semantic error.

A syntax error is caused by the incorrect use of the rules governing the structure of the language (grammar). For example, you may write LET A + B = C. The rules state that the assignment variable must be declared before the operation statement and there would be a syntax error if this were not done. A semantic error occurs when the meaning of the statement is

Exercises 9.5

1 A project, to computerise the timetabling of internal examinations in a large school is to be undertaken by a computer studies class. The main data needed is a file containing each student's name and subjects studied and a second file containing the details of staff timetables.

Give a brief description of each necessary step in the development of the project and, for each step, give a detailed description of the documentation which should be produced and which will form part of the final project. *(AEB, 1979)**

2 A software package is to be produced for your school's history department to be used for revising dates and other important historical facts. It will be an interactive program with display on a VDU only. The history teacher is not a computing specialist. Design and describe, fully, the documentation which would form part of this package. *

---

altered due to an error in the syntax. For example, LET X = Y − Z is a perfectly valid Basic statement but the operator − should have been +. Or you may write LET P = Q ∗ R + S when you meant to write LET P = Q ∗ (R + S), which has a different meaning.

(ii) Execution errors are errors which are detected during execution of the program, and they fall into two categories: arithmetic errors causing for example, division by zero, overflow (see Chapter 6.7), or insufficient or excessive data, and logical errors which are the most common type of programming error. Logical errors can themselves be grouped into two categories: simple errors in the program writing (eg. GOTO 380 where line 380 does not exist), and actual errors in the logic of the program. In this case, the program may run satisfactorily but give an incorrect result because the program design is incorrect. This type of error is the most difficult to detect as it is not always obvious that an error has occurred!

(b) Error detection

Compilation errors are detected by the compiler or interpreter and execution errors usually by the operating system. The method by which errors are reported and the type of error message generated varies between computer systems. Some examples are given below.

In most mainframe computers using a compiler, detected errors are stored until compilation is complete and then an error listing is provided. Fig. 9.17(*a*) shows the simplest type of listing stating only the line numbers where errors have been found. Fig. 9.17(*b*) shows a more

```
 40 ERROR
 60 ERROR
 90 ERROR
110 ERROR                        (a)
170 ERROR
Ready:

10 REM PROG TO FIND THE LARGEST NUMBER
20 INPUT L
30 IF L=1 THEN 70
40 IF L=2                        (b)
***STATEMENT INCOMPLETE***
```

Fig. 9.17 Compiler error messages
   (*a*) Simple
   (*b*) Diagnostic listing

helpful diagnostic listing in which a brief error message follows each identified error and a summary of the errors by line number appears at the end of the program listing.

As most microcomputers use an interpreter which interprets the program one line at a time, any 'compilation' errors are detected immediately the line is interpreted. An error message is generated and interpretation stops until the error is corrected. A typical error and error message are shown in Fig. 9.18.

```
10 FIR X=1 TO 20
20 PRINT X
30 NEXT X
RUN

Syntax error at line 10
```

Fig. 9.18 Interpreter error message

Once the program has been interpreted successfully, it is controlled by the operating system during program execution. Arithmetic and logical errors are detected as they occur in the program run and after a suitable error message has been generated, execution is halted. Fig. 9.19 shows a typical logical error message.

```
10 FOR X=1 TO 10
20 FOR Y=10 TO 0 STEP -2
30 PRINT X/Y
40 NEXT:NEXT
RUN
        0.1
        0.125
0.166666667
        0.25
        0.5

Division by zero at line 30
```

Fig. 9.19 Typical logical error message

As an interpreter attempts to execute each line of a program immediately following successful interpretation, execution errors can be detected at the same time as compilation errors. Again, following display of a suitable error message, further interpretation and execution cannot take place until the error is corrected (see Fig. 9.20).

```
Redimensioned array at line 85
Return without Gosub @ line 1234
Can't /0 at line 4721
```

Fig. 9.20 Typical execution error message

(c) Diagnostic aids
Despite all the above error detection routines, there is no guarantee that all errors in a program will be detected, let alone corrected by the time the program appears to run. Any remaining errors will, almost certainly, be logical errors and can often be very difficult to detect and correct. In order to help in this error detection, diagnostic aids are often provided with the computer software or, failing this provision, can be 'homemade'.

Most computers have a tracing facility. When the trace routine is switched on (usually by a system command, eg. TRACE ON), each line number is displayed in the order in which execution is taking place. It is therefore possible to detect when a program is going to the wrong line or if it is jumping over a section of program. Remember to switch the trace off otherwise your output may have hundreds of line numbers mixed up with the correct output. See Fig. 9.21.

A second trace facility offered by some computer systems is to display the values of all the variables during program execution. Detailed study of a printout of this information may then reveal, for example, that a controlled loop has not counted far enough to read all the data. A printout of a variable trace from a 380Z is shown in Fig. 9.22.

```
       LVAR
A=  0
B=  9
C=  8
X= -2
Z=  3

READY:
```
Fig. 9.22

```
                RUN
[10] [20]

[30] Input 3 heights in metres,eg 1.23
[40]
Note: this program does not accept any two identical heights
[50]
To end the program, input 0 for the first number
[60]
?3,5,2
[80] [90] [100]


[110] [120] [160] [170] [180] B IS THE TALLEST
```

Fig. 9.21 Output showing line number trace

```
10 REM PROG TO FIND THE TALLEST OF 3 PEOPLE.(BKHTS1)
15 MODE7:PRINT:PRINT
20 PRINT"Input 3 heights in metres,eg 1.23"
25 PRINT:PRINT "Note:this program does not accept any two identical heights"
30 PRINT:PRINT"To end the program, input 0 for the first number"
40 PRINT:INPUT A,B,C
50 CLS:IF A=0 THEN 170
60 IF A=B OR A=C OR B=C THEN 20
70 PRINT:PRINT:PRINT
80 X=A-B
90 IF X<0 THEN 130
100 Y=A-C
110 IF Y<0 THEN 160
120 PRINT"A IS THE TALLEST":PRINT:PRINT:GOTO 20
130 Z=B-C
140 IF Z<0 THEN 160
150 PRINT"B IS THE TALLEST":PRINT:PRINT:GOTO 20
160 PRINT"C IS THE TALLEST":PRINT:PRINT:GOTO 20
170 END
```

Fig. 9.23 Program written from flowchart in Fig. 9.12

96 COMPUTER STUDIES

```
 10 REM PROG TO FIND THE TALLEST OF 3 PEOPLE.(BKHTS2)
 20 MODE 7:PRINT:PRINT
 30 PRINT"<40>"
 40 PRINT"Input 3 heights in metres,eg 1.23"
 50 PRINT:PRINT "Note: this program does not accept any  two identical heights"
 60 PRINT:PRINT"To end the program, input 0 for the     first number"
 70 PRINT"<80>"
 80 PRINT:INPUT A,B,C:CLS
 90 PRINT:PRINT"<100>"
100 IF A=0 THEN END
110 PRINT"<120>"
120 IF A=B OR A=C OR B=C THEN 40
130 PRINT "<140>"
140 PRINT:PRINT:PRINT
150 X=A-B
160 PRINT"<170>"
170 IF X<0 THEN 250
180 PRINT"<190>"
190 Y=A-C
200 PRINT"<210>"
210 IF Y<0 THEN 310
220 PRINT"<230>"
230 PRINT"A IS THE TALLEST":PRINT:PRINT:GOTO 40
240 PRINT"<250>"
250 Z=B-C
260 PRINT"<270>"
270 IF Z<0 THEN 310
280 PRINT"<290>"
290 PRINT"B IS THE TALLEST":PRINT:PRINT:GOTO 40
300 PRINT"<310>"
310 PRINT"C IS THE TALLEST":PRINT:PRINT:GOTO 40

RUN
<40>
Input 3 heights in metres,eg 1.23
Note: this program does not accept any two identical heights
To end the program, input 0 for the first number
<80>

?1.64,1.51,1.47

<100>
<120>
<140>



<170>
<190>
<210>
<230>
A IS THE TALLEST

Input 3 heights in metres,eg 1.23
Note: this program does not accept any two identical heights
To end the program, input 0 for the first number
<80>

?0,9,8

<100>
```

Fig. 9.24 **Program with trace facilities**

PROBLEM SOLVING TECHNIQUES 97

The program in Fig. 9.23 is written from the flowchart in Fig. 9.12 and will be used as the basic program to demonstrate machine independent diagnostic aids.

Home-made trace facilities can be built into a program by adding a 'print line number statement' between active lines of the program as shown in the program segment in Fig. 9.24.

Although these may take some time to add to a long program, it is a simple and very effective way of detecting logical errors if the computer does not offer the trace facility. Variable tracing can be achieved in a similar way by adding print statements at selected points in the program (Fig. 9.25).

The above are diagnostic facilities for use on high-level language programs and are not normally available for assembly language or machine code programming. In these cases, errors would be detected by using a 'store dump'. This gives a printout of the contents of each store location—usually in hexadecimal—and is usually described as dumping. A dump of a large program can produce a vast amount of output, all of which may have to be examined to detect the errors (Fig. 9.26).

If all system and home-made debugging facilities fail to pin-point any error in the program, the last resort is a dry run. Using a print-out of the *actual program* which is

```
 10 REM PROG TO FIND THE TALLEST OF 3 PEOPLE.(BKHTS3)
 20 MODE 7:PRINT:PRINT
 30 PRINT"Input 3 heights in metres,eg 1.23"
 40  PRINT:PRINT "Note:this program does not accept any   two identical heights"
 50 PRINT:PRINT"To end the program, input 0 for the     first number"
 60 PRINT:INPUT A,B,C
 70 CLS
 80 IF A=0 THEN END
 90 IF A=B OR A=C OR B=C THEN 30
100 PRINT:PRINT:PRINT
110 X=A-B
120 PRINT"X= ";X:PRINT
130 IF X<0 THEN 180
140 Y=A-C
150 PRINT"Y= ";Y:PRINT
160 IF Y<0 THEN 220
170 PRINT"A IS THE TALLEST":PRINT:PRINT:GOTO 30
180 Z=B-C
190 PRINT"Z= ";Z:PRINT
200 IF Z<0 THEN 220
210 PRINT"B IS THE TALLEST":PRINT:PRINT:GOTO 30
220 PRINT"C IS THE TALLEST":PRINT:PRINT:GOTO 30

RUN

Input 3 heights in metres,eg 1.23

Note:this program does not accept any two identical heights

To end the program, input 0 for the first number

?1.64,1.51,1.47

X= 0.13

Y= 0.17

A IS THE TALLEST

Input 3 heights in metres,eg 1.23

Note:this program does not accept any two identical heights

To end the program, input 0 for the first number

?0,9,8
```

Fig. 9.25 Variable tracing

98 COMPUTER STUDIES

11011001	00100001	00001011	10111000
11111100	00101011	00001010	00011110
11001110	10110100	01101001	11100100
00100001	11000100	01110110	11101110
01010111	10001100	11011110	00001111
11100110	00100110	10010001	01100101
10011010	00000101	00010001	00010010
10011100	00010011	10100001	01001000
01110100	00011101	01010111	11100011
11101111	01110000	11110101	00000101
11111000	11101000	00100101	00001100
01111110	00100100	11010101	01100100
01110010	01000100	00101101	10010110
01111011	11111011	01110001	01110100
10001010	˙˙101010	˙1110000	˙˙01010C
˙˙101010	˙˙0˙	˙10110	˙˙01
˙˙0		˙000	
		˙1	

0	052E	+20645	*00050245	ADX	165(1)
1	00)H	+1640	*00003150	LDX	1640
2	002$	+148	*00000224	LDX	148
3	009,	+604	+00001134	LDX	604
4	00=\	+892	*00001574	LDX	892
5	@0=ˆ	−8387714	*40001576	LDX	894
6	000E	+37	*00000045	LDX	37
7	0000	+0	*00000000	LDX	0
8	@0=_	−8387713	*40001577	LDX	895
9	0000	+0	*00000000	LDX	0
10	74LD	+1854244	+07045444	SUSW	2852

Fig. 9.26 Two types of core dump

not running properly—not a previous copy which might be out-of-date—work through each line of the program yourself following each instruction exactly and performing each calculation just as if the computer were doing it. Write down the result of each action or calculation in a table showing all the variables, tests and line numbers (Fig. 9.27(*a*)).

All possible paths through the program have been tested by selecting different values for A, B and C. Note that both paths to line 160 have been tested.

Let us suppose that an error had been introduced when the program was being written and line 140 actually read IF Z > 0 THEN 160. The output from the first set of data in the dry run above would now have been 'C is the tallest' which is nonsense, as we can see that 1.54 is actually the smallest of the three input heights. The dry run table for the incorrect program would be as shown in Fig. 9.27(*b*).

We can see that all is well up to line 130 and that in line 140 the test 'is Z > 0?' should take the program to line 150, not 160, so we can either swap round lines 150 and 160, and jump line 90 to 150, or change the inequality sign on line 140.

Dry runs are particularly helpful in detecting errors in array manipulation when it is the only practical way of 'seeing' what is stored in each element of the array. It is, of course, possible to write a program to produce a dry run table by combining both techniques of 'home-made' tracing—line numbers and variable values—into the object program. This is shown in the program and output in Fig. 9.28.

Line no	A	A = 0	B	C	X	X < 0?	Y	Y < 0?	Z	Z < 0?	Output
40	1.62		1.73	1.54							
50		no									
80					−0.11						
90						yes					
130									+0.08		
140										no	
150											B is the tallest
40	1.73		1.62	1.54							
50		no									
80					+0.11						
90						no					
100							+0.19				
110								no			
120											A is the tallest
40	1.62		1.54	1.73							
50		no									
80					+0.08						
90						no					
100							−0.11				
110								yes			
160											C is the tallest
40	1.54		1.62	1.73							
50		no									
80					−0.08						
90						yes					
130									−0.19		
140										yes	
160											C is the tallest
40	0		0	0							
50		yes									
170											

Fig. 9.27(a) Trace table

Line no.	A	A = 0?	B	C	X	X < 0?	Y	Y < 0?	Z	Z < 0?	Output
40	1.62		1.73	1.54							
50		no									
80					−0.11						
90						yes					
130									+0.08		
140										yes	
160											C is tallest

Fig. 9.27(b) Dry run table for incorrect program

```
10 REM PROG TO CREATE A TRACE TABLE.(GCBKHTS4)
20 MODE 7:F=0
30 PRINT:PRINT"Note: This program does not accept any two identical heights"
40 PRINT:PRINT"To end the program,input 0 for A"
50 PRINT:PRINT:PRINT"Input 3 numbers separated by a comma"
60 INPUT A,B,C:IF F<>0 THEN 110
70 IF A=0 THEN END
80 PRINT:PRINT:PRINT
90 PRINT"LINE";TAB(5)"A";TAB(11)"B";TAB(17)"C";TAB(23)"X";TAB(29)"Y";TAB(34)"Z";TAB(37)"OUT"
100 PRINT"----------------------------------------"
110 PRINT"110";TAB(5)A;TAB(11)B;TAB(17)C
120 PRINT"120":IF A=0 THEN 240
130 X=A-B:PRINT"130";TAB(23)X
140 PRINT"140":IF X<0 THEN 190
150 Y=A-C:PRINT"150";TAB(29)Y
160 PRINT"160"
170 PRINT"170":IF Y<0 THEN 230
180 PRINT"180";TAB(38)"A":GOTO 240
190 Z=B-C:PRINT"190";TAB(34)Z
200 PRINT"200"
210 PRINT"210":IF Z<0 THEN 230
220 PRINT"220";TAB(38)"B":GOTO 240
230 PRINT"230";TAB(38)"C":GOTO 240
240 PRINT"240":GOTO 50
```

RUN

Note: This program does not accept any two identical heights

To end the program,input 0 for A

Input 3 numbers separated by a comma
?1.64,1.51,1.47

LINE	A	B	C	X	Y	Z	OUT
110	1.64	1.51	1.47				
120							
130				0.13			
140							
150					0.17		
160							
170							
180							A
240							

Input 3 numbers separated by a comma
?0,9,8

Fig. 9.28   (*a*) Program to create a trace table
              (*b*) Output from one run

PROBLEM SOLVING TECHNIQUES 101

Exercises 9.6

1. Explain, by giving examples, the difference between a *compilation* error and an *execution* error. *
2. The following algorithm can be used to convert an integer expressed in binary to its denary equivalent:
   (i) Multiply the most significant bit of the binary integer by 2 and call the result 'TOTAL'.
   (ii) Add the next bit to TOTAL.
   (iii) If this was the last bit, then TOTAL gives the required answer.
   (iv) If there are further bits, multiply TOTAL by 2 then return to step (ii).
   (a) Draw a flowchart from this algorithm.
   (b) Dry run the flowchart using 101110_2 as input, showing all working.
   (c) How can the flowchart be modified to convert a number in some other base, n, (where $n < 10$), to base 10?   (*AEB, 1977*)*
3. The flowchart shows the necessary steps to solve a particular problem.
   (a) Construct a table for values of A, C and T. Use this to dry run the flowchart, for A having values 3, 10, 6, 4, 2, −1.
   (b) What is the name given to the type of process carried out between the points P and Q in the flowchart?
   (c) What is the special name for the last piece of data?
   (d) What does T represent?
   (e) What does C represent?
   (f) What problem does the flowchart solve? *

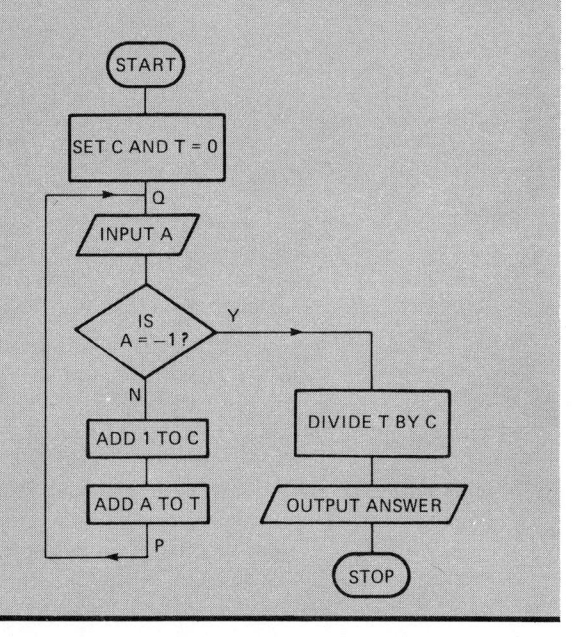

9.6 Test data

The use of test data to check a flowchart has previously been mentioned (Section 9.3). Test data can be used in a similar manner to check a program. It has two main purposes:
(a) to check all the logical paths in the program
(b) to check that the program produces the correct output.

The dry run in the previous section requires *four* sets of data to test all the logical paths, although there are only three possible outputs, and the test data must be chosen carefully with this in mind.

In order to check that the program produces the correct output, dummy data can be used as long as it is of the same type as the real data. For example, the dry run shown previously uses three real heights—with subsequent arithmetic calculation which could itself cause errors. The program will work equally well if the data is A = 3, B = 2, C = 0 and calculation is so much simpler and less likely to have errors. If the program is used to find the largest of three numbers, not heights, then it should be capable of dealing with any numbers including negative numbers.

Exercise 9.7

Check that the flowchart and program in Figs. 9.12 and 9.23 work if any, or all, of the input numbers are negative, by creating a dry-run table as on page 99.

If the program is only to find the tallest of three people, then there should be a test in the program to prevent negative data from being input—for obvious reasons! This could be:

25 IF A < 0 OR B < 0 OR C < 0 THEN PRINT "I've heard of pygmies but this is ridiculous! Try again":
GO TO 20

Now our test data must include negative numbers as well as positive ones and should be rejected by the program (see Fig. 9.29).

When you are using alpha data to test, for example, a file creation program, it is not necessary to input long names and addresses or other alphabetic data. The test data need only consist of a single letter for any string input. The output might look odd, but, after all, it is only test data!

In summary, test data should test all paths through the program and be simple enough to enable the processing and output to be checked manually. A large amount of test data is unnecessary.

```
 10 REM PROG TO FIND THE TALLEST OF 3 PEOPLE.(BKHTS5)
 20 MODE 7:PRINT:PRINT
 30 PRINT"Input 3 heights in metres,eg 1.23"
 40 PRINT:PRINT"Note: This program does not accept any  two identical heights"
 50 PRINT:PRINT"To end the program,input 0 for A"
 60 PRINT:INPUT A,B,C:CLS
 70 IF A=0 THEN END
 80 IF A=B OR A=C OR B=C THEN 30
 90 IF A<0 OR B<0 OR C<0 THEN PRINT"I´ve heard of pygmies but this is ridiculous!! Try again":PRINT:PRINT:GOTO 30
100 PRINT:PRINT:PRINT
110 X=A-B
120 IF X<0 THEN 160
130 Y=A-C
140 IF Y<0 THEN 190
150 PRINT"A IS THE TALLEST":PRINT:PRINT:GOTO 30
160 Z=B-C
170 IF Z<0 THEN 190
180 PRINT"B IS THE TALLEST":PRINT:PRINT:GOTO 30
190 PRINT"C IS THE TALLEST":PRINT:PRINT:GOTO 30


    RUN

Input 3 heights in metres,eg 1.23

Note: This program does not accept any two identical heights

To end the program,input 0 for A

?-1,2,3
I´ve heard of pygmies but this is ridiculous!!Try again

Input 3 heights in metres,eg 1.23

Note: This program does not accept any two identical heights

To end the program,input 0 for A

?0,9,8
```

Fig. 9.29 Final program including data check

Summary

- Not all problems can sensibly be solved by computers.
- Before a computer solution is attempted, the problem must be clearly defined in terms of output—input—processing.
- Always redefine the problem in terms of a flowchart *before* attempting to write a program.
- Documentation should be written to accompany every stage in the solution of the problem.
- Good user documentation will be capable of being understood by a non-specialist in computing without help from the author.
- Most program writing produces errors. Good system diagnostics will help to detect and analyse most types of error.
- 'Home-made diagnostics' can be of great benefit in tracing some faults.
- Test data should be selected to test *all* possible outcomes from a program (or flowchart).

10 Programming techniques

It is assumed that the reader of this section has spent some time learning to program in BASIC and is familiar with all the standard elements of the language. As the sub-set of BASIC which is common to all versions of the language is very small and quite inadequate for advanced programming, the discussion of the various techniques which follows will be centered on flowcharts rather than programs. Some programs, written in BBC BASIC are included and versions of these programs for RML, APPLE, and PET are to be found in Appendix 5.

10.1 Searching

When data is stored, it has to be recovered in order to be used. The process of retrieving the data from an array, a file, or other data store, is known as *searching*. If the data is stored in an array, then each element of the array has to be read to see if it contains the required data. If the array holds unordered data (i.e. not sorted alphabetically or numerically), then the whole array may have to be searched to find the required data. If the data is ordered in the array or file (as all data should be), then it is possible to start the search at some point close to where the data is stored and search either backwards or forwards for the required item. This item of data is called the *key* and a match between the key and an item of stored data is known as a *hit*. This technique of linear searching is used later to find specified data in a file. Linear searching can, however, be very inefficient if the amount of data to be searched is large and access is frequent.

'Sometimes our computer misbehaves but our teacher always says that it is our programs which are wrong.'

Binary searching is commonly used on a large quantity of ordered data and can reduce significantly the average time to a hit. The principle of a binary search is to compare the key with the record in the (approximate) middle of the file. This tells us in which half of the file the data is stored, so the key is compared with the middle item in this section, which tells us which half it is in . . . and so on until a hit is made. Fig. 10.1 shows the principle. This is shown in flowchart form in Fig. 10.2, from which the program in Fig. 10.3 has been written.

10.2 Sorting

All data should be sorted into order before storing for ease of access as above. There are a number of methods of sorting, each with advantages and disadvantages, and the choice of sort routine depends much on the type and quantity of data to be sorted. Two methods only will be discussed in this section: they are the *exchange* or *swop* sort and the *balanced two-way merge* sort.

Fig. 10.1 A binary search

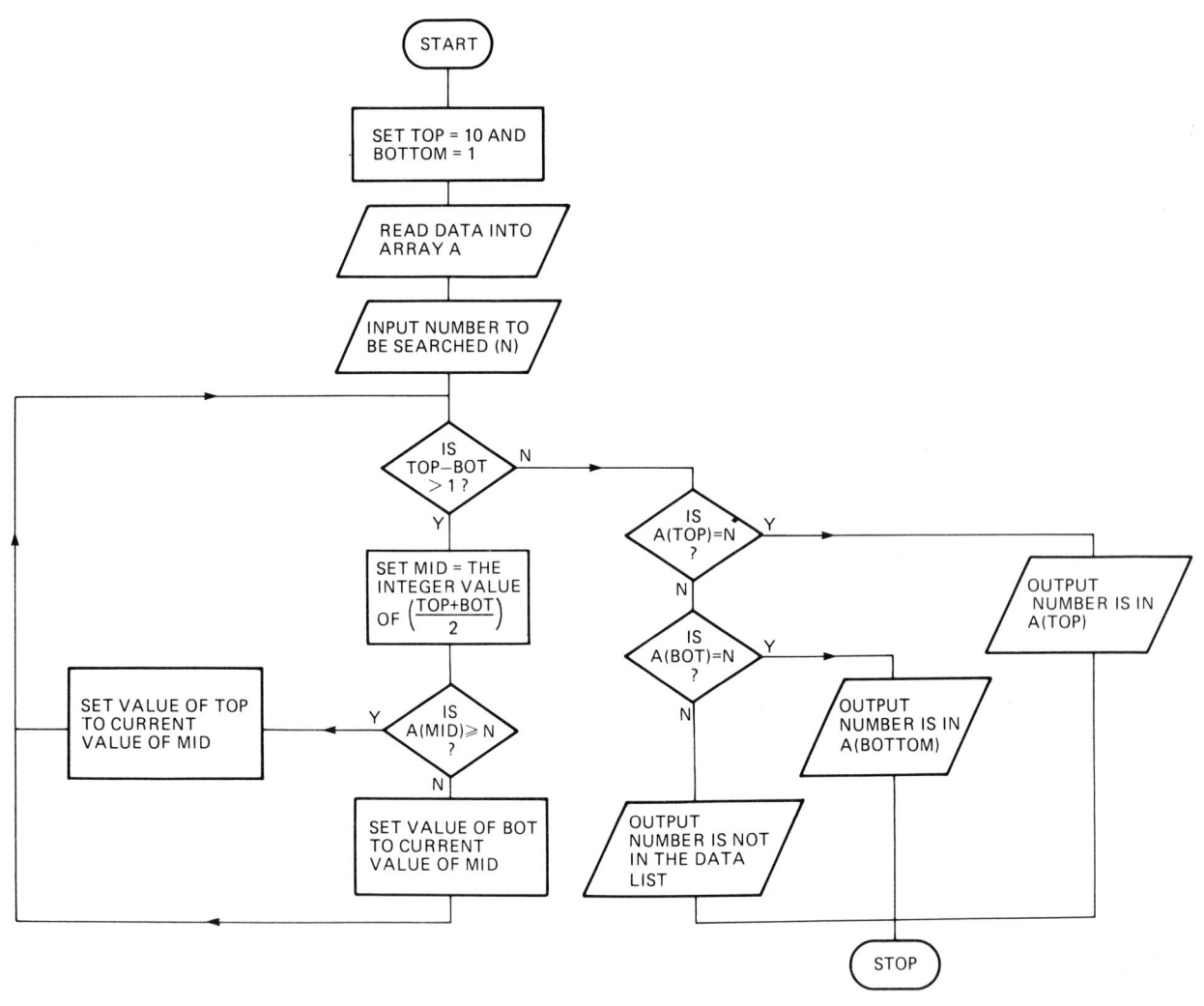

Fig. 10.2 Flowchart for a binary search

```
 10 REM BINARY SEARCH PROGRAM.BKCHOP(BBC BASIC)
 20 MODE 7:PRINT:PRINT:PRINT:DIM A(10)
 30 FOR B=1 TO 10:READ D:A(B)=D:NEXT B
 40 PRINT:PRINT:PRINT
 50 INPUT" What number do you wish to search for? "N
 60 PRINT:PRINT
 70 T=10:B=1
 80 IF T-B<=1 THEN 120
 90 M=INT((T+B)/2)
100 IF A(M)>=N THEN T=M:GOTO 80
110 B=M:GOTO 80
120 IF A(T)=N THEN PRINT"THE NUMBER ";N;" IS ELEMENT NO.";T:GOTO 160
130 IF A(B)=N THEN PRINT"THE NUMBER ";N;" IS ELEMENT NO.";B:GOTO 160
140 PRINT"THE NUMBER ";N;" IS NOT IN THE LIST"
150 DATA 1,5,6,11,14,26,31,33,39,50
160 END
```

Fig. 10.3 Program from flowchart in Fig. 10.2

Exchange sort

The principle of the exchange sort is as follows:
(i) The unordered data is stored in an array.
(ii) The first and second items in the array are compared.
(iii) If they are in order,* they are left in position; otherwise, they are exchanged.
(iv) The second and third items are now compared and either left alone or exchanged.
(v) This process continues until the last pair of data items in the array has been compared and adjusted.
(vi) The (largest) item in the array is now at the bottom of the array. This data item is now in its correct position in the ordered list so it is not considered again and therefore the 'list length' is reduced by one.
(vii) The sequence is restarted at step (ii) and repeats until no further exchanges are made. At this point, the data is completely sorted and in order and the routine finishes.

It is possible to sort A → Z or Z → A or numeric ascending from zero or vice versa. The flowchart in Fig. 10.4 is to sort A → Z. Fig. 10.5 shows a program and printout.

```
10  REM EXCHANGE SORT.BKEXCH(BBC BASIC)
20  MODE 7:DIM A$(13):C=0
30  READ A$:IF A$="XXX" THEN 80
40  A$(C)=A$
50  DATA DOG,RAT,MOUSE,BEE,HORSE,COW,HEN
60  DATA SHEEP,FOX,FISH,CAT,PIG,XXX
70  C=C+1:GOTO 30
80  PRINT:PRINT:PRINT"SORTING.....":PRINT:PRINT
90  Q=C
100 J=0:F=0
110 IF A$(J)<A$(J+1) THEN 150
120 X$=A$(J)
130 A$(J)=A$(J+1)
140 A$(J+1)=X$:F=1
150 IF J+1<C THEN 190
160 IF F=0 THEN 210
170 C=C-1
180 GOTO 100
190 J=J+1
200 GOTO 110
210 CLS:PRINT:PRINT
220 FOR I=0 TO Q:PRINTA$(I):NEXT I
230 PRINT:PRINT"SORT COMPLETE"
RUN
SORTING.....

BEE
CAT
COW
DOG
FISH
FOX
HEN
HORSE
MOUSE
PIG
RAT
SHEEP

SORT COMPLETE
```

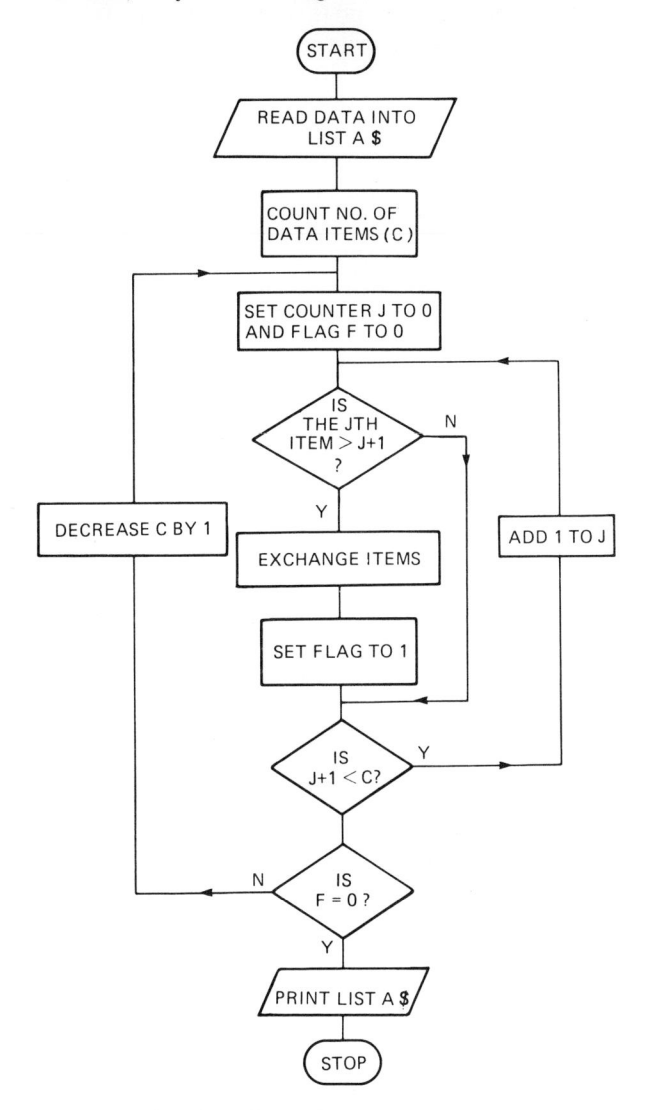

Fig. 10.4 Flowchart for exchange sort

* 'Order' means in the correct relative position in the ordered sequence, e.g. A–Z or in ascending numeric value. The ordering is made by comparing the ASCII values of the data being tested: For example Brown is less than Smith, because B has a lower ASCII value than S. If Smithson is compared with Smithers, the ASCII value of the first five characters is identical and the decision will be made on the sixth character. AB123 is 'less than' AB124 and AB123 is 'less than' AC123.

Fig. 10.5 Program and printout from flowchart in Fig. 10.4

The exchange sort is relatively easy to understand and lends itself to easy demonstration with numbered cards (held by pupils). It is also easy to program and is fast enough for most school projects which do not involve a large amount of data. However, it is a slow method of sorting a large amount of data. The number of passes through the data and the number of comparisons on each pass are directly proportional to the number of items to be sorted. The number of exchanges to be made depends on how 'disordered' the original data is.

two data files, two empty files are required during the sorting process.

The principle is as follows:
(i) Take the first data item from each file, order them and transfer both to a blank file, C.
(ii) Repeat with the second item from each file but transfer the ordered pair to the other blank file, D.
(iii) Continue steps (i) and (ii) until all the data is in files C and D, which can now be considered as the data files.

```
 10 REM EXCHANGE SORT & SEARCH.BKSOSE(BBC BASIC)
 20 MODE 7:PRINT:PRINT:PRINT:DIM A$(13):C=0
 30 READ A$:IF A$="XXX" THEN 80
 40 A$(C)=A$
 50 DATA DOG,RAT,MOUSE,BEE,HORSE,COW,HEN
 60 DATA SHEEP,FOX,FISH,CAT,PIG,XXX
 70 C=C+1:GOTO 30
 80 PRINT:PRINT:PRINT"SORTING.....":PRINT:PRINT
 90 Q=C
100 J=0:F=0
110 IF A$(J)<A$(J+1) THEN 150
120 X$=A$(J)
130 A$(J)=A$(J+1)
140 A$(J+1)=X$:F=1
150 IF J+1<C THEN 190
160 IF F=0 THEN 210
170 C=C-1
180 GOTO 100
190 J=J+1
200 GOTO 110
210 PRINT:PRINT"SORT COMPLETE"
220 REM BINARY SEARCH
230 PRINT:INPUT"What animal do you wish to search for?   "N$
240 T=12:B=1
250 IF T-B<=1 THEN 280
255 M=INT((T+B)/2)
260 IF A$(M)>=N$ THEN T=M:GOTO 250
270 B=M:GOTO 250
275 PRINT:PRINT
280 IF A$(T)=N$ THEN PRINT "THE ";N$;" IS ITEM NO.";T;" IN THE LIST":GOTO 310
290 IF A$(B)=N$ THEN PRINT "THE ";N$;" IS ITEM NO.";B;" IN THE LIST":GOTO 310
300 PRINT"THE ";N$;" IS NOT IN THE LIST"
310 GOTO 220  :REM OR END
```

Fig. 10.6 Program combining sorting and searching

The program in Fig. 10.6 combines the previous search and sort programs and shows how alpha data (animals names) can be found by using a binary search on an ordered file.

Balanced two-way merge sort
The balanced two-way merge sort is widely used in data processing where data is held on two files—the master file and the transaction file—which need to be merged and sorted to form a new master file. The sorting is achieved during the merging process. In addition to the

(iv) Repeat the process from (i) but merge and order the data in blocks of four—two from each data file—before transferring them to file A or B.
(v) When A and B are empty, repeat from step (i) but merge and order the data in blocks of eight—four from each file.
(vi) Continue doubling the number of data items merged on each pass until the files merge into one sorted file.

This process can be demonstrated more easily with a numerical example:

	File A contains:	2, 3, 7, 4, 1, 5, 3, 8
	File B contains:	6, 1, 0, 0, 5, 3, 2, 7
Pass 1	File C contains:	2, 6, 0, 7, 1, 5, 2, 3
	File D contains:	1, 3, 0, 4, 3, 5, 7, 8
Pass 2	File A contains:	1, 2, 3, 6, 1, 3, 5, 5,
	File B contains:	0, 0, 4, 7, 2, 3, 7, 8
Pass 3	File C contains:	0, 0, 1, 2, 3, 4, 6, 7
	File D contains:	1, 2, 3, 3, 5, 5, 7, 8
Pass 4	File A contains:	0, 0, 1, 1, 2, 3, 3, 3, 4, 5, 5, 6, 7, 7, 8

This sorting procedure is most efficient when both data files contain approximately equal data items and the number in either file is approximately a power of two (16, 32, 64 . . . .). This sort can also be used to sort a single unordered file of data by dividing the original data into approximately equal groups and considering one half as file A and the other as file B.

The following example shows the same procedure using files of differing lengths containing names.

	File A:	Anson, Andrews, Brown, Carter, Lewis, Rose, Smith, Turner.
	File B:	Dutton, Taylor, Peak, Jones, Hunt, Atkin
Pass 1	File C:	Anson, Dutton, Brown, Peak, Hunt, Lewis, Smith, Turner.
	File D:	Andrews, Taylor, Carter, Jones, Atkin, Rose
Pass 2	File A:	Andrews, Anson, Dutton, Taylor, Atkin, Hunt, Lewis, Rose
	File B:	Brown, Carter, Jones, Peak, Smith, Turner
Pass 3	File C:	Andrews, Anson, Brown, Carter, Dutton, Jones, Peak, Taylor
	File D:	Atkin, Hunt, Lewis, Rose, Smith, Turner
Pass 4	File A:	Andrews, Anson, Atkin, Brown, Carter, Dutton, Hunt, Jones, Lewis, Peak, Rose, Smith, Taylor, Turner.

This is typical of a transaction file (B) being merged with the master file (A). The sort would only be marginally quicker if the data in file B was ordered, as the number of passes and comparisons is fixed by the number of data items.

10.3 Simulation

Simulation is the art of 'make-believe' and despite the fact that a computer is somewhat prosaic, it is very good at simulating almost any event or situation.

The simplest simulation is that of a single event: tossing a coin, once, or throwing a dice, once. This may seem a rather trivial thing for a computer to do but it is just as easy to program a computer to toss a coin 1000 times as once. Have you ever tried tossing a coin 1000 times? A large computer would require about 2 seconds to simulate this and count the number of heads and tails as well!

A computer can also simulate events like landing a spaceship on the moon or driving a car round a racetrack but in both these examples, if they are interactive games, the data is provided by the player from a keyboard or other input device.

More complex simulations are based on a model so that the computer simulation is designed to reproduce the model as closely as possible. The model may be a chemistry experiment which requires the mixing of two or more chemicals in a laboratory. This experiment can be simulated on a computer without using any chemicals or apparatus. Some experiments are dangerous, others are costly and others take a long time to complete. However, with a computer to simulate the experiment all risks and use of chemicals are removed and the time reduced from days, or even years, to minutes or seconds.

The model we wish to simulate may be a road junction where traffic lights are to be installed. Using a simulation, the light settings can be varied to find the effect on the traffic flow. Actual measurements of the traffic flow at the road junction will have been taken previously, and this data forms an important part of the simulation.

Another type of model simulation is used to predict a pattern of events based on a mathematical model of, for example, a factory wishing to manufacture a new product. Many variable parameters can be built into the model, for example material costs, labour costs, profit margins, and number sold. These parameters can be adjusted to give maximum profit. By using a computer simulation it is possible to predict the likely return on investment without actually manufacturing the product or investing capital in new plant and machinery.

All computer simulations are based on probability. The probability of an unbiased tossed coin coming down heads is *always* $\frac{1}{2}$; the probability that a brick dropped from a height will not descend heavily on whatever is underneath it, is zero! The probability that we will all die sometime is a certainty, or 1. This probability factor, which can be any number between 0 and 1, is used to determine whether an event is likely to occur and, if so, what is the probability of the event taking place.

For example, the probability that a car will either arrive or not arrive at a petrol pump at any given instant of time is $\frac{1}{2}$, but, by recording when cars arrive, we may find that the probability of seven cars arriving in every 15 minute period is only 1/20. The first probability is fixed—it is always $\frac{1}{2}$—and is known as discrete. The second type is generated by a frequency distribution and is called continuous. We will use only the first type of probability in the worked example below.

The problem is to simulate a petrol station with *n* pumps and to examine the factors that cause a queue to develop. If the simulation shows that there is always an unacceptable length of queue then three factors can be considered to reduce the queue:

(i) Add more pump(s)—this would be costly.
(ii) Reduce the time each car is at a pump—this is not easy, but possible.
(iii) Reduce the number of cars buying petrol—and cut down your profits!

The first simulation will be based on the probability that a car will arrive in each time period being 1:2 (either a car will arrive or it will not). We will do this first simulation by hand using a coin to decide if a car arrives or not. The time periods are quite arbitrary—it doesn't matter what they are—1 min, 5 min etc., as long as each period is the same. It is usual to perform a simulation over a fixed time period. The other data required is as follows: the time each car is at the pump (cycle time) is three time periods; the time of simulation is 20 time periods.

The results can be set out in table form as shown below. Each car is numbered sequentially when it arrives and a toss of heads is taken to be 'car arrives' and a tail as 'no car'.

Period	Toss	Car?	Pump A	Pump B	Queue
1	T	N	—	—	—
2	H	Y	1	—	—
3	T	N	1	—	—
4	T	N	1	—	—
5	T	N	—	—	—
6	H	Y	2	—	—
7	T	N	2	—	—
8	H	Y	2	3	—
9	H	Y	4	3	—
10	H	Y	4	3	5
11	T	N	4	5	—
12	H	Y	6	5	—
13	T	N	6	5	—
14	H	Y	6	7	—
15	H	Y	8	7	—
16	H	Y	8	7	9
17	T	N	8	9	—
18	T	N	—	9	—
19	H	Y	10	9	—
20	T	N	10	—	—

This clearly shows that there were two occasions when there was a queue of one car for one period. It is certainly not worth installing a third pump on this evidence but, as the probability of a car arriving in any time period is 1 in 2, in 20 periods, 10 cars could arrive all in the first 10 time periods. Let us see what would happen then.

Period	Toss	Car?	Pump A	Pump B	Queue
1	H	Y	1	—	—
2	H	Y	1	2	—
3	H	Y	1	2	3
4	H	Y	3	2	4
5	H	Y	3	4	5
6	H	Y	3	4	5,6
7	H	Y	5	4	6,7
8	H	Y	5	6	7,8
9	H	Y	5	6	7,8,9
10	H	Y	7	6	8,9,10
11	T	N	7	8	9,10
12	T	N	7	8	9,10
13	T	N	9	8	10
14	T	N	9	10	—
15	T	N	9	10	—
16	T	N	—	10	—
17	T	N	—	—	—

This simulation shows that a third pump would have been put to good use as there was a queue for approximately 50% of the time and that the queue length was at least two cars for the majority of the queuing time and twice peaked at three cars. Let us see the effect of introducing a third pump and keeping the distribution badly skewed into the first 10 periods.

Period	Car?	Pump A	Pump B	Pump C	Queue
1	Y	1	—	—	—
2	Y	1	2	—	—
3	Y	1	2	3	—
4	Y	4	2	3	—
5	Y	4	5	3	—
6	Y	4	5	6	—
7	Y	7	5	6	—
8	Y	7	8	6	—
9	Y	7	8	9	—
10	Y	10	8	9	—
11	N	10	—	9	—
12	N	10	—	—	—

As the pump time is three time periods, three pumps will be able to keep up with the demand even if the arrival rate is always one car per period, and there will never be a queue.

A great deal can be learnt about the effectiveness of a simulation from this simple example and you could continue experiments by varying the parameters themselves: for example, what is the effect of every third car requiring an extra time period at the pump?

```
 10 REM PETROL STATION SIMULATION.BKSIM2(BBC BASIC)
 20 CLEAR:DIM P1(101),P2(101),Q(101),RD(101):F=0:Q2=0:P1=0:P2=0:T=0:QC=0:N=0
:Q=0:C=0:R=0
 30 MODE 7:PRINT:PRINT:PRINT
 40 IF F=1 THEN FOR X=1 TO RT:Q(X)=0:P1(X)=0:P2(X)=0:NEXT X:GOTO 60
 50 PRINT:PRINT:INPUT"WHAT IS THE PERIOD TO BE SIMULATED ? "RT
 60 PRINT:INPUT"HOW LONG IS EACH CAR ON A PUMP ? "CT
 70 IF F=1 THEN 100
 80 FOR Z=1 TO RT:RD(Z)=RND(2):NEXT Z
 90 IF F<>1 THEN 110
100 T=0:P1=0:P2=0:Q=0:N=0:C=0:R=0:QC=0:Q2=0
110 CLS:PRINT:PRINT
120 PRINT;"TIME        CAR       PUMPS        QUEUE"
130 PRINT;"PERIOD    OR NOT     A    B "
140 PRINT"---------------------------------"
150 T=T+1:IF P1(T)=0 THEN P1=0
160 IF P2(T)=0 THEN P2=0
170 IF QC=0 THEN 250
180 IF P1<>0 THEN 210
190 FOR X=T TO CT+T-1:P1(X)=Q(1):NEXT X
200 P1=1:GOSUB 490
210 IF QC=0 THEN 250
220 IF P2<>0 THEN 250
230 FOR X=T TO CT+T-1:P2(X)=Q(1):NEXT X
240 P2=1:GOSUB 490
250 REM ***
260 IF RD(T)=1 THEN 370
270 N=N+1:C=C+1
280 IF P1<>0 THEN 310
290 FOR X=T TO CT+T-1:P1(X)=N:NEXT X
300 P1=1:GOTO 370
310 IF P2<>0 THEN 340
320 FOR X=T TO CT+T-1:P2(X)=N:NEXT X
330 P2=1:GOTO 370
340 REM *** ADD 1 TO QUEUE ***
350 QC=QC+1:Q(QC)=N
360 IF QC<Q2 THEN 370 ELSE Q2=QC
370 IF RD(T)=1 THEN A$="NO CAR" ELSE A$="CAR"
380 PRINT;T;TAB(9)A$;TAB(18)P1(T);TAB(22)P2(T);TAB(27);
390 FOR X=1 TO QC:PRINT;Q(X);" ";:NEXT X
400 PRINT
410 IF T<>RT THEN 150
420 PRINT:PRINT:PRINT"NUMBER OF CARS IN ";RT;" PERIODS WAS ";C
430 PRINT:PRINT:PRINT"MAX.QUEUE LENGTH WAS ";Q2;" CARS"
440 PRINT:INPUT"Do you wish to use this simulation again? (Y/N) "A$
450 IF A$="N" THEN END ELSE 460
460 CLS:PRINT: PRINT:INPUT"Do you wish to use the same data as the previous
 simulation? (Y/N) "B$
470 IF B$="Y" THEN 480 ELSE 10
480 F=1:GOTO 40
490 REM *** MOVE UP THE QUEUE ***
500 FOR X=1 TO QC:Q(X)=Q(X+1):NEXT X
510 QC=QC-1
520 RETURN

RUN
```

Fig. 10.7(a) Petrol pump simulation program

Now let us look at a computer simulation of this situation where the coin tossing is simulated by a random number generator, and the petrol pumps and the queue by arrays. A program for this simulation is shown in Fig. 10.7 and following the program, there are three runs, showing the effect of increasing the time on the pump from three to five periods.

The technique outlined above could be described as 'simple simulation.' It is based on the occurence or non-occurence of an event within a fixed time period and takes no account of the probability distribution of the occurence of the event. This technique is beyond the scope of this book.

With the technique above, many 'situations' can be simulated: for example, the school dining-room (ideally, not practically!), bus queues, a supermarket checkout. The technique can provide a stimulating experience and the basis for a good coursework project.

```
WHAT IS THE PERIOD TO BE SIMULATED ? 15

HOW LONG IS EACH CAR ON A PUMP ? 3

TIME       CAR        PUMPS       QUEUE
PERIOD     OR NOT     A    B
----------------------------------------
1          NO CAR     0    0       0
2          NO CAR     0    0       0
3          NO CAR     0    0       0
4          NO CAR     0    0       0
5          CAR        1    0       0
6          CAR        1    2       0
7          CAR        1    2       3
8          NO CAR     3    2       0
9          CAR        3    4       0
10         NO CAR     3    4       0
11         NO CAR     0    4       0
12         CAR        5    0       0
13         CAR        5    6       0
14         CAR        5    6       7
15         CAR        7    6       8


NUMBER OF CARS IN 15 PERIODS WAS 8

MAX.QUEUE LENGTH WAS 1 CARS

Do you wish to use this simulation again? (Y/N) Y

Do you wish to use the same data as the previous    simulation? (Y/N) Y

HOW LONG IS EACH CAR ON A PUMP ? 4

TIME       CAR        PUMPS       QUEUE
PERIOD     OR NOT     A    B
----------------------------------------
1          NO CAR     0    0       0
2          NO CAR     0    0       0
3          NO CAR     0    0       0
4          NO CAR     0    0       0
5          CAR        1    0       0
6          CAR        1    2       0
7          CAR        1    2       3
8          NO CAR     1    2       3
9          CAR        3    2       4
10         NO CAR     3    4       0
11         NO CAR     3    4       0
12         CAR        3    4       5
13         CAR        5    4       6
14         CAR        5    6       7
15         CAR        5    6       7 8
```

Fig. 10.7(b) Output of simulation program

(*continued*)

Fig. 10.7(b) Continued

```
        NUMBER OF CARS IN 15 PERIODS WAS 8
        MAX.QUEUE LENGTH WAS 2 CARS

        Do you wish to use this simulation again? (Y/N) Y
        Do you wish to use the same data as the previous    simulation? (Y/N) Y

        HOW LONG IS EACH CAR ON A PUMP ? 5


        TIME        CAR         PUMPS          QUEUE
        PERIOD      OR NOT      A     B
        --------------------------------------------
        1           NO CAR      0     0        0
        2           NO CAR      0     0        0
        3           NO CAR      0     0        0
        4           NO CAR      0     0        0
        5           CAR         1     0        0
        6           CAR         1     2        0
        7           CAR         1     2        3
        8           NO CAR      1     2        3
        9           CAR         1     2        3 4
        10          NO CAR      3     2        4
        11          NO CAR      3     4        0
        12          CAR         3     4        5
        13          CAR         3     4        5 6
        14          CAR         3     4        5 6 7
        15          CAR         5     4        6 7 8


        NUMBER OF CARS IN 15 PERIODS WAS 8

        MAX.QUEUE LENGTH WAS 3 CARS

        Do you wish to use this simulation again? (Y/N) N
```

Exercises 10.1

1 Using the above distribution of one car per period for the first 10 periods, find the effect of increasing the cycle time to four periods. Do you think a third pump is necessary under these circumstances?

What would be the effect if cars continued to arrive in bunches, i.e. 1 per time period for the first 10 periods then none for the next, and so on? Clearly, this odd distribution presents problems, but it can happen in the early morning, as people travel to work, or on their way home at night.

2 Repeat the first simulation (two pumps and a three period cycle) using your own data obtained by tossing a coin. Compare all the results obtained. If enough people take part, at least some of the results should show roughly similar queuing patterns.

3 Modify the program to allow for varying the number of pumps used.

10.4 Iteration

Iteration is the process of repeatedly performing a sequence of operations until a specified condition or result is obtained. This process is best illustrated with an example: If we wish to find the square root of any number, B, we can make a guess at it; call this guess x. To find how close we are to being correct we must square x and compare the result with B.

If x^2 is greater than B then we choose a new value of x, less than the previous one, and square it. This will again give a value either greater than, less than or equal to B and by continuing this process we should obtain successive values for x which are becoming closer and closer to $\sqrt{B}$.

If B has a finite root, we can obtain it by this method, although it may take a large number of guesses before the accurate result is obtained, but if B does not have a finite root, we could continue this process all our lives and still not obtain an absolute answer. In this case, we must be content with an approximation and when we are satisfied with the accuracy of this approximation, we stop the process.

This process can be shown to be given by the iteration formula:

$$x_{n+1} = \tfrac{1}{2}(x_n + B/x_n)$$

Where x_{n+1} is the most recent approximation to $\sqrt{B}$ and x_n the previous approximation. The table below shows the calculation of $\sqrt{18}$ by this method.

$B = 18$; $x_0 = 4$ (first guess at root)

N	x_n	B/x_n	$(x_n + B/x_n)$	x_{n+1}
0	4	4.5	8.5	4.25
1	4.25	4.235	8.485	4.2426
2	4.2426	2.2426	8.4852	4.2426

There is no point in continuing the process any further as the result will always be 4.2426. This is $\sqrt{18}$ *correct* to four decimal places and it required three iterations to obtain the answer. The number of iterations needed depends on the required accuracy of the answer and how good the initial 'guess' is.

Example: Find $\sqrt{97}$ correct to seven decimal places.

$B = 97$; $x_0 = 10$

N	x_n	B/x_n	$(x_n + B/x_n)$	x_{n+1}
0	10	9.7	19.7	9.83
1	9.83	9.86775	19.69775	9.84887589
2	9.84887589	9.848839713	19.6977156	9.8488578
3	9.8488578	9.848857803	19.6977156	9.8488578

There is no difference between the last two values of the root so the process stops.

It is worth noting that if the starting guess had been 8, it would have required only one more iteration to obtain the root as above. Calculation of square roots by this method is particularly suited to computational techniques as it doesn't take much longer in human terms of time, for a program to loop 100 times than only three times and computers *always* get the arithmetic correct, as well!

A program to calculate the square root of any number to a chosen degree of accuracy is shown in Fig. 10.8.

An iterative process can also be used to solve equations such as $x^3 - 6x + 1 = 0$ by rearranging the equation as:

$$x = \frac{1 + x^3}{6}$$

```
 10 REM SQUARE ROOTS.BKROOT(BBC BASIC)
 20 MODE 7:PRINT:PRINT:PRINT
 30 PRINT"THIS PROGRAM WILL FIND THE SQUARE ROOT  OF ANY POSITIVE NUMBER.":PRINT
 40 PRINT"TO STOP THE PROGRAM,   INPUT A NEGATIVE NUMBER":PRINT
 50 CLEAR:INPUT"WHAT NUMBER DO YOU WANT THE SQUARE ROOT OF ?"B:PRINT
 60 IF B<1 THEN 130
 70 INPUT"WHAT IS YOUR INITIAL GUESS ?"X:PRINT
 80 C=C+1:X1=.5*(X+B/X)
 90 PRINT"APPROXIMATION ";C" IS "X1
 100 IF ABS(X-X1)<.0001 THEN 110 ELSE X=X1:GOTO 80
 110 PRINT:PRINT"THE SQUARE ROOT OF ";B" IS "X1:PRINT
 120 GOTO 50
 130 PRINT"BYE!"
```

(a)

```
RUN


THIS PROGRAM WILL FIND THE SQUARE ROOT
OF ANY POSITIVE NUMBER.

TO STOP THE PROGRAM,   INPUT A NEGATIVE
NUMBER

WHAT NUMBER DO YOU WANT THE SQUARE ROOT
OF ?20

WHAT IS YOUR INITIAL GUESS ?5

APPROXIMATION 1 IS 4.5
APPROXIMATION 2 IS 4.47222222
APPROXIMATION 3 IS 4.47213596

THE SQUARE ROOT OF 20 IS 4.47213596

WHAT NUMBER DO YOU WANT THE SQUARE ROOT
OF ?79

WHAT IS YOUR INITIAL GUESS ?8

APPROXIMATION 1 IS 8.9375
APPROXIMATION 2 IS 8.88833042
APPROXIMATION 3 IS 8.88819442
APPROXIMATION 4 IS 8.88819442

THE SQUARE ROOT OF 79 IS 8.88819442
```

(b)

Fig. 10.8 Calculation of the square root of any number (a) Program   (b) Output from run

This is usually written as

$$x_{n+1} = \frac{1 + x_n^3}{6}$$

for solution by iteration, where x_{n+1} is the most recent approximation and x_n the previous one. It is left to the mathematically inclined reader to solve this by iteration, (let $x_n = 0$ for the first guess at the solution), and to ponder over the fact that both the following rearrangements of the original formula must produce further values for x (roots):

$$x = (6x - 1)^{1/3}$$

$$x = \frac{(6x - 1)^{1/2}}{x}$$

The three values of x obtained are, in fact, the three solutions of a cubic equation.

A program for the solution of polynomials is given in Fig. 10.9.

The use of iteration is by no means limited to the solution of equations or finding square roots. A program to land a spaceship on the moon uses iteration to 'test' the height of the spaceship above the surface. When this equals zero, the iterations stop and, depending on the speed of impact, a landing, or a crater, will have been achieved!

```
 10 REM ITERATION PROGRAM.BKITER(BBC BASIC)
 20 DIM A(10),N(10)
 30 MODE 7:B=1:F1=0:PRINT:PRINT
 40 PRINT:INPUT"HIGHEST POWER OF X ",N
 50 PRINT:PRINT"INPUT COEFFICIENT OF X^";N;" ";
 60 INPUT A(B):N(B)=N
 70 IF N=1 THEN X1=A(B)
 80 N=N-1:B=B+1
 90 IF N>-1 THEN 50
100 C=B:B=1
110 PRINT"****************************"
120 PRINT
130 IF A(B)=0 THEN 190
140 IF A(B)=1 AND N(B)=1 THEN PRINT;"X";:GOTO 180
150 IF N(B)=1 THEN PRINT; A(B) ;"X";:GOTO 180
160 IF A(B)=1 THEN PRINT;"X^";N(B);:GOTO 180
170 PRINT; A(B);"X^";N(B);
180 IF A(B+1)>0 THEN PRINT; " + ";
190 IF B<>C THEN B=B+1:GOTO 130
200 B=1:IF F1=1 THEN 250
210 FOR X=1 TO C:A(X)=A(X)/(-X1)
220 IF N(X)=1 THEN A(X)=0
230 NEXT X
240 F1=1:PRINT:PRINT:PRINT; "X=";:GOTO 130
250 PRINT:PRINT:INPUT"HOW MANY DECIMAL PLACES OF ACCURACY ",DP
260 IF DP<1 OR DP>6 THEN PRINT"BETWEEN 1 AND 7":GOTO 250
270 DP=INT(DP)
280 PRINT:INPUT"STARTING VALUE ",X
290 CLS:PRINT:PRINT
300 B=1:P=X:Y=0
310 U=A(B)*X^(N(B)):Y=Y+U:IF B<>C THEN B=B+1:GOTO 310 ELSE X=((INT((Y*10^DP)+.5))/10^DP):PRINTX:T=T+1
320 ON ERROR PRINT "DIVERGING.TRY ANOTHER STARTING VALUE":T=0:PRINT:PRINT:GOTO 280
330 IF INT(P*10^DP)-INT(X*10^DP)<>0 THEN 300
340 PRINT:PRINT"THE SOLUTION IS ";(INT((P*10^DP)+.5)/10^DP)
350 IF T-1=1 THEN A$=" ITERATION" ELSE A$=" ITERATIONS"
360 PRINT:PRINT:PRINT"IT TOOK ";T-1;A$
370 PRINT:PRINT
380 INPUT"DO YOU WANT ANOTHER ITERATION (Y/N) ",E$
390 IF E$="N" THEN END
400 PRINT:PRINT:INPUT"USING THE SAME EQUATION (Y/N) ",E$
410 IF E$="Y" THEN 430 ELSE 420
420 CLS:S=0:P=0:X=0:T=0:GOTO 30
430 CLS:S=0:P=0:X=0:T=0:GOTO 250
```

Fig. 10.9 Solution of polynomials
(*a*) Program

(*Continued*)

```
RUN
HIGHEST POWER OF X ?3

INPUT COEFFICIENT OF X^3 ?1

INPUT COEFFICIENT OF X^2 ?3

INPUT COEFFICIENT OF X^1 ?-4

INPUT COEFFICIENT OF X^0 ?-12
******************************

X^3 + 3X^2-4X-12X^0

X=0.25X^3 + 0.75X^2-3X^0

HOW MANY DECIMAL PLACES OF ACCURACY ?3

STARTING VALUE ?0
        -3
        -3

THE SOLUTION IS -3
IT TOOK 1 ITERATION
DO YOU WANT ANOTHER ITERATION (Y/N) ?Y
USING THE SAME EQUATION (Y/N) ?Y


HOW MANY DECIMAL PLACES OF ACCURACY ?3

STARTING VALUE ?-1
     -2.5
    -2.219
    -2.039
    -2.001
       -2
       -2

THE SOLUTION IS -2
IT TOOK 5 ITERATIONS
DO YOU WANT ANOTHER ITERATION (Y/N) ?Y
USING THE SAME EQUATION (Y/N) ?Y


HOW MANY DECIMAL PLACES OF ACCURACY ?3

STARTING VALUE ?3
     10.5
   369.094
DIVERGING.TRY ANOTHER STARTING VALUE
STARTING VALUE ?1.8
    0.888
   -2.234
   -2.044
   -2.001
      -2
      -2

THE SOLUTION IS -2
IT TOOK 5 ITERATIONS
DO YOU WANT ANOTHER ITERATION (Y/N) ?N
```

Fig. 10.9 Solution of polynomials (*Continued*)   (*b*) Output from run

The programs that conclude this chapter have been included to show various practical programming techniques.

Fig. 10.10 shows a dice throwing simulation with an option to print a bar chart displaying the number of occurrences of each number on the dice. Features of this program are the 'maximum number seive' in lines 280-330 and the scaling in line 350 to ensure that the bar chart always fits on to the screen irrespective of the number of throws.

```
 10 REM DICE THROWING PROGRAM WITH HISTOGRAM PLOTTING.BKDICE(BBC BASIC)
 20 MODE 7:A=0:B=0:C=0:D=0:E=0:F=0:G=0
 30 PRINT:"THIS PROGRAM SIMULATES THE TOSSING OF A SINGLE DICE AND COUNTS THE NUMBER OF    OCCURENCES OF EACH NUMBER."
 40 PRINT"YOU HAVE A CHOICE OF DISPLAYING THE RESULTS AS TOTALS OR AS A BAR CHART."
 50 INPUT"DO YOU WANT A BAR CHART?-Y/N "A$
 60 PRINT:PRINT:INPUT"HOW MANY THROWS?   "X
 70 IF A$="Y" OR A$="y" THEN G=1
 80 IF X>2000 THEN PRINT:PRINT"IVE BETTER THINGS TO DO!!!!":GOTO 60
 90 PRINT:PRINT"PLEASE WAIT....."
100 PRINT"..WHILE I THROW THE DICE ";X;" TIMES..."
110 FOR Z=1 TO X
120 Q=RND(6)
130 REM COUNTERS FOR EACH THROW OF THE DICE.
140 ON Q GOTO 150,160,170,180,190,200
150 A=A+1:GOTO 210
160 B=B+1:GOTO 210
170 C=C+1:GOTO 210
180 D=D+1:GOTO 210
190 E=E+1:GOTO 210
200 F=F+1
210 NEXT Z
220 IF G=1 THEN 290
230 PRINT:PRINT
240 PRINT"NO.OF 1s= ";A,"NO.OF 4s= ";D:PRINT
250 PRINT"NO.OF 2s= ";B,"NO.OF 5s= ";E:PRINT
260 PRINT"NO.OF 3s= ";C,"NO.OF 6s= ";F:PRINT
270 IF G<>1 THEN END
280 REM TESTS TO FIND GREATEST RESULT-NUMBER OCCURING MOST IS ASSIGNED TO H.
290 H=A:IF H>B THEN 300 ELSE H=B
300 IF H>C THEN 310 ELSE H=C
310 IF H>D THEN 320 ELSE H=D
320 IF H>E THEN 330 ELSE H=E
330 IF H>F THEN 340 ELSE H=F
340 REM SCALING TO ENSURE HISTOGRAM ALWAYS FITS ON SCREEN.
350 S=INT(700/H)
360 MODE 1
370 REM PLOT AXES
380 MOVE 150,300:DRAW 150,1000
390 MOVE 150,300:DRAW 1100,300
400 DRAW 1100,300
410 REM PLOTTING ROUTINES-EACH BAR IS PLOTTED AS TWO TRIANGLES.
420 GCOL 0,1:MOVE 150,300:MOVE 300,300
430 PLOT 85,150,A*S+300:PLOT 85,300,A*S+300
440 GCOL 0,2:MOVE 300,300:MOVE 450,300
450 PLOT 85,300,B*S+300:PLOT 85,450,B*S+300
460 GCOL 0,3:MOVE 450,300:MOVE 600,300
470 PLOT 85,450,C*S+300:PLOT 85,600,C*S+300
480 GCOL 0,1:MOVE 600,300:MOVE 750,300
490 PLOT 85,600,D*S+300:PLOT 85,750,D*S+300
500 GCOL 0,2:MOVE 750,300:MOVE 900,300
510 PLOT 85,750,E*S+300:PLOT 85,900,E*S+300
520 GCOL 0,3:MOVE 900,300:MOVE 1050,300
530 PLOT 85,900,F*S+300:PLOT 85,1050,F*S+300
540 PRINT TAB(5,24);A,TAB(10,24);B,TAB(15,24);C,TAB(20,24);D,TAB(25,24);E,TAB(30,24);F
```

Fig. 10.10 Dice throwing simulation

Exercise 10.2

Add to the program in Fig. 10.10 to display a suitable vertical axis scale for any number of throws.

```
 10 REM LECTURE HEADER PROGRAM. BKDEMO (BBC BASIC)
 20 DELAY=28:TIMES=0:CC=1
 30 MODE 6:READ M$
 40 VDU19,1,CC,0,0,0
 50 VDU 23,1,0;0;0;0;
 60 TIMES =1
 70 PRINT TAB(2,10);M$
 80 L=1:R=39:Y=1:REM SETS PARAMETERS FOR TOP LINE OF ANIMATED DISPLAY.
 90 FOR X=L TO R
100 VDU 23,255,24,60,126,219,126,36,66,129
110 PRINT TAB(X,Y);CHR$(255):REM PRINTS CHAR DEFINED ABOVE AT THE TAB POSITION
120 PRINT TAB(X-1,Y);CHR$(32):REM BLACKS OUT THE PREVIOUS SQUARE.
130 FOR D=1 TO DELAY:NEXT:REM SETS SPEED OF ANIMATION.
140 NEXT
150 T=1:B=20:X=39:REM PARAMETERS FOR R.H.VERTICAL LINE.
160 FOR Y=T TO B
170 PRINT TAB(X,Y);CHR$(255)
180 PRINT TAB(X,Y-1);CHR$(32)
190 FOR D=1 TO DELAY:NEXT
200 NEXT
210 L=1:R=39:Y=20:REM PARAMETERS FOR BOTTOM LINE.
220 FOR X=R TO L STEP -1
230 PRINT TAB(X,Y);CHR$(255)
240 PRINT TAB(X+1,Y);CHR$(32)
250 FOR D=1 TO DELAY:NEXT
260 NEXT
270 B=20:T=1:X=1:REM PARAMETERS FOR L.H.VERTICAL LINE.
280 FOR Y=B TO T STEP -1
290 PRINT TAB(X,Y);CHR$(255)
300 PRINT TAB(X,Y+1);CHR$(32)
310 FOR D=1 TO DELAY:NEXT
320 NEXT
330 TIMES=TIMES+1:IF TIMES<>3 THEN 80:REM COUNTER FOR NUMBER OF FRAMES OF DISPLAY
340 CC=CC+1:IF CC=8 THEN CC=1
350 C=C+1:IF C<4 THEN 30:REM COUNTER TO RESET DATA DISPLAY
360 RESTORE:C=0
370 GOTO 30

 380 DATA GOOD EVENING,WELCOME TO THE COURSE,TONIGHT IS BASIC 1 - INPUT & OUTPUT..,..AND DEMONSTRATION PROGRAMS
```

Fig. 10.11 Low resolution graphics program

Fig. 10.11 shows another low resolution graphics program to display messages on the screen while an 'animated border', made from a character defined in line 100, is displayed round the edge of the screen. Line 70 is the text-plotting line, and lines 150–320 plot the 'border'.

Fig. 10.12 shows a high resolution graphics program to plot the sine, cosine and tangent curves from 0 to 360. Line 200 is required to 'catch' the tangent curve as it heads to and from infinity.

```
 10 REM HIGH RES.GRAPHICS PROG.BKSCTN(BBC BASIC)
 20 MODE 0:VDU23,1,0;0;0;0;
 30 MOVE 0,0:DRAW 0,1023:MOVE 0,500:DRAW 1279,500:MOVE 0,500
 40 PRINT TAB(0,3);"+1"
 50 PRINT TAB(0,28);"-1"
 60 PRINT TAB(18,16);"90"
 70 PRINT TAB(37,16);"180"
 80 PRINT TAB(57,16);"270"
 90 PRINT TAB(76,16);"360"
100 FOR D=0 TO 360   STEP 10:DRAW D*3.5,500+SIN(RAD(D))*400:NEXT
110 PRINT TAB(28,5);"SIN X"
120 Q=INKEY(500)
130 MOVE 0,500
140 FOR D=0 TO 360 STEP 10:DRAW D*3.5,500+COS(RAD(D))*400:NEXT
150 PRINT TAB(20,24);"COS X"
160 Q=INKEY(500)
170 MOVE 0,500
180 FOR D=0 TO 360   STEP 10
190 E=500+TAN(RAD(D))*400
200 IF E>1000 OR E<-1000 THEN 250
210 DRAW D*3.5,E
220 NEXT
230 PRINT TAB(50,4);"TAN X"
240 VDU30:END
250 MOVE 0,0:GOTO 220
```

Fig. 10.12 High resolution graphics program

Exercises 10.3

1 Add to the program in Fig. 10.12 to display the *x* axis values every 90°.
2 Modify the program to draw the same graphs for $x = 0$ to $720°$.

Fig. 10.13 shows a data processing program to input data items from the keyboard and after verification, sorts the data 0–999 ... or A → Z, then prints it as a single field record, to a named file. Input is from lines 30–130: verification from lines 150–240; sorting from lines 250–280; print to file at line 310, and output routines from lines 320–350.

Exercise 10.4

As the program in Fig. 10.13 is written, each record has a single field. Alter the program to accept multi-field records.

Fig. 10.14 shows a program that produces ranked exam or test results from marks, input to the program as data, which are matched with student names held on files. The details relating to the exam are input from the keyboard following a series of prompts. The various sections of the program are explained briefly, in REM statements preceeding the section but two programming features require further explanation.

The marks are input to the data lines in the same order as the students' names are stored in the file. The sort, into rank order, is done using the marks as the key (i.e. highest mark first). At output, the program is required to attach the correct name to each mark. This is achieved by adding a 'tail' to the % mark in line 300. The 'tail' consists of the *position* of the mark in the data (corresponding to the name of the student obtaining that mark, in the names file), divided by 100. For example, if the seventh person obtained 59%, the actual mark assigned to list B is 59.007. This 'mark' is decoded in line 630 by subtracting the integer value of the number (59) from the actual number (giving 0.007) and multiplying this by 100 to give the original number 7. (The addition of 0.1 is necessary to ensure that the number is rounded up to a whole number). This number is assigned to P and used as the subscript to the list A$ to identify the student's name.

As written, the program can deal with up to 120 students in a maximum of four class groups. When dealing with over 60 marks, the exchange sort in lines 340–410 is slow (120 marks require $1\frac{1}{2}$ min to sort), and this routine could be replaced by a faster sorting technique.

```
 10 REM BKSORT.FOR SERIAL DISK FILES.(BBC BASIC)
 20 MODE7:PRINT:PRINT:PRINT:F=0
 30 PRINT"This program accepts alphanumeric data from the keyboard & sorts it A-Z or 0-9 then prints it to the named file"
 40 PRINT:PRINT"When the sorted data has been printed to the file,it will be shown on the screen& a hard copy option offered."
 50 PRINT:PRINT:PRINT "Press space bar to continue":PRINT:IF GET<>32 THEN 50
 60 CLS:PRINT:PRINT
 70 DIMX$(200),B$(200)
 80 INPUT"What is the name of the file to be used ?"F$:PRINT
 90 PRINT"Now  type in one data item after the prompt,then RETURN, & continue until allthe data has been input then finish with XXX"
100 PRINT:PRINT
110 INPUT"NEXT ITEM ?"B$
120 IF B$="XXX" THEN 140
130 PRINT:C=C+1:X$(C)=B$:GOTO 110
140 CLS:PRINT:PRINT
150 PRINT"You now have an opportunity to check & amend any item of data.":PRINT"After the item is displayed, check and type Y if OK."
160 PRINT"If you wish to alter the data type N, then,after the prompt, retype the item correctly.":PRINT:PRINT
170 FOR Q=1 TO C:PRINT"DATA ITEM ";Q;" IS "X$(Q) ;
180 PRINT " : Please check-OK ? ":X=X+1:PRINT
190 IF GET<>89 THEN 200 ELSE 230
200 INPUT"Please input the correct version "C$:PRINT:PRINT
210 IF C$=X$(Q) THEN PRINT "You haven't changed anything! Is that correct? ":GOTO 180
220 X$(Q)=C$:PRINT"Data to be filed is "X$(Q):PRINT:GOTO 180
230 NEXT Q:CLS:PRINT:PRINT
240 PRINT"All data items have now been checked and will be sorted and written to the file  "F$
250 FOR J=1 TO C-1:FOR K=J+1 TO C
260 IF X$(J) <= X$(K) THEN 280
270 T$=X$(J):X$(J)=X$(K):X$(K)=T$
280 NEXT K:NEXT J
290 PRINT:PRINT:PRINT
300 X=OPENOUT(F$)
310 FOR Z=1 TO C:PRINT#X,X$(Z):NEXT Z:CLOSE#X
320 PRINT:PRINT:PRINT "Do you want a hard copy of the file(Y/N)? ":IF GET<>89 THEN 330 ELSE VDU2
330 PRINT:PRINT:PRINT"FILE "F$" NOW CONTAINS THE FOLLOWING RECORDS:-":PRINT
340 FOR Z=1 TO C:PRINT X$(Z):NEXT Z
350 PRINT:PRINT:PRINT"FILE "F$" CONTAINS ";C;" RECORDS"
360 VDU3
```

Fig. 10.13 Sorting and printing data to a file

```
 10 REM BKRANK. FOR SERIAL DISK FILES.(BBC BASIC)
 20 MODE7:PRINT:PRINT
 30 PRINT"The input to this program is a set of exam marks from DATA lines."
 40 PRINT"The program calls for files of names to match the marks."
 50 PRINT"The output is a list of names and percentages ranked in descending order."
 60 PRINT"The program will accept up to 4 files with a maximum of 120 names."
 70 PRINT:PRINT "Enter the marks for each class on lines 770,800,810,820 as follows:-"
 80 PRINT"   770 DATA 45,57,73,80,..........(one set of marks per data line)"
 90 PRINT"Any absentees must be given the mark -1.This will be interpreted as absent in   the ranked order"
100 PRINT:PRINT "When this input is complete, delete line 110 then RUN the program again"
110 STOP
120 DIM A$(120),B(120):CLS:PRINT:PRINT
130 Q1=0
140 REM ***************INPUT
150 INPUT"How many files are to be included? "QQ
160 PRINT:PRINT "What are the names of the files ? (YOU MUST INPUT 4 NAMES EVEN IF SOME ARE DUMMY eg:5A1MATHS,5A2MATHS,N,M)"
170 INPUT F1$,F2$,F3$,F4$
180 PRINT:INPUT "How many names in each file? (IN THE SAME ORDER AS THE FILE NAMES. YOU MUST INPUT 4 NUMBERS eg 27,30,0,0)"RR,SS,TT,UU
190 PRINT:INPUT"What is the max mark for this exam? "T
200 PRINT:INPUT"What title do you wish to be printed at the top of the ranked listing? "C$
210 PRINT:INPUT "Do you want a hard copy of the results? (Y/N) "I$: IF I$="Y" THEN Q1=1
220 REM Q1 is a flag which is set to 1 if a hard copy is required.
230 CC=RR+SS:CD=CC+TT:C=CD+UU:Q=C:Q2=C
240 REM RR,SS & TT are the number of records in each file to be used.
250 REM CC is the total if 2 files are used; CD is the total if 3 files are used & C if 4 are used
260 FOR I=1 TO C:READ R:IF R=-1 THEN C=C-1
270 REM If R=-1 then this person was absent and the total C must be reduced by 1 for subsequent calculations
280 REM ********** CALCULATION OF MEAN,VARIANCE & STD.DEV.
290 S=INT(R*100/T+.5)
300 S1=S1+S*S:B(I)=S+I/100:T1=T1+S
310 NEXT I
320 A1=T1/C:V1=(C*S1-T1*T1)/C/(C-1)
330 LET D=SQR(V1)
340 REM ********** SWOP ROUTINE
350 M=0
360 Q=Q-1:J=1
370 IF B(J)>B(J+1) THEN 390 ELSE Z=B(J)
380 B(J)=B(J+1):B(J+1)=Z:M=1
390 J=J+1
400 IF J <=Q THEN 370
410 IF M=1 THEN 350
420 PRINT:PRINT:PRINT:PRINT
```

Fig. 10.14 Ranked examination or test results

(*Continued*)

120 COMPUTER STUDIES

```
430 REM ********** OPEN the required files for reading and assign each name
    to the Nth element of array A$
440 REM ********** SELECTION OF FILES
450 W=OPENUP(F1$)
460 FOR N=1 TO RR:INPUT#W,B$:A$(N)=B$:NEXT N
470 IF QQ=1 THEN 560
480 X=OPENUP(F2$)
490 FOR N=RR+1 TO CC:INPUT#X,B$:A$(N)=B$:NEXT N
500 IF QQ=2 THEN 560
510 Y=OPENUP(F3$)
520 FOR N=CC+1 TO CD:INPUT#Y,B$:A$(N)=B$:NEXT N
530 IF QQ=3 THEN 560
540 Z=OPENUP(F4$)
550 FOR N=CD+1 TO Q2:INPUT#Z,B$:A$(N)=B$:NEXT N
560 CLOSE #0
570 REM ********** OUTPUT
580 CLS
590 IF Q1=1 THEN VDU2
600 PRINT C$:PRINT
610 PRINT"POS.";TAB(7)" NAME ";TAB(24);"%"
620 PRINT:FOR J=1 TO Q2
630 P=(B(J)-INT(B(J)))*100+.1
640 IF J=1 THEN 680
650 IF INT(B(J))>0 THEN 670
660 PRINT TAB(7);A$(P);TAB(23);"ABS":GOTO 710
670 IF INT(B(J))=INT(B(J-1)) THEN 700
680 PRINT; J;TAB(7);A$(P);TAB(23);INT(B(J))
690 GOTO 710
700 PRINT TAB(7);A$(P);TAB(23);INT(B(J))
710 NEXT J
720 PRINT:PRINT:PRINT
730 PRINT "MEAN MARK =";A1;"%"
740 PRINT
750 PRINT "STD.DEV.  =";D
760 VDU3
770 DATA 57,72,59,64,39,51,41,30,13,38,29,34,17,14,60,66,25,46,10
780 DATA 79,69,35,50,86,68,56,35,62,59,70,44,56,62,67,68,55,59,50,70,86,40,43
790 DATA -1,60,37,61,28,40,29,49,38,28,-1,27,40,56,42,42,49,60,38,16,43
800 DATA 35,11,20,47,-1,22,-1,14,25,47,35,18,-1,22,15,29,25,23,26,32
```

Fig. 10.14 Continued

Exercise 10.5

The number of names in each file used (in the program in Fig. 10.14) is required as input to this version of the program (line 150). Modify the program to use files in which the first field contains the number of records in the file (see Fig. 11.35).

Figs. 10.15 and 10.16 show programs that are slightly more mercenary in that they are designed to make money!

The program in Fig. 10.15 is basically a very simple program to try and guess, in five goes, a number below 50 selected by the computer. Line 110 produces a random number, less than 50 and stores it in X. Lines 150–170 compare this number with the player's guess, N, and output encouraging messages. The rest of the program 'clothes' the 'skeleton' program and turns it into a game that offers an even chance of winning to clever players.

Fig. 10.16 shows another use for the school computer. The random number generator in line 80 picks three lucky numbers from the number of subscribers, E. The second and third numbers drawn are compared with previously selected number(s) and rejected if they are the same, at line 100, to ensure that no number wins two prizes.

PROGRAMMING TECHNIQUES

```
   10 REM BKGESS.(BBC BASIC)
   20 MODE 7:PRINT:PRINT
   30 PRINT "Hello! My name is MICRO & I want to help to make some money for
SCHOOL FUND":PRINT
   40 PRINT "I'm going to think of a number between 1& 50 and I want you to try
and guess it."
   50 PRINT "You can have up to 5 guesses and after  each guess I will give you
a clue.":PRINT
   60 PRINT "It will cost you 10p per go and IF you win you can either have your
money back or another go.":PRINT
   70 PRINT "Of course,I am going to change my number between goes!!  So who is
going to play?"
   80 PRINT:INPUT"PLEASE TYPE YOUR NAME THEN PRESS RETURN "N$:PRINT
   90 CLS:PRINT:PRINT "Hello ";N$;",I've thought of a number.":PRINT
  100 PRINT "You must now type in your guess then    press RETURN":PRINT
  110 PRINT:PRINT:X=RND(50):C=0
  120 C=C+1
  130 IF C<5 THEN 140 ELSE 200
  140 PRINT "GUESS NUMBER ";C;" ";:INPUT N
  150 IF N>50 THEN PRINT "Don't be daft!! I said LESS than 50!!":GOTO 120
  160 IF N<X THEN PRINT "Your guess is too low,try again":GOTO 120
  170 IF N>X THEN PRINT "Your guess is too high,try again":GOTO 120
  180 PRINT "Well done ";N$;" !"
  190 PRINT "You have guessed my number in ";C;" goes":GOTO 230
  200 PRINT "LAST GO!!!....THINK!!!";:INPUT N
  210 IF N=X THEN 180 ELSE 220
  220 PRINT:PRINT "Sorry,you have had your 5 goes & you    did'nt guess my number
which was ";X:GOTO 250
  230 PRINT:PRINT "Do you want another go?  (or your money back?)  Type YES for
another go";
  240 INPUT A$:IF A$<>"YES" THEN 250 ELSE PRINT "Type in your number":CLS:PRINT:
PRINT:GOTO 110
  250 D=D+10
  260 PRINT "Thank you for playing. I have now collected ";D;"p for the SCHOOL
FUND.":PRINT
  270 PRINT "Anybody else want to play?":PRINT "PRESS SPACE BAR TO CONTINUE"
  280 IF GET=32 THEN 20
  290 END
```

Fig. 10.15 Guessing a number

```
   10 REM PRIZE DRAW.BKDRAW(BBC BASIC)
   20 MODE 7:PRINT:PRINT:PRINT:DIM W(3)
   30 PRINT "        KNUTSFORD COUNTY HIGH SCHOOL
":PRINT
   40 PRINT "           200 CLUB MONTHLY DRAW":
PRINT:PRINT:PRINT
   50 INPUT"WHAT MONTH IS IT? "M$:PRINT
   60 INPUT"HOW MANY ENTRANTS FOR THIS MONTHS
DRAW? "E
   70 FOR X=1 TO 3
   80 R=RND(E)
   90 W(X)=R:IF X=1 THEN 110
  100 IF W(X)=W(X-1) OR W(X)=W(X-2) THEN 80
  110 NEXT X
  120 PRINT:PRINT:PRINT
  130 FOR Z=1 TO 3
  140 PRINT"          WINNER NO. ";Z;" IS ";W(Z)
:PRINT
  150 NEXT Z
  160 PRINT:PRINT:PRINT
  170 PRINT"      END OF THIS MONTHS DRAW"
```

Fig. 10.16 Lucky number draw

> **Summary**
>
> - A binary search is particularly easy to implement on an index-sequential file and can be very time saving when you are searching through a very large file.
> - Sorting techniques are widely used in data processing. Many different 'sorts' have been devised; the exchange sort is the easiest to understand and use and is fast enough for sorting small files of data.
> - Many different 'real-life' situations can be simulated using simple techniques.
> - Many useful programming techniques do not require very advanced programming skills. They should be used wherever possible in your own work.

11 File handling

11.1 Introduction

We have seen, in the previous chapter, that a program needs data. This can be provided in one of three ways:
 (i) From within the program, e.g. in a BASIC program from data statements to be READ.
 (ii) As interactive input during the program run, e.g. in BASIC-INPUT
(iii) From files created previously and accessible by the program.

Each of these methods of data input has its advantages and disadvantages.

The first method is simple to use. The data is input once and the program can be run many times (using the same data). If the data needs to be changed, part of the *program* has to be rewritten.

With the second method, the data has to be input 'on-line' and to run the program a second time requires the data to be input again. The advantage of this method is that different data *can* be input each time the program is run.

You will probably have used both these methods of data input in your program writing and you will probably have realised that both are satisfactory methods—if the amount of data to be input is small.

Let us take the example of a payroll program and look at the effectiveness of each method of data input. Given that the program will do the necessary calculations based on the number of hours each employee works, the input need only consist of an employee number and hours worked (by that employee), to give an output of employee number and amount of pay. For a small number of employees, either method (i) or (ii) could be used equally effectively. As the employee number is fixed from week to week, method (i) would involve inputting this, and the hours worked, for each employee, once. If the number of employees and the hours they worked never changed, this method could be used for every pay calculation. Method (ii), however allows for any variations to be input at the time of processing. So changing the hours worked is easy with method (ii), but now the employee numbers also have to be input each time the

'You only use files in special circumstances.'

program is run. But for a small number of employees, this method could be used.

However, a payroll program which only used an employee number and hours worked is almost unthinkable and it is when we start adding more data items and increase the number of employees that both methods (i) and (ii) become slow and cumbersome and we have to look to a more efficient method of data input (and storage).

A real pay roll program is likely to contain the following data about each employee: name, employee number, works dept. number, tax code, National Insurance number, basic rate of pay, overtime rate of pay, bonus rate, contributions to: (*a*) holiday fund, (*b*) National Savings, (*c*) works club, (*d*) union fund.

All this data is fixed from week to week and can be stored so that it can be used, when required, for calculating the employees' pay with only one other item of data needed—the hours worked in that particular week. Such a store, containing permanent or semi-permanent data is called a *file*. In commercial data processing, the hours worked would also be put into a file and both files used in the program. The first file containing all the employee data, (called the master file), would be kept and the temporary one containing 'this week's hours worked' (called the transaction file), would be scrapped. Next week, a new temporary file (containing hours worked) would be created and run with the same master file. Of course, this master file will need to be changed from time to time as staff change or their 'permanent details' alter. This updating of a file is dealt with in Section 8 of this chapter.

11.2 What is a file?

'A file is an organised collection of related records'. Two important words in the above definition are 'related' and 'organised'.

All the data in any one file should be related: you could have files of employees in a factory; pupils in the fourth year; British butterflies; houses for sale, etc. It would be nonsense to make a single file which contained the names of fourth year pupils, the price of houses for sale, the eating habits of butterflies and the tax code of a factory's employees! Such a file would make no sense as it could not be used for any purpose.

Secondly, all the related data in a file should, ideally, be organised, i.e. put into some order. All alpha data should be filed in alphabetical order (usually A–Z), and numeric data in (usually) ascending number order. Obviously, some data is a mixture of both alpha and numeric data e.g. batsmen's names and runs scored. In such a case we must decide how the data is to be filed. If we choose name first followed by score, the file would be organised (or *ordered*), to contain an alphabetically sorted list of names with scores. If the scores are to come first, the data would be sorted and put into the file so that the highest score came first, followed by the name of the batsman, and so on down to the lowest score, plus batsman's name. The item of data on which the ordering of a file is based is known as the *key*.

Before we consider a computer file we shall create a simple manual file containing the name, address, telephone number, age, sex and form of a small group of pupils. For this, we need:

(i) *Data*.
(ii) Cards or paper on which we can *write* each data item.
(iii) Some sort of *file* or folder in which we can *store* the data.

Here is the data we will use to put into our file:

Mary Brown, 45 Townfields Knutsford, 0565 2468, 16, F, 5U

John Young, 3 Green Lane Northwich, No telephone, 16, M, 5S
Alan Green, 17 Town Lane Mobberley, MOB 1234, 15, M, 5V
Fiona Jones, 43 Tree Way Knutsford, 0565 74812, 16, F, 5U
John Bloggs, 339 Ashworth Park Knutsford, 0565 9999, 16, M, 5V
Roy Smith, 99 Manchester Rd. Knutsford, 0565 7887, 16, M, 5T
Ann White, 'The Cottage' Plumley Rd. Knutsford, No telephone, 16, F, 5T
Peter Evans, 1 The Talbots Mobberley, MOB 2345, 15, M, 5U

Each item of data is now written on a separate card so that the details can be read easily:

Brown Mary	16
45 Townfields	F
Knutsford	5U
0565 2468	

This set of data, relating to one person, is called a *record* and when we have written a record for each of the eight people and put them together in a box or folder, we have created a *file*. Each record card must be set out in the same way to ensure accuracy of reading when we need to use the file. Note that the surname is written before the christian name. This is common practice to enable a record to be found quickly as there is far less likelihood of surnames being the same than there is of finding two or more people with the same christian name.

If we now sort the cards alphabetically by surname so that Bloggs John is first and Young John is last, we have *ordered* the file so that we can quickly find the details from any record if we are given just the surname.

Clearly, most of the data relating to one person can, and, in some cases, will change. Age and form will change annually and address, telephone number and even name, could change at any time. Consider how you would do this for a manual system. Would you cross out and over-write, or write out a completely new card, or would it be possible to have the card pre-marked for age and form?

Once a file is created, there must be provision for modifying it by adding more records, deleting records or modifying existing records. This is called *updating*. We must also be able to use the data in the file by reading one or more records. This is called *accessing* the file. We may perhaps wish to access the file just to copy down the details, e.g. what is Ann White's address? Or we may wish to manipulate the data to answer a particular query. This is known as file *interrogation*. Examples of this are questions such as 'How many pupils are in 5T?'

or 'How many girls are in 5U?' In order to answer the first question we simply need to go through the file counting the number of records showing 5T. The second question can be answered only by checking two items of data on each card. First, is the pupil in 5U? There are three records which satisfy that interrogation but when we ask the second question we find that, of the three records picked out, only two of them are girls.

There are many possible ways in which we could interrogate this file, some of which would be 'nonsense', e.g. 'How many people live at MOB 2345?'

A useful 'feel' for computer file-handling can be obtained by creating a form file using similar data and interrogating the file in all possible ways. Pets, hobbies, sports etc. can all be added to make a more interesting file to read.

We have seen that a file consists of a number of records and that each record contains a number of separate items of data. These sub-divisions of a record are known as *fields*, and all the records in a file will have the *same number* of fields and the *n*th field in each record will store the *same type* of data. For example, if the first field of the first record holds the *name* of the pupil, then the first field of *every* record in the file must hold the *name* of a pupil. If the second field is the pupil's address, then the second field of *every* record will hold the appropriate address to match the name. If the pupil's form is the sixth field in the first record then the appropriate form must always be in the sixth field of each record. It cannot be in any other field of any record for reasons we will see later in the chapter.

Using the data mentioned in the introduction for the employee records, we can now build up a picture of what a computer file looks like (see Table below).

Note first that all 12 fields *must exist* for each record even if some contain nothing (zero), and secondly that a single field (in any record) is the smallest element of the file which can be handled by the program. In the example given above, it will not be possible except by further complex programming, to separate the christian name and surname of any employee because these two items of data are recorded in the same field. This is a very important point which you must remember when you are creating a file (Section 4).

11.3 Types of computer file

Four types of computer file are commonly used to store data:
(*a*) Serial
(*b*) Sequential
(*c*) Indexed sequential
(*d*) Random.

(a) Serial access

With a serial access file each record is printed to the file serially. As the data for the next record is input, it is printed to the file immediately following the previous record. There is no attempt to organise the records into alphabetical or numerical order. This is the simplest form of file to create but may not be the most efficient method in terms of access to the data, as the data to be read could be anywhere in the file. An example of such a file is given below:

```
Record 1:    SMITH PETER      4T  15
Record 2:    EVANS JUDITH     5K  16
Record 3:    GREEN JOHN       4K  15
Record 4:    COOPER JANE      4K  16
Record 5:    TAYLOR ERIC      5U  16
Record 6:    DEAN TIM         5T  16
```

The type of file is normally referred to by the method of access to the records. Thus the first type above is usually called a serial access file.

	Record 1	Record 2	Record 3	Record N
Field 1 (Name)	Brown John	Coates Roy	Dixon Alan	Young Albert
Field 2 (Works no.)	47835	16743	52444	87742
Field 3 (Dept. no.)	38	17	17	26
Field 4 (Tax code)	124H	103H	107H	205H
Field 5 (NI code)	3	3	5	7
Field 6 (Basic rate)	55	50	62	88
Field 7 (Overtime rate)	2.4	1.8	2.4	–
Field 8 (Bonus rate)	1.6	3.3	1.8	4.0
Field 9 (Holiday fund)	–	100	150	–
Field 10 (Nat. Savings)	200	50	–	–
Field 11 (Wks. club)	–	–	50	–
Field 12 (Union)	–	–	125	–

The three fields used in each record in this file are surname and Christian name; form; and age. We will create a similar student file with more records in Section 11.4.

A serial access file is often used to hold data for a short time and is referred to as a transaction file (see Section 11.9). Before the data in the file is used, it will almost certainly be organised to create a sequential access file.

(b) Sequential access

A much more useful version of a straightforward serial access file is an organised serial file where each record is sequenced in some order, hence the name sequential access file.

Using the example above, each record would be sorted on a particular, chosen, key and a new file created in which the records could be alphabetically sequenced on, for example, the surname. The surname is the key for the sort. (See Chapter 10.2 for sorting procedures.) The file would then appear as:

Record 1:	COOPER JANE	4K	16
Record 2:	DEAN TIM	5T	16
Record 3:	EVANS JUDITH	5K	16
Record 4:	GREEN JOHN	4K	15
Record 5:	SMITH PETER	4T	15
Record 6:	TAYLOR ERIC	5U	16

Both serial and sequential access files have one big disadvantage in that to find *any* record, all preceding records must be searched. As the records in a sequential access file are now in a predetermined order, access to any particular record can be much quicker than in a straight serial file as the data can be 'searched for' in an organised manner (see Chapter 10.1).

(c) Indexed sequential

An indexed sequential file is a form of sequential file where the first record of the file is an index which holds the address of each record in the file. In use, the address of a record is 'read' from the index and can then be accessed directly by 'reading' at the address given in the index. This type of file is widely used in commercial data processing because it can be accessed either sequentially or randomly.

The file above would now appear as:

Record 1:	INDEX		
Record 2:	COOPER JANE	4K	16
Record 3:	DEAN TIM	5T	16
Record 4:	EVANS JUDITH	5K	16
Record 5:	GREEN JOHN	4K	15
Record 6:	SMITH PETER	4T	15
Record 7:	TAYLOR ERIC	5U	16

(d) Random access (also called direct access)

In a random access file each record is written to the file in what appears to be a random manner. There is no obvious relationship between records (as with (b) and (c) above). The record key is used to generate an address where the record is to be stored (on magnetic disk—see below) and, therefore use of this same key will enable access to be made directly to the required record.

11.4 File storage media

Although all forms of backing store (see Chapter 7.3) can be used to store files, only magnetic tape and disk will be considered here.

(a) Magnetic tape

Magnetic tape is particularly suitable for storing serially organised files where each record is written to the tape immediately following the previous one. This means, of course, that the last record of a large file will be at the other end of a large reel of tape to the first record and subsequent access to the $(n+1)$th record can only be achieved by 'reading through' the length of tape holding the first n records (see p. 67).

An advantage of using magnetic tape to store files is that no storage is wasted: each record follows the previous one throughout the file. The time taken to get to any record depends first on its position on the tape and secondly the current position of the tape. Therefore it can take a long time (average of 2 min) to access any record on the tape, but a serially organised file should only be used for serial access: i.e. the next record to be read is the next record in the file.

An employee payroll file, (as in Section 11.2) is a good example of such a file. In use, each record will need to be read to obtain the data necessary to calculate the employee's salary, and, as each employee requires paying, a serially ordered file on magnetic tape is quite satisfactory for this purpose. All types of serial access file can be held on cassette tape and accessed satisfactorily but, as most microcomputers only control the tape recorder when it is running at read/write speed, i.e. very slowly, it can take a very long time to read all the records in a file.

(b) Magnetic disk

Disks can be used to store all four types of file, described in Section 11.3, but it is possible to read/write to any part of a disk at any time. A disk is particularly suitable for the storage of random access files.

When a serially organised file is created, the first record is written to the first available sector of the first available track (and on the first available disk on a multi-disk system). Successive records are written to the following sectors on the same track. When this track is full, writing continues (on the same numbered track) on the next disk surface until that also is full, when writing continues in a similar manner on the next disk surface, and so on until the file is completely written.

This method of writing produces a *cylinder* of data and has been created without moving the read/write heads (unless more than one cylinder is required to store all the file). This, of course, means that reading *any record* stored on a single cylinder can be achieved by selecting the correct read/write head and, at worst, waiting one revolution for the required sector to come round under the head. This takes less than 20 ms.

On a single disk system, the file is usually written on consecutive tracks but if the 'next track' already has data written on it, the disk operating system will move the head to the next available track and continue to write the file (on a number of different tracks if necessary). The desk operating system takes note of where each record is on the disk and it is therefore possible to access an individual record directly. Each record in a random access file is allocated its position on the disk(s) by using the record key to generate the address of the disk, track and block number to be used.

This can be a simple system like record 123 is written to disk 1, track 2, block 3 or it can be based on a mathematical formula known as a hashing algorithm. For example the record number could be divided by 7: $123 \div 7 = 17$, remainder 4. This could mean that record 123 would be stored on disk 4, track 17. The same 'formula' when applied to the required record key, gives the address to be accessed directly in order to read the record.

When a disk is being used for file storage, serially organised files can be accessed randomly by searching on a record number key which was allocated (by the program) to each record as it was printed to the file. A typical example of the use of a random access file stored on magnetic disk is a stock file used by a business for the control of stock (see Chapter 12). Any record on the file is equally likely to be accessed in any order and, if it is an online system, the record could then be updated or deleted as necessary.

Most microcomputers will support a floppy disk system and it is the version of BASIC, (or other high-level language being used), that determines the type of file access available. (At the time of writing, most microcomputers only support serial access files.)

In Sections 11.5–11.8 we are going to see how to create, access and update a *serial* file to be stored on a cassette tape or on a disk. The file has deliberately not been made into a sequential file to avoid the complication of sorting after deletion or addition of any record. The final program in this chapter uses a sequential file and the sorting routine can be found towards the end of the program.

11.5 Creating a file

We are going to create a typical school file using the same data as for the manual file in Section 11.2, and use it subsequently for interrogation, record addition or deletion and amendment. We will create the computer file with only eight records, although this would typically be 30 for one form.

We could put all the data for each record into one field, i.e. a one-field record, but we could not then isolate any particular item of data from all the others in the record. For example we could not find how many 15 year old boys there are in the fourth year unless the age and sex are put into separate fields. We will put our data into a six-field record with the christian name and surname occupying the same field. This means that we cannot easily separate christian names and surnames, e.g. we cannot find how many pupils in the file are named Alison. We must therefore think carefully of how the file is to be used before we actually create it. If we put each item of data into a separate field, some space may be wasted, but we will be able to use the file in the maximum number of different ways.

A file can normally be created in one of two ways: (*a*) by using a specially written program or (*b*) by using an editor. We are going to consider only the first method in this chapter.

The creation of the file is very simple and can best be shown in flowchart form (Fig. 11.1). When the file has been opened and named, it is empty. Each record is put

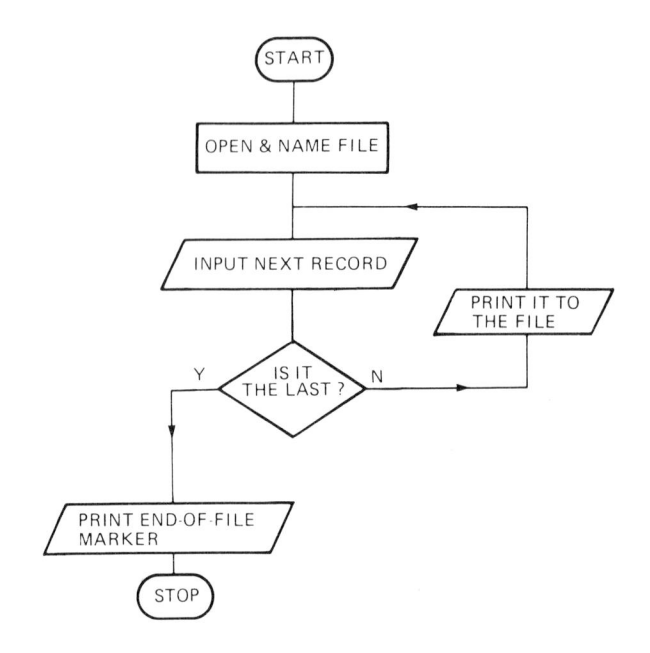

Fig. 11.1 Flowchart for the creation of a file

into the file sequentially and after the last record, an end-of-file marker is written to the file to close it. These records will stay in the file until they are erased or overwritten and can be used as often as needed by any program which calls for the file by name.

Let us now look at the process of programming from this flowchart. Unfortunately, the commands and statements used in file handling differ considerably between different versions of Basic. The syntax used in this chapter is for the BBC Micro, (tape or disk). Some of the main file handling programs written in RML BASIC, APPLE BASIC and PET BASIC are to be found in Appendix 5.

First, here is the data we wish to put in the file:—

Mary Brown, 45 Townfields Knutsford, 0565 2468, 16, F, 5U
John Young, 3 Green Lane Northwich, No telephone, 16, M, 5S
Alan Green, 17 Town Lane Mobberley, MOB 1234, 15, M, 5V
Fiona Jones, 43 Tree Way Knutsford, 0565 74812, 16, F, 5U
John Bloggs, 339 Ashworth Park Knutsford, 0565 9999, 16, M, 5V
Roy Smith, 99 Manchester Rd. Knutsford, 0565 7887, 16, M, 5T
Ann White, 'The Cottage' Plumley Rd. Knutsford, No telephone 16, F, 5T
Peter Evans, 1 The Talbots Mobberley, MOB 2345, 15, M, 5U

Notice that commas mark the end of each field and, therefore, they can only be used in the data if the field is enclosed in speech marks—see line 180 of Fig. 11.2. Note also that J. Young does not have a telephone number, but there must be a field with either zero in it, if it is a numeric field or '—' or 'none' if it is a string field.

Each line of data represents one record and each record has six fields, which are name, address, telephone number, sex, age and form. The data for each record has to be read into the program before it can be printed into the file. The 6 fields of record 1 are read into the 6 elements of the first line of the array N $, (N $ (Q, R) where Q = 1 and R varies between 1 and 6); record 2 is read into the second line of the array, ie Q = 2, and so on for all 8 records.

We now have to open a file and print the data to it. The command used to open a file, named "STUDENTS", for writing is: X = OPENOUT (F $) where X is the channel number and F $ is the name to be given to the file. The # sign is used to represent 'the file' so the command PRINT#X means 'Print to the file allocated previously to channel X'. See lines 40 and 80 of Fig. 11.2.

The program must then read the next record and print that to the file and continue until all records have been printed to the file. Following the last record, an end-of-file marker is printed to the file (CLOSE#X), and the file creation process is complete. Note that the end-of-file marker is generated by the system software. We do not need to know what it is; we cannot read it or print it out; it is a feature which we cannot miss out of our file, but its generation is done for us.

The complete program to create a file containing the above data is shown in Fig. 11.2. Note the inclusion of the counter C. This counts the number of records printed to the file and can be very useful in subsequent checking and processing.

Fig. 11.2 also shows the result of running the program. The output tells us that the file has been written and how many records it contains, but it does not print out the actual contents of the file. In order to find out what is in the file we must now read the file.

11.6 Reading the file

We need to read the file first to see if it really does contain the data we put into it and then on any subsequent occasion when we want to know something about the pupils. We need a further program in order to read the file and before writing the program we will see the necessary steps by using another flowchart.

The flowchart in Fig. 11.3 is very similar to that used for writing the file and, just as we input *all* the fields for one record, we must now read *all* the fields for each record, one record at a time. It is not possible to read only part of a record. This is a fundamental concept of reading from a file; we have to read the *whole* record, but, having read the whole record, we can then print out, or use in some other way, the field(s) in which we are interested.

As a record is read, each field is assigned to a separate variable and held until the next record is read. As we want to check the file to see if it contains all the data put into it, the program must print out all the fields, as shown in Fig. 11.4.

Note again, the inclusion of the counter, C. This time the counter totals the number of records in the file which should, of course, agree with the number put in. When the logical end-of-file marker is found, in line 60, the file

128 COMPUTER STUDIES

```
 10 REM WRITING A SERIAL FILE TO DISK,(OR TAPE).PROG01(BBC BASIC)
 20 MODE 0:DIM N$(9,6)
 30 PRINT:PRINT:INPUT"WHAT IS THE NAME OF THIS NEW FILE?        "F$
 40 X=OPENOUT(F$)
 50 PRINT: PRINT"EACH * INDICATES THAT A RECORD HAS BEEN WRITTEN":PRINT
 60 Q=1
 70 FOR R=1 TO 6:READ N$(Q,R):IF N$(Q,1)="XXX" THEN 90
 80 PRINT#X,N$(Q,R):NEXT:PRINT"*";:Q=Q+1:GOTO 70
 90 CLOSE #X
100 PRINT:PRINT:PRINT"FILE WRITING IS COMPLETE"
110 PRINT:PRINT"FILE ";F$;" CONTAINS ";Q-1;" RECORDS"
120 DATA BROWN MARY,45 TOWNFIELDS KNUTSFORD,0565 2468,16,F,5U
130 DATA YOUNG JOHN,3 GREEN LANE NORTHWICH,--,17,M,5S
140 DATA GREEN ALAN,17 TOWN LANE MOBBERLEY,MOB 1234,15,M,5V
150 DATA JONES FIONA,43 TREE WAY KNUTSFORD,0565 74812,16,F,5U
160 DATA BLOGGS JOHN,39 ASHWORTH PARK KNUTSFORD,0565 9999,17,M,5V
170 DATA SMITH ROY,99 MANCHESTER RD KNUTSFORD,0565 7887,15,M,5T
180 DATA WHITE ANN,"THE COTTAGE, PLUMLEY RD KNUTSFORD",--,16,F,5T
190 DATA EVANS PETER,1 THE TALBOTS MOBBERLEY,MOB 2345,15,M,5U
200 DATA "XXX"


RUN

WHAT IS THE NAME OF THIS NEW FILE?        GHJ456

EACH * INDICATES THAT A RECORD HAS BEEN WRITTEN

********

FILE WRITING IS COMPLETE

FILE GHJ456 CONTAINS 8 RECORDS
```

Fig. 11.2 Program to create a file

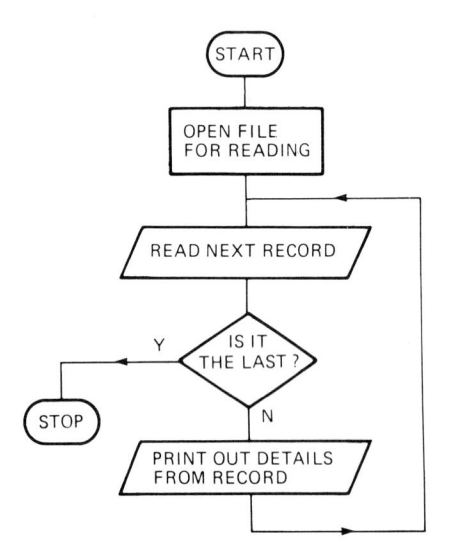

Fig. 11.3 Flowchart for reading a file

```
 10 REM READING A FILE-PROG02 (BBC BASIC)
 20 MODE 0:DIM A$(30,6)
 30 INPUT TAB(4,8)"WHAT IS THE NAME OF THE FILE YOU WISH TO READ ? "N1$
 40 PRINT:PRINT "     READING THE FILE...."
 50 X=OPENUP(N1$):Q=1
 60 FOR R=1 TO 6:INPUT#X,A$(Q,R):IF EOF#X THEN 90
 70 NEXT
 80 Q=Q+1:GOTO 60
 90 CLOSE#X
100 PRINT:PRINT
110 FOR A=1 TO Q
120 PRINT A$(A,1);TAB(16);A$(A,2);TAB(54);A$(A,3);TAB(67);A$(A,4);TAB(72);A$(A,5);TAB(77);A$(A,6)
130 NEXT
140 PRINT"FILE LISTING COMPLETE"
150 PRINT"FILE "N1$" CONTAINS ";Q;" RECORDS"
```

Fig. 11.4 Program for reading a file

FILE HANDLING 129

is closed and the array A$ is printed out at line 120. A run of this program is shown in Fig. 11.5.

If we only want the names of the pupils in the file then line 120 would be altered to print out only the name field, A$ (A,1), and the output from a run would be as shown in Fig. 11.6. We can alter line 120 to get any output we want e.g. name and form (Fig. 11.7), or name, sex and form (Fig. 11.8). However, the output can only be one or more fields from *every record* in the file. If we want to get some data which may only be contained in one or two records, we must learn how to *interrogate* the file.

```
RUN
WHAT IS THE NAME OF THE FILE YOU WISH TO READ ? GHJ456

   READING THE FILE....

   BROWN MARY        45 TOWNFIELDS KNUTSFORD         0565 2468     16    F    5U
   YOUNG JOHN        3 GREEN LANE NORTHWICH          --            17    M    5S
   GREEN ALAN        17 TOWN LANE MOBBERLEY          MOB 1234      15    M    5V
   JONES FIONA       43 TREE WAY KNUTSFORD           0565 74812    16    F    5U
   BLOGGS JOHN       39,ASHWORTH PARK KNUTSFORD      0565 9999     17    M    5V
   SMITH ROY         99 MANCHESTER RD KNUTSFORD      0565 7887     15    M    5T
   WHITE ANN         THE COTTAGE PLUMLEY RD KNUTSFORD --            16    F    5T
   EVANS PETER       1 THE TALBOTS MOBBERLEY         MOB 2345      15    M    5U


FILE LISTING COMPLETE

FILE GHJ456 CONTAINS 8 RECORDS
```

Fig. 11.5 Output from a run of the program shown in Fig. 11.4

```
110 FOR A=1 TO Q
120 PRINT A$(A,1)
130 NEXT
RUN
WHAT IS THE NAME OF THE FILE YOU WISH TO
READ ? GHJ456

   READING THE FILE....

BROWN MARY
YOUNG JOHN
GREEN ALAN
JONES FIONA
BLOGGS JOHN
SMITH ROY
WHITE ANN
EVANS PETER

FILE LISTING COMPLETE

FILE GHJ456 CONTAINS 8 RECORDS
```

```
110 FOR A=1 TO Q
120 PRINT A$(A,1);TAB(19);A$(A,6)
130 NEXT
RUN
WHAT IS THE NAME OF THE FILE YOU WISH TO
READ ? GHJ456

   READING THE FILE....

BROWN MARY        5U
YOUNG JOHN        5S
GREEN ALAN        5V
JONES FIONA       5U
BLOGGS JOHN       5V
SMITH ROY         5T
WHITE ANN         5T
EVANS PETER       5U

FILE LISTING COMPLETE

FILE GHJ456 CONTAINS 8 RECORDS
```

Fig. 11.6 Program segment and output printing only the name field

Fig. 11.7 Program segment and output giving name and form

130   COMPUTER STUDIES

```
110 FOR A=1 TO Q
120 PRINT A$(A,1);TAB(19);A$(A,5);
    TAB(25);A$(A,6)
130 NEXT
RUN
WHAT IS THE NAME OF THE FILE YOU WISH TO
   READ ? GHJ456

   READING THE FILE....
BROWN MARY          F     5U
YOUNG JOHN          M     5S
GREEN ALAN          M     5V
JONES FIONA         F     5U
BLOGGS JOHN         M     5V
SMITH ROY           M     5T
WHITE ANN           F     5T
EVANS PETER         M     5U


FILE LISTING COMPLETE

FILE GHJ456 CONTAINS 8 RECORDS
```

Fig. 11.8 Program segment and output giving name, sex and form

11.7 Interrogating the file

One of the ways in which we can use our file is to 'ask it questions'. For example:
 (i) How many pupils are there in 5V?
 (ii) How many pupils are not on the telephone?
 (iii) What are the names of all the 15 year olds?
 (iv) What are the telephone numbers of all the 17 year old boys?
 (v) What are the names and addresses of all the 16 year old girls in 5U?
This is called *interrogation*.
The first two example questions above do not require any actual data from the file: the answer to the question will tell us *how many* records in the file fit the specification given in the question.

The answer to any of the last three questions will be actual data from the file. If we look at page 128 to remind ourselves of the data we have put into the file, we can see that the answers to question (iii) are: Alan Green and Roy Smith.

We achieved this by reading the *age field* of *each record* and when we found one that was *15* we wrote down the *name* from the *name field* in that record. This procedure is called a single-field interrogation and each time we find a record with a matching field to the one we

want, this is called a *hit*. Therefore the interrogation of our file using question (iii) above, gave two hits.

Question (iv) is an example of a double-field interrogation, i.e. the age field has to be 17 *and* the sex field has to be M before a hit is scored. Such an interrogation on our file would give two hits and from these we can find the telephone numbers of all the 17 year old males in the file.

The last question is an example of a triple-field interrogation, i.e. the age field has to be 16 *and* the sex field F *and* the form field 5U, before a hit is scored. In our file this interrogation would give us the names and address of Mary Brown and Fiona Jones.

Let us look again at two of these interrogations in flowchart form. Fig. 11.9 shows interrogation (i) in

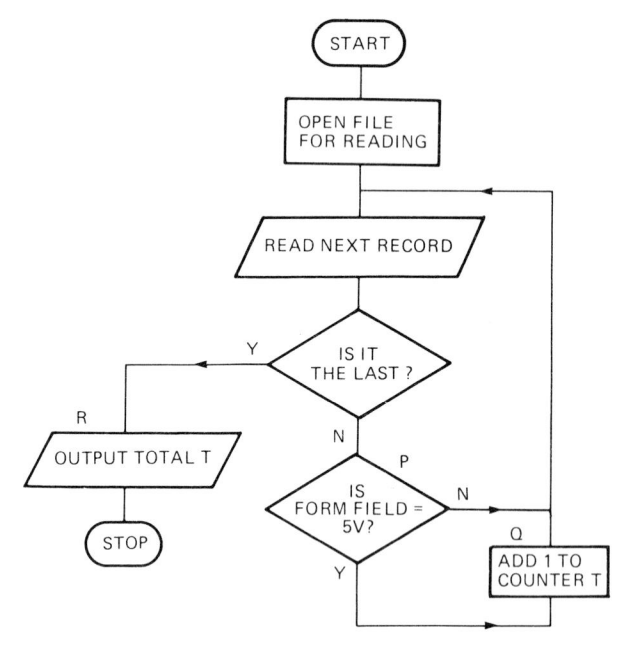

Fig. 11.9 Flowchart for single field interrogation

flowchart form. Compare this flowchart with the one on p. 128 for reading a whole file. It is the same but with the addition of boxes P, Q and R: P is the single interrogation; Q is the recording of a hit and R is the output.

We can see from the flowchart for interrogation in Fig. 11.10 that if the interrogation fails on *any one* of the three requirements of age, sex or form, further interrogation of the record is abandoned and the next record is read to see if it matches all the requirements. Multi-field interrogations, as they are normally called, need not be limited to only three fields. Theoretically, there is no limit to the number of fields of a record that must match given requirements before a hit is made. It should also be realised, that, once a hit is made, any field(s) or the whole record can be output as required by the user.

FILE HANDLING 131

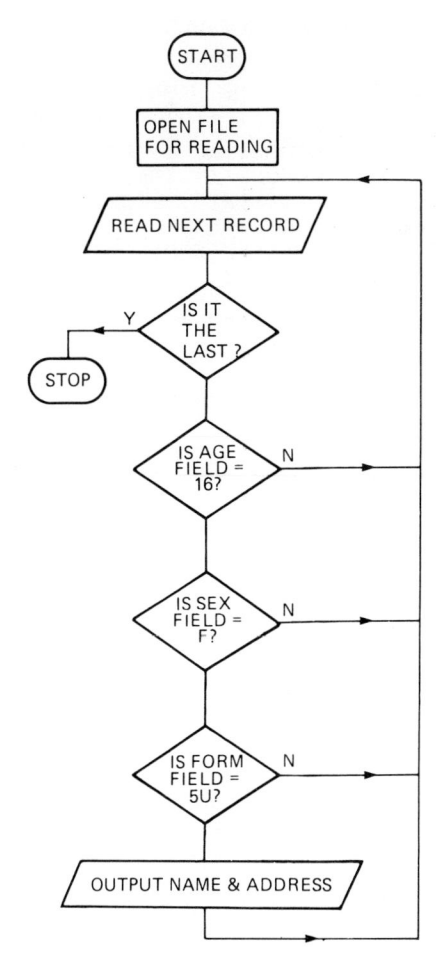

Fig. 11.10 Flowchart for triple field interrogation

```
10 REM INTERROGATING A SERIAL DISK FILE
ON A SINGLE FIELD.PROG03.(BBC BASIC)
20 MODE 0:PRINT:PRINT:PRINT:DIM A$(8,6)
30 X=OPENUP("GHJ456")
40 Q=1
50 FOR R=1 TO 6
60 IF EOF#X THEN 110
70 INPUT#X,A$(Q,R)
80 IF A$(Q,6)="5V" THEN C=C+1
90 NEXT R
100 Q=Q+1:GOTO 50
110 CLOSE #X
120 CLS:PRINT TAB(0,6);"THE NUMBER OF PUP
ILS IN 5V IS ";C
130 PRINT"FILE INTERROGATION COMPLETE"
140 END
```

Fig. 11.11 How the form field is checked

```
10 REM INTERROGATING A SERIAL DISK FILE
ON 3 FIELDS.PROG3.1(BBC BASIC)
20 MODE 0:PRINT:PRINT:PRINT:DIM A$(8,6)
30 X=OPENUP("GHJ456"):Q=1
40 FOR R=1 TO 6:IF EOF#X THEN 150
50 INPUT#X,A$(Q,R)
60 IF A$(Q,4)="16" THEN 80
70 GOTO 140
80 IF A$(Q,5)="F" THEN 100
90 GOTO 140
100 IF A$(Q,6)="5U" THEN 120
110 GOTO 140
120 FOR K=1 TO 2:PRINT A$(Q,K);"    ";:NEXT
130 PRINT:PRINT:C=C+1
140 NEXT R:Q=Q+1:GOTO 40
150 CLOSE#X
160 PRINT"FILE INTERROGATION COMPLETE"
170 PRINT:PRINT C;" HITS SCORED"
```

Fig. 11.12 Program for triple field interrogation

```
10 REM INTERROGATING A SERIAL FILE ON 3
FIELDS.PROG3.2(BBC BASIC)
20 MODE 0:PRINT:PRINT:PRINT:DIM A$(8,6)
30 X=OPENUP("GHJ456"):Q=1
40 FOR R=1 TO 6:IF EOF#X THEN 120
50 INPUT#X,A$(Q,R)
60 IF A$(Q,4)<>"16" THEN 110
70 IF A$(Q,5)<>"F" THEN 110
80 IF A$(Q,6)<>"5U" THEN 110
90 FOR K=1 TO 2:PRINT A$(Q,K);"    ";:NEXT
100 PRINT:PRINT:C=C+1
110 NEXT R:Q=Q+1:GOTO 40
120 CLOSE#X
130 PRINT"FILE INTERROGATION COMPLETE"
140 PRINT:PRINT C;" HITS SCORED"
```

Fig. 11.13 Program using inequality logic

Programming for file interrogation

Two different programming techniques can be used for file interrogation: multiple interrogation statements and Boolean operators.

Multiple interrogation statements, used with all versions of Basic, are based on the IF ... THEN statement. For a single interrogation, one IF ... THEN statement is used to check if a specified field matches the requirement. The program in Fig. 11.11 shows, on line 60, how the form field of each record is checked to see if it is '5V'. If it is, one is added to the counter C and this total is output after the whole file has been read.

Fig. 11.12 shows a program for a three-field interrogation where IF ... THEN occurs three times. Line 60 checks whether the age field is 16 and if it is not, interrogation of this record is abandoned. The program then returns to line 40 and reads the next record. If the age field is 16, the program advances to the next check, at line 80. Here, if the sex field is female, line 90 is jumped, and at line 100 a final check is made. If this is 5U, then all checks have matched and the information from the record is output.

This program uses the IF ... THEN statements simply but the program jumps out of sequence if a statement is satisfied, so three 'GOTO 140' lines are needed to read the next record when the statement is not satisfied.

The program in Fig. 11.13 uses the logic of inequality (< >). The program is shortened by three lines and line 60 now reads: 'If A$ (Q,4) is *not equal* to 16, then go back to line 110.'

Programs using 'inequality logic' are usually more efficient and should be used whenever possible.

Boolean operators, available in most versions of Basic, are compounds of the relational operators AND and OR. To find all the girls aged 15 in our file, each record must be tested for sex field and age field. Line 60 becomes:

60 IF A$ (Q,4) = 15 AND A$ (Q,5) = "F" THEN.

The program is shown in Fig. 11.14.

```
10 REM INTERROGATING A SERIAL FILE ON 3
FIELDS.PROG3.3(BBC BASIC)
20 MODE 0:PRINT:PRINT:PRINT:DIM A$(8,6)
30 X=OPENUP("GHJ456"):Q=1
40 FOR R=1 TO 6:IF EOF#X THEN 110
50 INPUT#X,A$(Q,R)
60 IF A$(Q,4)="16" AND A$(Q,5)="F" AND
A$(Q,6)="5U" THEN 80
70 GOTO 100
80 FOR K=1 TO 2:PRINTA$(Q,K);"   ";:NEXT
90 PRINT:PRINT:C=C+1
100 NEXT R:Q=Q+1:GOTO 40
110 CLOSE#X
120 PRINT"FILE INTERROGATION COMPLETE"
130 PRINT:PRINT C;" HITS SCORED"
```

Fig. 11.14 Program using Boolean operators

When inequality logic is used with Boolean operators, the operator changes from AND to OR (Fig. 11.15).

```
10 REM INTERROGATING A SERIAL FILE ON 3
FIELDS.PROG3.4(BBC BASIC)
20 MODE 0:PRINT:PRINT:PRINT:DIM A$(8,6)
30 X=OPENUP("GHJ456"):Q=1
40 FOR R=1 TO 6:IF EOF#X THEN 100
50 INPUT#X,A$(Q,R)
60 IF A$(Q,4)<>"16" OR A$(Q,5)<>"F" OR
A$(Q,6)<>"5U"  THEN 90
70 FOR K=1 TO 2:PRINTA$(Q,K);"   ";:NEXT
80 PRINT:PRINT:C=C+1
90 NEXT R:Q=Q+1:GOTO 40
100 CLOSE#X
110 PRINT"FILE INTERROGATION COMPLETE"
120 PRINT:PRINT C;" HITS SCORED"
```

Fig. 11.15 Program using inequality logic and Boolean operators

It is also possible to manipulate data retrieved from a file. For example, to find and compare the average age of boys in 5V with that of girls in 5U, the program first interrogates each record. When the form field is 5V, and the sex field is M, the age field is added to a total age counter. After reading all the records, the program calculates the average age (Fig. 11.16).

```
10 REM INTERROGATING A SERIAL FILE ON 2
FIELDS AND MANIPULATING THE DATA.PROG4.0
20 MODE 0:PRINT:PRINT:PRINT:DIM A$(8,6)
30 X=OPENUP("GHJ456"):Q=1
40 FOR R=1 TO 6:IF EOF#X THEN 80
50 INPUT#X,A$(Q,R)
60 IF A$(Q,5)="M" AND A$(Q,6)="5V" THEN
T2=T2+VAL(A$(Q,4)):C2=C2+1
70 NEXT:Q=Q+1:GOTO 40
80 CLOSE#X
90 PRINT TAB(0,8);" THE AVERAGE AGE OF
THE BOYS  IN 5V IS ";T2/C2
```

Fig. 11.16 Calculating the average age

To find the average age of the girls in 5U, we need only re-write line 260 and run the program again (Fig. 11.17).

```
10 REM INTERROGATING A SERIAL FILE ON 2
FIELDS AND MANIPULATING THE DATA.PROG4.1
20 MODE 0:PRINT:PRINT:PRINT:DIM A$(8,6)
30 X=OPENUP("GHJ456"):Q=1
40 FOR R=1 TO 6:IF EOF#X THEN 80
50 INPUT#X,A$(Q,R)
60 IF A$(Q,5)="F" AND A$(Q,6)="5U" THEN
T1=T1+VAL(A$(Q,4)):C1=C1+1
70 NEXT:Q=Q+1:GOTO 40
80 CLOSE#X
90 PRINT TAB(0,6);" THE AVERAGE AGE OF
THE GIRLS IN 5U IS ";T1/C1
```

Fig. 11.17 The average age of girls in form 5U

The two lines can be written into the same program if some of the variables are changed (Fig. 11.18).

```
10 REM INTERROGATING A SERIAL FILE ON 2
FIELDS AND MANIPULATING THE DATA.PROG4.2
20 MODE 0:PRINT:PRINT:PRINT:DIM A$(8,6)
30 X=OPENUP("GHJ456"):Q=1
40 FOR R=1 TO 6:IF EOF#X THEN 90
50 INPUT#X,A$(Q,R)
60 IF A$(Q,5)="F" AND A$(Q,6)="5U" THEN
T1=T1+VAL(A$(Q,4)):C1=C1+1
70 IF A$(Q,5)="M" AND A$(Q,6)="5V" THEN
T2=T2+VAL(A$(Q,4)):C2=C2+1
80 NEXT:Q=Q+1:GOTO 40
90 CLOSE#X
100 PRINT TAB(0,6);" THE AVERAGE AGE OF
THE GIRLS IN 5U IS ";T1/C1
110 PRINT TAB(0,8);" THE AVERAGE AGE OF
THE BOYS  IN 5V IS ";T2/C2
```

Fig. 11.18 Single program calculating both averages

11.8 File updating

The previous section has dealt with the interrogation of the data held in a file. The data itself has not changed: each field in each record is exactly the same as when the file was created but even in a simple file such as this one, some of the data will need to be changed at some time. For example, someone may leave the school, in which case their record will need to be *deleted* from the file. Another pupil may come new into the school in the fifth year and would have to be *added* to the file. Lastly, part of a record may require *amending* if some of the data changes such as a change of address or telephone number.

These three techniques of addition, deletion and amendment of one or more records in a file will be dealt with separately, but before we look at these in detail we must look at a technique that is common to all file updating and is fundamental to the way in which we are going to manipulate our files.

Whether we are going to add, delete or amend one or more records in the file, we will first read the whole file into an *array*. Data manipulation will take place whilst the data is in the array. New data will be added to the array and data deleted from the array, then the array will be printed to a new file. We may then choose to kill the old version of the file or save it as security. It is good practice to save the original version of a file *and* the updated version—known as the *father file* and the *son file* respectively—until a new version of the updated file is made. The original file is then killed, so that the most recent version *and* the previous version are always kept. This process is shown in flowchart form in Fig. 11.19.

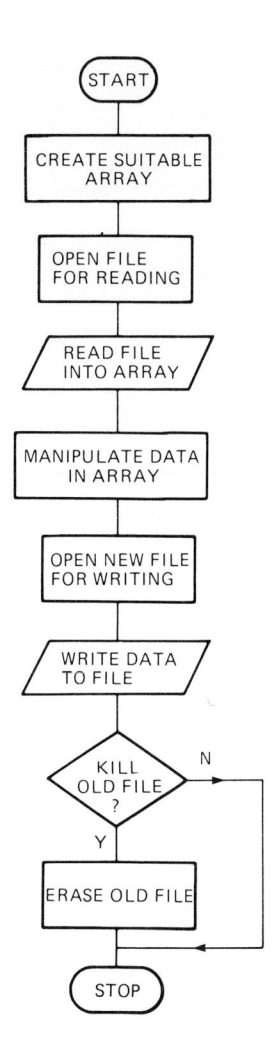

Fig. 11.19 Flowchart for reading file into an array for manipulation, then into a new file

Creating a new file identical to the old one

With the flowchart in Fig. 11.19 as a guide, Fig. 11.20 shows a program that will read the file into a two-dimensional array then print it without any alteration, to a new file.

Note that in this program:
(a) A$ is a 2-dimensional array used to store the data from each record as it is read from the file at line 80.
(b) In line 350, the numeric variable D is changed into a string variable D$, so that it can be held in a string array, and back to a numeric variable in line 430.

As each record is read from the file at line 340, each field is assigned to one element of the array A$.

The name from the first record is assigned to A$ (1,1).
The address from the first record is assigned to A$ (1,2).
The telephone number from the first record is assigned to A$ (1,3).

The name from the second record assigned to A$ (2,1).

The age from the second record is assigned to A$ (2,4).

The form from the fifth record is assigned to A$ (5,6) and so on until all 48 elements (6 × 8) of the array are filled with data.

A new file is opened at line 160 and the process reversed at line 180 where each element of the array is printed to the new file, one record at a time. When all the data has been printed to the file we have two files holding identical data, GHJ456 and RST789. At line 230 we are offered the option to kill the original file. Any default on the word YES will prevent the file from being erased.

134 COMPUTER STUDIES

```
 10 REM PROG TO READ A SERIAL FILE INTO ONE ARRAY THEN INTO A NEW FILE.
PROG05(BBC BASIC)
 20 MODE 0: DIM A$(9,6)
 30 REM READING FROM THE FILE INTO AN ARRAY A$
 40 PRINT TAB(0,4); "PLEASE WAIT WHILE THE FILE IS READ....":PRINT
 50 X=OPENUP"GHJ456"
 60 Q=1
 70 FOR R=1 TO 6
 80 INPUT#X,A$(Q,R)
 90 IF EOF#X THEN 120
100 NEXT R
110 Q=Q+1:GOTO 70
120 CLOSE#X
130 PRINT "FILE <GHJ456> HAS NOW BEEN READ":PRINT
140 REM WRITING FROM THE ARRAY TO THE NEW FILE
150 PRINT "WRITING THE NEW FILE....":PRINT
160 Y=OPENOUT"RST789"
170 FOR A=1 TO Q:FOR B=1 TO 6
180 PRINT#Y,A$(A,B)
190 NEXT:NEXT
200 CLOSE#Y
210 PRINT:PRINT"NEW FILE-<RST789>-NOW COMPLETE":PRINT:PRINT
220 REM OPTION TO KILL THE OLD FILE
230 INPUT"DO YOU WISH TO KILL THE OLD FILE?(YES or NO) "K$:PRINT
240 IF K$<>"YES" THEN 310
250 INPUT"ARE YOU SURE??! "KK$:PRINT:PRINT
260 PRINT:PRINT
270 IF KK$<>"YES" THEN 310
280 *DELETE"GHJ456":PRINT:PRINT
290 PRINT"FILE GHJ456 IS NOW ERASED AND THE NEW FILE-RST789-IS SAVED"
300 GOTO 320
310 PRINT"BOTH FILES ARE SAVED"
320 END
```

Fig. 11.20 A program to create a new file

```
 RUN
PLEASE WAIT WHILE THE FILE IS READ....

FILE <GHJ456> HAS NOW BEEN READ

WRITING THE NEW FILE....

NEW FILE-<RST789>-NOW COMPLETE

DO YOU WISH TO KILL THE OLD FILE?(YES or NO) NO

BOTH FILES ARE SAVED

 RUN
PLEASE WAIT WHILE THE FILE IS READ....

FILE <GHJ456> HAS NOW BEEN READ

WRITING THE NEW FILE....

NEW FILE-<RST789>-NOW COMPLETE

DO YOU WISH TO KILL THE OLD FILE?(YES or NO) YES

ARE YOU SURE??! YES

FILE GHJ456 IS NOW ERASED AND THE NEW FILE-RST789-IS SAVED
```

Fig. 11.21 Runs from program in Fig. 11.20

FILE HANDLING

Deleting a record from the file

First we have to identify *which* record we wish to delete. For the type of file we are using—name, address etc.— it is probable that we would always use the person's name in order to identify the record to be deleted, although we could use any one of the unique fields of a record—a name, address or telephone number—or a combination of fields if we needed to. In flowchart form this process becomes as shown in Fig. 11.22. A more detailed flowchart is shown in Fig. 11.23, and a program from this flowchart appears in Fig. 11.24.

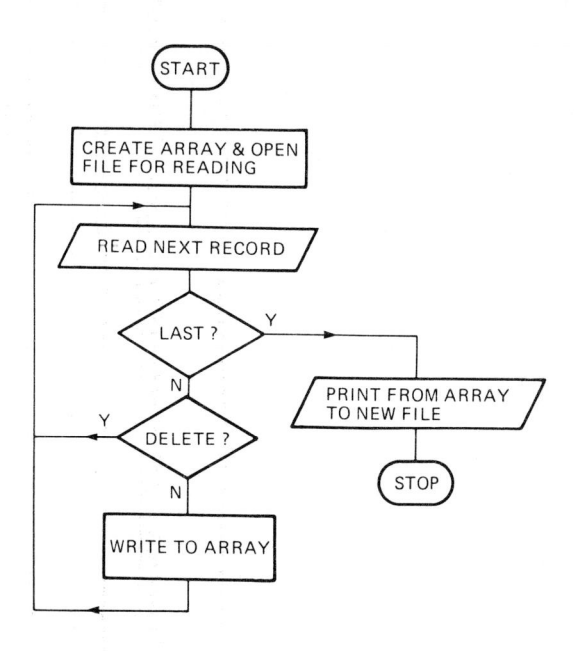

Fig. 11.22 Flowchart to delete a record from a file

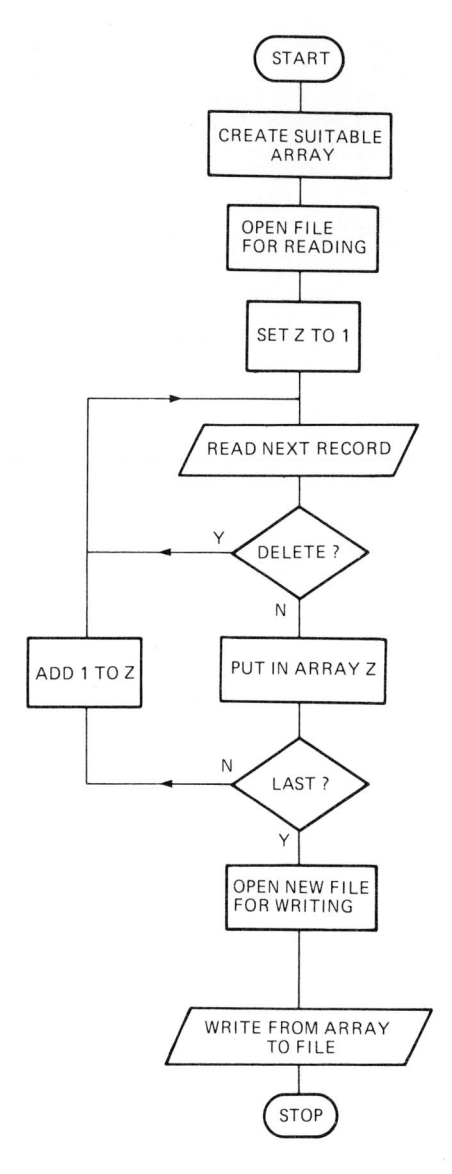

Fig. 11.23 A more detailed flowchart for record deletion

Notes on the program. The name to identify the record to be deleted is input as a variable, 'NAME$', so that different records can be deleted. If the selected record is simply deleted, there will be a gap, or a blank record, left in the file. This is unacceptable, and therefore after the record is identified (line 70), it is *not* copied to the array and each succeeding element of the array is shifted up by one place. The Qth record is copied to the (Q-1)th element of the array thereby ensuring that all the elements of the array contain one record of the new file.

The data is then read from the array, and printed to the new file at line 150. Lines 190-210 read the new file and print out the name and address only from each record in the file.

The output in Fig. 11.25 shows different records deleted each time. A version of this program with an option to delete any record is given in Fig. 11.26.

Notes on the program in Fig. 11.26. This version of the program to delete more than one record offers each record in turn for deletion. The record to be deleted is *not* written to the array A$ and the subscript L is *not* incremented, thereby closing up the array to its new size. Note that this is not a practical method of deleting records from a large file. The program in Fig. 11.24 can easily be modified to loop back to line 30 to delete more than one record—but the records to be deleted *must* be input in the order they appear in the file.

136 COMPUTER STUDIES

```
 10 REM PROG TO DELETE ONE RECORD FROM A SERIAL FILE.PROG06(BBC BASIC)
 20 MODE 0:DIM N1$(30,6)
 30 INPUT TAB(0,4)"WHAT IS THE NAME IN THE RECORD YOU WISH TO DELETE? "NAME$
 40 PRINT TAB(0,7);"READING THE FILE....":PRINT
 50 X=OPENUP("GHJ456"):Q=1
 60 FOR R=1 TO 6:INPUT #X,N1$(Q,R):IF EOF#X THEN 100
 70 IF N1$(Q,1)=NAME$ THEN Q=Q-1
 80 NEXT
 90 Q=Q+1:GOTO 60
100 CLOSE#X
110 REM WRITING THE NEW FILE
120 PRINT:PRINT "WRITING THE NEW FILE....":PRINT
130 Y=OPENOUT("RST789")
140 FOR A=1 TO Q:FOR B=1 TO 6
150 PRINT #Y,N1$(A,B):NEXT:NEXT
160 CLOSE #Y
170 CLS:PRINT:PRINT"NEW FILE-RST789-NOW COMPLETE":PRINT
180 REM PRINTING OUT THE NEW FILE
190 FOR C=1 TO Q
200 PRINT N1$(C,1);TAB(15);N1$(C,2)
210 NEXT
220 PRINT:PRINT"FILE RST789 NOW CONTAINS ";Q;" RECORDS"
```

Fig. 11.24 **A program to delete a record**

```
 RUN
WHAT IS THE NAME IN THE RECORD YOU WISH TO DELETE? BLOGGS JOHN
READING THE FILE....


WRITING THE NEW FILE....


NEW FILE-RST789-NOW COMPLETE

BROWN MARY      45 TOWNFIELDS KNUTSFORD
YOUNG JOHN      3 GREEN LANE NORTHWICH
GREEN ALAN      17 TOWN LANE MOBBERLEY
JONES FIONA     39,ASHWORTH PARK KNUTSFORD
SMITH ROY       99 MANCHESTER RD KNUTSFORD
WHITE ANN       THE COTTAGE PLUMLEY RD KNUTSFORD
EVANS PETER     1 THE TALBOTS MOBBERLEY


FILE RST789 NOW CONTAINS 7 RECORDS
```

Fig. 11.25 **Output from the program in Fig. 11.24**

FILE HANDLING

```
 10 REM PROG TO DELETE ONE OR MORE RECORDS FROM A SERIAL FILE.PROG6.1(BBC BASIC)
 20 MODE 0:DIM A$(30,6),B$(30,6)
 30 PRINT TAB(0,4);"READING THE FILE....":PRINT
 40 REM READING THE FILE
 50 X=OPENUP("GHJ456"):Q=1:L=1
 60 FOR R=1 TO 6:INPUT#X,A$(Q,R):IF EOF#X THEN 80
 70 NEXT:Q=Q+1:GOTO 60
 80 CLOSE#X
 90 PRINT:PRINT
100 REM DELETING FROM THE ARRAY & CLOSING UP
110 FOR K=1 TO Q
120 CLS:PRINT TAB(0,8);"NAME IN RECORD IS ";A$(K,1):PRINT
130 INPUT "DO YOU WISH TO DELETE THIS RECORD(Y/N)? "AA$
140 IF AA$="Y" THEN 170
150 FOR M=1 TO 6:B$(L,M)=A$(K,M):NEXT
160 L=L+1
170 NEXT
180 REM WRITING THE NEW FILE
190 CLS:PRINT TAB(0,4);"WRITING THE NEW FILE....":PRINT
200 Y=OPENOUT("RST789")
210 FOR A=1 TO L-1:FOR B=1 TO 6
220 PRINT #Y,B$(A,B):NEXT:NEXT
230 CLOSE #Y
240 CLS:PRINT:PRINT"NEW FILE-RST789-NOW COMPLETE":PRINT:PRINT
250 REM PRINTING OUT THE NEW FILE
260 FOR C=1 TO L-1
270 PRINT B$(C,1);TAB(15);B$(C,2):NEXT
280 PRINT:PRINT"FILE NOW CONTAINS ";L-1;" RECORDS"
```

(a)

```
RUN
READING THE FILE....


NAME IN RECORD IS BROWN MARY

DO YOU WISH TO DELETE THIS RECORD(Y/N)? N
NAME IN RECORD IS YOUNG JOHN

DO YOU WISH TO DELETE THIS RECORD(Y/N)? Y
NAME IN RECORD IS GREEN ALAN

DO YOU WISH TO DELETE THIS RECORD(Y/N)? Y
NAME IN RECORD IS JONES FIONA

DO YOU WISH TO DELETE THIS RECORD(Y/N)? N
NAME IN RECORD IS BLOGGS JOHN

DO YOU WISH TO DELETE THIS RECORD(Y/N)? Y
NAME IN RECORD IS SMITH ROY

DO YOU WISH TO DELETE THIS RECORD(Y/N)? Y
NAME IN RECORD IS WHITE ANN

DO YOU WISH TO DELETE THIS RECORD(Y/N)? N
NAME IN RECORD IS EVANS PETER

DO YOU WISH TO DELETE THIS RECORD(Y/N)? Y
WRITING THE NEW FILE....

NEW FILE-RST789-NOW COMPLETE

BROWN MARY     45 TOWNFIELDS KNUTSFORD
JONES FIONA    43 TREE WAY KNUTSFORD
WHITE ANN      THE COTTAGE PLUMLEY RD
               KNUTSFORD

FILE NOW CONTAINS 3 RECORDS
```

(b)

Fig. 11.26 Program with an option to delete any record
      (*a*) Program
      (*b*) Output

Adding a record to the file

Throughout the whole of this chapter we are using a non-organised file, i.e. it has not been put into alphabetic or numeric order, and therefore it clearly does not matter where we add the new record. For simplicity of programming, new records will be added to the beginning of the file.

The new record is supplied as data and is read into the first element of the array, and the other records from the file into the remainder of the array. The whole of the array is then printed to the new file. This process is shown in flowchart form in Fig. 11.27, and a program from this flowchart is given in Fig. 11.28. The version of this program given in Fig. 11.29 uses interactive input to enable more than one record to be added to the file.

```
 10 REM PROG TO ADD ONE RECORD TO A SERIA
L FILE.PROG07(BBC BASIC)
 20 MODE 0: Z=1:DIM A$(9,6)
 30 FOR R=1 TO 6:READ A$(Z,R):NEXT R
 40 DATA "NEWBY MALCOLM","7 PARK PLACE LI
NDOW","LIN 437402",16,"M","5U"
 50 PRINT TAB(0,4); "READING THE FILE....
":PRINT
 60 X=OPENUP("GHJ456")
 70 FOR Q=Z+1 TO Z+8:FOR R=1 TO 6
 80 INPUT#X,A$(Q,R)
 90 IF EOF #X THEN 110
100 NEXT:NEXT
110 CLOSE#X
120 PRINT:PRINT "WRITING THE NEW FILE....
":PRINT
130 Y=OPENOUT("RST789")
140 FOR A=1 TO Q:FOR B=1 TO 6
150 PRINT#Y,A$(A,B)
160 NEXT:NEXT
170 CLOSE #Y
180 PRINT:PRINT" NEW FILE-RST789-WRITTEN
 AND CLOSED"
190 PRINT:PRINT" FILE NOW CONTAINS ";Q;"
 RECORDS"
200 PRINT:FOR C=1 TO Q
210 PRINT A$(C,1);TAB(15);A$(C,2)
220 NEXT
```

(a)

```
RUN
READING THE FILE....

WRITING THE NEW FILE....

NEW FILE-RST789-WRITTEN AND CLOSED

FILE NOW CONTAINS 9 RECORDS

NEWBY MALCOLM  7 PARK PLACE LINDOW
BROWN MARY     45 TOWNFIELDS KNUTSFORD
YOUNG JOHN     3 GREEN LANE NORTHWICH
GREEN ALAN     17 TOWN LANE MOBBERLEY
JONES FIONA    43 TREE WAY KNUTSFORD
BLOGGS JOHN    39,ASHWORTH PARK KNUTSFORD
SMITH ROY      99 MANCHESTER RD KNUTSFORD
WHITE ANN      THE COTTAGE PLUMLEY RD KNUTSFORD
EVANS PETER    1 THE TALBOTS MOBBERLEY
```

(b)

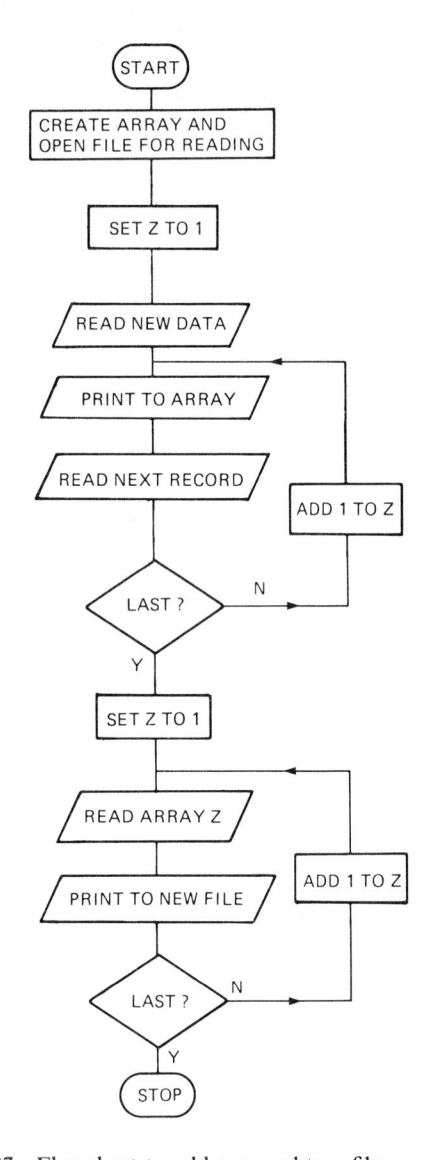

Fig. 11.27 Flowchart to add a record to a file

Fig. 11.28 A program for adding a record to a file
(a) Program   (b) Output

FILE HANDLING   139

```
 10 REM PROG TO ADD ONE OR MORE RECORDS TO A SERIAL FILE.PROG7.1(BBC BASIC)
 20 MODE 0:PRINT:PRINT:PRINT:DIM A$(30,6):Z=1
 30 REM INPUT THE NEW DATA
 40 PRINT"INPUT THE DATA FOR THE NEXT NEW RECORD":PRINT
 50 INPUT"NAME     ? "A$(Z,1):PRINT
 60 INPUT"ADDRESS ? "A$(Z,2):PRINT
 70 INPUT"TEL.NO. ? "A$(Z,3):PRINT
 80 INPUT"AGE      ? "A$(Z,4):PRINT
 90 INPUT"SEX      ? "A$(Z,5):PRINT
100 INPUT"FORM     ? "A$(Z,6):PRINT
110 INPUT"DO YOU WISH TO ADD ANOTHER RECORD (Y/N) ? "W$
120 IF W$<>"Y" THEN 140
130 Z=Z+1:CLS:PRINT:PRINT:GOTO 40
140 REM READING FROM THE FILE
150 CLS:PRINT:PRINT:PRINT "READING THE FILE....":PRINT
160 X=OPENUP("GHJ456")
170 FOR Q=Z+1 TO Z+9:FOR R=1 TO 6
180 INPUT#X,A$(Q,R)
190 IF EOF#X THEN 210
200 NEXT:NEXT
210 CLOSE #X
220 REM WRITING THE NEW FILE
230 PRINT "WRITING THE NEW FILE....":PRINT
240 Y=OPENOUT("RST789")
250 FOR A=1 TO Q-1:FOR B=1 TO 6
260 PRINT#Y,A$(A,B)
270 NEXT:NEXT
280 CLOSE#Y
290 CLS:PRINT:PRINT:PRINT"NEW FILE-RST789-WRITTEN AND CLOSED":PRINT
300 PRINT"FILE NOW CONTAINS ";Q-1;" RECORDS"
310 PRINT:FOR C=1 TO Q-1
320 PRINT A$(C,1);TAB(15);A$(C,3);TAB(32);A$(C,4)
330 NEXT
```

(a)

```
INPUT THE DATA FOR THE NEXT NEW RECORD

NAME      ? GREY MAVIS

ADDRESS ? 23 HALE RD HALE CHESHIRE

TEL.NO. ? 061 000 1234

AGE      ? 16

SEX      ? F

FORM     ? 5S

DO YOU WISH TO ADD ANOTHER RECORD (Y/N) ? N


READING THE FILE....

WRITING THE NEW FILE....
```

```
NEW FILE-RST789-WRITTEN AND CLOSED

FILE NOW CONTAINS 8 RECORDS


GREY MAVIS     061 000 1234    16
BROWN MARY     0565 2468       16
YOUNG JOHN     --              17
GREEN ALAN     MOB 1234        15
JONES FIONA    0565 74812      16
BLOGGS JOHN    0565 9999       17
SMITH ROY      0565 7887       15
WHITE ANN      --              16
```

(b)

Fig. 11.29 Adding a record using interactive input
(a) Program
(b) Output

Updating (amending) a record

We will consider two different types of record updating:
(a) when only one record requires updating, eg. a change of address and/or telephone number
(b) when all the records require updating, eg. a change of form at the beginning of a year.

We will also consider two methods of amending a record:
(a) by re-writing the *whole* of the record
(b) by re-writing only the fields that need to be amended.

A flowchart for updating one or more records of a file is shown in Fig. 11.30. Note that this flowchart applies both to re-writing a whole record or to re-writing one or more fields of a record.

The program in Fig. 11.31 shows how a record is amended by inputting a complete new record as a new *data* line in the program. It could equally be input interactively. Although the program shown only amends one record of the file—John Young has a new address and telephone number—this technique can be used to amend any one, or more, fields in one, or more, records, of the file by including the amended records as *data* and identifying the records to be amended in the same way as John Young is found in line 100. Note that the names of the records to be modified must be written from line 100

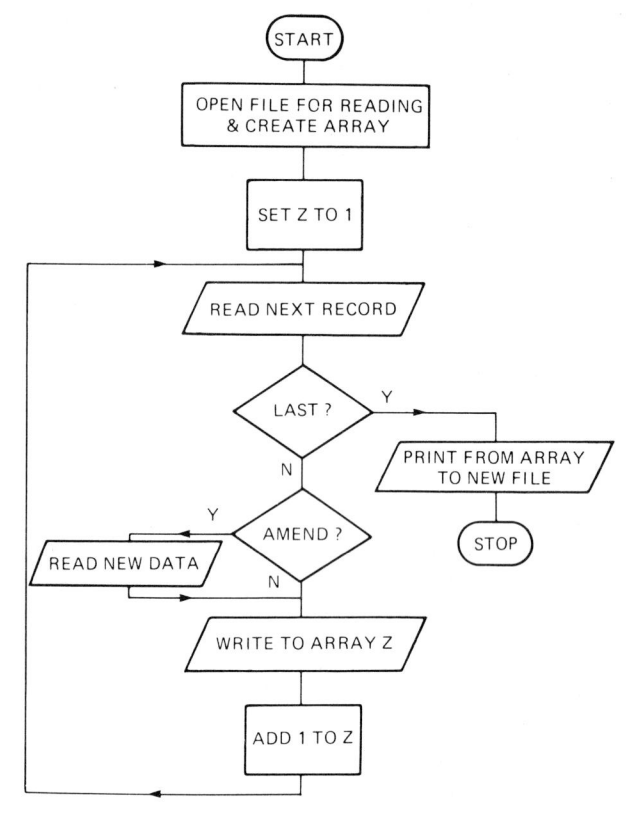

Fig. 11.30 Flowchart to update any record in a file

```
10 REM PROG TO AMEND ONE RECORD OF A SERIAL FILE.PROG08(BBC BASIC)
20 MODE 0:PRINT:PRINT:PRINT:DIM A$(8,6):Q=1
30 PRINT "READING THE FILE....":PRINT
40 X=OPENUP("GHJ456")
50 FOR R=1 TO 6:INPUT#X,A$(Q,R):NEXT:IF EOF#X THEN 70
60 Q=Q+1:GOTO 50
70 CLOSE#X
80 REM READING FROM THE ARRAY A$ & INSERTING THE NEW RECORD WHEN IDENTIFIED
90 FOR A=1 TO Q:FOR B=1 TO 6
100 IF A$(A,1)<>"YOUNG JOHN" THEN 110 ELSE 140
110 NEXT B
120 NEXT A
130 GOTO 170
140 FOR E=1 TO 6:READ A$(A,E):NEXT E
150 DATA YOUNG JOHN,2 MELLOR CRES GOOSTREY,0650 9753,17,M,5S
160 GOTO 120
170 REM WRITING THE NEW FILE
180 PRINT "WRITING THE NEW FILE....":PRINT
190 Y=OPENOUT("RST789")
200 FOR C=1 TO Q:FOR D=1 TO 6:PRINT#Y,A$(C,D):NEXT:NEXT
210 CLOSE#Y:CLS:PRINT:PRINT
220 PRINT"NEW FILE-RST789-NOW COMPLETE":PRINT
230 REM PRINTING OUT THE NEW FILE
240 FOR C=1 TO Q
250 PRINT A$(C,1);TAB(15);A$(C,2)
260 NEXT
270 PRINT "FILE CONTAINS ";Q;" RECORDS"
```

Fig. 11.31(a) How a record is amended by inputting a new record

```
RUN
READING THE FILE....
WRITING THE NEW FILE....
NEW FILE-RST789-NOW COMPLETE

BROWN MARY        45 TOWNFIELDS KNUTSFORD
YOUNG JOHN        2 MELLOR CRES GOOSTREY
GREEN ALAN        17 TOWN LANE MOBBERLEY
JONES FIONA       43 TREE WAY KNUTSFORD
BLOGGS JOHN       39,ASHWORTH PARK KNUTSFORD
SMITH ROY         99 MANCHESTER RD KNUTSFORD
WHITE ANN         THE COTTAGE PLUMLEY RD
                  KNUTSFORD
EVANS PETER       1 THE TALBOTS MOBBERLEY
FILE CONTAINS 8 RECORDS
```

Fig. 11.31(b) The output from the program in Fig. 11.31(a)

```
    10 REM PROG TO AMEND ONE OR MORE RECORDS
OF A SERIAL FILE (BY BATCH).PROG8.1
    20 MODE 0:PRINT:PRINT:DIM A$(8,6):Q=1
    30 PRINT "READING THE FILE....":PRINT
    40 X=OPENUP("GHJ456")
    50 FOR R=1 TO 6:INPUT#X,A$(Q,R):NEXT
    60 IF EOF#X THEN 80
    70 Q=Q+1:GOTO 50
    80 CLOSE#X
    90 REM READING FROM THE ARRAY A$ AND INSE
RTING THE NEW RECORD WHEN IDENTIFIED
   100 FOR A=1 TO Q:FOR B=1 TO 6
   110 IF A$(A,1)="BROWN MARY" THEN 170
   120 IF A$(A,1)="JONES FIONA" THEN 170
   130 IF A$(A,1)="EVANS PETER" THEN 170 ELSE
 150
   140 NEXT B
   150 NEXT A
   160 GOTO 220
   170 FOR E=1 TO 6:READ A$(A,E):NEXT E
   180 DATA BROWN MARY,45 TOWNFIELDS KNUTSFOR
D,0565 2468,16,F,5S
   190 DATA JONES FIONA,43 TREE WAY KNUTSFORD
,0565 74812,17,F,5U
   200 DATA EVANS PETER,1 THE TALBOTS MOBBERL
EY,MOB 9999,15,M,5U
   210 GOTO 150
   220 REM WRITING THE NEW FILE
   230 PRINT "WRITING THE NEW FILE....":PRINT
   240 Y=OPENOUT("RST789")
   250 FOR C=1 TO Q:FOR D=1 TO 6:PRINT #Y,A$(
C,D):NEXT:NEXT
   260 CLOSE#Y:CLS:PRINT:PRINT
   270 PRINT"NEW FILE-RST789-NOW COMPLETE"
   280 REM PRINTING OUT THE NEW FILE
   290 FOR C=1 TO Q
   300 PRINT A$(C,1);TAB(15);A$(C,3);TAB(30);
A$(C,4);TAB(38);A$(C,6)
   310 NEXT:PRINT
   320 PRINT "FILE CONTAINS ";Q;" RECORDS"
```

(a)

Fig. 11.32 Three records to be modified (by 'batch')
        (a) Program
        (b) Output

in the same order as the records in the file. Also the *data* lines must hold the new records in this same order.

The program in Fig. 11.32 shows three records to be modified: Mary Brown's form; Fiona Jones' age and Peter Evans' telephone number. This type of file amendment program is often used commercially when each new record is input as data to the program from a transaction file. A disadvantage of this program is that the whole record must be input again, even if only one field is to be amended. However, if the amendment applies to all the records in the file, e.g. all the forms change at the end of an academic year, the program can easily be modified to effect this change.

In the program shown in Fig. 11.33 the technique is altered slightly. As *each* record has to be altered, there is no need to identify any particular record and the *form* field of each record is changed immediately after it is read from the file and printed directly to the new file without storing it in an array.

```
RUN


READING THE FILE....

WRITING THE NEW FILE....


NEW FILE-RST789-NOW COMPLETE

BROWN MARY     0565 2468     16     5S
YOUNG JOHN     --            17     5S
GREEN ALAN     MOB 1234      15     5V
JONES FIONA    0565 74812    17     5U
BLOGGS JOHN    0565 9999     17     5V
SMITH ROY      0565 7887     15     5T
WHITE ANN      --            16     5T
EVANS PETER    MOB 9999      15     5U

FILE CONTAINS 8 RECORDS
```

(b)

142 COMPUTER STUDIES

```
 10 REM PROG TO AMEND ONE FIELD IN ALL RE
CORDS OF A SERIAL FILE.PROG8.2(BBC BASIC)
 20 MODE 0:PRINT:PRINT:DIM A$(8,6):Q=1
 30 PRINT "READING THE FILE....":PRINT
 40 X=OPENUP("GHJ456")
 50 FOR R=1 TO 6:INPUT#X, A$(Q,R):NEXT R:
IF EOF#X THEN 70
 60 Q=Q+1:GOTO 50
 70 CLOSE#X
 80 FOR A=1 TO Q:FOR B=1 TO 6
 90 IF A$(A,6)="5U" THEN A$(A,6)="6U"
100 IF A$(A,6)="5S" THEN A$(A,6)="6S"
110 IF A$(A,6)="5V" THEN A$(A,6)="6V"
120 IF A$(A,6)="5T" THEN A$(A,6)="6T"
130 NEXT:NEXT
140 PRINT"WRITING THE NEW FILE....":PRINT
150 Y=OPENOUT("RST789")
160 FOR C=1 TO Q:FOR D=1 TO 6
170 PRINT #Y,A$(C,D)
180 NEXT D:NEXT C
190 CLOSE#Y:CLS:PRINT:PRINT
200 PRINT"NEW FILE-RST789-NOW COMPLETE"
210 FOR C=1 TO Q
220 PRINT A$(C,1);TAB(15);A$(C,4);TAB(25)
;A$(C,6)
230 NEXT:PRINT
240 PRINT "FILE CONTAINS ";Q;" RECORDS"
```

(a)

```
READING THE FILE....

WRITING THE NEW FILE....


NEW FILE-RST789-NOW COMPLETE

BROWN MARY       16        6U
YOUNG JOHN       17        6S
GREEN ALAN       15        6V
JONES FIONA      16        6U
BLOGGS JOHN      17        6V
SMITH ROY        15        6T
WHITE ANN        16        6T
EVANS PETER      15        6U

FILE CONTAINS 8 RECORDS
```

(b)

Fig. 11.33 Amendment of the same field in *all* records
 (a) Program
 (b) Output

A disadvantage of both these programs is that the actual program has to be altered to amend the file. This is bad practice: the program should be written to allow new data to be input from the keyboard or from a transaction file without altering the program.

The program in Fig. 11.34 allows one or more fields in any record to be amended from the keyboard.

```
 10 REM TO AMEND SELECTED FIELDS IN 1 OR
MORE RECORDS IN A SERIAL FILE.PROG09
 20 MODE 0:PRINT:DIM A$(9,6),R$(8):Q=1
 30 PRINT "PLEASE WAIT WHILE THE FILE IS
READ..."
 40 X=OPENUP("GHJ456")
 50 FOR R=1 TO 6:INPUT#X,A$(Q,R):NEXT R
 60 IF EOF#X THEN 80
 70 Q=Q+1:GOTO 50
 80 CLOSE#X:CLS:PRINT:PRINT
 90 PRINT:INPUT "WHAT IS THE NAME IN THE
RECORD YOU WISH TO AMEND ? "N1$:PRINT
100 FOR A=1 TO Q
110 IF A$(A,1)<>N1$ THEN 120 ELSE 130
120 NEXT A
130 PRINT:INPUT"DO YOU WISH TO AMEND THE:
-NAME(TYPE 1); ADDRESS (2);TEL NO (3);AGE (
4);FORM (5) "I
140 INPUT "NOW INPUT THE NEW DATA "R$(I)
150 A$(A,I)=R$(I)
160 INPUT " DO YOU WISH TO AMEND ANOTHER
FIELD IN THIS RECORD? (Y/N) "B$
170 IF B$<>"Y" THEN 190
180 GOTO 130
190 CLS: INPUT TAB(0,4) " DO YOU WISH TO
AMEND ANOTHER RECORD?  (Y/N) "C$
200 IF C$<>"Y" THEN 210 ELSE 90
210 REM READING FROM THE ARRAY TO THE NEW
 FILE
220 CLS:PRINT:PRINT
230 PRINT "PLEASE WAIT WHILE THE NEW FILE
 IS WRITTEN..."
240 Y=OPENOUT("RST789")
250 FOR A=1 TO Q:FOR B=1 TO 6
260 PRINT#Y,A$(A,B)
270 NEXT B:NEXT A
280 CLOSE#Y:CLS:PRINT
290 PRINT:PRINT" NEW FILE-RST789-WRITTEN
AND CLOSED":PRINT
300 REM PRINTING OUT THE NEW FILE
310 FOR C=1 TO Q:FOR D=1 TO 6
320 PRINT A$(C,D);" ";
330 NEXT D
340 PRINT:NEXT C
```

Fig. 11.34(a) Allowing one or more fields to be amended from the keyboard

FILE HANDLING   143

```
RUN


PLEASE WAIT WHILE THE FILE IS READ...


WHAT IS THE NAME IN THE RECORD YOU WISH TO AMEND ? WHITE ANN

DO YOU WISH TO AMEND THE:-NAME(TYPE 1); ADDRESS (2);TEL NO (3);AGE (4);FORM (5) 2

NOW INPUT THE NEW DATA : 6 TALBOT RD SALE


DO YOU WISH TO AMEND ANOTHER FIELD IN THIS RECORD? (Y/N) Y

DO YOU WISH TO AMEND THE:-NAME(TYPE 1); ADDRESS (2);TEL NO (3);AGE (4);FORM (5) 3

NOW INPUT THE NEW DATA : 061 000 9876


DO YOU WISH TO AMEND ANOTHER FIELD IN THIS RECORD? (Y/N) N
DO YOU WISH TO AMEND ANOTHER RECORD?     (Y/N) N


PLEASE WAIT WHILE THE NEW FILE IS WRITTEN...

NEW FILE-RST789-WRITTEN AND CLOSED

BROWN MARY           45 TOWNFIELDS KNUTSFORD            0565 2468
YOUNG JOHN           3 GREEN LANE NORTHWICH             --
GREEN ALAN           17 TOWN LANE MOBBERLEY             MOB 1234
JONES FIONA          43 TREE WAY KNUTSFORD              0565 74812
BLOGGS JOHN          39,ASHWORTH PARK KNUTSFORD         0565 9999
SMITH ROY            99 MANCHESTER RD KNUTSFORD         0565 7887
WHITE ANN            6 TALBOT RD SALE                   061 000 9876
EVANS PETER          1 THE TALBOTS MOBBERLEY            MOB 2345
```

Fig. 11.34 (b) Run from program 09

All the techniques and programs in this chapter have been shown separately so that students will find them easy to follow. A good file manipulation program should have the capability of adding or deleting records, or amending any part of any record and ordering the file subsequent to any amendment. (The files used in this chapter have been deliberately kept as non-ordered files so that students can follow the various techniques of file handling without adding the complexity of sorting routines).

The final program in this chapter (Fig. 11.35) is a practical one for creating, editing, interrogating and ordering a student record file. The program is interactive and all data is entered from the keyboard in response to prompts from the program. An existing file is read into the array M$ at line 150 prior to manipulation and the ending routine sorts the records on the surname key, alphabetically, at lines 1540–1700 before printing to the file. The new file name is the same as the old one with the addition of a suffix 'M' (line 1760). *Note* that in **BBC BASIC**, the original file name must contain less than six characters to remain legal when the 'M' is added. As written, the program can create, edit etc. a file similar to the one used in this chapter, containing up to 100 records. It is a relatively simple matter to alter the program to deal with a file containing different fields with different data and it is left to the interested student to adopt the program to suit his own requirements.

144 COMPUTER STUDIES

```
 10 REM SERIAL DISK FILE HANDLER.PROG10(BBC BASIC)
 20 MODE 7
 30 MR=100:VU=1:F1=0:F2=0
 40 DIM M$(MR,6),F$(6),T(12),K$(6)
 50 FOR I=1 TO 6:READ F$(I):NEXT I
 60 FOR I=1 TO 12:READ T(I):NEXT I
 70 DATA "NAME","ADDRESS","TEL.NO.","AGE","SEX","FORM"
 80 DATA 0,15,55,68,73,76,0,15,55,68,72,76
 90 INPUT TAB(0,9)"Do you wish to create a new file(TYPE N)or edit an existing one (TYPE E)? "A1$
100 PRINT:INPUT"What is the name of the file you are     going to create or use ? "F$:PRINT
110 IF A1$="N" THEN F1=1:GOTO 830
120 PRINT"Please wait while the file is read ...":PRINT
130 X=OPENUP(F$)
140 INPUT#X,R
150 FOR RC=1 TO R:FOR I=1 TO 6:INPUT#X,M$(RC,I):NEXT I:NEXT RC
160 CLOSE#X
170 REM****** MAIN MENU ******
180 CLS
190 PRINT: PRINT:PRINT"There are ";R;" records in the file ";F$
200 PRINT:PRINT"MAIN MENU"
210 PRINT:PRINT"1   ADD A RECORD"
220 PRINT:PRINT"2   DELETE A RECORD"
230 PRINT:PRINT"3   EDIT A RECORD"
240 PRINT:PRINT"4   SEARCH THE FILE"
250 PRINT:PRINT"5   SORT THE FILE"
260 PRINT:PRINT"6   END "
270 PRINT:INPUT"Type in the number of your chosen option "A$
280 A=VAL(A$):IF A<1 OR A>6 OR A<>INT(A) THEN 270
290 CLS
300 ON A GOTO 850,980,640,1110,1540,1730
310 REM****** RESPONSE SECTION ******
320 Q$=Q$+" (Y/N) "
330 PRINT:PRINTQ$;:INPUT A$
340 CLS
350 IF LEFT$(A$,1)="Y" THEN YES =1:RETURN
360 IF LEFT$(A$,1)="N" THEN YES =0:RETURN
370 PRINT:PRINT"YES OR NO PLEASE!":GOTO 330
380 REM****** PRINT RECORDS ******
390 CLS:IF VU=0 THEN VDU2
400 PRINT:PRINT"RECORD NO.";RC
410 FOR I=1 TO 6
420 PRINT:PRINTF$(I);TAB(10);":";M$(RC,I)
430 NEXT I
440 PRINT:PRINT:VDU3
450 IF VU=1 THEN RETURN
460 IF NOHEAD =1 THEN 480
470 RETURN
480 REM****** RECORD SEARCH ******
490 VU=1
500 INPUT TAB(1,8)"What is the name in the record you wish to find? "K$
510 RC=1
520 S=1:S$=M$(RC,1):GOTO 550
530 IF MID$(S$,S,LEN(K$))=K$ THEN 620
540 S=S+1
550 IF S+LEN(K$)<=LEN(S$)+1 THEN 530
560 RC=RC+1
570 IF RC<=R THEN 520
```

Fig. 11.35 Program for creating, editing, interrogating and ordering a student record file

(*Continued*)

FILE HANDLING 145

```
580 PRINT:PRINT"** RECORD NOT FOUND **"
590 Q$="Do you wish to search the file again":GOSUB 310
600 IF YES =1 THEN 500
610 NF=1:RETURN
620 GOSUB 380
630 NF=0:RETURN
640 REM****** EDIT RECORD ******
650 PRINT:PRINT TAB(13);"EDIT A RECORD"
660 VU=1
670 GOSUB 480
680 PRINT
690 IF NF=1 THEN 180
700 FORI=1TO6
710 PRINTI;" ";F$(I)
720 NEXTI
730 PRINT:INPUT"Which field do you want to change? "Y$
740 Y=VAL(Y$):IF Y>6 OR Y<1 OR Y<>INT(Y) THEN 730
750 PRINT:PRINT"OLD ";F$(Y);" : ";M$(RC,Y)
760 PRINT:PRINT"NEW ";F$(Y);" ";:INPUTM$(RC,Y)
770 GOSUB 380
780 Q$="Do you want to change another field":GOSUB 310
790 IF YES=1 THEN 700
800 Q$="Do you want to change another record   ":GOSUB 310
810 IF YES=1 THEN 670
820 GOTO 180
830 REM ******ADD A RECORD******
840 CLS
850 CLS:PRINT:PRINT TAB(14,2);"ADD A RECORD"
860 IF F2=1 THEN 880
870 IF A1$="N"THEN R=0
880 CLS:R=R+1
890 PRINT TAB(10,3)"ADD A RECORD NO. ";R:PRINT
900 FORI=1TO6
910 PRINT:PRINTF$(I);TAB(10);:INPUTM$(R,I)
920 NEXT I
930 Q$="Do you want to add another record       ":GOSUB 310
940 IF YES=0 THEN F2=1:GOTO 180
950 IF R<MR THEN 880
960 PRINT:PRINT"MAXIMUM OF ";MR;" RECORDS ONLY":GOTO 190
970 REM****** DELETE A RECORD ******
980 PRINT:PRINT TAB(13);"DELETE A RECORD"
990 GOSUB 480
1000 IF NF=1 THEN 180
1010 Q$="Do you want to delete this record":GOSUB 310
1020 IF YES =0 THEN 190
1030 R=R-1
1040 FOR I=RC TO R:FOR J=1 TO 6
1050 M$(I,J)=M$(I+1,J)
1060 NEXT J:NEXT I
1070 Q$="another record":GOSUB 310
1080 IF YES=0 THEN 190
1090 IF R=1 THEN PRINT"ONLY ONE RECORD REMAINING!":GOTO 190
1100 GOTO 990
1110 REM ******SEARCH & LIST******
1120 CLS:PRINT:PRINT TAB(14);"SEARCH DATA"
1130 PRINT:PRINT"MENU :"
1140 PRINT:PRINT"1 SEARCH 1 OR MORE FIELDS"
1150 PRINT:PRINT"2 LIST ALL RECORDS"
1160 PRINT:PRINT"3 RETURN TO MAIN MENU"
1170 PRINT:INPUT"Type in the number of your chosen option "A$
1180 A=VAL(A$):IF A<1 OR A>3 OR A<>INT(A) THEN 1170
1190 ON A GOTO 1200,1450,180
1200 PRINT
1210 FOR I=1 TO 6:PRINT I;" ";F$(I):NEXT I
1220 FOR I=1TO6:K$(I)=CHR$(255):NEXTI
1230 Z=1:PRINT
```

Fig. 11.35 continued

146 COMPUTER STUDIES

```
1240 INPUT"Which field do you wish to search? "Y$
1250 Y=VAL(Y$):IF Y>6 OR Y<1 OR Y<>INT(Y) THEN 1240
1260 PRINT:PRINT"Enter the search key for "F$(Y)" ";
1270 INPUT K$(Y)
1280 Q$="´AND´ WITH ANOTHER FIELD":GOSUB310
1290 IF YES=1 THEN Z=Z+1:PRINT:GOTO1240
1300 Q$="Do you want to list to the printer":GOSUB 310
1310 VU=1:IF YES=1 THEN VU=0:NOHEAD=0
1320 FOR RC=1TOR
1330 HITS=0
1340 FORJ=1 TO 6
1350 S=1:S$=M$(RC,J):K$=K$(J):GOTO1380
1360 IF MID$(S$,S,LEN(K$))=K$ THEN HITS=HITS+1:GOTO1390
1370 S=S+1
1380 IF S+LEN(K$)<=LEN(S$)+1 THEN 1360
1390 NEXTJ
1400 IF HITS=Z THEN GOSUB 380:IFVU=1 THEN PRINT:INPUT"PRESS ´RETURN´ TO CONTINU
E "A$
1410 PRINT"*";
1420 NEXT RC
1430 PRINT:IF HITS=0 THEN PRINT" There is no record to match the input key" ELS
E PRINT"** END OF SEARCH **"
1440 D=INKEY(200):GOTO1120
1450 REM ******LIST ALL RECORDS******
1460 Q$="Do you want to list to the printer":GOSUB 310
1470 VU=1:IF YES=1 THEN VU=0:NOHEAD=0
1480 FOR RC=1TOR
1490 GOSUB380
1500 IF VU=1 THEN PRINT:INPUT"PRESS ´RETURN´ TO CONTINUE "A$
1510 NEXT RC
1520 PRINT:PRINT "** END OF FILE **"
1530 D=INKEY(200):GOTO1120
1540 REM ******SORT ON NAME KEY******
1550 CLS
1560 PRINT TAB(2,9);"SORTING";
1570 C=R-1
1580 F=0
1590 J=1
1600 IF M$(J,1)<=M$(J+1,1) THEN 1670
1610 FORI=1TO6
1620 X$=M$(J+1,I)
1630 M$(J+1,I)=M$(J,I)
1640 M$(J,I)=X$
1650 NEXT I
1660 F=1
1670 J=J+1:IFJ<=C THEN 1600
1680 C=C-1:PRINT".";
1690 IF F=1 THEN 1580
1700 PRINT"Sorting complete":K=INKEY(100)
1710 GOTO 180
1720 REM ******ENDING ROUTINES******
1730 PRINT TAB(2,9);"PLEASE WAIT WHILE THE FILE IS WRITTEN..."
1740 IF F1=1 THEN 1770
1750 O$=F$
1760 F$=F$+"M"
1770 Y=OPENOUT(F$)
1780 PRINT #Y,R
1790 FOR RC=1 TO R:FOR I=1 TO 6
1800 PRINT #Y,M$(RC,I)
1810 NEXT I:NEXT RC
1820 CLOSE #Y
1830 IF F1<>1 THEN 1860
1840 PRINT:PRINT"THE DATA HAS BEEN WRITTEN TO "F$
1850 GOTO 1880
1860 PRINT:PRINT"THE NEW VERSION OF THE FILE IS "F$
1870 PRINT:PRINT"THE OLD FILE IS STILL "O$
1880 PRINT:PRINT"BYE !":END
```

Fig. 11.35 continued

11.9 Security of files

A lot of time and effort is put into creating a file: anybody who has made a file with more than about 12 records, each with five or six fields, will know this. Anybody who has made such a file and then 'lost' it, will know this very well indeed and probably wished they had taken some precautions to make their file secure.

File security can be considered at two levels:
(i) Protection of a complete file against total, or even partial, loss.
(ii) Protection of a file against unauthorised use.

The first risk can be minimised easily by making a copy of the file and storing this quite separately from the original version, for example, *not* on the same disk or tape which might be accidently lost, damaged or even erased! If the file is updated in some way then the copy must also be updated or a copy of the new file kept in place of the old one. Such a system is known as the family system, or the ancestral system of file protection.

When a new file is created it is known as the master file and, for security, a copy is made. When this file is updated, the copy is kept along with the transaction file and the new file. These two versions of the file are known as father and son and hold the previous and the latest versions of the file, respectively, but they must be stored on different disks or tapes.

If the father file were to be lost or corrupted, it would not matter as the son file still exists, but it would be necessary to make another copy of the son file, quickly. If the son is corrupted, the father file (and the transaction file) can be used to re-create the son file. When the son file is itself updated, it is copied (to make the new father file), and the updated file becomes the new son file. The old father is destroyed, or for even greater security, kept as the grandfather file. If this is done, three generations of the file exist at all times, which may be costly in terms of storage space, but can be 'project saving' if accidental erasure or damage to a file occurs.

This technique is shown in flowchart form on page 133 and in detail in Fig. 11.20. At line 210, the father file is GHJ456 and the son file is RST789. The option to kill the father file is offered in line 230, with a small added security in line 250, just in case you have made a mistake! These nine lines of program should, of course, be added to all the file updating programs in this chapter.

Protection of a file against unauthorised use can be achieved in a number of ways. The two most practical methods are to make the file name secret or by using 'secret' characters embedded in the file name. Keeping the file name secret is not easy if you are going to use it with other people around who can read your file name. Some mainframe computer systems achieve this by making the file name 'appear' on the VDU or teletypewriter on top of previously written characters, typically XXXXXXXX on a teletype or 'black squares' on a VDU, so that the characters of the file name are undecipherable to the human eye, but not to the computer. This technique does not, however, prevent somebody from obtaining a listing of all the file names and working through each one if he so desires.

The second method uses control characters in the file name which do not print either on a VDU or on a line printer. Control characters are allocated the first 33 values in the ASC11 code and can be seen in columns 1 and 2 of the table in Appendix 4. Not all these control characters are available on all 'standard' teletype keyboards. On some keyboards of both teletypes and microcomputers there is a special key called control, (marked CTRL), which, when depressed at the same time as a second key, generates a control character which is not 'echoed' in visible form anywhere. Care must be taken in selecting suitable control characters as many computer systems, both mainframe and microcomputers, use some control characters to control the computers. Reference should be made to the system manual before choosing control characters for use in file names. A word of warning, however, about using 'secret characters': make sure *you* have a record of what characters you have used, otherwise even you will not be able to access the file!

In the business and commercial world, files may contain many hundreds, or even thousands, of records and the time taken to create such files is measured in terms of man-years. Large files may take hundreds of man-years to create and not only represent an enormous financial investment to a company, but would be almost impossible to re-create if the master file was destroyed. It is not surprising, therefore, to find that companies go to considerable lengths to protect their files. Three generations of each file would normally be kept in a fire and waterproof safe and copies of the files kept under similar conditions in a completely separate safe. There are many stories told of a company's buildings and contents, including the computer, being totally destroyed by fire and the master files recovered, undamaged, from a safe still intact among the rubble.

11.10 Data processing

The preceeding sections of this chapter have dealt with the handling of data in computer files in some detail and in a practical programming manner, to encourage students to undertake some data processing. A great many excellent examination projects can be based on a data processing application and, with the advent of the microcomputer in the home, the number of data processing applications that can be tackled is almost limitless.

However much we try though, it is almost impossible to get the 'feel' of commercial data processing in an educational or home environment. When you are looking at commercial data processing, the following should be realised:

(i) The amount of data to be handled is many orders of magnitude greater than is normally handled in schools.
(ii) The method of data input is different (p. 22-25).
(iii) The method of updating files is different (see below).
(iv) Files are updated frequently, possibly more than once a day, if many records are constantly changing.
(v) Time means money in the commercial world and there is a constant pressure to get data processed quickly.
(vi) Specially trained staff are employed to prepare data for computer input and to handle the throughput of jobs in the computer.

File updating

Section 11.8 dealt with a number of different methods of updating a file. None of these techniques is really practical if we have to amend many records in a large file. Consider, for example, a master file of a car insurance company. Such a file would contain many thousands of records holding details of every car and its owner, insured with that company. On any day, new insurance policies are issued, necessitating the addition of records to the file, existing policies require amending when a car is changed or the type of insurance covered is altered, and policies require cancelling if a person changes his insurance company or ceases to own a car. All this is quite apart from the daily task of processing claims, but if the master file is not up to date, it can become a liability to the company, not an asset.

The method used to update a master file is to make small files containing all the amendments generated during, typically, a working day, and to update the master file at the end of the day so that the following

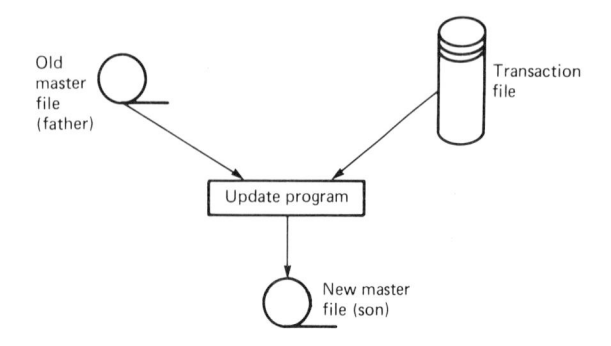

Fig. 11.36 Simple system flowchart for file updating

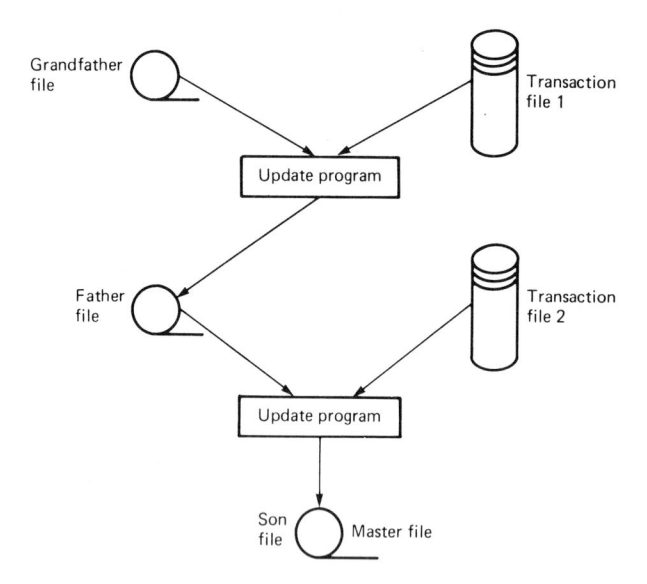

Fig. 11.37 System flowchart showing grandfather, father, son concept

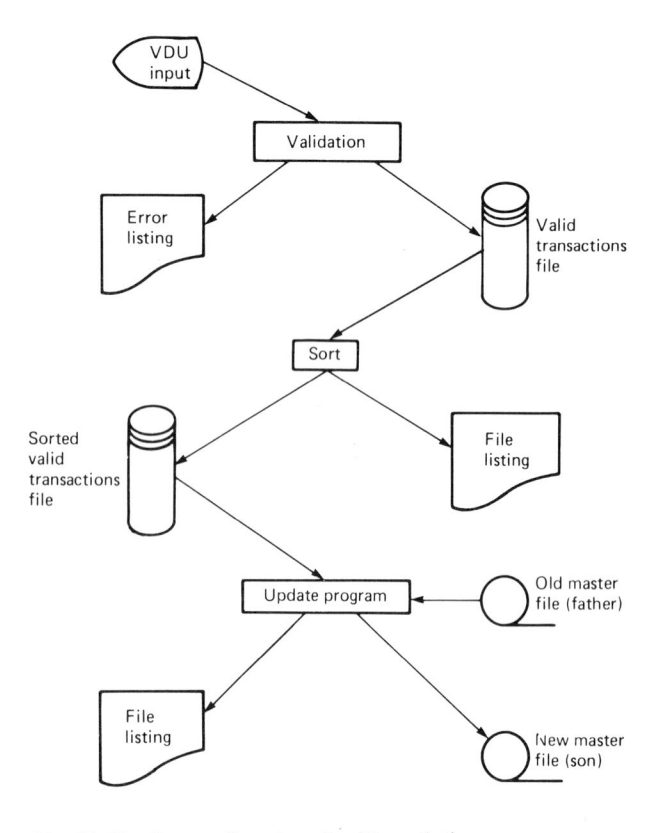

Fig. 11.38 System flowchart for file updating

day's work is done using the latest version of the master file. In a car insurance company, separate files would be made for holding details of new policies, amended policies and deleted policies. Such files are known as transaction files and as soon as they have been used to update the master file, they are erased. In many data processing departments where file updating is frequent, the transaction files themselves are kept until after the next updating run, again as added security in case the master file is destroyed. This type of file updating is shown diagrammatically in Fig. 11.36.

If this process takes place twice before any files are over written, then three generations of file exist at the same time (Fig. 11.37). All files need to be organised in order to speed up the process of searching for a given data item (see p. 106), and therefore the transaction files themselves need to be similarly organised. A typical data flowchart for file updating is shown in Fig. 11.38.

Summary

- Data should be stored in files for ease of access and editing.
- Data stored in a file should normally be organised (alphabetically or numerically).
- Four types of file are commonly used: serial access; sequential access; indexed sequential access; and random access.
- Serially organised files can be stored on both magnetic tape and disk. Each record is written to the file immediately following the preceding record.
- Random access files would not (sensibly) be stored on magnetic tape. Each record is written 'at random' to a 'calculated' block on a disk surface.
- All the records in one file must have the same number of fields, which must contain data, even if the data is dummy.
- Interrogation involves reading one, or more, fields of all the records in a file looking for specified data. When a record matches this data a 'hit' is recorded.
- A file may be amended by adding or deleting one or more records or altering one or more fields in existing records.
- File security can be achieved by writing a 'secret password' into the file name.
- Protection against loss of an updated file is achieved by keeping a copy of the previous version(s) of the file (father – son).
- Transaction files are used to update master files.

Exercises 11.1

1 A file consisting of a number of records, is to be held on the following media:
(i) punched cards; (ii) paper tape; (iii) magnetic tape; (iv) magnetic disc.
Explain, with the aid of sketches, the structure of the file in each case, including its division into records, fields, etc. (*AEB, 1978*)*

2 In a certain school it is decided to keep pupils' records on a magnetic tape file.
(*a*) What items could usefully be included in the record? Indicate clearly which of these items would need to be altered at the beginning of a school year, and how this could be achieved.
(*b*) Discuss briefly the advantages and disadvantages of using a tape system or a disk system for this type of data processing. (*AEB, 1974*)*

3 (*a*) What is a *master file*?
(*b*) Describe, briefly, how a master file is updated.

4 A second-hand car dealer wishes to keep a record of the cars he has for sale on a computer file. Each record is to contain the following details about each car: year; make; model; colour; condition; price.
(*a*) Show, by means of a detailed diagram, exactly how this particular data would be structured into a file for subsequent interrogation.
(*b*) State which type of file (random or serial access) would be most suitable for this particular application, and why.
(*c*) State briefly how the file would be created; how it would be interrogated for a particular enquiry and how data in the file could be changed. (*AEB, 1979*)*

5 A clothing warehouse keeps a list of its contents on index cards. The information consists of:

Item number	(6 digit integer)
Item name	(up to 20 characters)
Manufacturer code	(5 characters)
Location code	(6 digits)

The information is to be stored on magnetic backing storage media, so that it becomes part of an on-line stock control computerised system.
(*a*) Devise a suitable data capture form for this information.
(*b*) Describe the data in terms of fields and records.
(*c*) Which backing storage medium would be most suitable and why?

(d) What other field is normally added when such a system is computerised?
(e) What other information relevant to this application could be stored on the backing storage?

(*AEB, 1980*)*

6 In designing a system to hold personal information about students in a school, it is decided that the first two fields of each record will consist of a student's name and address and that their date of birth, sex and form will be coded numerically to form a single, *n*-bit, third field.
(a) Suggest a method of encoding the data to form the third field, using as few bits as possible. Explain the coding system used and give two examples.
(b) Show how this data can be validated by using one extra bit. Illustrate this by using one of the examples from (a).

7 A file is to be set up to store criminal records. The layout of each record is as follows:
Surname (15 characters);
Height (in cm) (3 characters);
Eye colour (1 character);
Hair colour (1 character);
Crime (1 character).

The codes used for the last 3 fields are as follows:

Eye colour	Hair colour	Crime
1 Brown	1 Brown	1 Murder
2 Blue	2 Black	2 Assault
3 Grey	3 Fair	3 Armed robbery
4 Green	4 Grey	4 Theft
5 Hazel	5 White	5 Embezzlement

(a) Draw a flowchart to show how to create the file, with 100 records.
(b) Write a program segment to print the names of all criminals on the file over 170 cm tall who also have fair hair and who have committed murder.

8 Complete the following paragraph by inserting the appropriate word from the list below in the spaces. (You may use a word more than once.)

generations, father, master, grandfather, duplicated, transaction, son, corrupted.

Most data-processing applications require a ..... file which is the main reference file and is usually updated using a ..... file. It is normal to retain three ..... of file; the most recent version is the ..... file, the ..... file is the previous version of the file and the oldest version is known as the ..... file. The ..... file would be used to produce a new son file should that file become ......*

12 The use of computers

12.1 General uses in business

Writing this chapter in the early 1950s would not have taken very long. The few computers that existed at that time were purpose-built to do, usually, one job—scientific or mathematical calculations. LEO (Lyons Electronic Office, 1951) was the first computer used for commercial/business applications and this was limited in the first years of its use to calculate the payroll and for stock control. By 1954 IBM had developed the first general-purpose computer (IBM 650) and gradually many different jobs which had previously been done by hand methods were computerised.

Anyone making an inventory during the early 1970s of the different uses for computers could have been forgiven for thinking that the list was complete and that there could be no more ways in which a computer could be used. They would have been very wrong. New uses are being thought of continuously and the introduction of the microcomputer has meant that whole new areas of activity, like the home and education, are finding new uses for computers, almost daily. Whatever job a computer does, however big and complex the computer system is, whatever speed of operation is achieved, the system can always be considered as:

$$\text{Input} \rightarrow \text{Process} \rightarrow \text{Output}$$

The method of getting data into, and information out of, the processing unit, may require any of the peripheral devices discussed in Section 7.1. The CPUs used in widely differing applications may have the same basic architecture and only differ in minor details, and even some of the software will be 'standard'. Most computers today are general-purpose computers, like the ICL 2900 series, and it is the particular application and use to which the computer system will be put, which dictates the choice of peripherals and software.

Virtually every computer that is used in a business or commercial environment performs 'standard functions' of payroll, stock control, invoicing, accounting, and staff records as well as the 'particular use' for which the system has been designed. The standard jobs could be described as 'the bread and butter' of all businesses and

'Not all computers uses are sensible.'

need to be carried out either manually or using a computer.

Scrooge was not the only one to keep accounts in a manual ledger. Until the introduction of computers, *every* company kept all its accounts, details of stock, staff records etc. in manual systems and the wages office in many factories started work on next week's wages almost before the current week's wages were paid! As all these standard jobs, as above, *had* to be carried out if the company was to continue in business, they were the first to be 'computerised'.

Payroll

Every company has to pay its employees and every employees wages or salary may be made up in a different way (as discussed in Chapter 11). All the employee records are stored in one (master) file and the data for each employee, relating to the current week (or month) is input into a second (transaction) file. The data relating to hours worked may be automatically recorded on to magnetic tape or disk at the clocking-in station or the employees' clock-card may have a magnetic stripe built into it on which the times of clocking in and out are recorded for subsequent direct data entry to the computer (Fig. 12.1).

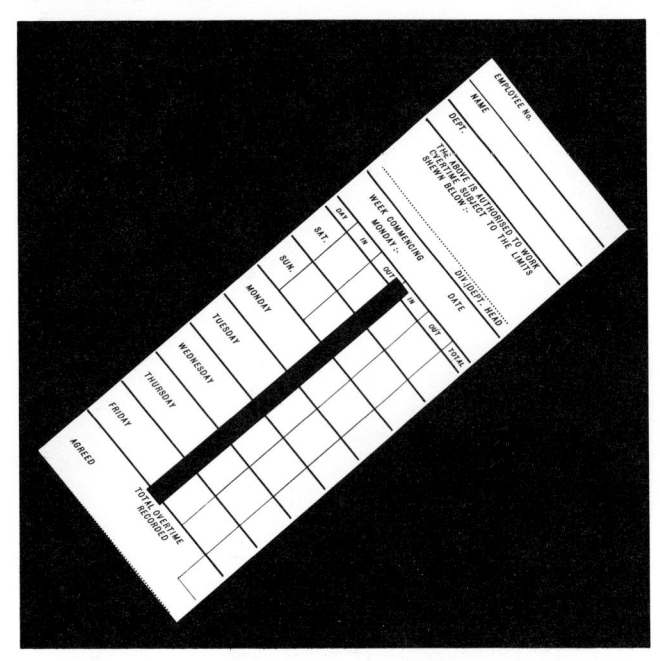

Fig. 12.1 Clock card with magnetic stripe

The output from a payroll program is in the form of a pay-slip giving all the relevant details of salary and deductions which can be printed on special 'private' stationery, where only the employee name and number appears on the outside of the payslip and all personal details appear only on the inside of the payslip (Fig. 12.2).

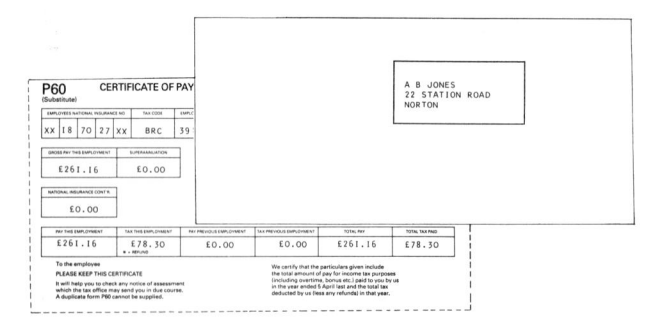

Fig. 12.2 Payslip printed on 'private' computer stationery

If salaries are being paid directly into the employees' bank accounts, or payment is made by cheque, the cheques are printed directly from the computer output.

If payment is to be made in cash, the program may total the amount of money required to pay all the employees and break this down into the number of notes and coins required for each pay packet, and the total notes and coins that need to be drawn from the bank. Machines are available which dispense the required coins and notes automatically.

Invoicing and accounting

Invoicing and accounting are practised by every company that buys and sells goods. Goods which are purchased from another supplier have to be paid for when the supplier's account is presented and goods sold by the company require invoicing to the purchaser before payment will be made.

In manufacturing an aeroplane, for example, many thousands of different parts are required from dozens of different suppliers and every item, from rivets to jet engines, will have to be paid for and accounted for in the manufacture of the plane. The systems used before computers were introduced relied entirely on many thousands of pieces of paper which had to be checked and re-checked and read and re-read (and very often lost), before the final entry was made in some account book.

As well as dealing with all accounts sent by outside suppliers in respect of goods supplied and invoicing every customer for goods sold, a typical accounts department of a manufacturing company will be expected to look beyond the day-to-day operations of the company. It will be expected to advise on pricing structures for new products, design a strategy to ensure profitability of operation, advise on investments and keep a tight control on credit to ensure a steady cash flow. The complexity and competitiveness of modern business is such that manual implementation of such activities as those given above is virtually unthinkable.

A typical computerised accounting system will be closely linked to a purchasing and stores system where every item supplied to the company is input to backing store from a VDU terminal and checked when the supplier's account arrives. If. the record of goods received matches the account, the computer is 'authorised' to pay the supplier either by cheque or credit transfer. Equally, when goods are supplied to a customer, the invoice is prepared automatically from files containing details of all products, their prices, discount codes, and customers' names and addresses. The use of computers in accounting has greatly speeded-up the process of preparing and checking all output; reduced the number of errors due to lost documents; significantly reduced the number of people involved in what was a labour intensive, but largely routine job, and provided a database on which many financial calculations may be based.

Stock control

The control of stock in any business or company is vital to its ability to make a profit or even to its survival. Whether the company is a large manufacturing organisation or a small retail shop, stock control must be efficiently practised.

Ideally, a shop should not need to hold any more stock than can be sold in one day, or until the next delivery of supplies, and a factory should only need to stock as much material as can be used before the next delivery is due. Unfortunately, the ideal situation is not the practical one, and varying demands for goods, and delays in delivery of components or other supplies, force shop-keepers and factory owners alike to keep a stock of goods which are *likely* to sell, and material which *may be* required, before the next delivery.

Whatever stock is purchased, it has to be paid for, and the business ordering the stock will not get its money back until the stock is sold. Too much stock may guarantee customer satisfaction, because they can be supplied without delay, but may tie up too much of the company's ready cash. Too little stock may save paying out too much cash but may lose customers if their order cannot be fulfilled immediately. Somewhere between these two extremes lies the happy medium and stock control is an attempt to achieve an optimum level of stock to suit supply and demand.

Stock control by computer is much more accurate and efficient than by hand methods because of the amount of data the computer can access, without error, such as price structures, delivery dates and alternative suppliers. A computer can also examine and adjust a number of different variables before producing an optimum result, such as target production dates; altered work schedules to allow for changed delivery dates; and component re-ordering dates to fit in with new schedules. The actual ordering is, of course, automatically done at the correct time by the computer!

As stock control is so important to business, industry, commerce and the retail trade, many stock control packages have been produced, usually for a specific application, varying from Tesco's 'fresh food at low price' package, which is used weekly by all Tesco branches to re-stock their supplies, to a complex design and manufacturing package used by ICL.

ICL have used a system known as Pericles for many years to help in the design and manufacture of computers. This system embraces the applications of stock control and accounting which may be required by any of the factories and offices throughout the United Kingdom. The master files holding information relating to every component required to make any ICL computer or associated equipment are held on disk, with the main computer system at Stevenage in Hertfordshire and are accessed remotely from VDU terminals via dedicated Telecom lines. Although the system is interactive, the files can only be interrogated via the VDU, and updating is done by batch operation every night so the files are correct at the start of every day. Although this may seem a reasonable time scale for file updating, in a manufacturing company which may buy, use, or modify many thousands of items in a single day, out-of-date information can cause many production problems as well as waste large amounts of money. A further disadvantage of this system is that any data which is required to be accessed in more than one way has to be held on more than one file and, because of the type of file structure used, a file may have to be fully searched to find the required item of data.

The new version of this system is the basis for a very sophisticated design and manufacturing information system which can be used to help in the design and manufacture of cars, aeroplanes, trains etc. as well as computers. The data that was previously held on up to 14 files, is now held on one database with no duplication, and updating is now performed online by authorised users of the system. As the files are now structured in terms of a comprehensive database, enquiries can be made at many 'levels'. Enquiries could range from 'What components are required to make a 2900?' to 'Where is this component used and who supplies it?'. Three hundred ICL 7500 VDU terminals, situated in 10 sites throughout the UK, have access to 400 000 000 characters of data held on 2×200 Mbyte exchangeable disk stores, controlled by one 2960 central processor. The average response time to any query is less than 5 seconds. ICL estimate that use of this system, where the data files are always up-to-date, can save £1 000 000 per day in 'lost opportunity' (to make a new product) and has achieved a saving of £3 000 000 per year in non-wasted (out of date or incorrect) stock.

12.2 Banking

The banks were among the first to realise the great savings that could be achieved by using a computer. In the simplest possible terms, a bank's operation could be described as 'processing figures (payments, credits etc.), written on paper (cheques, standing orders, currencies etc.), to buy and sell money'. By the late 1950s, much of the old handwritten ledger work had been transferred to accounting machines and in the early 1960s the computer was introduced, enabling branches of the same bank to be linked to a central computer system, using teleprinters and paper tape for input which had been prepared off-line. Since these early beginnings, the banks' use of computers has steadily grown and one of the largest users of computers, Barclays Bank, has an investment of over £70 000 000 in its computer systems, which are used, among many other more sophisticated jobs, to clear almost 3 000 000 cheques every day.

Until the early 1970s, the computers were used solely to automate existing manual procedures such as cheque clearing, standing order payments, salary payments and branch customer accounts. With the advancing technology, Barclays were able to evolve new uses for their computers and new and more efficient methods of implementing old procedures. Among these is the automatic reading of cheques using sorters employing the technique of MICR; on-line terminals networked to enable any terminal in the UK to be connected to the main computer centre; Barclaybank cash dispensing service; and 'customer terminals' (Fig. 12.3).

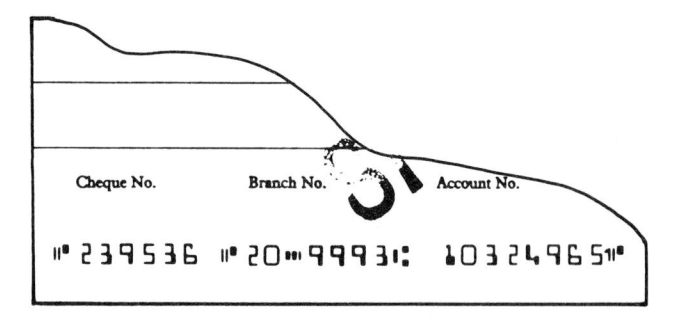

Fig. 12.4 Cheque showing characters printed in magnetic ink

Fig. 12.3 Bank counter terminal

All cheques paid into all branches of Barclays bank are sent to the cheque clearing department in London, every day. Cheques from other banks are taken out and sent to the central Bankers Clearing House from whom Barclays will receive cheques presented through any of the other banks. All the Barclays cheques are then sorted into the branches holding the actual accounts on which the cheques are drawn. The data used as the sorting key is encoded on each cheque in magnetic ink characters (Fig. 12.4) (see p. 54).

Barclaybank is the name given to a 24-hour cash dispensing service which enables authorised users to obtain up to £50 cash per day from cash dispensing terminals situated outside banks, in universities, shopping precincts etc., or to pay cash into their account, or simply to ask for an up-to-date statement. Authorised users have an embossed plastic card with a magnetic stripe permanently attached to the card. The stripe contains encoded data which identifies the customer and holds details of his account. It is 'read' when the card is inserted into the dispensing unit. Each unit is connected directly to the main computer centre, using private telephone lines and the data read from the card is checked against the master files held on the computer. If the user is authorised, and his account holds more than the minimum limit, the computer asks which service is required and then either pays out the requested amount in notes, or accepts cash into the dispenser, or issues a printed statement of the balance of the account. The details of the transaction are recorded on disk at the computer centre which is subsequently used to update the master file daily (Fig. 12.5).

Fig. 12.5 Cash dispenser (IBM 3624 Auto-teller)

Very many more people are now paid by cheque or by direct credit to a bank that was the case only a few years ago; the use of credit cards grew enormously during the latter half of the 1970s; the use of standing orders and direct debit mandates is growing daily; and last, but by no means least, the number of traveller's cheques issued has almost doubled each year during this same period. Without the use of computers to assist in this work most of it could not be done in a realistic time-scale in our modern society.

Barclays Bank maintains that most of the routine clerical work, which is a normal part of banking, can be done much more quickly and more precisely using computers, thereby releasing staff for more satisfying and creative aspects of their work.

12.3 Garment design and manufacture

A fascinating, and quite different, use of computers is in garment design. Courtaulds use a computing system developed by the Hughes Aircraft Corporation of America to help in the design and manufacture of clothes.

The first items of a new product range are designed and made by hand, using only the expertise and skill of the designer and the cutter. After the designs have been approved by the buyer, the first paper pattern is produced by hand, using the approved garments as an accurate guide. It is at this point that the computer comes into the operation. Each piece of the pattern is placed on a pattern digitizer table, and the co-ordinates of selected points around the edge of the pattern are read using a cursor and fed into the computer (Fig. 12.6).

In order to store a straight edge on the pattern, only two sets of co-ordinates need to be read—the two ends of the straight line—but to store curves, many points around the curve need to be digitised. Whatever the pattern shape, sufficient points to enable the pattern to be reproduced are fed into the computer and stored. This procedure is repeated for each piece of the pattern for one garment, the whole operation taking a skilled operator about a minute per pattern shape.

The next step is to grade this basic pattern into sizes. The human body is an awkward shape and does not obey any sensible mathematical rules for sizing. All mass-produced garments are made in a variety of sizes to suit the individual and the rules for grading these sizes are complex and are based on years of experience of altering a 'standard size' pattern to suit other requirements. The grading rules are given to the computer which then calculates the size of each piece of the pattern for each standard size required. This data is also stored and is subsequently used to produce patterns of all the various sizes without the need for any further design work.

The next step is to fit all the pieces of the pattern onto the 'material' from which the garment is to be made. Many students will have seen this done, or done it themselves, on the kitchen table or the bedroom floor and spent hours trying to fit all the pieces of the pattern onto the minimum length of material whilst preserving technicalities like pattern match and direction of the nap. With a computer, this process takes only minutes, and there are no paper patterns to blow away and no material is needed.

The computer system used to do this job uses a VDU with graphics tablet (see Chapter 7.1). The 'material' is shown on the screen as two horizontal lines representing the width of the material from which the garment is to be made. The left hand edge of the material is shown as a vertical line whilst the right hand edge remains undefined at this stage. All the pieces of the pattern are now called from store and appear, reduced by the same scale as the material, in a spare area at the top of the screen. Using a 'wand' and the data tablet, a skilled marker operator 'takes' each piece of pattern from the screen storage area and positions it between the lines marking the edges of the material. It is this operator's job to position the pieces of the pattern to use the maximum width and minimum length of material. When all the pieces have been positioned, the computer calculates the 'percentage fit', i.e. the amount of material that has been used, expressed as a percentage of the total area used. A target 'fit' of 85% is aimed for and if the calculated figure is much below this, the operator re-positions the pieces

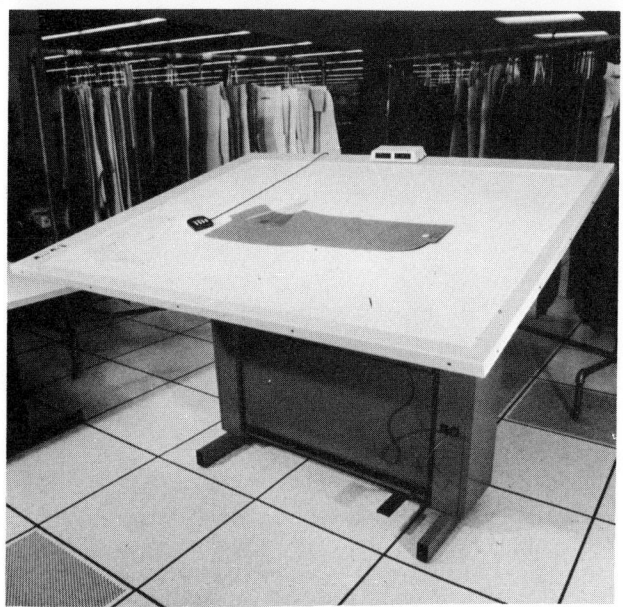

Fig. 12.6 Digitiser table

on the screen in an attempt to improve the current figure. The process can be repeated as often as required to try and achieve the maximum utilisation of the material and, therefore, minimum waste. Fig. 12.7

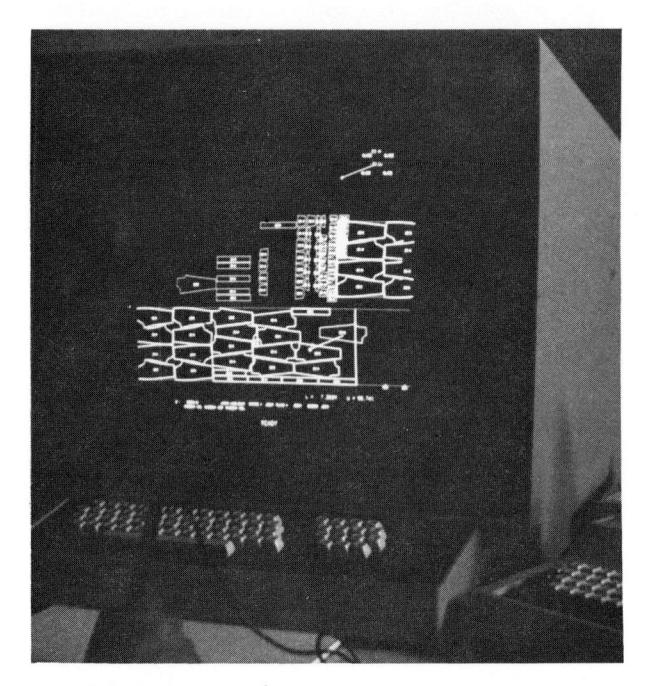

Fig 12.7 Pattern market

shows an almost complete marker; the pieces at the top of the screen have still to be fitted.

When the operator is satisfied that he connot effect any further improvement in the marker layout, all the co-ordinates of each piece of the pattern, as they now appear on the screen, are stored on magnetic tape and disk and a full size pattern is drawn using a graph plotter with paper 2.1 m wide.

The garment manufacturing industry uses fabrics of standard widths, which are supplied in 50–100 m rolls, so the final marker pattern will be for as many garments as can be cut out of a manageable length of material (5–10 m), thus allowing the pieces for many identical garments to be cut out of one piece of material. Depending on the thickness of the material, up to 300 pieces can be cut at one time, so it is possible to cut out enough pattern pieces to make approximately 6000 garments in one operation. The machine used to cut out the pieces of material is a Gerber cutting table, shown in Fig. 12.8.

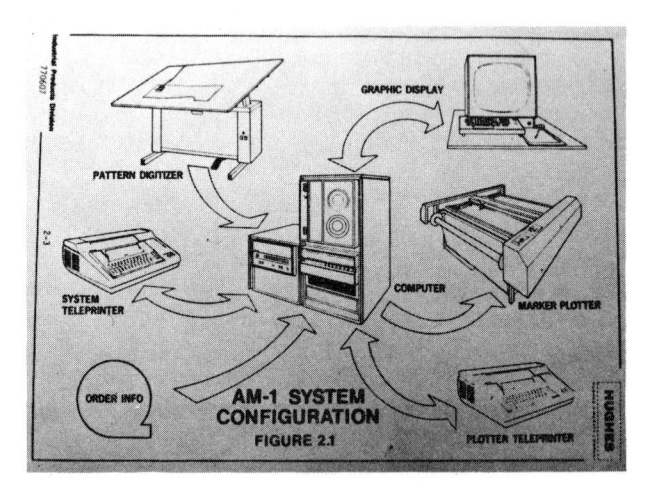

Fig. 12.9 Overview of complete system

All the lengths of material to be cut are laid on top of each other on the table and covered with the full size pattern and a sheet of clear plastic. The 'sandwich' of layers of material is held down to the table by suction, hence the need for the plastic sheet. A very sharp rotating knife is suspended above the table, which can be moved to any position above the material by controlling the longitudinal and transverse movements of the knife using special electric motors known as stepper motors. The knife can be lowered to cut into the 'sandwich' of material or raised to be moved to a new cutting position. Signals to effect control of the knife are fed into the system from the magnetic tape on which the final marker was stored at an earlier stage. The cutting mechanism faithfully, and accurately, follows the full size version of this marker and cuts out each piece of the pattern in turn.

Fig 12.8 Cutting table

The approximate time to cut out enough pieces of material to make 1000 garments is 30 minutes. A new version of the cutting table uses a laser beam instead of a rotating knife, but this cannot be used on certain thermoplastic materials as the heat from the laser melts the material and joins the layers together!

The system described above has many advantages over a manual system: ease and speed of producing 'master patterns' from the original design; automatic grading for different sizes; permanent storage of all manufacturing data with easy and quick access; ease of alteration of any stored patterns; and optimum use of material. Fig. 12.9 shows an overview of the complete system.

It is only when we see the costs involved in production of garments that we can see the savings achieved by producing the marker by computer. If an 85% 'fit' is obtained, obviously, 15% of the material is wasted. In one group involved in garment design the cost of this wasted material is estimated at £7 500 000! The system described above can improve the 'fit' by 1-2%, depending on the particular pattern, enabling a saving of approximately £100 000 per annum to be made. The use of a computer system, which is described below, can therefore easily be justified in terms of cost effectiveness.

Details of the computer system are as follows:

(i) The central processor is a Hewlett Packard 21 MX which uses a 16 bit word and has 64 K of IAS with 650 ns access time.
(ii) The disk storage capacity is 20 Mbytes.
(iii) The graphic display terminal has its own microprocessor which contains 16 K words of IAS.
(iv) The digitiser table has a working surface of approximately 1.5 m × 1.1 m and, within this area, an accuracy of ±0.2 mm can be obtained.

12.4 Airlines

The airlines were another group who were quick to realise the advantages of using computers. By the early 1960s, the volume of traffic using the major airlines had become so large that unless some automation could be introduced, delays in passenger booking, and over-booking would be inevitable. To some extent, these problems could be overcome by employing more staff to handle the rapidly growing business, but that was only a partial solution. The full solution was provided by introducing computers.

British Overseas Airways Corporation (BOAC) introduced a comprehensive seat reservation system in 1968 which used online terminals at Heathrow airport, and the main air terminals, which were connected to a central computer system situated at Heathrow. With the introduction of VDU terminals, this system was quickly expanded to link the major UK airports into the system. Thus the time required to book a seat was substantially reduced and the possibility of over booking was reduced to almost zero as the seats for any flight were stored on disk and *immediately* a booking was confirmed, that seat was removed from the availability list and not offered to the next enquirer.

Fig. 12.10 A British Airways check-in desk

British European Airways (BEA), meanwhile, had produced a similar system linking all the UK airports and terminal buildings and many of the large travel agencies. When these two airlines were merged in 1972 to form British Airways (BA), the existing systems were merged to form BABS (British Airways Booking System), which is recognised as one of the world's leading, comprehensive, booking systems. The communications network now extends around the world and it is possible to access the system directly from Australia, or America and obtain a response in the same few seconds as from a travel agent in London. As well as handling seat reservations, BABS can issue tickets and give all possible fare quotations and flight times for any route. It can also make any necessary hotel reservations along with any personal requirements, e.g. vegetarian meals, use of wheelchairs, baby-in-arms etc. The system also deals with check-in procedures, baggage weight control, cargo control, and provides the data for flight operations and flight planning. It is only when some of the statistics involved in the above operations, are quoted that the advantages of using a computer can be appreciated. Indeed it should be realised that continued expansion of airline business would have been quite impossible without the use of computers.

BABS handles an average of about 1 000 000 enquiries per day and during the summer peak, about 2 000 000 per day. Approximately 400 000 different routes and fare structures are stored in the system and can be accessed immediately. On average, 1000 passengers per hour are checked in at Heathrow. BABS provides up-to-the-second data for weight control and after check-in has closed, can immediately provide a list of passengers who are actually on the flight.

All flight operations and movements are controlled by a real-time computer system known as FICO (flight information and control of operations). Starting simply from a scheduled flight number, this system gradually builds up a complete 'dossier' on the flight, allocating aircraft, crew, food, fuel, etc., and receiving information from BABS relating to passengers on the flight. The system feeds into the operations control centre at Heathrow, and provides the data necessary for flight planning.

Early in 1981, BA announced a new cargo handling system, BA80, which will be installed at Manchester and Glasgow as well as London airport. It will be integrated into the existing BA worldwide network to provide international cargo handling facilities and by integrating with the existing customs clearance system, ACP80, it is hoped to speed up cargo shipments and reduce the present mass of necessary documents to a minimum.

12.5 Police

The police use computers widely in their fight against crime, in dealing with prosecutions and court proceedings and to assist in traffic handling.

The main computer resource is the Police National Computer (PNC), which is housed at Hendon in North London and connected to all divisional police headquarters in the UK via direct Telecom lines. Each divisional unit has one or more VDUs which are used in most communications with the PNC, and a teletype which is used when printed output is required. The average time of response to a routine enquiry for registration details of a suspected car, from anywhere in the UK, is within a few seconds. If the enquiry has come from a patrol car via the radio, a further minute might be added to the enquiry time. Before the PNC was introduced in 1974, a similar enquiry could have taken hours to complete (Fig. 12.11).

Fig. 12.11 Police National Computer

The PNC has an enormous storage capacity and its files store the names and addresses of the legal owner of every vehicle registered in the UK (some 25 million records); details of every reported stolen car or car 'under suspicion' of having been involved in a crime; the name, and brief details of anybody convicted of a serious offence or wanted by the police; persons missing or found; and details of all disqualified drivers. The system also stores a coded version of the national fingerprint files held at Scotland Yard.

The system can also be used as a fast communications network where urgent messages can be sent to all police forces within seconds of, for example, a serious crime being reported.

The PNC is 'on-line' 24 hours a day and is designed, as far as possible, to maintain a service to forces even in the event of partial failure of equipment. This support and reliability are achieved by duplication of vital components of the system such as the central processor and by using small processors to control the input and output to and from the CPU, and the communications network. Duplication also means that routine maintenance can be carried out by closing down selected units when required.

The central processing unit consists of three Burroughs B7700 processors which normally work together in harness, but can also operate in dual or single processor mode, the former when a processing unit is required for maintenance. The processors operating in any mode have access to over six million bytes of fast memory. Over 40 million records are stored on 52 dual disc drives with a total capacity of over 12 000 megabytes. This data is protected by periodic 'dumping' to magnetic tape on any of 13 magnetic tape units. These units also provide a facility for maintaining a running audit on what is happening on the machine and a record of all messages received from terminals operated by police forces throughout Great Britain. Peripheral devices include four-line printers and card and paper tape readers and punches. The system is controlled and monitored from four console display units.

Most police forces throughout the UK have either their own small computer or access to the local council computer but only police controlled local systems can be linked in to the PNC system. Local forces use their own computers in many ways; two examples are:
(a) to record details of all crimes and accidents in the area for subsequent detailed analysis
(b) by the prosecutions department to issue summonses and all the legal documents required before a prosecution and then to follow-up the court hearing with notices of sentence etc.

The police also make a wide and growing use of computers to help in traffic control. In some inner city areas, all the traffic lights controlling the flow of traffic through the area are linked to, and controlled by, a computer. Data relating to traffic flow is constantly fed into the computer which then sets the traffic signals to suit the traffic conditions prevailing at that time. Priority can be given to city-bound traffic during the morning rush-hour and vice versa at night. Remotely controlled television cameras provide visual information of traffic patterns to the officer on duty. In the event of any occurrence which could interrupt the traffic flow, such as an accident or slow-moving lorry, this data can be fed into the computer which would then work out the best solution to keep the traffic flowing and set the signals accordingly.

In April 1981, a new scheme to update the traffic control computers in London was announced. When the first phase is completed, in 1983, over 2000 traffic signal installations in north London will be controlled by computer. By 1990 this will have been extended to cover the whole of the Greater London area.

Most of the motorways are now under varying degrees of computer control, which can give speed restriction warnings in the event of bad road conditions or an accident, or re-routing where this is possible to avoid a congested or dangerous section of motorway.

12.6 Supermarkets

Supermarkets almost owe their very existence to computers. As the name implies, a supermarket tries to stock everything that will sell and, as anyone who has fought his way past trollies containing margarine, meat, mops or melons will know, at peak times, the assistants are hard pressed to to keep the shelves stocked with goods. This is a perfect example of the need for effective stock control.

Since the first supermarkets appeared in the middle 1950s, the detailed use of computers has changed considerably and many new methods of data collection have been introduced, but the overall aim has been the same: to supply every branch with the goods it orders with the minimum of delay. From the branch point of view the aim is to order the minimum amount of goods consistent with the known demands for those goods. To meet these criteria, the essentials of any system must be:
(a) generation and dispatch of orders from the branches to the main warehouse or other suppliers
(b) fulfilment of orders and dispatch of goods to branches
(c) re-ordering of stock by warehouse.
The method by which these aims have been achieved has changed during recent years and is likely to be the subject of considerable development in the future.

Orders from the branches are made daily and the most common method in use at the time of writing is to record the quantity of any item *left* on the shelves. If this is below a pre-determined minimum, then that item must be reordered. The recording is usually done using a barcode reader to identify a particular product by reading a bar-code on the shelf and manually counting the items remaining on the shelf. This data is keyed in and recorded on a magnetic tape cassette carried by the assistant.

At the end of each day, the cassette is fitted into a terminal connected to the main computer via the Telecom network and the data from each cassette from the different branches is sent, in turn, to the main computer during the evening. Orders for each branch and the total order for each product item are available at the warehouse, to be made up and dispatched, the following morning. Items from the main warehouse that have fallen below the minimum stock level (stored on disk) are automatically re-ordered from the suppliers. From the data stored in the main computer files, branch and group accounting can be easily done. Information on product lines, particularly sales promotions, can be available daily and management has at its finger-tips all the data required to forecast and schedule.

Another method of establishing what items have been sold is to identify every item sold at the checkout point.

Cash registers have been in use for many years in every retail selling environment to record the individual items purchased and their total cash value. Many modern point-of-sale devices, based on the cash register, have been developed, and a typical modern terminal can be used on its own as a single retail outlet or can be linked to similar satellite terminals for a multi-checkout system in a large supermarket. The details relating to each item checked out can be keyed in directly or read in using an OCR or UPC wand attached to the terminal (see Section 7.1).

An advanced version of the read-out station was introduced in 1980 where, at the checkout point, the bar code identifying the product is read by a laser scanner which can read a code correctly even if it is upside down or back to front. When the product has been 'identified', the computer looks up the price in its memory, which is then displayed instantly at the checkout and printed on the customer's receipt. The system produces a cash total of the items purchased and, at the same time, records the details on to tape or disk. This data is used for reporting at the local level and for re-ordering daily. It is also sent to the main computer weekly with data from other branches to produce full information on weekly sales, product promotions, profitability of selected lines, branch costs etc. (Fig. 12.12).

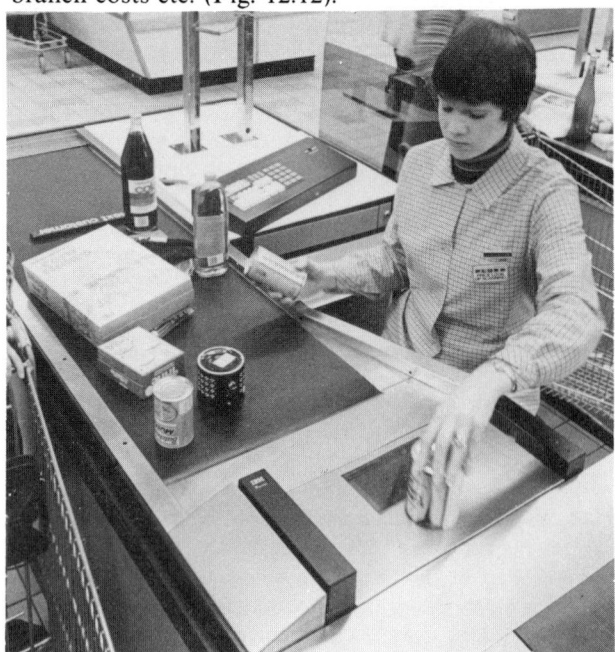

Fig. 12.12 Laser scanner checkout in use at Sainsburys

At present, the most common methods of paying for goods in a supermarket are by cash or cheque. This means that many people are carrying large amounts of money with them and checkout tills require emptying of cash many times in a busy day. One supermarket in Limoges in France, has collaborated with the largest local bank and each customer, with an account at that bank, is issued with a special credit card. When checkout is complete, the customer need only present the card, which is inserted in a special badge-reader connected directly to a minicomputer in the supermarket. After the card has been checked to see that it is not stolen, lost or discredited, the customer is asked to key in his personal identification number. This is, in effect, an electronic signature, and authorises deduction of the amount recorded from the individual's bank account and credit for the same amount to the supermarket account.

No cash or cheques change hands, customers spend less time queuing at checkouts and the bank has far fewer cheques to process. Details of the transactions are recorded on magnetic tape and at the end of each day, the data is sent to the bank to update its customers' accounts and the supermarket account. Although such a system could easily be on-line this would mean installing a special communication network and new terminals and it is intended to enlarge the off-line scheme to include other supermarkets and stores in the Limoges district as the next step in development.

At least one experiment, again in France, of on-line supermarket purchasing is being validated. The main objection to such a scheme is purely human—it may be necessary to reveal the current state of a customer's account in public! Until such human frailties can be safeguarded, such schemes, however advanced and sensible, will remain schemes, not realities.

12.7 Hospitals

Hospitals use computers to help them in a very wide range of different jobs from medical records to clinical diagnosis. Many hospitals now have a data communications network radiating from the central computer system into all the wards, operating theatres, clinical laboratories and administration departments, so that access to the computer files is available to authorised personnel using a portable terminal, plugged in to the network at the patient's bedside or by the operating table. The files contain all the necessary 'standard' personal information, along with a complete medical record of every patient and standard clinical diagnostic procedures. Whilst a person is an 'in-patient' a record of his treatment, drugs, diet and therapy are also retained.

Holding such personal information on a computer system presents problems of security in that not everybody who needs access to *some* of the data, should have access to *all* of it. This security is usually achieved by storing the data at different 'levels', each requiring a password, so that the 'name and address level' is

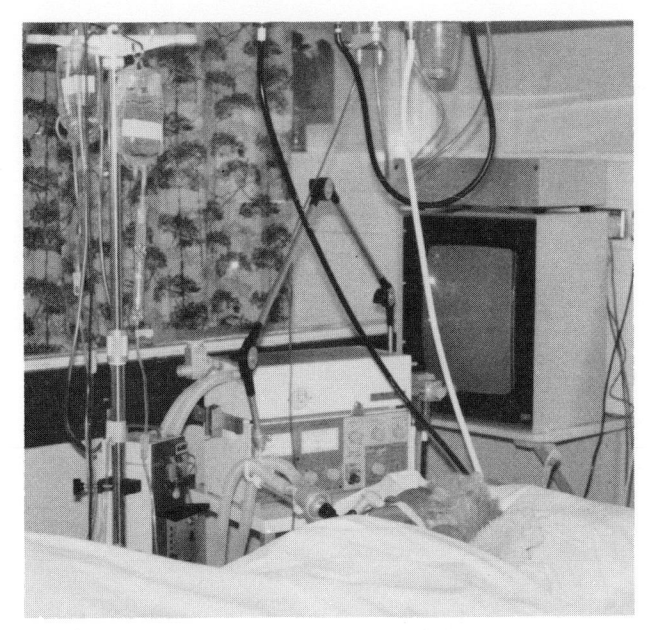

Fig. 12.13 Microcomputer used to control and monitor the patient environment in an intensive care unit

available to anybody with access to the system, whilst the clinical record may only be accessed by the patient's consultant and his medical team.

Much work has been done, particularly in the USA, to provide 'computer clinical diagnostics' where, after the doctor inputs the patient's symptoms, the computer will search through its files in an attempt to diagnose the disease or illness. When it reaches a medical area covered by the symptoms, the computer will ask the doctor more detailed questions, or for more data, and again search the files with the additional data as a new key. This dialogue between doctor and computer continues until the computer has sufficient data to be able to make a diagnosis. Such a system requires many man-years of 'medical programming' to give the computer the medical knowledge, but it does mean that junior doctors are able to draw on, and use, medical knowledge which they may not normally acquire without many years of research and practice in their profession.

Computer diagnosis from exact factual data is much easier and is practised in many hospitals. For example an electrocardiagram can be analysed by a computer as it is being recorded from the patient and at the end of the recording, the computer will display, visually, a message stating 'heart performance OK' or giving a defect diagnosis.

Since the introduction of microcomputers, the use of computers by the medical profession is not now restricted to large hospitals. Individual doctors and dentists are using microcomputers to store all patient records, which can then be used to generate lists of 'innoculations due', reminders of patient visits etc. A dentist can also store a dental chart of each patient which can be displayed on a VDU whilst the treatment is being given. Such a system obviously saves all written records and many filing cabinets of patient records would be easily stored on relatively few floppy disks. Other advantages, to both the hospital doctor and the local general practitioner are speed of access to any record and security of storage of data. The system can *automatically* provide reminders of visits, clinic lists, re-ordering of medical supplies, etc., all of which are vital to the running of a medical service but are very time-consuming when they are implemented manually.

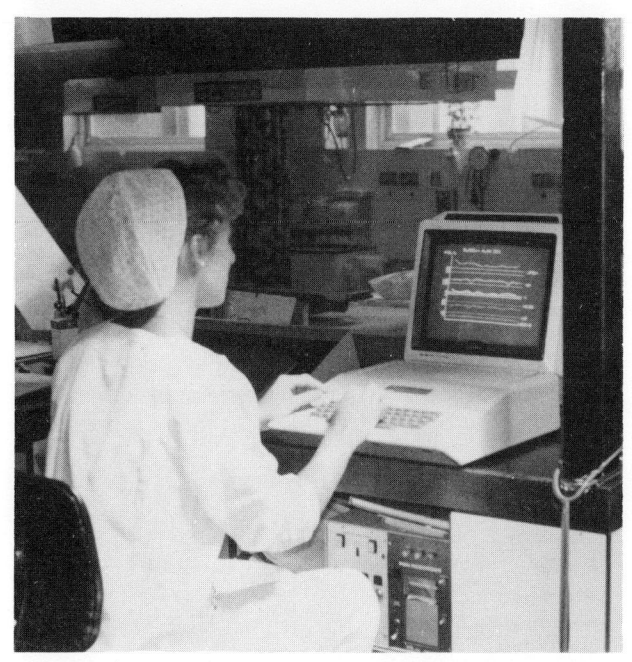

Fig. 12.14 A microcomputer is used in a Manchester hospital to give a graphical display of a patient's clinical record

12.8 Small businesses

At the other end of the 'business size' scale, there are many small businesses which are only now able to take advantage of 'computerisation' as minicomputers become cheaper and microcomputers are readily available. Examples of 'small users' can be found in most high streets, varying from solicitors using their computer for legal conveyancing and their word processor for compiling legal documents, to the two examples given below of estate agents and employment agencies.

Estate agents took a surprisingly long time to take advantage of the great benefits available to them of using a computer. An estate agent's entire stock-in-trade is on paper, which is duplicated many times for each different house, and details of many houses to be sold are stored at any given time. This is a perfect situation where a computer can be of great benefit. Some estate agents have cut out all paper duplication of house details and rely entirely on prospective buyers coming into their offices to use the VDU terminals. The buyer keys in sufficient details to identify the type of house he wishes to purchase and the computer responds with some details of any properties which match the input keys. Further details and a hard copy output are then available for properties selected from the list. A microcomputer is ideal for the small to medium sized business with all the house details held on floppy disks.

Another type of business which is benefitting in many ways from the introduction of computers, is employment and secretarial agencies. As details of each vacancy are supplied to the agency, these are input to disk storage and immediately available to any prospective employee accessing the job file through a VDU terminal. When a vacancy is filled, that job can be removed from the computer file within seconds of the agency being notified. A big advantage of such a system is that a 'job hunter' can look through the job files on the VDU without assistance from anyone else. For such a system to be effective, access to the files would need to be from more than one terminal, which precludes the use of a standard microcomputer, at least at the time of writing.

12.9 Computers in the home

Many microcomputers have been bought for 'home use' but most are used for program writing or for playing games! However many interesting programs, for use in the home have been written, from household budgeting and income tax calculation, to providing a daily engagement diary.

An important 'use of computers' in the home, without actually having a computer in the home, is *teletext*. This is a computer based information retrieval system which utilises a modified domestic television set to display text or graphics requested from the computer.

Two types of system are in use. The first, which is transmitted along with the ordinary television signals, by BBC Television, (Ceefax), and the IBA (Oracle), can be received in any home with a modified television set. The 'pages' of data are stored on disk in a small computer and are transmitted sequentially. Approximately 100 'main' pages are transmitted by BBC1 and a similar number of BBC2. Independent television transmits approximately 200 pages (1981 figures).

As the 'pages' are transmitted sequentially, the user has to wait for the selected page to 'come round', which can take up to 30 seconds on either BBC channel, or 1 minute on independent television. The slowness of this 'refresh' time is one reason why only 200 'pages' of information are stored. Note that a 'page' may consist of many hundreds of lines of information which can only be presented 40 lines at a time on the television screen. The type of information stored varies from up-to-date news and financial reports to recipes, gardening hints and jokes, *but* the information presented can only be read.

The second type of teletext system is known as Viewdata and this system differs from the television based systems above in that it is possible to communicate interactively with the computer holding the information files. The largest public system is British Telecoms Prestel. The method of communication between the computer and a user's television set is via the telephone network, which allows data to be sent in two directions.

Thousands of pages of information are available and, because a large computer system with approximately 1120M bytes of disk storage is used, the time to get at any page is roughly the same. Prestel is not only a vast information source, it can be used to purchase goods, book theatre tickets, airline reservations or holidays. To purchase a calculator, for example, the viewer keys in the catalogue number, followed by his credit card number and name and address, which appear in a special 'response frame' on the television screen.

At the time of writing, this order has to be collected by the supplier of the goods from the Prestel computer, but a development will enable the supplier to access the computer remotely to find out what orders have been placed. Prestel charges for each 'page' requested (3p per page in 1981), as well as the standard phone charges, so it is perhaps not surprising that by early 1981 only 12% of Prestel users were in the home. Travel companies account for approximately one-third of the 88% of business users.

12.10 Computers in education

In this section more emphasis will be put on what *can be done* in education than on what is being done, in the hope that students and teachers alike will realise that there is much work to be done in this area and that they may be able to contribute to this development.

Computers have been used in education for many years and many schools have used their computing facilities for purposes other than simply teaching computing. Unfortunately, until microcomputers came on the scene, few schools owned their own computer and relied on batch processing or online terminals for computer power. Neither mode of operation is very good for data processing. Time-tabling and options programs have been used successfully by some schools, but these have usually been commercial programs requiring a large computer system to run them.

With the introduction of microcomputers, much more work is being done and this can be considered under four headings: administration, teaching, computer aided learning and testing.

(a) Administration

Many programs have been written to assist in administration. Unfortunately these have usually been written for one specific application in one school and may not even be known to exist outside the school. Uses in this area can themselves be split into three groups:

(i) School organisation, including timetabling, option selection, staff cover, and, from a comprehensive database, school records, class lists, exam entries.

(ii) School administration. In this respect, a school has some of the same problems as any other business and as schools become more autonomous, they will be required to do work which is now done centrally. School accounts, whether they are PTA or tuck shop, can be administered by a computer. Stock records and control and ordering of stock can be done effectively by computer, and standard letters can be produced easily and quickly by word processors.

(iii) Departmental administration can equally benefit from being 'computerised' and records (subject), set lists and exam results are all capable of being produced by a computer.

(b) Teaching

In many schools, the computer is used only as a resource to teach computer studies and one of the main objectives must be to disseminate the work that has already been done in using the computer as a teaching resource and expand the development into every subject taught in our schools.

Many programs have been written covering most subject areas, but again developments have, in the main, been confined within a school and rarely fully documented and published. Much interesting and useful work is being done by the ITMA (Investigation on Teaching with Microcomputers as an Aid) project team and some of this work has been published (see Appendix 7). The computer is an ideal resource for simulation of science experiments, modelling in economics, graphics in art and design and accessing a large data base in geography, history or geology.

(c) Computer aided learning

The concept of a computer being used to teach has been in the forefront of many people's minds for many years. After all, a computer is tireless, it doesn't forget facts

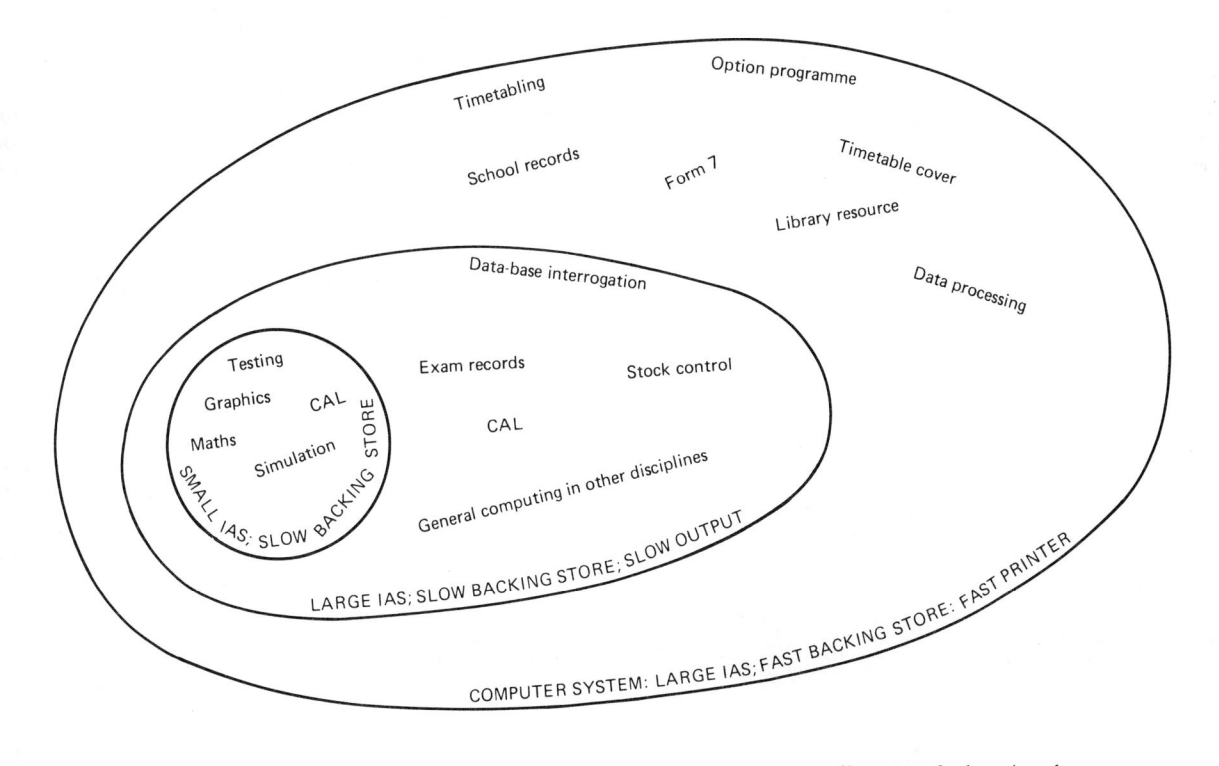

Fig. 12.15 Venn diagram of educational uses

and it never makes a mistake in calculations. Sometimes teachers are not quite able to live up to being such a paragon of virtue! Some very sophisticated programs have been produced which enable students to learn from information presented to the student by the computer. Poor learning programs simply present facts which the student has to learn. Good programs allow the student to question the computer about the presented data and ask for related data to be considered, thereby creating a dialogue between student and computer. Some experiments are being undertaken in the USA where students are only taught by computer and the teacher is there to discuss points raised in seminar sessions and to support the computer, but not to teach.

From a more practical point-of-view, it is possible to design programs which will teach facts, like vocabulary, chemical element tables, dates and names of monarchs, composers' works etc., and use them very effectively for class teaching. Some very good work is being done to enable very slow learners to learn simple numeracy, for example, utilising the fact that a computer *does* have limitless patience and is prepared to go over the same lesson as many times as the individual requires. Such work requires a dedicated computer and the Sinclair ZX81 is proving very effective for this type of work.

(d) Testing

Testing is the sort of work a computer is good at. Once a test has been programmed into a computer, anybody can use it, keying in their answers in response to each question. At the end of the test, the result is immediately available, if required. Otherwise it can be stored, along with other test results, to give a profile of each student through, for example, an academic year. Multiple choice questions, requiring only a single character to indicate the selected answer, as input, are ideal to program, but questions requiring one or two, (exact) word answers can be asked. Needless to say, questions requiring long answers, or essays, should not be asked.

Before attempting to implement any of the above in your own school, consideration must be given to the computing system available. Whereas all the above could be run on a large system, some could not be run at all on a small microprocessor and some not sensibly run if, for example, the system does not support a fast printer. The 'Venn diagram' in Fig. 12.15 shows the type of activity that can be undertaken within three specified types of computer system.

12.11 Real-time computing

Real-time computing uses a system that is able to receive continuously changing data from outside sources and that is able to process the data sufficiently rapidly to be capable of influencing the source of data. A real-time computing system may use a general purpose digital computer or a computer system designed especially for real-time applications, such as the Ferranti Argus series.

The most common use of a real-time system is to control a process. The process may be a steel rolling-mill, a chemical plant or an electricity generating station. Whatever the process, sensors in the plant measure a physical quantity, such as temperature, pressure, thickness or voltage, and convert this into a digital signal, (using an analogue to digital convertor), which is input to the central processor. By comparing this (actual) signal with a stored (theoretical) value, an error signal may be produced which is then used to operate the necessary controls in the plant to, for example, increase the temperature, or reduce the pressure, to return the process to its correct operating condition. This continuous monitoring and immediate response to any change in input, means that it is possible to use such a system to control complex and potentially dangerous plants such as atomic power stations and petroleum producing plant. Emergency shut-down can occur within a quarter of a second after 'danger' signals are received by the computer. (See Chapter 5.5.)

Other examples of real-time process control are in North Sea oil exploration and drilling, control of electricity and water distribution, and control of food preparation.

The volume of air traffic has now grown to the point that safe control of aircraft flying the world's air-routes, and particularly close to major airports, would be

Fig. 12.16 The computer department at Knutsford County High School in a lunch time session

almost impossible if real-time computers were not used for control. When an aircraft enters the controlled zone, data relating to the aircraft's height, speed, position and destination is fed automatically into the controlling computer, which then positions and controls the aircraft at a safe distance from all other aircraft, either until it leaves the zone or arrives safely at its destination.

Both the British Airways Booking System and the police traffic control system described earlier in this chapter use real-time computing systems. The traffic control system has continuous input of traffic flow from sensing devices in the roads. This data is used to control traffic lights which, in turn, control the traffic flow and so on. Input to BABS is a booked seat which is immediately removed from the availability file for that flight. Neither system could operate effectively if the speed of response of the system was less than immediate.

12.12 The future

There are so many changes constantly taking place in computer technology, computing techniques and in the use of computers, that it is very difficult to keep up with the present situation, let alone try and look into the future! Nevertheless, there are a number of areas that will be directly affected by projects currently in the development stage. There are other areas where further predictable developments in current technology will enable completely new techniques to be exploited.

Chip technology

The ubiquitous 'chip' will play an ever-increasing role in almost anything to do with computing—and in almost everything else as well! The technology is advancing so fast that the number of circuits that can be packed onto a single chip has been doubling every year. This means that within 10 years it could be possible to have a computer, far more powerful than any in existence now, made on a single chip! It will also mean that the cost of processing power will be reduced dramatically as the packing density per chip increases. This reduction in cost will result in more and more devices having chips fitted in them: model railways, electronic organs, washing machines, cars and calculators are only a few of the things that have already benefited from chip technology. At the same time, the increase in power of the chip will enable it to do much more in processing, controlling or storing data.

Voice response systems will really 'take-off' when the density of a chip allows large vocabularies to be stored at low cost. This development should have reached an active stage by the time digital transmission is available in the next few years and will enable 'digital messages' (from a computer), to be sent and stored for later playback in voice format.

Technological advances will also have a big part to play in creating what has been called 'the cashless

---

Exercises 12.1

1 Choose *two* computer applications from the following selection and describe with the aid of diagrams, a suitable computer system for:
 (i) machine tool control
 (ii) weather forecasting
 (iii) theatre seat reservation
 (iv) medical diagnosis.
The system described should include details of data collection, input and output devices, any special requirements for the central processor and storage devices and brief notes on any important human elements of the system. (*AEB, 1975*)*

2 Describe, in detail, a computer application with which you are familiar. The system described should include details of data collection; input and output devices used; details of the central processor relevant to the application described; storage devices used and any important human elements of the system.
(*AEB, 1976*)

3 A school has a teletype terminal linked to a large computer system via an acoustic coupler.
 (*a*) Suggest two applications in each of the following categories:
  (i) school administration
  (ii) teaching in disciplines other than computer studies
  (iii) testing
  (iv) teaching slow learners.
 (*b*) Choose *one* of the applications mentioned in (*a*) and describe, with the aid of diagrams, implementation of the system used. (*AEB, 1976*)*

4 A program has been written for an application in some subject at school. (You may choose the subject.) Outline the application you have chosen and then describe, in detail, the documentation which must accompany this program to make it usable by anybody with minimal computing knowledge.
(*AEB, 1978*)

5 (*a*) Outline suitable computer facilities for use in schools, explaining which hardware, software and processing methods might be used.
 (*b*) For any *two* of the following show how in one way the computer may be used to help them.
  (i) head teacher
  (ii) secretary
  (iii) librarian
  (iv) subject teacher
  (v) teacher in charge of 'tuck' shop. (*AEB, 1980*)

society'. Point-of-sale devices will become more sophisticated, accepting 'electronic money' instead of cheques and directly updating bank accounts on, first, a national basis, but probably before the turn of the century, through an international network to a bank in any country.

Storage

During the last decade, the cost of fast access storage has reduced by a factor of almost 300 to 1 and, with ever increasing packing density and faster access speeds, the cost per bit will continue to fall, enabling the storage capacity of computer systems to be increased significantly. This will enable much faster manipulation of large amounts of data and will involve new techniques of data manipulation and storage. Continued development of bubble memory will offer a very large capacity, medium speed, backing store. The 1 Mbyte bubble store, on a chip, is already a reality and the big advance in this development will be to reduce the access time to be similar to, or better than, present disk systems.

One significant change which will result from the ability to store vast amounts of data on a single chip will be to introduce a new form of book. The words will be stored on one, or more, chips which can be 'plugged into' a 'chip reader' equipped with controls to select which page is to be displayed on a visual display screen. The screen itself will be small and flat like the page out of a conventional printed book and any 'chip book' from the library can be plugged in and read. If a voice output system is connected to this book, a genuine 'talking book' will be available for the blind.

The possibility of storing all human knowledge, so that anyone in their own home can access the various data banks where this would be stored, will become quite feasible with cheap, mass storage. Further development of laser techniques will result in the video disk becoming a more widely used method of mass storage despite the fact that a disk is not re-useable. When video disks are as cheap as floppy magnetic disks, they will be used widely as semi-permanent storage then thrown away when no longer required.

Communications

A third area that will see considerable change during the next few years is that of communication. The telephone system in the UK uses a complex network which can be used to transmit voice, data and text at a very slow speed. Special cables are required to allow transmission of pictures (facsimile transmission) and to allow computers to communicate with each other in real time instead of waiting during the slow transmission of data.

An entirely new system using optical fibres instead of wires will probably be operational by the late 1980s. Such a system has a much greater transmission capability (and the added bonus that it is more difficult to tap), and, using digital signals instead of analogue signals, will allow high speed transmission of data in any form.

It is probable that a communications network will be established throughout the UK which will enable users to access different computers connected to the network to utilise the particular power or resources of that computer, or to access its data banks. Once such a system is established, it is possible to link into an international network so that data banks in other countries can be accessed via the local networks and communications satellites, thus bringing the power and resources of what will become a total information system, to everybody's home.

The age of data processing is over and the age of information processing is beginning.

Exercise 12.2

'By the year 2000, every home will have a computer.' Discuss this statement giving your views on the various issues involved with particular reference to the computing system used and the jobs such a system could usefully accomplish. *(AEB, 1974)**

Summary

- The uses to which a computer can be put are almost limitless.
- The same general-purpose computer can be used in many different applications simply by changing the software.
- Microcomputers are rapidly extending the use of computers in the home and in education.
- Real-time computer systems are used in applications where the processing is used to influence the source of the data being processed.
- Many exciting, and far-reaching changes will take place in the next few years as the technology advances.

13 The impact of computers on society

13.1 Individual appreciation

Society is made up from many individuals, each of whom may have a very different view of computers and their effect on their own life or of society in general. Views will vary from 'not very much' from someone who is totally unaware of what computers do, to 'affects us in every part of our lives' from someone who works with computers. The average man-in-the-street is surely aware that computers exist and that they are used in many different ways by many different people, but he is probably unaware of the capabilities and limitations of the computer, who actually does use them and what they are used for.

We live in a society where only bad news is news. Stories of computers that send exhorbitant accounts to people or send out bills for £0 and then reminders and threats until presented with a cheque for £0, (which is duly receipted!), are the ones that get into the newspapers and on television, and which the average person reads and believes. In the next few years, the individual will find computers playing an ever increasing role in his life. To understand the part that they can play, and what they can and cannot do, people will need to be quietly educated in the ways of the computer.

13.2 Effect on employment

Much of the 'bad news' about computers has centred on the fact that in many people's minds the introduction of computers means unemployment. Whilst this is true, we should also appreciate that many of the jobs that have been 'lost to a computer' were dull and repetitive and often dirty or dangerous. Technical innovation is not new, it has been with us since the industrial revolution, but the rate of change due to the 'new technology' is much faster and more far reaching.

The introduction of computers, and allied technology, has created many new jobs and whole new industries, from 'chip' manufacturing to medical research body scanning. A huge new industry of software design and manufacture grew up during the late 1970s because even the most sophisticated computer hardware

'The impact of computers on society is so great, it will go on for ever.'

was quite useless without supporting software. Computers desperately need people to help them!

Much has been written and said about the attitude of the trades unions to the introduction of computers and associated technology. Generally, trade unionists are opposed to computers because they see the computer only as a threat to their jobs, but there is a growing number who realise that computers have come to stay. They realise that, if they do not accept the benefits which must come from introducing new technology, perhaps in the long-term, the very jobs which they are frightened of losing now, will be lost anyway as other, more forward looking, people become the major suppliers of goods and services, produced and offered much cheaper using computers.

13.3 Effect on freedom

In the western world an individual has almost complete freedom to say and write what he likes and to protest and demonstrate in almost any way, against anybody or any organisation which does not speak, act, or think as they do. There is a fear, perhaps held only by those who rebel against the status quo, that computers can, and are, taking away some of this right of freedom. Certainly, there have been reported cases of seemingly unwarranted, and unnecessary surveillance and recording of quite innocuous and harmless demonstrations.

If such surveillance is being undertaken indiscriminately, then we may indeed consider that some of our freedom is being eroded, but we must also consider that many meetings and demonstrations held these days, become violent and cause damage and physical injury, even death. Surveillance of such events with recording of faces, names, attitudes, acts etc. could only be good if it helped to prevent the reoccurrence of violence and riots. But, what data is to be stored; who is responsible for deciding what is to be stored; who checks it and who has access to it in the future, are all questions which must be asked and should be answered—but who by?

13.4 Effect on privacy

The census of 1981 provided some information about everybody resident in the UK on the 5th April. Every householder in the UK was bound, by law, to answer 21 questions relating to his family, home and work. All this information will be used to make a huge database which will be stored on magnetic tapes and disks until the next census in 1991. It will be accessed time and time again in the intervening years to process the data to give somebody, somewhere, information about *us*. Considerable precautions have been taken to ensure that the information regarding some 50 000 000 persons in the UK is kept secure and we must assume that it *will* be kept secure. However, with the growing number of files containing information about us—medical records, salary records, social security records, police records, driving licence records—who is to *guarantee* privacy of all this information. A growing fear is that all these different files may, sooner or later, be linked and that private information is available to persons who have no right to it, whatsoever. If we are to make and keep files containing private information then each individual should know what the file contains.

Laws have been passed in the USA to make it a right for anybody to see what 'their record' contains. In the UK, many 'privacy committees' have considered the questions being asked but have not provided any answers or passed any legislation to give any protection to citizens. As well as knowing what 'our record' contains, we should know who has access to it. This latter is much more difficult to control and as networks linking computer systems throughout the UK, Europe or the world, are created, the problem becomes bigger and more difficult to control.

It is possible to make files very protected with passwords and other user identifications, but even the most sophisticated security system can be broken by a determined and clever criminal. Therefore it would seem that privacy must be preserved by ensuring that personal files only contain corroborated facts which we have agreed are correct and that files containing, for example, medical records are *never* accessible by other than authorised medical staff.

Exercises 13.1

1 'Computers have dramatically changed our lives'. Comment on this statement, with particular reference to the actual effect on the individual now and the likely effect in the future. *(AEB, 1977)**

2 'The increasing development of the use of data banks gives considerable cause for concern.'
(a) Explain fully the term *data bank*.
(b) Describe briefly three applications in which data banks are used.
(c) Give three causes for concern shown about data banks, and suggest how they may be overcome.
(AEB, 1980)*

3 A company proposes to create a file containing details of all its employees. Each record will consist of: 1. Name 2. Address 3. Telephone number 4. Age 5. Sex 6. Works number 7. Marital status 8. Number of children 9. Qualifications 10. Experience 11. Salary 12. Employee's bank and account number 13. Company medical record 14. Promotion prospects.
(a) Who should create this file? Suggest a method of preserving the privacy of the information.
(b) Who should have access to the file? Suggest a method of ensuring that only authorised users can access the data. *

4 It has been suggested that the increasing use of computers and computer controlled machinery will very soon produce a society where most people are unemployed.
(a) Name three different jobs where a computer has replaced people and give a brief description of each job before and after computerisation.
(b) Name one job which you think is 'safe from computerisation' and explain why you think it is safe.
(c) Give three reasons why 'computerisation' will *not* produce mass unemployment. *

THE IMPACT OF COMPUTERS ON SOCIETY

'Every computer requires human support to survive.'

It has been estimated that by the turn of the century, computing will be the world's largest industry. If this is to be so, it is vital that it grows to this size in an informed society because such an industry *must* exist for the good of mankind as a whole. Computers can, and will, bring increasing benefits to society but we must learn to *use* them, not *abuse* them!

A last word (of hope) from a student: 'Every computer requires human support to survive!'

Summary

- Computers effect our lives as individuals and as a society.
- Most of the effects are for the good. Acceptance of the 'computer age' and education in the use and abuse of computers and allied technology is vital if we are to reap the undoubted benefits that computers have to offer.

Appendix 1
Coursework

Computing is a practical subject. The whole essence of making a computer work for you is embodied in writing, or using, programs to enable the computer to perform specified functions which may range from making a printer print to solving a complex data processing problem.

The importance of this vital aspect of computer studies—practical programming—is recognised by every examination board and all syllabuses include a section devoted to coursework. The actual detailed requirements for coursework differ between exam boards but, basically, students are required to design, implement and document one, or more, programming projects.

The subject matter of the project is largely the choice of the student, given the natural constraints of the computing facilities available. Not all coursework has to be programming—the growing use of microcomputers in schools and the availability of a wide range of integrated circuits, has allowed the fascinating study of 'process control' to be brought into schools. Whether the 'process' to be controlled is a model railway, a lift, or the mixing of two chemicals, writing the software (and probably designing the hardware) makes an excellent piece of coursework. Projects based on existing software will become more widely acceptable as useful software packages become generally available to schools. For example, the ICL FIND package for information retrieval has been very successfully used to produce interesting projects on such widely differing topics as the television viewing habits of a whole school and packaged holidays.

An in-depth, critical appraisal of some aspect of computer development or usage can make an excellent project for those students who perhaps do not find program writing as fascinating as some. Students should be warned, however, against simply copying from text books and manufacturers' information leaflets. Such a project must involve some personal research into the selected topic. This can be very rewarding not only in terms of coursework marks, but in a wider and deeper understanding of some computing topic.

However, the only type of coursework that is acceptable to *all* exam boards is practical programming, so the rest of this chapter will be devoted to considerations of this type of coursework.

Getting started

Coursework is normally started during the third term of a two-year course and continues during the fourth and fifth terms, for completion during the early part of the last term. By the third term, most students will have been taught enough programming to enable them to make a start on their coursework. All students should have a steadily growing experience of using the computing facilities available but, whereas this will have been limited to programming so far, all practical work should now be considered in the light of examination structured coursework.

The first requirement is an idea! *What* is the first piece of coursework going to be about? The list below gives approximately 100 suggestions for coursework topics which are divided into six broad subject areas.

Ideas for programming projects

1 Mathematical
Printing bar chart*, generating normal and frequency distribution curves, coefficient of correlation†, scatter diagram, rank order correlation†, statistics package of some, or all, of these. Solving quadratic equations*, solving simultaneous equations, calculating surface area and volume of standard solids*, calculation of square roots*, finding prime numbers, calculation of π†, conversion between bases, calculation of area of a triangle, finding Pythagorean triples, calculation of complex area*, generation of number series, numerical integration, factorials†, permutations and combinations, roots of equations, right-angle check, trajectory calculations, calculations of triangle type.

2 Games
Noughts and crosses, hangman, nim, snakes and ladders, dice throwing*, card dealing and playing,

Mastermind, Monopoly, target shooting, lunar landing, car racing, show jumping, battleships, Mastermind quiz, roulette, chess†, Escape from Colditz.

3 Simulation
Flying a glider, landing a plane, cricket, population growth/decay, North Sea oil explorations, various science experiments, fruit machine, traffic-light control*, petrol station, factory production, economic modelling†.

4 Data processing
Wages calculation and pay-slip printing, calculation and printing of invoices*, stock control, PERT network analysis, gas/electricity bill calculation and printing*, bank accounts, job cost analysis, market trends, stock market trends and forecasts, rotation and growing of crops, MOT vehicle check, school tuck shop sales*, mock election.

5 Programs involving files
All the ideas in Section 4 could also be included here. Subject tests, computer dating, criminal records interrogation, text analysis, timetable compilation (traffic)†, language translation†, survey or opinion poll and analysis, hotel menu preparation, quiz, compilation of league tables.

Various subject problems: field studies in geography or biology, population growth in history or economics, geological survey and analysis, chemical elements table*.

6 Others
CESIL compiler†, route calculations from a map, code making and breaking, solving anagrams, maze-running (two dimensional and three dimensional)†, perpetual calendar, magic square generation, contour analysis and sectional drawing, music composition or analysis, Kirchoff's laws*, morse code generation and reading, text justification, cross-word compilation†, converting Roman to Arabic and vice-versa, best buy supermarket survey*, bio-rhythms.

7 Graphics
Many of the ideas suggested above can be enhanced by the addition of graphical output, such as snakes and ladders. Some rely heavily on a graphical output but are not, of themselves, graphics programs, for example, any board game like 'Escape from Colditz' is of this type. Others will benefit from the use of high resolution graphics, e.g. any plotting involving curves (like sine/cosine). It is unlikely that a 'graphics only' project would qualify for O level unless it involved animation, three-dimensional graphics or some fairly complex manipulation of graphical modules. An example could be building design.

All of these topics have been used in coursework at O level. Those marked with an asterisk (*) are relatively simple and should not be considered for a final exam submission but make excellent mini, or dummy, projects which can be attempted before the main project work is started. Or they can be a first project, which can be used for experience only, and replaced with a more ambitious project later in the course.

The most important criterion governing the choice of topic for coursework is that it should be chosen by the student and be a subject in which the student is interested and has some knowledge. Most hobbies, from fishing to morris dancing, can provide an interesting and worthwhile subject for coursework. A word of warning—*don't* choose a topic that is going to prove too difficult, or too time consuming, to implement. Almost every computer studies student considers that there is not enough time for coursework so few students can afford to throw away possibly half a term's work simply because of a bad subject choice.

The topics marked † in the list above are more difficult and should not be considered for first projects or even by the average student for any project. They do, however, represent very worthwhile projects for the 'dedicated computing enthusiast'.

Once you have selected a suitable topic, the next step is exactly as discussed in Chapter 9.2. *What* is the program going to do? What output is required and therefore what input is needed, and how is this to be achieved in processing? You need to think how the problem is to be solved. Rough documentation should be started and every piece of paper relating to the project should be kept at this stage. Some of this will be used to provide the final, *legible, coherent, indexed, well presented* documentation required by the examination board.

The next step is to define the algorithm for the solution of the problem in flowchart form and from this flowchart, write the *simplest possible program*, i.e. one that will solve the problem but need not contain hundreds of REM or PRINT statements, or line after line of DATA statements! Many a good project is ruined at this stage by confusing the essential elements of the program with irrelevant detail. A program can be built up as the project develops and thoroughly tested at each stage before the next one is added.

Reference to the way the sports day project from Chapter 9 was written will show this idea of a sectional build-up:

(i) Event input—lines 120–190
(ii) Awarding points—lines 330–380
Test
(iii) Score totalling—lines 410–440
Test
(iv) Simple output—teams and scores
Test

(v) More than one event
Test
(vi) Improved output
Test
(vii) Data verification
Test data
(viii) Improved output
(ix) Sort routine
Test
(x) Improved presentation (clearing screen and adjusting output)
(xi) Final testing and runs.

At each stage a printout of a program listing and run (where applicable), showing both input and output, should be obtained and should be kept to form part of the documentation – project development.

If a particular line of development looks like becoming too difficult or too time-consuming, abandon pursuit of the idea before spending too much time, or losing heart, or both! But include notes on the idea, the development undertaken, and the reasons for its unsuccessful conclusion in the documentation.

At all stages, the program should be tested with carefully selected test data. This should be chosen to try to 'break' the program and show up any errors or deficiencies in the routines. Every possible situation should be allowed for and suitable default routines and error messages written into the program. In the sports-day program there are three such routines. The final program should be carefully tested and the results of all testing, and the data used, should form an important part of the project documentation.

If the documentation has been planned as suggested in Section 9.3 and has *evolved as the project has developed*, even if only in rough form, then it should prove relatively easy to modify to fit in with the exam marking scheme of any particular examination board. All boards have at least one common requirement for project work—that it should be presented in a legible and coherent form! Coursework can, and does, vary from 50 or more pages of typewritten script, diagrams, flowcharts, annotated listings, output and even photographs, to two-thirds of a page of illegible scrawl, sometimes accompanying an interesting, complex, untested, program and often 'padded-out' with page after page of hand-written program listing! All documentation should be produced in such a manner that a third party can understand what you have done, and why, and can follow through the complete development and testing with the absolute minimum of trouble.

At least one examination board requires that coursework is continually assessed by the subject teacher. Whether it is a formal examination requirement, or not, this is good practice. It allows a teacher to keep closely in touch with what his students are doing, to monitor progress and to suggest new ideas or lines of development which may help to turn an 'ordinary' project into a good one. Continued assessment should also prevent a 'mad panic' from developing in the few weeks prior to submission!

If we assume that project work is undertaken in terms 3, 4 and 5 of a two year course, there are two ways in which this work can be programmed. First as follows:

term 3 | holiday | term 4 | term 5
project 1 | | project 2 | project 3 ↑submission

This method has the advantage that projects 2 and 3 can benefit from previously gained experience, and there is great satisfaction in knowing that one or more projects are complete and can give students much encouragement for remaining work.

The second way is

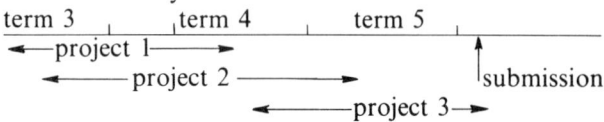

term 3 | term 4 | term 5
←—project 1—→
←———— project 2 ————→ ↑submission
←———— project 3 —→

This scheme is more practical as the demands for computer time are spread out and it helps those students who want to modify their first project, or change it completely, after embarking on their second one.

The scheme adopted by any student, or group of students, may have to be modified to suit the availability of computer time and the number of students wanting to use the available facilities. Computer use should be carefully time-tabled, rationed and monitored to ensure that the best use is made by *all* computing students and not just those who can, so easily, hog the facilities.

An often asked question is 'How big/long should a project be?', to which the only answer is that it is not possible to state quantitative criteria like 'x pages of documentation', or 'a 200 line program'. Every project must be considered individually and guidelines can only be given here, but one overriding statement can be made, that it is *quality* and not quantity that makes a good project. Some projects do not require long programs and can only support a minimum amount of documentation; for example, a program to solve a quadratic equation can be written in a few lines and everything to be said about it can be said in one or two pages of documentation. Conversely, a comprehensive file manipulation program could run to 200 lines of program and the supporting documentation could, and should, run to many pages. Remember, a data file need only contain enough records to fully test the program or to make the project interesting and, possibly, useful as well.

If we quote the appropriate part of just one syllabus (AEB) we should get a 'qualitative feel' for what constitutes good coursework:

> 'The projects submitted should demonstrate the candidate's ability to understand and to make appropriate use of a variety of programming techniques. .... programs consisting of only a few simple statements, i.e. a programming exercise, should not be submitted. An attempt should be made to realise the potential of the language used.'

Do's and Don'ts for coursework.

1 DO start to think about your coursework in advance of the formal starting date and try and have at least one idea, or topic, in mind.

2 DO choose a subject, or topic, with which you are familiar and in which you are interested.

3 DON'T tackle anything too complex.

4 DON'T start by writing a program.

5 DO keep the documentation up-to-date at all times.

6 DO design your project to fit in with the appropriate exam marking scheme.

7 DON'T despair when things seem to go wrong.

8 DON'T be afraid to abandon a project that isn't going well.

9 DO ask for help.

10 DO try and enjoy *all* aspects of the practical work—not just the program writing.

Appendix 2
Computer staff

The computer industry, whether it is the design and manufacturing side of the industry or the user side, has created its own job titles and job descriptions. Some details of the more common ones are given below. The 'family tree' shows the relationships between the various jobs which might exist in a typical computer department. It is only typical and it should not be assumed that all computer departments have the same structure. The actual structure and size of a department depends to a large extent on the size of the company, the size of the computer system and the use to which the computer is being put.

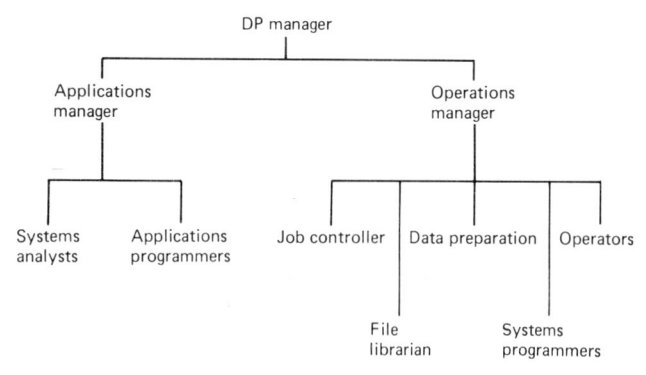

Fig. A2.1 Relationships between jobs in a typical computer department

The *data processing manager* is the person with overall responsibility for the successful running of the computer department. In a large commercial company, he may well be a director with a seat on the board controlling the company. He is responsible for the efficient use of the computer and, in many companies, ensuring that the computer department makes a profit on its operations.

The *operations manager* is responsible for the day-to-day running of the computer, its associated equipment and the operations staff. He will probably be the department's technical expert, whereas the data processing manager will probably be trained in finance, business or administration.

A *systems analyst* has the responsibility for analysing a business system to assess its suitability for a computer application. He may also be responsible for the design of a computer system to perform specific tasks and to implement this design through to its realisation in terms of hardware and software. A systems analyst would probably act as leader in a project team which may be charged with the responsibility for part of a large project.

The main task of a *programmer* is, of course, to write programs. These are based on the various procedures defined by the systems analyst for the solution of the problem. The programmer details these procedures in a suitable programming language. He will also be responsible for the documentation to accompany the program.

Although there are many different types of program, they can be divided into two broad categories of applications programs and systems software, and job titles exist in these two areas. An *applications programmer* would be writing programs concerned with different applications of computer useage, e.g. payroll or stock control. A programmer writing systems software would be creating programs to help run the computer system, such as compilers and operating systems. In the computer industry, there will also be programmers writing programs to assist in the design of computers (computer aided design).

A *computer operator* runs jobs on the computer. He is responsible for input and output; communication with the computer via the operators' console; ensuring that all the component parts of the computer system are in good working order and loading backing storage devices with the correct tapes or disks for the particular job being run.

A *data controller* is responsible for the preparation and collection of the necessary material for each job to be processed. He will arrange (computer) work schedules and allocate priorities where necessary. He will also be responsible for initial validation of the data to be input for each job.

Data preparation staff are responsible for preparing data for input to the computer. This may be by punching cards or paper tape or using a VDU terminal as described in Section 4.3.

The *file librarian* is responsible for keeping all files correctly catalogued and stored for immediate use and for ensuring that all files are up to date, and the necessary copies made and stored safely. He may also be required to issue updated copies of any files generated by the computer department to other users of the files.

Appendix 3
Nomograms of history of data processing

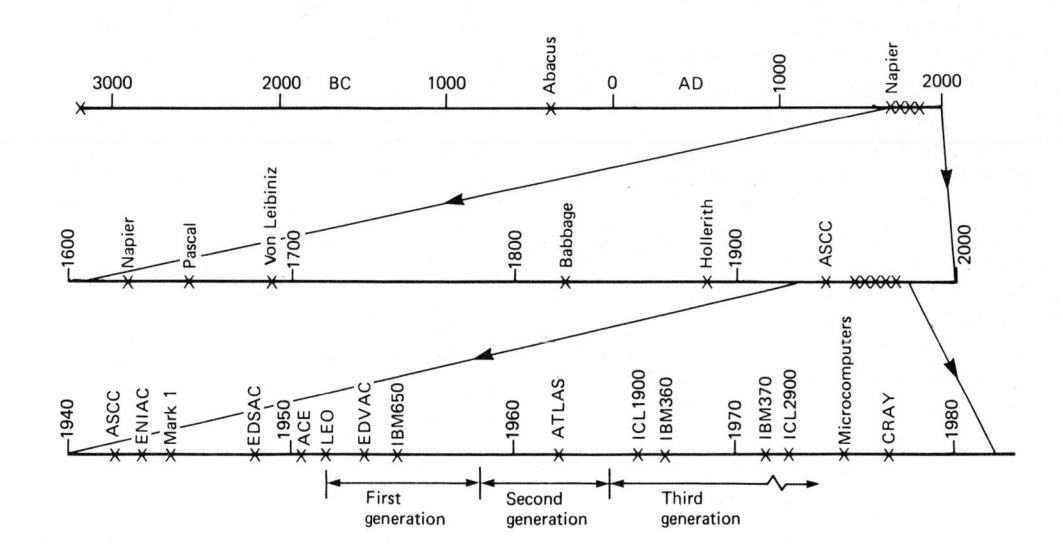

175

Appendix 4
ISO 7 bit code

							0	0	0	0	1	1	1	1	
							0	0	1	1	0	0	1	1	
							0	1	0	1	0	1	0	1	
bits	b7	b6	b5	b4	b3	b2	b1								
				0	0	0	0	NUL	DLE	SP	0	@	P	`	p	1
				0	0	0	1	SOH	DC1	!	1	A	Q	a	q	2
				0	0	1	0	STX	DC2	"	2	B	R	b	r	3
				0	0	1	1	ETX	DC3	£	3	C	S	c	s	4
				0	1	0	0	EOT	DC4	$	4	D	T	d	t	5
				0	1	0	1	ENQ	NAK	%	5	E	U	e	u	6
				0	1	1	0	ACK	SYN	&	6	F	V	f	v	7
				0	1	1	1	BEL	ETB	'	7	G	W	g	w	8
				1	0	0	0	BS	CAN	(	8	H	X	h	x	9
				1	0	0	1	HT	EM	)	9	I	Y	i	y	10
				1	0	1	0	LF	SUB	*	:	J	Z	j	z	11
				1	0	1	1	VT	ESC	+	;	K	[	k		12
				1	1	0	0	FF	FS	,	<	L	\	l		13
				1	1	0	1	CR	GS	-	=	M	]	m		14
				1	1	1	0	SO	RS	.	>	N	^	n	—	15
				1	1	1	1	SI	US	/	?	O	_	o	DEL	16
								1	2	3	4	5	6	7	8	

Appendix 5
File handling programs in other languages

All the programs in Chapters 9, 10 and 11 are written in BBC BASIC and will run on any BBC Micro with cassette tape or disk drive. Unfortunately, they will not run on any other computer without modification. Whilst there is some compatability between the different dialects of 'basic BASIC' there is none as far as file handling is concerned. Not only are the BASIC file commands different, but the disk, or tape, operating systems used by different computers show virtually no compatibility.

This appendix contains versions of five of the file handling programs suitable for direct implementation on APPLE (or ITT 2020), RML 380/480Z and PET. Using these programs as a guide, any of the programs in Chapters 10 and 11 can easily be written for a particular system.

See page (vi) for details of the software available.

RML BASIC

Writing a file

```
 10 REM WRITING A FILE. PROG01 (BASICS)
 20 CLEAR 100
 30 PRINT:PRINT:INPUT"WHAT IS THE NAME OF THIS NEW FILE?        ";F$
 40 PRINT "PLEASE WAIT..."
 50 PRINT: PRINT"EACH * INDICATES THAT A RECORD HAS BEEN WRITTEN":PRINT
 60 CREATE£10,F$
 70 QUOTE£10,34
 80 Q=1
 90 FOR R=1 TO 6:READ N$(Q,R):IF N$(Q,1)="XXX" THEN 110
100 PRINT£10,N$(Q,R):NEXT R:PRINT"*";:Q=Q+1:GOTO 90
110 CLOSE£10
120 PRINT:PRINT:PRINT"FILE WRITING IS COMPLETE"
130 PRINT:PRINT"FILE ";F$;" CONTAINS ";Q-1;" RECORDS"
140 DATA "BROWN MARY","45 TOWNFIELDS KNUTSFORD","0565 2468",16,"F","5U"
150 DATA "YOUNG JOHN","3 GREEN LANE NORTHWICH","--",17,"M","5S"
160 DATA "GREEN ALAN","17 TOWN LANE MOBBERLEY","MOB 1234",15,"M","5V"
170 DATA "JONES FIONA","43 TREE WAY KNUTSFORD","0565 74812",16,"F","5U"
180 DATA "BLOGGS JOHN","39 ASHWORTH PARK KNUTSFORD","0565 9999",17,"M","5V"
190 DATA "SMITH ROY","99 MANCHESTER RD KNUTSFORD","0565 7887",15,"M","5T"
200 DATA "WHITE ANN","THE COTTAGE, PLUMLEY RD KNUTSFORD","--",16,"F","5T"
210 DATA "EVANS PETER","1 THE TALBOTS MOBBERLEY","MOB 2345",15,"M","5U"
220 DATA "XXX",X,X,X,X,X
```

Reading from a file

```
 10 REM READING A FILE.PROG02 (BASICS)
 20 CLEAR 100:PRINT:PRINT
 30 INPUT TAB(4,8)"WHAT IS THE NAME OF THE FILE YOU WISH TO READ ? "N1$
 40 PRINT:PRINT "     READING THE FILE...."
 50 OPEN£10,N1$:Q=1
 60 FOR R=1 TO 6:INPUT£10,A$(Q,R):ON EOF GOTO 80:NEXT
 70 Q=Q+1:GOTO 60
 80 PRINT:PRINT
 90 FOR A=1 TO Q
100 PRINT A$(A,1);TAB(16);A$(A,2);TAB(54);A$(A,3);TAB(67);A$(A,4);TAB(72)
;A$(A,5);TAB(77);A$(A,6)
110 NEXT
120 PRINT:PRINT:PRINT"FILE LISTING COMPLETE":PRINT
130 PRINT"FILE "N1$" CONTAINS ";Q;" RECORDS"
```

Reading a file into one array then into a new file

```
 10 REM READ A FILE INTO ONE ARRAY THEN INTO A NEW FILE.PROG05.1 (BASICS)
 20 CLEAR 80
 30 PRINT TAB(0,4); "PLEASE WAIT WHILE THE FILE IS READ....":PRINT
 40 OPEN£10,"DEF456"
 50 Q=1
 60 FOR R=1 TO 6
 70 INPUT£X,A$(Q,R)
 80 NEXT R
 90 Q=Q+1:GOTO 60
100 PRINT "FILE <DEF456> HAS NOW BEEN READ":PRINT
110 REM WRITING FROM THE ARRAY TO THE NEW FILE
120 PRINT "WRITING THE NEW FILE....":PRINT
130 CREATE£10,"UVW789"
140 QUOTE£10,34
150 FOR A=1 TO Q:FOR B=1 TO 6
160 PRINT£Y,A$(A,B)
170 NEXT B:NEXT A
180 CLOSE£10
190 PRINT:PRINT"NEW FILE-<RST789>-NOW COMPLETE":PRINT:PRINT
200 REM OPTION TO KILL THE OLD FILE
210 INPUT"DO YOU WISH TO KILL THE OLD FILE (YES or NO)";K$:PRINT
220 IF K$<>"YES" THEN 290
230 INPUT"ARE YOU SURE??! ";KK$:PRINT:PRINT
240 PRINT:PRINT
250 IF KK$<>"YES" THEN 290
260 RENAME "UVW789","DEF456":ERASE"DEF456"
270 PRINT"FILE DEF456 IS NOW ERASED AND THE NEW FILE SAVED UNDER THE OLD FILE NAME"
280 GOTO 300
290 PRINT"BOTH FILES ARE SAVED"
300 END
```

APPENDIX 5 FILE HANDLING PROGRAMS

Deleting one record from a file

```
 10 REM DELETE ONE RECORD FROM A FILE.PROG06 (BASICS)
 20 CLEAR100
 30 INPUT TAB(0,4)"WHAT IS THE NAME IN THE RECORD YOU WISH TO DELETE? ";NAME$
 40 PRINT TAB(0,7);"READING THE FILE....":PRINT
 50 OPEN£10,"DEF456":Q=1
 60 ON EOF GOTO 110
 70 FOR R=1 TO 6:INPUT £X,N1$(Q,R)
 80 IF N1$(Q,1)=NAME$ THEN Q=Q-1
 90 NEXT
100 Q=Q+1:GOTO 70
110 REM WRITING THE NEW FILE
120 PRINT:PRINT "WRITING THE NEW FILE....":PRINT
130 CREATE£10,"UVW789"
140 QUOTE£10,34
150 FOR A=1 TO Q:FOR B=1 TO 6
160 PRINT£10,N1$(A,B):NEXT B:NEXT A
170 CLOSE£10
180 PRINT:PRINT"NEW FILE-UVW789-NOW COMPLETE":PRINT
190 REM PRINTING OUT THE NEW FILE
200 FOR C=1 TO Q
210 PRINT N1$(C,1);TAB(15);N1$(C,2)
220 NEXT C
230 PRINT:PRINT"FILE UVW789 NOW CONTAINS ";Q;" RECORDS"
```

Adding one or more records to a file

```
 10 REM ADD ONE OR MORE RECORDS TO A FILE.PROG7.1(BASICS)
 20 CLEAR 100:DIM A$(20,6)
 30 PRINT"INPUT THE DATA FOR THE NEXT NEW RECORD":PRINT
 40 INPUT"NAME       ";A$(Z,1):PRINT
 50 INPUT"ADDRESS    ";A$(Z,2):PRINT
 60 INPUT"TEL.NO.    ";A$(Z,3):PRINT
 70 INPUT"AGE        ";A$(Z,4):PRINT
 80 INPUT"SEX        ";A$(Z,5):PRINT
 90 INPUT"FORM       ";A$(Z,6):PRINT
100 INPUT"DO YOU WISH TO ADD ANOTHER RECORD (Y/N) ";W$
110 IF W$<>"Y" THEN 140
120 Z=Z+1:PRINT:PRINT:GOTO 30
130 PRINT:PRINT:PRINT "READING THE FILE....":PRINT
140 OPEN£10,"DEF456"
150 FOR Q=Z+1 TO Z+9:FOR R=1 TO 6
160 INPUT£10,A$(Q,R)
170 NEXT R:NEXT Q
180 PRINT "WRITING THE NEW FILE....":PRINT
190 CREATE£10,"UVW789"
200 QUOTE£10,34
210 FOR A=1 TO Q-1:FOR B=1 TO 6
220 PRINT£10,A$(A,B)
230 NEXT B:NEXT A
240 CLOSE£10
250 PRINT:PRINT"NEW FILE-UVW789-WRITTEN AND CLOSED":PRINT
260 PRINT"FILE NOW CONTAINS ";Q-1;" RECORDS"
270 PRINT:FOR C=1 TO Q-1
280 PRINT A$(C,1);TAB(15);A$(C,3);TAB(32);A$(C,4)
290 NEXT
300 END
```

APPLE II   BASIC

Writing a file

```
20   REM   WRITING A FILE(APPLE II).PROG 01.1
30  C$ =  CHR$ (4)
40   PRINT C$;"OPEN GHJ456"
50   PRINT C$;"WRITE GHJ456"
60  Q = 1
70   FOR R = 1 TO 6
80    READ N$(Q,R)
90    IF N$(Q,R) = "XXX" THEN 130
100   PRINT N$(Q,R)
110   NEXT R
120  Q = Q + 1: GOTO 70
130   PRINT C$;"CLOSE GHJ456"
140   PRINT : PRINT : PRINT "FILE WRITING COMPLETE": PRINT
150   PRINT "FILE (GHJ456) CONTAINS "Q - 1" RECORDS"
160   DATA "BROWN MARY","45 TOWNFIELDS KNUTSFORD","0565 2468",16,"F","5U"
170   DATA  "YOUNG JOHN","3 GREEN LANE NORTHWICH","--",17,"M","5S"
180   DATA  "GREEN ALAN","17 TOWN LANE MOBBERLEY","MOB 1234",15,"M","5V"
190   DATA "JONES FIONA","43 TREE WAY KNUTSFORD","0565 74812",16,"F","5U"
200   DATA  "BLOGGS JOHN","39 ASHWORTH PARK KNUTSFORD","0565 9999",17,"M","5V"
210   DATA  "SMITH ROY","99 MANCHESTER RD   KNUTSFORD","0565 7887",15,"M","5T"
220   DATA "WHITE ANN","THE COTTAGE PLUMLEY RD KNUTSFORD","--",16,"F","5T"
230   DATA  "EVANS PETER","1 THE TALBOTS MOBBERLEY","MOB 2345",15,"M","5U"
235   DATA  "DUMMY",0,0,0,0,0
240   DATA  "XXX","0","0",0,"0","0"
```

Reading from a file

```
200   REM   READING FROM A FILE(APPLE II).PROG 02
205  C = 0:C$ =  CHR$ (4): PRINT : PRINT
207   INPUT "WHAT IS THE NAME OF THE FILE YOU WISH TO READ? ";N1$: PRINT : PRINT

210   PRINT C$;"OPEN";N1$
215   PRINT C$;"READ";N1$
220  Z = 1
225   FOR Q = 1 TO 6: INPUT A$(Z,Q): NEXT Q
230  Z = Z + 1: IF A$(Z - 1,1) = "DUMMY" THEN 245
240   GOTO 225
245   PRINT C$;"CLOSE";N1$
250   FOR X = 1 TO Z - 1
252   PRINT A$(X,1),A$(X,2),A$(X,3)
253   PRINT
254   NEXT X
260   PRINT : PRINT : PRINT : PRINT "FILE LISTING COMPLETE"
270   PRINT : PRINT "FILE ";N1$;" CONTAINS ";Z - 1;" RECORDS"
```

APPENDIX 5 FILE HANDLING PROGRAMS   181

Reading a file into one array then into a new file

```
300  REM   PROG TO READ A FILE INTO AN ARRAY THEN
305  REM   INTO A NEW FILE(APPLE II).PROG 05
310  C$ =  CHR$ (4): DIM A$(9,6)
320  PRINT C$;"OPEN GHJ456"
325  PRINT C$;"READ GHJ456"
330  FOR Z = 1 TO 9: FOR Q = 1 TO 6
340   INPUT A$(Z,Q)
350  NEXT Q: NEXT Z
375  PRINT C$;"CLOSE GHJ456"
380  REM   READING FROM ARRAY A$ INTO NEW FILE
390  PRINT C$;"OPEN RST789"
395  PRINT C$;"WRITE RST789"
400  FOR Z = 1 TO 9: FOR Q = 1 TO 6
410   PRINT A$(Z,Q)
420  NEXT Q: NEXT Z
450  PRINT C$;"CLOSE RST789"
455  PRINT
460  PRINT "NEW FILE-RST789-NOW COMPLETE"
470  REM   OPTION TO KILL OLD FILE
475  PRINT
480  INPUT "DO YOU WISH TO KILL THE OLD FILE?";K$
490  IF K$ ( ) "YES" THEN 550
500  INPUT "ARE YOU SURE?!!";KK$
510  IF KK$ ( ) "YES" THEN 550
520  PRINT C$;"DELETE GHJ456"
530  PRINT "GHJ456 IS NOW ERASED"
540  GOTO 560
550  PRINT : PRINT "BOTH FILES ARE SAVED"
560  END
```

Deleting one record from a file

```
300  REM   PROG TO DELETE ONE RECORD FROM A FILE(APPLE II).PROG 06
310  C$ =  CHR$ (4): DIM A$(9,6)
315  PRINT : INPUT "WHAT IS THE NAME IN THE RECORD YOU WISH TO DELETE ?";NAME$
320  PRINT C$;"OPEN GHJ456"
330  PRINT C$;"READ GHJ456"
335  Z = 1
340  FOR Q = 1 TO 6: INPUT A$(Z,Q): NEXT Q
342  IF A$(Z,1) = NAME$ THEN Z = Z - 1
345  Z = Z + 1: IF A$(Z - 1,1) ( ) "DUMMY" THEN 340
350  PRINT C$;"CLOSE GHJ456"
360  PRINT C$;"OPEN RST789"
370  PRINT C$;"WRITE RST789"
380  Z = 1
390  FOR Q = 1 TO 6: PRINT A$(Z,Q): NEXT Q
400  Z = Z + 1: IF A$(Z - 1,1) ( ) "DUMMY" THEN 390
410  PRINT C$;"CLOSE RST789"
420  PRINT C$;"OPEN RST789"
430  PRINT C$;"READ RST789"
440  Z = 1
450  FOR Q = 1 TO 6: INPUT A$(Z,Q)
460  PRINT A$(Z,Q): NEXT Q
465  PRINT
470  Z = Z + 1: IF A$(Z - 1,1) ( ) "DUMMY" THEN 450
480  PRINT C$;"CLOSE RST789"
490  PRINT : PRINT "LISTING OF FILE (RST789) COMPLETE"
```

Adding one or more records to a file

```
300  REM   PROG TO ADD ONE OR MORE RECORDS TO A FILE(APPLE II).PROG 07.1
320  C$ =  CHR$ (4): DIM A$(30,6)
340  PRINT
350  PRINT "NOW INPUT THE DATA FOR THE NEXT RECORD": PRINT : PRINT
360  INPUT "NAME ?";N$: PRINT
370  INPUT "ADDRESS ?";A$: PRINT
380  INPUT "TEL.NO. ?";T$: PRINT
390  INPUT "AGE ?";D: PRINT
400  INPUT "SEX ?";S$: PRINT
410  INPUT "FORM ?";F$: PRINT
420  T = T + 1:Z = Z + 1
430  GOTO 490
440  F = 1
450  PRINT C$;"OPEN GHJ456"
460  PRINT C$;"READ GHJ456"
470  FOR Z = 1 + T TO 9 + T
480  FOR Q = 1 TO 6: INPUT A$(Z,Q): NEXT Q
482  NEXT Z
490  D$ =  STR$ (D)
500  A$(Z,1) = N$:A$(Z,2) = A$:A$(Z,3) = T$:A$(Z,4) = D$:A$(Z,5) = S$:A$(Z,6) = F$
510  IF F = 1 THEN 550
520  INPUT "DO YOU WISH TO ADD ANOTHER RECORD(Y/N)? ";W$
530  IF W$ = "Y" THEN 340
540  GOTO 440
550  PRINT C$;"CLOSE GHJ456"
552  PRINT C$;"OPEN RST789"
554  PRINT C$;"WRITE RST789"
555  FOR Q = 1 TO 9 + T
557  FOR R = 1 TO 6
560  PRINT A$(Q,R)
562  NEXT R: NEXT Q
590  PRINT C$;"CLOSE RST789"
595  PRINT : PRINT
600  PRINT "NEW FILE (RST789) WRITTEN AND CLOSED"
610  FOR A = 1 TO 9 + T: FOR B = 1 TO 6
620  PRINT A$(A,B)
630  NEXT B: PRINT : NEXT A
```

APPENDIX 5 FILE HANDLING PROGRAMS 183

Amending selected fields in one or more records

```
300  REM    PROG TO AMEND SELECTED FIELDS IN ONE
305  REM    OR MORE RECORDS(APPLE II).PROG 09
320  C$ =   CHR$ (4): DIM A$(9,6)
350  Z = 1
382  PRINT C$;"OPEN GHJ456"
384  PRINT C$;"READ GHJ456"
390  FOR Q = 1 TO 6: INPUT A$(Z,Q): NEXT Q
400  IF A$(Z,1) = "DUMMY" THEN 410
405  Z = Z + 1: GOTO 390
410  PRINT C$;"CLOSE GHJ456"
415  PRINT : PRINT : INPUT "WHAT IS THE NAME IN THE RECORD YOU WISH TO AMEND? ";
N1$
420  Z = 1
430  IF A$(Z,1) = N1$ THEN 447
440  Z = Z + 1: IF A$(Z,1) < > "DUMMY" THEN 430
445  PRINT : PRINT "NAME NOT ON FILE": GOTO 415
447  PRINT : PRINT : PRINT "DO YOU WISH TO AMEND THE:-": PRINT "NAME(TYPE 1)": P
RINT "ADDRESS(TYPE 2)": PRINT "TEL NO.(TYPE 3)": PRINT "AGE(TYPE 4)": PRINT "FOR
M(TYPE 6)": INPUT I
450  PRINT : PRINT "NOW INPUT THE NEW DATA"
460  INPUT R$(I)
470  A$(Z,I) = R$(I)
480  PRINT : INPUT "DO YOU WISH TO AMEND ANOTHER FIELD IN THIS RECORD? ";B$
490  IF B$ < > "Y" AND B$ < > "YES" THEN 510
500  GOTO 447
510  PRINT : PRINT : INPUT "DO YOU WISH TO AMEND ANOTHER RECORD? ";B1$
520  IF B1$ < > "Y" AND B1$ < > "YES" THEN 530
525  GOTO 415
530  PRINT C$;"OPEN RST789"
540  PRINT C$;"WRITE RST789"
550  Z = 1
560  FOR Q = 1 TO 6: PRINT A$(Z,Q): NEXT Q
570  Z = Z + 1: IF A$(Z - 1,1) < > "DUMMY" THEN 560
590  PRINT C$;"CLOSE RST789"
600  FOR Q = 1 TO 8: FOR P = 1 TO 6
610  PRINT A$(Q,P)
620  NEXT P: NEXT Q
```

PET BASIC

Writing a file

```
10 REM WRITING A FILE.PROG 01(PET BASIC)
20 PRINT"■":DIM N$(9,6)
30 PRINT:INPUT"WHAT IS THE NAME OF THIS NEW FILE ";F$
40 DOPEN#8,(F$),W
50 PRINT:PRINT"EACH * INDICATES THAT A RECORD HAS BEEN WRITTEN TO THE FILE"
60 Q=1
70 FOR R=1 TO 6:READ N$(Q,R)
80 IF N$(Q,1)="XXX" THEN 120
90 PRINT#8,N$(Q,R):NEXT R
100 PRINT"*";
110 Q=Q+1:GOTO 70
120 DCLOSE
130 PRINT:PRINT"FILE WRITING COMPLETE":PRINT
140 PRINT"FILE CONTAINS";Q-1;"RECORDS"
150 DATA "BROWN MARY","45 TOWNFIELDS KNUTSFORD","0565 2468",16,"F","5U"
160 DATA "YOUNG JOHN","3 GREEN LANE NORTHWICH","--",17,"M","5S"
170 DATA "GREEN ALAN","17 TOWN LANE MOBBERLEY","MOB 1234",15,"M","5V"
180 DATA "JONES FIONA","43 TREE WAY KNUTSFORD","0565 74812",16,"F","5U"
190 DATA "BLOGGS JOHN","39 ASHWORTH PARK KNUTSFORD","0565 9999",17,"M","5V"
200 DATA "SMITH ROY","99 MANCHESTER RD KNUTSFORD","0565 7887",15,"M","5T"
210 DATA "WHITE ANN","THE COTTAGE PLUMLEY RD KNUTSFORD","--",16,"F","5T"
220 DATA "EVANS PETER","1 THE TALBOTS MOBBERLEY","MOB 2345",15,"M","5U"
230 DATA "XXX"
```

Reading from a file

```
200 REM READING FROM A FILE.PROG02(PET BASIC)
210 PRINT"■":DIM A$(8,6)
220 PRINT:INPUT"WHAT IS THE NAME OF THE FILE THAT YOU   WISH TO READ ";N1$
230 PRINT:PRINT "READING THE FILE.....":PRINT
240 DOPEN#8,(N1$)
250 Q=1
260 FOR R=1 TO 6:INPUT#8,A$(Q,R)
270 IF ST=64 THEN 300
280 NEXT R
290 Q=Q+1:GOTO 260
300 DCLOSE
310 FOR A=1 TO Q:FOR B=1 TO 6
320 PRINT A$(A,B);" ";:NEXT B
330 PRINT:NEXT A
340 PRINT:PRINT"FILE LISTING COMPLETE"
350 PRINT:PRINT"FILE CONTAINS ";Q;" RECORDS"
```

Reading a file into one array then into a new file

```
10 REM PROG TO READ A SERIAL DISK FILE INTO AN ARRAY THEN TO A NEW FILE.
20 REM PROG 05(PET BASIC)
30 PRINT"■":PRINT:PRINT:DIM A$(8,6)
40 PRINT:INPUT"WHAT IS THE NAME OF THE INPUT FILE ";R1$:PRINT
50 INPUT"WHAT IS THE NAME OF THE OUTPUT FILE ";W1$:PRINT
60 PRINT "READING THE FILE...":PRINT
70 DOPEN#8,(R1$)
80 Q=1
90 FOR R=1 TO 6:INPUT#8,A$(Q,R)
100 IF ST=64 THEN 130
110 NEXT R
120 Q=Q+1:GOTO 90
130 PRINT"FILE ";R1$;" HAS NOW BEEN READ":PRINT
140 DCLOSE
150 DOPEN#8,(W1$),W
160 FOR A=1 TO Q:FOR B=1 TO 6
170 PRINT#8,A$(A,B)
180 NEXT B:NEXT A
190 DCLOSE
200 REM OPTION TO KILL THE OLD FILE
210 PRINT:INPUT"DO YOU WISH TO KILL THE OLD FILE (Y/N) ";A$
220 PRINT:IF A$<>"Y" THEN 280
230 INPUT"ARE YOU SURE??!!(Y/N) ";KK$
240 PRINT:IF KK$<>"Y" THEN 280
250 SCRATCH (R1$)
260 PRINT"FILE ";R1$;" IS NOW ERASED"
270 GOTO 63999
280 PRINT"BOTH FILES ARE SAVED"
```

Deleting one record from a file

```
10 REM PROG TO DELETE ONE RECORD FROM A SERIAL DISK FILE.PROG06 (PET BASIC)
20 PRINT"■":PRINT:PRINT:DIM N1$(8,6)
30 PRINT:INPUT"WHAT IS THE NAME IN THE RECORD YOU WISH TO DELETE? ";NAME$:PRIN
40 PRINT "READING THE FILE...":PRINT
50 DOPEN#8,"GHJ456"
60 Q=1
70 FOR R=1 TO 6
80 INPUT#8,N1$(Q,R)
90 IF ST=64 THEN 130
100 IF N1$(Q,1)=NAME$ THEN Q=Q-1
110 NEXT R
120 Q=Q+1:GOTO 70
130 DCLOSE
140 REM WRITING THE NEW FILE
150 DOPEN#8,"RST789",W
160 FOR A=1 TO Q:FOR B=1 TO 6
170 PRINT#8,N1$(A,B)
180 NEXT B:NEXT A
190 DCLOSE
200 PRINT:PRINT"NEW FILE COMPLETE":PRINT
210 REM PRINTING OUT THE NEW FILE
220 FOR C=1 TO Q:FOR D=1 TO 6
230 PRINT N1$(C,D)
240 NEXT D:NEXT C
250 PRINT:PRINT"FILE NOW CONTAINS ";Q;" RECORDS"
```

Adding one or more records to a file

```
10 REM PROG TO ADD ONE OR MORE RECORDS TO A FILE.
20 REM PROG7.1 (PET BASIC)
30 PRINT"■":DIM A$(30,6):Z=1
40 REM INPUT THE NEW DATA FROM THE KEYBOARD
50 PRINT:PRINT"INPUT THE DATA FOR THE NEXT NEW RECORD":PRINT
60 INPUT"NAME     ";A$(Z,1):PRINT
70 INPUT"ADDRESS  ";A$(Z,2):PRINT
80 INPUT"TEL.NO.  ";A$(Z,3):PRINT
90 INPUT"AGE      ";A$(Z,4):PRINT
100 INPUT"SEX      ";A$(Z,5):PRINT
110 INPUT"FORM     ";A$(Z,6):PRINT
120 PRINT:INPUT"DO YOU WANT TO ADD ANOTHER RECORD (Y/N)";N$
130 IF N$<>"Y" THEN 150
140 Z=Z+1:PRINT"■":PRINT:PRINT:GOTO 50
150 PRINT"■":PRINT:PRINT
160 PRINT:PRINT"READING THE OLD FILE & WWRITING THE NEW FILE...":PRINT
170 DOPEN#8,"GHJ456"
180 FOR Q=Z+1 TO Z+8:FOR R=1 TO 6
190 INPUT#8,A$(Q,R)
200 IF ST=64 THEN 220
210 NEXT R:NEXT Q
220 DCLOSE
230 REM WRITING THE NEW FILE FROM THE ARRAY
240 DOPEN#8,"RST789"
250 FOR A=1 TO Q-1:FOR B=1 TO 6
260 PRINT#8,A$(A,B)
270 NEXT B:NEXT A
280 DCLOSE
290 PRINT"NEW FILE-RST789-WRITTEN & CLOSED":PRINT
300 PRINT"FILE CONTAINS ";Q;" RECORDS"
```

Appendix 6
Comparison between ENIAC and 380Z

Item	Parameter	ENIAC	BBC
1	size	85 m³	0.0083 m³
2	power consumption	140 kW	50 W
3	ROM	16 K bits (relays and switches)	unlimited
4	RAM	1 K bits (flip–flops)	32 K
5	clock rate	100 kHz	2 MHz
6	components	18 000 valves 70 000 resistors 10 000 capacitors 7 500 relays	86 'chips' (The 6502 CPU 'chip' alone contains approximately 10 000 'transistors')
7	add time	200 µs	200 ns
8	mean time between failures	hours	years
9	weight	30 000 kg	3.1 kg
10	backing store	none	disks and tapes

Appendix 7
Suggested reading material

1. *Computer Weekly*
   Published by IPC. Full of news of who's doing what, buying what, selling what, making what. Must be in the classroom.
2. *Computing*
   The professional computing newspaper. Published weekly and available to British Computer Society members including institutional affiliates.
3. *Computer Education*
   Published three times a year by the Computer Education Group. Mainly written by teachers and students for teachers and students.
4. The following centres produce useful materials (payment or subscription is sometimes required):
   (*a*) ILEA School and College Computer Service
   Room 231c, County Hall, London SE1 7PB
   (*b*) Hertfordshire Advisory Unit for Computer Based Education Endymion Road, Hatfield, Herts AL10 OHU
   (*c*) Birmingham Educational Computing Centre
   Camp Hill, Stratford Road, Birmingham B11 1AR
   (*d*) ITMA College of St. Mark and St. John,
   Deriford Road, Plymouth PL6 8BH
   (*e*) British Computer Society (Schools Committee)
   13 Mansfield Street, London W1M OBP, for the book list and the computing terms glossary.
5. For further reading:
   (*a*) *Computers at Work* by J. O. E. Clark
   (Hamlyn, ISBN 0 600 32204 1)
   (*b*) *Computer Peripherals* by B. Wilkinson and
   D. Horrocks (Hodder and Stoughton,
   ISBN 0 340 32652 3)
   (*c*) *Data Processing Made Simple* by S. Wooldridge
   (Heinemann, ISBN 0 491 01875 4)
   (*d*) *Glossary of Computing Terms* (British Computer Society, ISBN 0 901 86523 0).

Revision questions

1 (a) The East Wessex Electricity Board use a computer to produce consumers' electricity bills. List all the items of data required in order to calculate the amount due and to print a bill on a special form.
(b) **Draw a data flowchart for the system needed to produce the electricity bills above.**
(c) State which of the items of data listed in part (a) would be input (i) at the time when the bill is being prepared, and (ii) at an earlier stage and held in a backing store. *(AEB, 1975)**

2 Explain, in detail, the most important features of 'first generation'; 'second generation'; and 'third generation' computers and the distinguishable differences between these generations.
   Your answer should include dates, names or types of computers, hardware and software features and reference to the type of processing carried out, where applicable. *(AEB, 1976)**

3 (a) Explain, with the aid of diagrams, the essential differences between batch processing and interactive computing.
(b) Give a commercial/business application for which each of the above modes of operation is advantageous and state why. *(AEB, 1977)*

4 'The speed, power and reliability of computers have increased greatly over the past 20 years.' Justify this statement, explaining the changes which have taken place in hardware and software to make such advances possible. *(AEB, 1979)**

5 For each of the application stated below, say whether the method of processing would be *off-line, on-line, real-time*. In each case explain one reason for your choice.
(a) A water authority's flood warning system.
(b) A branch of a large clothing firm using Kimball tags.
(c) One of a series of car components warehouses linked to the head office by terminal. *(AEB, 1980)**

6 Write a program in any high level language for a geography test as follows:
   The program, which must be interactive, is to ask for the capital city of the following countries, one at a time: France, Wales, Spain, Australia and Japan (capitals are Paris, Cardiff, Madrid, Canberra and Tokyo respectively).
Two points are to be awarded for a correct answer and the program must state this. An incorrect answer must be stated as incorrect. After the last answer, the program must print out the score as a percentage. *(AEB, 1978)**

7 A UK firm manufactures spare parts for agricultural machinery. It has four distributors within a 60 km radius of the factory and 15 other distributors over 200 km away. The firm's catalogue lists over 500 different items and the sales records show that approximately one-third of these items are bought frequently and the remainder not more than half-yearly with some only once in 2 or 3 years. 10% of the firm's employees work in the stores and despatch departments and 20% are sales representatives covering the whole of the UK.
(a) Discuss the implications of the above company installing a computing system, listing any advantages and disadvantages such a system would have over the old manual system.
(b) Design a computing system suitable for the above application. Give your answer as a system flowchart with each 'symbol' carefully annotated. *(AEB, 1976)**

8 An invoice is to be prepared by a builder for sending to a client. The builder has used his own labour and that of a number of sub-contractors, e.g. for plumbing and electrical wiring. Each sub-contractor and the builder has incurred costs for labour and materials.
(a) (i) Prepare an invoice, using your own figures, under the heading of 'A. Bloggs & Co.' in a typical invoice format, including all the items detailed above. (Marks will not be awarded or deducted for the correctness of prices of materials or costs of labour.)
(ii) State clearly how each item is dealt with by hand in the course of preparation of the invoice.
(b) If this invoice was to be prepared by a computer, what differences would be necessary in the handling of the data items used in part (a)? *(AEB, 1977)**

9 Give

(*a*) *one* example of the type of program where a VDU would be a more advantageous form of input/output device (than a teletype) and,

(*b*) *one* example where the use of a teletype would be better.

State why in each case. (*AEB, 1978*)

10 (*a*) Choose *one* of the following types of backing store and explain how data is stored and retrieved referring to speed, capacity and cost.

    magnetic tape; floppy disk; magnetic bubble store.

(*b*) Using suitable examples explain how the following are stored in computers:

(i) numbers used for arithmetic purposes

(ii) characters.

(*c*) Give *two* methods of data validation.

(*AEB, 1980*)*

11 (*a*) If the function part of an instruction word consists of one byte (8 bits, not including parity, how many different functions can be specified.

(*b*) If the code for the instruction PRINT is 00011011, show

(i) in a diagram how this signal would be decoded on the execute cycle

(ii) by means of a second diagram, how the output from the decoder is used to get the contents of the specified location copied to the accumulator.

(*c*) Copy and complete the section of the truth table shown here for the lettered points in the logic circuit.

(*AEB, 1979*)

12 A vote is to be taken in a school to decide whether or not the school should have a uniform. The results of the voting are to be processed by a computer.

(*a*) Design a form/questionnaire to enable the raw data to be collected, and which would make it suitable for easy coding.

(*b*) Draw a simple systems flowchart showing how the results of the survey would be processed to give the total number of votes cast for each possible answer; the total number of votes cast and the votes cast for each answer as a percentage of the total votes cast.

(*c*) Draw a detailed programming flowchart of the above to enable the coding (in BASIC) to be taken directly from the flowchart.

13 In a certain computer, a location consists of 3 bytes, each of 8 bits, and can be used to hold either a binary integer or three 8 bit characters. Show by means of a diagram how the denary number 247 would be stored if

(*a*) it was being used in a mathematical calculation

(*b*) it was part of a house address e.g. 247 London Road.

State any codes used.

14 Using the AEB code on page 75, write a program from the flowchart below. The first instruction will be stored in location 100. The first items of data will be stored in locations 500, 501.

The first two items of data will be 1000, 0.

(*AEB, 1980*)

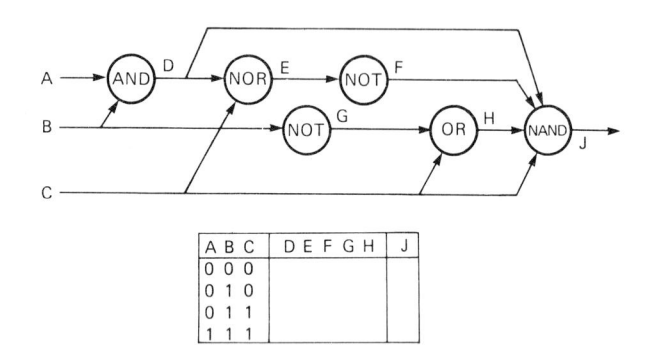

A B C	D E F G H	J
0 0 0		
0 1 0		
0 1 1		
1 1 1		

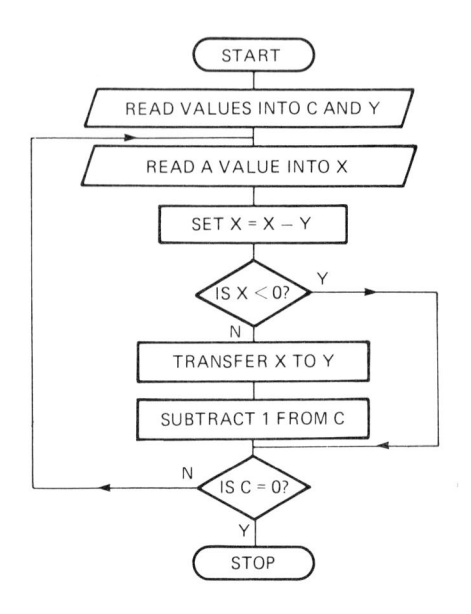

Multiple choice questions

The answers to all these questions are given in the answers section.

1. Punched cards were originally developed by
   (a) Jacquard.
   (b) Hollerith.
   (c) Lady Lovelace.
   (d) Napier.
2. Which of the following is *not* an output device
   (a) A line printer.
   (b) A visual display unit.
   (c) A graph plotter.
   (d) A light pen.
3. Which of the following is a peripheral device
   (a) A central processing unit.
   (b) A program.
   (c) A line printer.
   (d) A compiler.
4. The console typewriter is used by
   (a) the programmer.
   (b) the operator.
   (c) the punch operator.
   (d) the systems analyst.
5. Which of the following is *not* a high level language
   (a) Cobol.
   (b) Cesil.
   (c) Basic.
   (d) Algol.
6. Which language would most likely be used in business
   (a) Cobol.
   (b) Fortran.
   (c) Algol.
   (d) Plan
7. A compiler is
   (a) a computer operator.
   (b) a programmer.
   (c) an item of hardware.
   (d) an item of software.
8. Second generation computers used
   (a) transistors.
   (b) valves.
   (c) printed circuits.
   (d) integrated circuits.
9. An assembler would most likely be written in
   (a) Cobol.
   (b) machine code.
   (c) Fortran.
   (d) Cesil.
10. The type of computer storage with the quickest access time is
    (a) magnetic tape.
    (b) core store.
    (c) magnetic disc.
    (d) magnetic drum.
11. Our present computers are types of
    (a) analogue device.
    (b) adding machine.
    (c) abacus.
    (d) digital device.
12. A utility program is
    (a) a piece of software used to control the computer.
    (b) a program used to change a low level language into machine code.
    (c) an engineer's testing program.
    (d) a piece of software used to carry out routine jobs.
13. A dry run is
    (a) a program without any data.
    (b) a check on a program using test data.
    (c) a check on a flow-chart using test data.
    (d) none of these.
14. A multi-access system
    (a) allows data to be accessed quickly.
    (b) allows several programs access to the computer, apparently simultaneously.
    (c) is a computer with many on-line terminals.
    (d) is a type of real-time system.
15. Which of the following Basic instructions contains an error
    (a) 10 IF N > 38 THEN 40
    (b) 10 READ P, Q, R,
    (c) 10 LET X = P*Q/12
    (d) 10 PRINT P, Q, R,
16. A rogue value is
    (a) a piece of data punched incorrectly.
    (b) a piece of test data.
    (c) used to tell the computer that the last piece of data has been dealt with.
    (d) used to cause an unconditional jump.
17. A verifier is
    (a) a person who is in charge of the punch room.
    (b) a program sent through the computer to test it.
    (c) a person who checks the punching of a card or tape.
    (d) a machine used to check the punching on tape or card.
18. A variable is
    (a) a piece of data which changes value during the running of a program.
    (b) the name given to a store location in Basic.
    (c) a single letter, or a single number followed by a single letter.
    (d) a piece of a logic circuit.
19. 39_{10} written as a binary number is
    (a) 111001
    (b) 101001
    (c) 100111
    (d) none of these.
20. 101011_2 converted to denary is
    (a) 86
    (b) 45
    (c) none of these.
    (d) 43

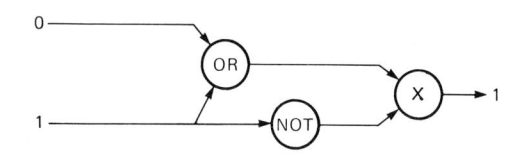

21 In the logic circuit above the gate marked X is a
(a) OR gate. (c) AND gate.
(b) NOT gate. (d) The circuit has no possible solution.

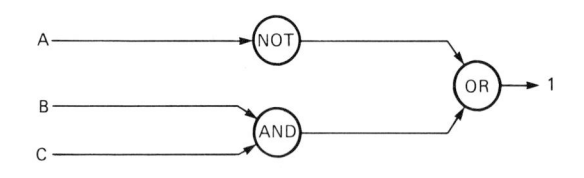

22 Which of the following inputs would *not* produce an output of 1
(a) A = 1 B = 0 C = 1 (c) A = 0 B = 0 C = 0
(b) A = 1 B = 1 C = 1 (d) A = 0 B = 0 C = 1

23 A third generation computer uses
(a) transistors. (c) micro-integrated circuits.
(b) valves. (d) electricity.

24 Which of the following is *not* a BASIC variable
(a) S9 (c) P
(b) R∅ (d) 2I

25 Charles Babbage was famous for inventing
(a) programming instructions. (c) the abacus.
(b) the punch card. (d) the analytical engine.

26
```
10 READ A,B
20 LET M = 3*A + B
30 LET N = (A+B)*A - 2
40 PRINT "M = ", M,
50 PRINT "N = ", N
60 DATA 5, 2
99 END
```
Which of the following represents the print out of the program above?
(a) M = 17   (c) M = 21
    N = 33   N = 12
(b) M = 17 N = 33 (d) None of these.

27 Line printer paper is divided into
(a) 15 zones each 8 characters wide.
(b) 13 zones each 8 characters wide.
(c) 8 zones each 13 characters wide.
(d) none of these.

28 Which of the following print statements could cause the output PAY = £48.
(a) 40 PRINT "PAY =£", "48"
(b) 40 PRINT "PAY = " "£"; P
(c) 40 PRINT "PAY = ", "£", P
(d) 40 PRINT "PAY = ", "£P"

29 Diagnostics are
(a) programs used to test the functioning of the computer.
(b) logic circuits in the control unit which activate a signal on the operators console when a problem occurs in the running of a program.
(c) tests written into compilers and assemblers to locate coding errors and warn the programmer.
(d) none of these.

30 A group of travel agencies are connected to a central airline booking computer. The most useful form of terminal for them to have is a
(a) teleprinter. (c) graphical display unit.
(b) video display unit. (d) document reader.

31 The operation code is
(a) the number representing the operation in a program instruction.
(b) the number representing the store location used in a program instruction.
(c) a very low level language.
(d) an advanced form of control program.

32 $10111_2 + 1011_2$ gives
(a) 100000_2 (c) 11110_2
(b) 100010_2 (d) none of these.

33 Which type of software would you except to use for organising a company's complete payroll?
(a) Applications package. (c) Executive program.
(b) Utility package. (d) Operating system.

34 Run time is
(a) the time when signals are transmitted to the computer.
(b) the time when the program is run.
(c) the time when the program is compiled.
(d) the time when the signals are transmitted to the peripheral units.

35 An abacus is
(a) a mechanical adding machine.
(b) a type of computer.
(c) an early form of adding device.
(d) a type of peripheral.

36 Hollerith was famous for
(a) the analytical engine.
(b) the punched card.
(c) Napier's bones.
(d) the stored program concept.

37 Which of the following is an output device?
 (a) Paper tape reader.
 (b) Teletypewriter.
 (c) Card punch.
 (d) Acoustic coupler.
38 A compiler is
 (a) a part of the computer hardware.
 (b) an object program.
 (c) a person who compiles.
 (d) none of the above.
39 Which of the following are high-level languages?
 (a) BASIC
 (b) Machine code.
 (c) CESIL.
 (d) ALGOL.
40 Which of the following storage devices is known as 'direct access'?
 (a) Magnetic tape.
 (b) Magnetic disc.
 (c) Paper tape.
 (d) Core store.
41 11111_2 expressed in denary is:
 (a) 31
 (b) 62
 (c) 11111
 (d) none of these
42 Which type of software would you expect to use for controlling a company's orders of stock control?
 (a) Utility package.
 (b) Applications package
 (c) Operating system.
 (d) Executive program.
43 In BASIC, the instruction PRINT X/Y
 (a) prints the value of X and Y.
 (b) prints X/Y.
 (c) prints the value of X/Y.
 (d) does nothing.
44 LEO is
 (a) the name of a person connected with computing.
 (b) the first transistorised computer.
 (c) the first commercial computer system.
 (d) a command in Basic.

45 A line printer *prints*
 (a) a word at a time.
 (b) a letter at a time.
 (c) a line at a time.
 (d) a page at a time.
46 The accumulator is
 (a) where programs are permanently stored.
 (b) where data is stored.
 (c) where arithmetic is performed.
 (d) where cards are accumulated.
47 A half-adder is
 (a) an adder which adds halves.
 (b) a full adder without the carry bit.
 (c) an adder with carry.
 (d) none of these.
48 A trace routine is
 (a) printing diagnostic messages.
 (b) instructions included in the program to enable the flow of data manipulation to be followed.
 (c) error messages.
 (d) a software routine used to plot curves.
49 Teletypewriter output is
 (a) 60 characters divided into 12 zones.
 (b) 72 characters divided into 5 zones.
 (c) 72 characters, one zone.
 (d) an unspecified number of characters, 5 zones wide.
50 An acoustic coupler is
 (a) a magetic device used for transmitting messages to a computer.
 (b) an electronic device used for connecting a telephone to a computer.
 (c) a mechanical device used for connecting a peripheral unit to the computer.
 (d) an electronic device used to transmit signals to a computer via the telephone network.

Answers

Note that answers are given only to those questions marked with an asterisk.

Exercises 3.1

1 (a) 26 alphabetic characters need ($2^5 \equiv 32$) 5 bits
(b) 999 numbers need ($2^{10} \equiv 1024$) 10 bits
(c) 9999 numbers need ($2^{14} \equiv 16384$) 14 bits
(d) (i) ABC 123 R

| 3 bits | 15 bits | 10 bits | 5 bits |

maximum 33 bits

(ii) ABC 123

| 3 bits | 15 bits | 10 bits |

maximum 28 bits

(iii) 123 ABC

| 3 bits | 10 bits | 15 bits |

maximum 28 bits

(iv) AB 1234

| 3 bits | 10 bits | 14 bits |

maximum 27 bits

(v) 1234 AB

| 3 bits | 14 bits | 10 bits |

maximum 27 bits

In each case, the first three bits are used to identify the bit pattern of the coding, e.g. 101 is the fifth coding pattern and states that the next 14 bits are numerals etc.
(e) Assume A ≡ 00001
B ≡ 00010 etc.

The coding for WNO 205 F is type (i) above.

| 001 | 10111 | 01110 | 01111 | 0011001101 | 00110 |

Code 1 W ≡ 23 N ≡ 14 O ≡ 15   205   F ≡ 6

Exercises 5.1

(i) $3F \equiv 3 \times 16 + 15 \times 1 = 48 + 15 = 63$
(ii) $BB \equiv 11 \times 16 + 11 \times 1 = 176 + 11 = 187$
(iii) $44 \equiv 4 \times 16 + 4 \times 1 = 64 + 4 = 68$
(iv) $100 \equiv 1 \times 256 + 0 \times 16 + 0 \times 1 = 256$
(v) $FFFF \equiv 15 \times 4096 + 15 \times 256 + 15 \times 16 + 15 \times 1 = 65535$
(vi) 16 | 27 | 11   Answer = 1B
         | 1 | 1

(vii) 16 | 99 | 3   Answer = 63
         | 6 | 6

(viii) 16 | 3135 | 15
       16 | 195 | 3   Answer = C3F
          | 12 | 12

(ix) 16 | 431 | 15
     16 | 26 | 10   Answer = 1AF
        | 1 | 1

(x) 16 | 43788 | 12
    16 | 2736 | 0
    16 | 171 | 11   Answer = AB0C
       | 10 | 10

Exercises 5.2

1 (a) $18.0625 = 18\frac{1}{16} = 10010.0001$
(b) $92_{10} = (5 \times 16) + 12 = 5C$ (hex)
(c) $901_{10} = 1001\,0000\,0001$ (BCD)

2 (a) Binary 100000001
       BCD   001001010011
(b) Either, because double word length is necessary
8 bits = 0–255 (binary), 0–99 (BCD)

194

ANSWERS

Exercises 5.3

1

A	B	C	D	Z
0	0	0	0	1
0	1	1	1	0
1	0	1	0	0
1	1	1	1	0

2

A	B	C	D	Z
0	0	0	1	0
0	1	0	1	0
1	0	0	0	1
1	1	1	0	0

3

A	B	C	D	Z
0	0	1	1	1
0	1	1	0	0
1	0	1	0	0
1	1	0	0	0

4

A	B	C	D	E	F	Z
0	0	0	1	1	1	1
0	0	1	1	1	1	0
0	1	0	1	1	1	1
0	1	1	1	0	0	1
1	0	0	1	1	1	1
1	0	1	1	1	1	0
1	1	0	1	1	1	1
1	1	1	0	1	0	1

5

A	B	C	D	E	Z
0	0	1	1	0	0
0	1	0	1	0	0
1	0	0	1	0	0
1	1	0	0	1	0

Exercises 5.4

1

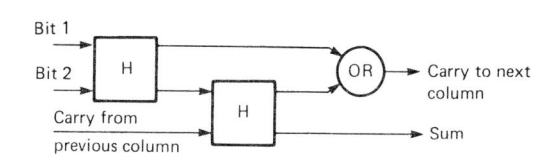

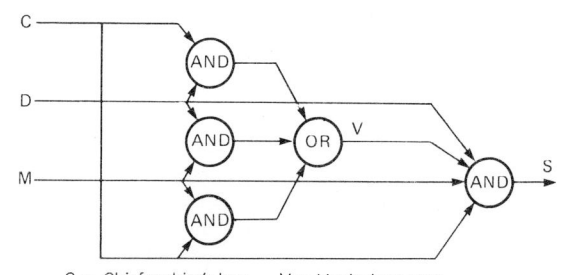

Bit 1, Bit 2 → H; Carry from previous column → H; outputs feed OR → Carry to next column; Sum output.

2 (diagram with NOT, AND, OR gates; inputs B, C, D, E, A, F; output 1)

3 (diagram with inputs A, C, D, E, F; AND, OR, AND, OR gates)

4

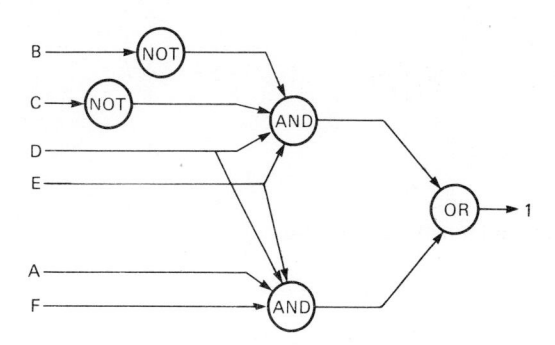

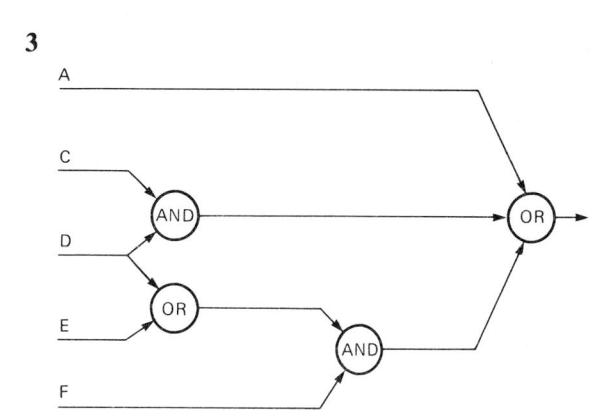

A	B	C	D	E	F	G
0	0	0	0	1	0	0
0	1	0	1	1	1	1
1	0	0	1	1	1	1
1	1	1	1	0	1	0

Circuit diagram:
C = Chief cashier's key
D = Deputy's key
M = Manager's key
V = Vault door open
S = Strong room door open

Exercises 6.1

(i) 0.00011 (ii) 0.1$\dot{1}$10$\dot{0}$ (iii) 0.1$\dot{1}$00$\dot{1}$
(iv) 0.0010010 (v) 0.010000111101011 ...
(vi) 0.010$\dot{1}$10101111000010100011$\dot{1}$

Exercises 6.2

1
(i) $+81 \equiv 01010001$ (ii) $+100 \equiv 01100100$
$-81 \equiv 10101111$ $-100 \equiv 10011100$
(iii) $+15 \equiv 00001111$ (iv) $+49 \equiv 00110001$
$-15 \equiv 11110001$ $-49 \equiv 11001111$
(v) $+123 \equiv 01111011$
$-123 \equiv 10000101$

2
(i) $+91 \equiv 01011011$ (ii) $+9 \equiv 001001$
$-91 \equiv 10100101$ $-9 \equiv 110111$

(iii) $+222 \equiv 011011110$
$-222 \equiv 100100010$

(iv) $+120 \equiv 0001111000$
$-120 \equiv 1110001000$

(v) $+654 \equiv 01010001110$
$-654 \equiv 10101110010$

(vi) $+1023 \equiv 001111111111$
$-1023 \equiv 110000000001$

Exercises 6.3

(i) $\quad 34 \equiv 0100010$
$+31 \equiv 0011111$
$-31 \equiv 1100001$
$\overline{1\ 0000011 \equiv 3}$

(ii) $107 \equiv 01101011$
$+69 \equiv 01000101$
$-69 \equiv 10111011$
$\overline{1\ 00100110 \equiv 38}$

(iii) $277 \equiv 0100010101$
$+17 \equiv 0000010001$
$-17 \equiv 1111101111$
$\overline{1\ 0100000100 \equiv 260}$

(iv) $514 \equiv 01000000010$
$+512 \equiv 01000000000$
$-512 \equiv 11000000000$
$\overline{1\ 00000000010 \equiv 2}$

(v) $1904 \equiv 011101110000$
$+360 \equiv 000101101000$
$-360 \equiv 111010011000$
$\overline{1\ 011000001000 \equiv 1544}$

Exercises 6.4

1 (a) | 3 bits | 9 bits |
function code   address/operand

(b)
256 128 64 32 16 8 4 2 1. ½ ¼

| 0 | 1 | 1 | 1 | 1 | 1 | 1 | 1 | 1 | 1 | 1 | $\equiv +511.75$

↑ sign bit   ↑ binary point

| 1 | 0 | 0 | 0 | 0 | 0 | 0 | 0 | 0 | 0 | 0 | $\equiv -512.00$

(c) $\quad -7.25 = -512 + 504.75$
$-512\ 256\ 128\ 64\ 32\ 16\ 8\ 4\ 2\ 1\ \tfrac{1}{2}\ \tfrac{1}{4}$

| 1 | 1 | 1 | 1 | 1 | 1 | 1 | 0 | 0 | 0 | 1 | 1 |
↑

2 (a) (i) 2) 133 (1   (ii) 8)133(5 $\tfrac{1}{8} = .1$
    2) 66 (0   8) 16(0
    2) 33 (1   2(2   Answer $= 205.1$
    2) 16 (0
    2)   8 (0
    2)   4 (0
    2)   2 (0
         1 (1

$0.125 = \tfrac{1}{8} = .001$
Answer $= 10000101.001$

(b) (i) $6\tfrac{3}{4} = 6 + \tfrac{1}{2} + \tfrac{1}{4} = 110.11 = 0.11011 \times 2^3$
(ii) $9.5 = 9 + \tfrac{1}{2} = 1001.1 = 0.10011 \times 2^4$

(c) 2.4 cannot be converted into binary because
(i) 0.4 or $\tfrac{2}{5}$ is not an exact fractional power of 2 i.e. it lies between 0.1 ($\tfrac{1}{2}$) and 0.01 ($\tfrac{1}{4}$)
(ii) It cannot be 'made up' of any combination of fractional powers of 2
(iii) When 0.4 is converted, a recurrence takes place after the fourth binary digit

$2.4 \quad = 2\ \ +0.4$
$0.4 \times 2 = 0.8 \qquad 0$
$0.8 \times 2 = 1.6 \qquad 1$
$0.6 \times 2 = 1.2 \qquad 1$
$0.2 \times 2 = 0.4 \qquad 0$
$0.4 \times 2 = 0.8$ etc.

$2.4 = 10.0\dot{1}10\dot{0}$
If represented as 10.0110 this is equivalent to $2 + \tfrac{1}{4} + \tfrac{1}{8} = 2.375$, so error $= 0.025$

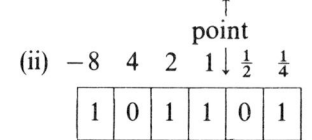

3 (a) (i) $-32\ 16\ 8\ 4\ 2\ 1$

| 0 | 1 | 1 | 1 | 1 | 1 | $= +31$

(ii) | 1 | 0 | 0 | 0 | 0 | 0 | $= -32$

(b) (i) $-8\ 4\ 2\ 1\ \tfrac{1}{2}\ \tfrac{1}{4}$

| | | | | | |
↑ point

(ii) $-8\ 4\ 2\ 1\!\downarrow\ \tfrac{1}{2}\ \tfrac{1}{4}$

| 1 | 0 | 1 | 1 | 0 | 1 |

4 $77_{10} \equiv 01001101 \qquad 145_{10} \equiv 010010001$
Add leading zero to make
9 bits: $\qquad\qquad\qquad 77_{10} \equiv 001001101$
One's complement = 110110010
Two's complement = 110110011
$$\begin{array}{r} 145 \quad 010010001 \\ -77 \quad 110110011 \quad\text{ADD} \\ \hline 1001000100 \quad 64+4=68_{10} \end{array}$$
The most left hand bit is dropped.

5 (a) | 0 | 1 | 1 | 0 | 1 | 0 | (b) | 1 | 0 | 1 | 1 | 1 | 0 |

6 Because register B shows the *two's complement* of $+2$. Using this form of notation, the operand is *add* not subtract.

Exercises 6.5
Note: In the following answers, the most left hand bit of both the mantissa and the exponent is a sign bit.
 (i) 01000011×0111 (ii) 01001101×0101
 (iii) 01110001×011 (iv) 0100110101×01000
 (v) $0100101101100001 \times 01010$
 (vi) 0111111111×0111 (vii) 01×00
 (viii) 01×101 (ix) 01111×00
 (x) 01111111×0100

Exercises 6.6
1 (a) In floating point representation fractional numbers are represented by a mantissa and an exponent, i.e. a power of 10 or 2.
$$4.5 = 0.45 \times 10^1 \quad\text{or}\quad .45E+01$$
$$4.5 = 100.1 \times 2^{-3} \quad\text{or}\quad .1001 \times 2^3$$

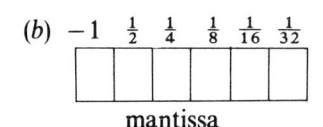

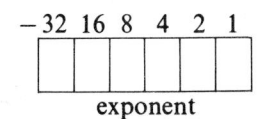

(b) $-1 \quad \frac{1}{2} \quad \frac{1}{4} \quad \frac{1}{8} \quad \frac{1}{16} \quad \frac{1}{32}$

mantissa

Range -1 to $+\frac{31}{32}$

$-32 \quad 16 \quad 8 \quad 4 \quad 2 \quad 1$

exponent

Range -32 to $+31$

2 (a) (i) Binary integer.
 (ii) Number of bits available.
 (iii) Sign and magnitude bit—two's complement form.
 (iv) Floating point mantissa.

 (v) Accuracy of mantissa is direct result of word length.
(b) $3\frac{3}{4} \equiv \quad 011.11 = 0.1111 \times 2^2$
$\qquad\qquad\qquad\qquad = 011110 \quad 000010$
$7\frac{1}{2} \equiv -111.1 = 110001 \times 2^4$
$\qquad\qquad\qquad = 110001 \quad 000100$

Exercises 6.7
 (i) 011110×0111
  Error = 3
 (ii) 100100×0101
  Error = 0.5
 (iii) 10110101101×011
  Error = 0.025
 (iv) 01100000011×01000
  Error = 0.125
 (v) 0111×0110
  Error = 0.75
 (vi) 010011110011×0100
  Error = 0.0015625
 (vii) 0110×1100
  Error = 0.003125
 (viii) 100111111×01000
  Error = 0.125

Exercises 7.1
1 (a) Data is captured at source—there are no intermediate documents. With commodity coding, stock control can be automated. It may reduce the number of employees. There is more regular statistical information for management. Helps prevent petty crime by staff.
(b) Advantages: fewer errors in bill totals; lists the items bought; development of money transfer systems.
Disadvantages: delay if breakdown occurs; lack of personal touch.
3 (a) *Cheque*. Characters are previously encoded on the cheque in magnetic ink in 'reserved areas'. The value of the cheque is typed into a reserved space using magnetic ink when the cheque is presented for payment. The ink is read using MICR devices and data is input directly to a processor.
 Advantages—all standard information (account number, cheque number) is pre-recorded on the cheque; only encoding in magnetic ink of the amount is necessary by humans; approximately 80% of data preparation is eliminated.
(b) *Credit card* (two forms). (i) 'Barclaycard type': Data relating to the customer (only) is embossed into a small plastic card. In use, this data is transferred by carbon, along with details of the transaction, onto a punched card. The data written on the card is then

encoded by punching onto the card. It is processed in the normal way. (ii) 'National Westminster type'. Characters are encoded onto a magnetic stripe which is read as for magnetic tape along with details of the transaction.

Advantages—a very small amount of data preparation is necessary. Details and summary of '*n*' transactions are available to the bank/customer almost as soon as the source documents are sent to the computer centre.

(c) *Mark sense card.* It is similar in appearance to an ordinary punched card but only 40 columns wide because of the extra space taken up by 'bubbles'. These correspond to hole positions and are marked with a soft pencil to encode the data. These marks are read by electrical sensing (carbon marking) or by an optical method (reflection of a light beam from the mark). One type is punched as a punched card (the punchings corresponding to the marks) and read as a normal punched card. Cards can (and usually do) have a special code, e.g. BASIC statements.

Note that the reader only reads *marks*. The position of the marks on the card determines what the mark means. The reader *does not* read characters or numbers.

(d) *Kimball tag.* This is a point of sale device, usually used on clothing sales. Data relating to the garment is punched (by the garment manufacturer) into a small card which is attached to the garment. When sold, the punched card is removed and fed into a computer for stock control etc., either directly using a special card reader at the cash desk, or in batch, once per day.

Advantages—enables automatic stock control, invoicing, accounting etc. No data preparation is needed.

5 (i) *Exchangeable disc store*
(a) Function: backing store device.
(b) Operation: see text.
(c) Use: large volume, fast access storage, importance of random versus sequential organisation.
(ii) *Visual display unit*
(a) Function: input/output device; normally interactive.
(b) Operation: see text.
    VDUs can be of two types: character only, or storage tube (for line drawings, etc.).
(c) Use: interactive device where hard-copy is not essential silent; fast output; use of light pen/storage tube for interactive graphics, e.g. design drawings.
tube for interactive graphics, e.g. design drawings.
(iii) *Teletypewriter*
(a) Function: slow input/output device.
(b) Operation: see text.
(c) Use: hardwired or via modem interface; as slow input/output device, often in interactive situations;

hardcopy provided; noisy; cheap. In a school or college it can be used for input of programs and output of results.
(iv) *Graphical plotter*
(a) Function: graphics output device.
(b) Operation: see text.
(c) Use: in any situation where a permanent record output device is required for a graphical application; production of an architectural drawing.
(v) *Paper tape reader*
(a) Function: medium speed (primary) input device.
(b) Operation: see text.
(c) Use: for the input of programs and other data to a system.

Exercise 8.1

1(a)

Instruction location	Instruction code	Instruction address	Comments
1000	B	2001	Read Y into acc.
1001	S	2000	Subtract X from Y
1002	J	1200	Jump to 1200 if acc. = 0
1003	K	1500	Jump to 1500 if acc. < 0
1004	P	1001	Jump to 1001 for next subtraction

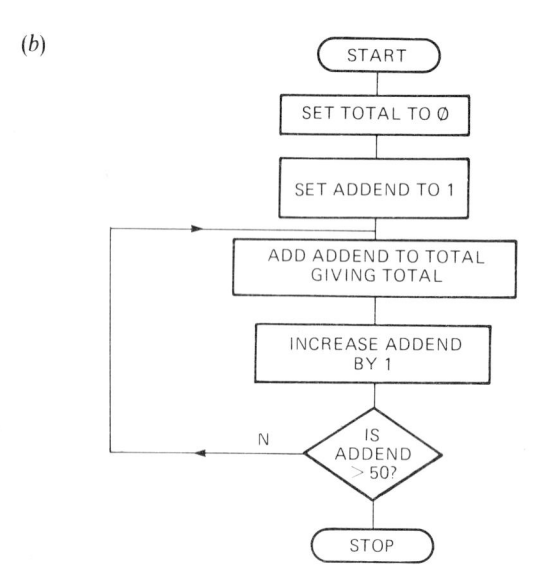

(b)

```
         START
           │
    SET TOTAL TO ∅
           │
    SET ADDEND TO 1
           │
    ┌─────▶│
    │  ADD ADDEND TO TOTAL
    │    GIVING TOTAL
    │      │
    │  INCREASE ADDEND
    │      BY 1
    │      │
    │    IS
    └──N── ADDEND
          > 50?
           │
          STOP
```

Instruction location	Instruction code	Instruction address	Comments
123	L	300	Add 1 to addend
124	B	302	Copy total to acc.
125	A	300	Add in addend
126	C	302	Store total in 302
127	B	300	Copy addend to acc.
128	S	301	Subtract +50
129	K	123	Jump to 123 if acc < 050
130	T		

(c)

```
        START
          │
   SET LAST TO 1
          │
  SET PREVIOUS TO 1
   SET TOTAL TO 2
          │
    ADD LAST TO
     PREVIOUS
    GIVING NEXT
          │
     ADD NEXT
     TO TOTAL
          │
    SET PREVIOUS
     TO LAST
          │
     SET LAST
     TO NEXT
          │
     ADD 1 TO
      COUNT
          │
       IS
     COUNT < 18  ──Y──┐ (loop back)
        ?
        │N
       STOP
```

Exercise 9.1

Data to be collected

(a) Number of pedestrians crossing the road in 15 minute periods.

(b) Number of vehicles using the road throughout the day over a large number of days.

How data is obtained

(a) By survey: manual observation/recording.

(b) By remote recorder: a pneumatic pulse counter records on to cassette.

How data is input to computer

(a) It is punched from special forms used by recording observers to capture pedestrian data on to paper tape/cards/direct entry to mangetic disc/tape.

(b) It is encoded from cassette on to paper tape.

Type of program

Statistical analysis with 'plotter' output, giving graphs of both sets of data—say, as histograms—on the same axes.

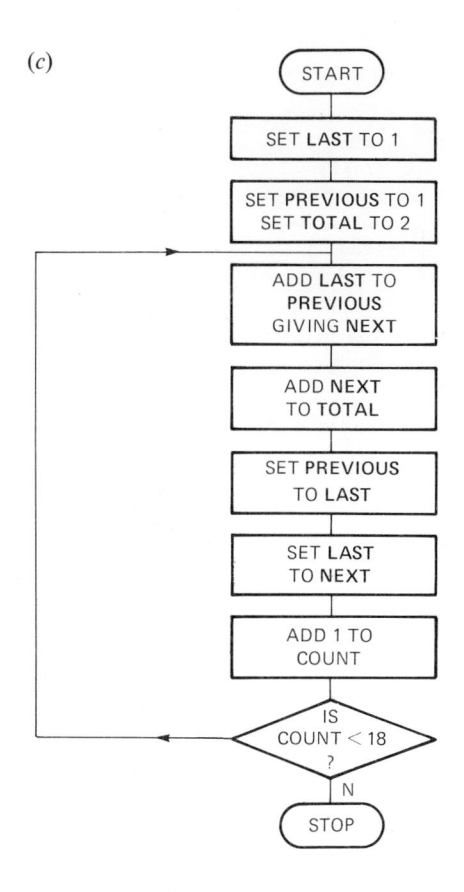

1000	L	105
1001	L	105
1002	L	105
1003	L	105
1004	L	105
1005	B	105
1006	A	105
1007	A	105
1008	A	105
1009	C	105
1010	B	101
1011	A	100
1012	C	103
1013	B	102
1014	A	103
1015	C	102
1016	B	101
1017	C	100
1018	B	103
1019	C	101
1020	L	104
1021	B	104
1022	S	105
1023	K	1010

200 COMPUTER STUDIES

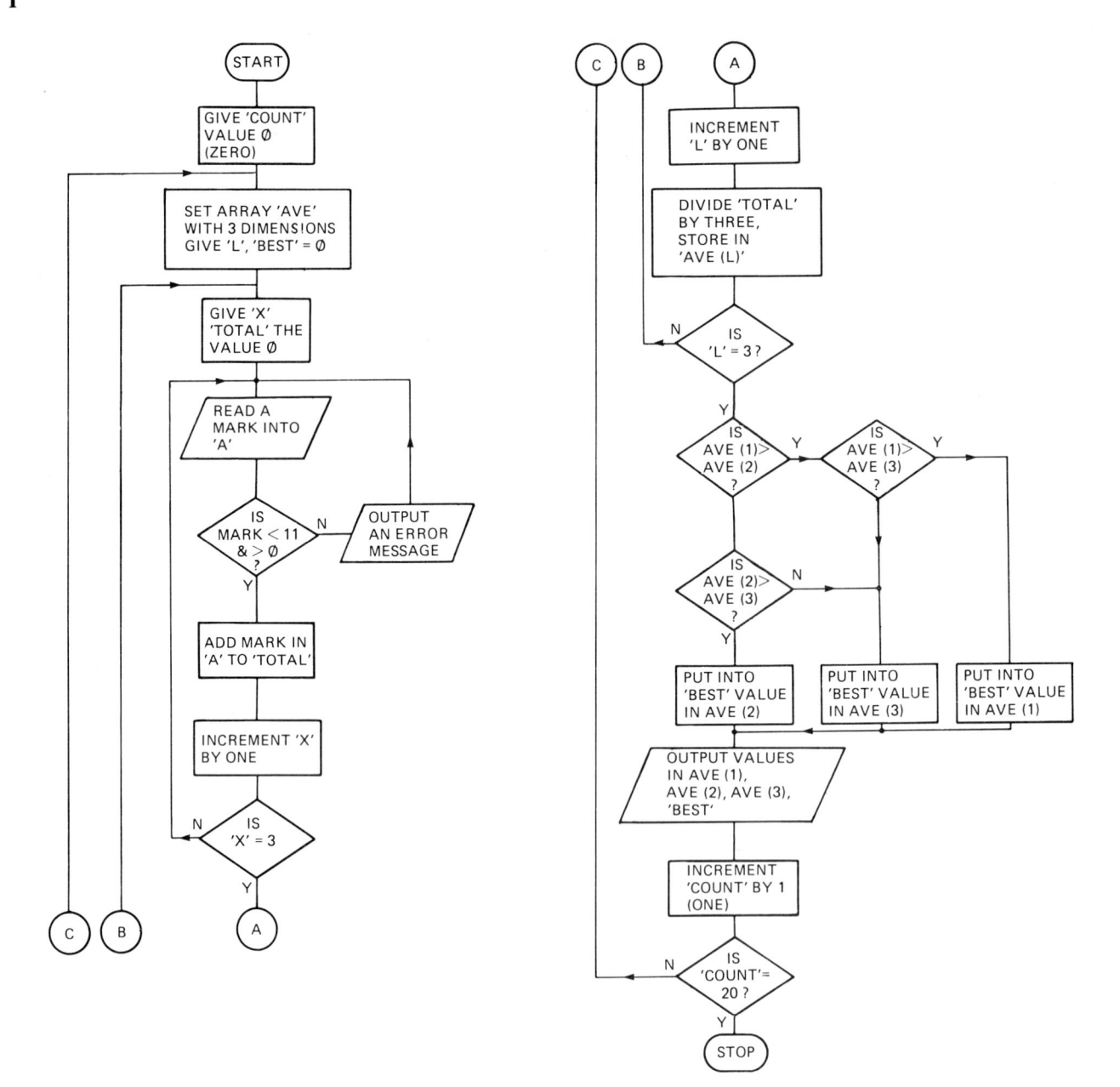

Exercises 9.4

1

```
START
  │
  ▼
GIVE 'COUNT' VALUE Ø (ZERO)
  │
  ▼
SET ARRAY 'AVE' WITH 3 DIMENSIONS
GIVE 'L', 'BEST' = Ø
  │
  ▼
GIVE 'X' 'TOTAL' THE VALUE Ø
  │
  ▼
READ A MARK INTO 'A'
  │
  ▼
IS MARK < 11 & > Ø ? ──N──▶ OUTPUT AN ERROR MESSAGE
  │Y
  ▼
ADD MARK IN 'A' TO 'TOTAL'
  │
  ▼
INCREMENT 'X' BY ONE
  │
  ▼
IS 'X' = 3 ──N──▶
  │Y
  ▼
  A
```

(C) (B)

```
C   B   A
            │
            ▼
        INCREMENT 'L' BY ONE
            │
            ▼
        DIVIDE 'TOTAL' BY THREE, STORE IN 'AVE (L)'
            │
            ▼
        IS 'L' = 3 ? ──N──▶
            │Y
            ▼
        IS AVE(1) > AVE(2) ? ──Y──▶ IS AVE(1) > AVE(3) ? ──Y──▶ PUT INTO 'BEST' VALUE IN AVE (1)
            │N                           │N
            ▼                            ▼
        IS AVE(2) > AVE(3) ? ──N──▶ PUT INTO 'BEST' VALUE IN AVE (3)
            │Y
            ▼
        PUT INTO 'BEST' VALUE IN AVE (2)
            │
            ▼
        OUTPUT VALUES IN AVE (1), AVE (2), AVE (3), 'BEST'
            │
            ▼
        INCREMENT 'COUNT' BY 1 (ONE)
            │
            ▼
        IS 'COUNT' = 20 ? ──N──▶
            │Y
            ▼
        STOP
```

ANSWERS

2

[Flowchart:]

START → PUT NAMES OF CARDS INTO A 52 ELEMENT ARRAY CALLED 'AVAILABLE CARDS' → SET NO. OF CARDS AVAILABLE TO 52 → SET PLAYER INDICATOR TO 1 → GENERATE RANDOM NUMBER IN RANGE 1 TO NO. OF CARDS AVAILABLE → LOOK UP NAME OF CARD FROM 'DICTIONARY' AND ADD TO PLAYER LIST GIVEN BY PLAYER INDICATOR → DELETE CARD FROM AVAILABLE CARDS LIST AND CLOSE-UP FROM BELOW THIS POSITION → SUBTRACT 1 FROM NO OF CARDS AVAILABLE → IS NO' OF CARDS AVAILABLE >0?

If Y → ADD 1 TO PLAYER INDICATOR → IS PLAYER INDICATOR ≤4? If Y, loop back to GENERATE RANDOM NUMBER; if N, loop back to SET PLAYER INDICATOR TO 1.

If N → PRINT OUT EACH PLAYER'S LIST OF CARDS → STOP

3

[Flowchart:]

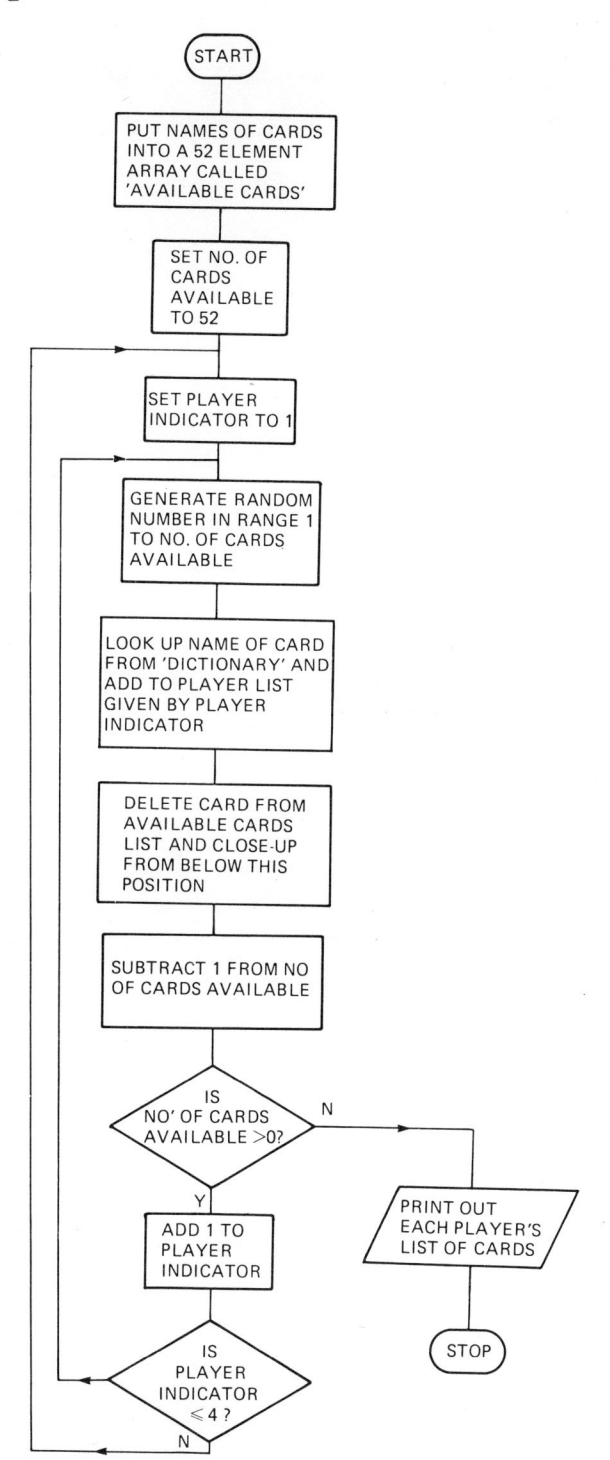

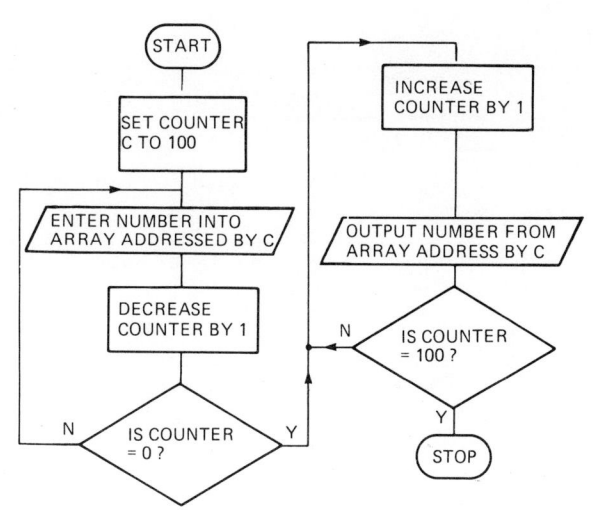

START → SET COUNTER C TO 100 → ENTER NUMBER INTO ARRAY ADDRESSED BY C → DECREASE COUNTER BY 1 → IS COUNTER = 0? If N, loop back to ENTER NUMBER. If Y → OUTPUT NUMBER FROM ARRAY ADDRESS BY C → IS COUNTER = 100? If N → INCREASE COUNTER BY 1 → loop back to OUTPUT NUMBER. If Y → STOP.

Note: First box could be C = 0, then fourth IS C > 100, then need to reset counter to 100 and count down to zero, etc.

4

```
START
  ↓
Stage 1: INPUT a,b,c
  ↓
IS a = 0 ?  —Y→ STOP
  ↓ N
IS a+b > c ?  —N→ ──┐
  ↓ Y                │
IS b+c > a ?  —N→ ──┤
  ↓ Y                │
IS a+c > b ?  —N→ ──┤
  ↓ Y                ↓
                OUTPUT "NO △ POSSIBLE"
Stage 1
  ↓
LET P = a+b+c
  ↓
OUTPUT 'PERIMETER EQUALS P'   ─ Stage 2
  ↓
LET S = P/2
  ↓
LET D = s(s−a)(s−b)(s−c)
  ↓
AREA = √D
  ↓
OUTPUT 'AREA = AREA'   ─ Stage 3
  ↓
(loop back to START)

Stage 4
```

5

```
START
  ↓
SET DAYS TO 1
  ↓
EXAMINE TICKET TYPE
  ↓
INCREASE TOTAL PASSENGERS BY 1
  ↓
1ST CLASS ? —Y→ SINGLE ? —Y→ INCREASE 1ST SINGLE BY 1
  ↓ N              ↓ N
SINGLE ? —Y→ INCREASE 2ND SINGLE BY 1
  ↓ N          DAY RETURN ? —Y→ INCREASE 1ST DAY BY 1
DAY RETURN ? —Y→ INCREASE 2ND DAY BY 1   ↓ N
  ↓ N                                  INCREASE 1ST PERIOD BY 1
INCREASE 2ND PERIOD BY 1
  ↓
ANY MORE TICKETS TODAY ? —Y→ (loop)
  ↓ N
OUTPUT TOTAL PASSENGERS
  ↓
OUTPUT ALL TICKET-TYPE SUB-TOTALS
  ↓
ADD 1ST DAY TO 2ND DAY, AND DIVIDE RESULT BY TOTAL OF DAYS
  ↓
OUTPUT DAY RETURN AVERAGE
  ↓
STOP

ANY MORE DAYS LEFT ? —Y→ INCREASE DAYS TOTAL BY 1
```

6

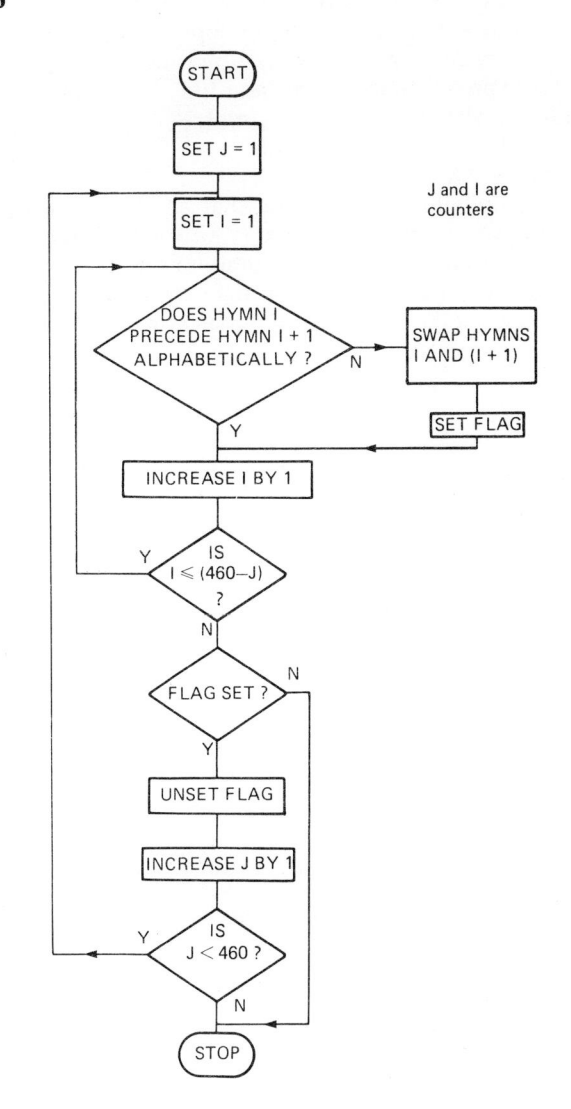

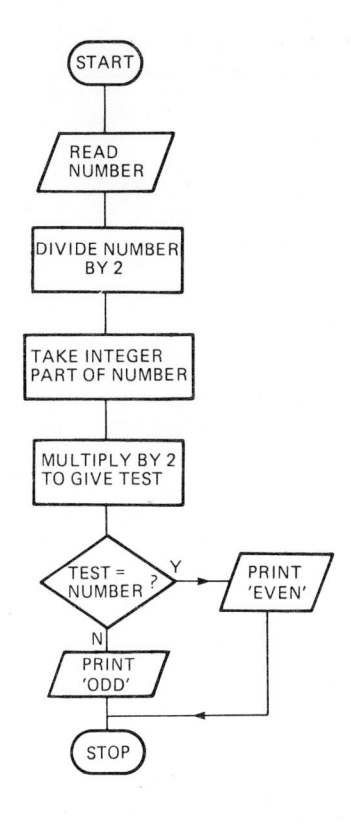

[Flowchart for sorting hymns:
START → SET J = 1 → SET I = 1 → DOES HYMN I PRECEDE HYMN I+1 ALPHABETICALLY?
- N → SWAP HYMNS I AND (I+1) → SET FLAG → (join)
- Y → INCREASE I BY 1 → IS I ≤ (460−J)?
  - Y → back to DOES HYMN I PRECEDE...
  - N → FLAG SET?
    - N → back to SET I = 1 area (via IS J < 460?)
    - Y → UNSET FLAG → INCREASE J BY 1 → IS J < 460?
      - Y → back to SET I = 1
      - N → STOP

J and I are counters]

7(a)

[Flowchart:
START → READ NUMBER → DIVIDE NUMBER BY 2 → TAKE INTEGER PART OF NUMBER → MULTIPLY BY 2 TO GIVE TEST → TEST = NUMBER?
- Y → PRINT 'EVEN' → STOP
- N → PRINT 'ODD' → STOP]

(b) Two versions of a program in **BASIC** are shown here. Any program that is correct, written in any dialect of *any* high level language is acceptable.

```
10 READ N
20 DATA 1,7,13,24,35,46,-1
30 IF N=-1 THEN END
40 T=INT(N/2)*2
50 IF T=N THEN 80
60 PRINT N" IS ODD":GOTO 10
80 PRINT N" IS EVEN":GOTO 10
```

```
10 FOR Q=1 TO 6
20 INPUT "NEXT NUMBER ",N
30 IF N>100 THEN 20
40 T=INT(N/2)*2
50 IF T=N THEN 70
60 PRINT N" IS ODD":GOTO 80
70 PRINT N" IS EVEN":GOTO 80
80 NEXT
```

8

A	B	C	Is B = 3?	Is A = 3?	Output
1	2	0	N		3
1	3	3	Y	N	
2	2	4	N		4
2	3	4	Y	N	
3	2	5	N		5
3	3	5	Y	Y	3 3 6
		6			

Exercises 9.5

1 Steps in project: (i) feasibility study (ii) system specification (iii) program specifications (iv) coding (v) testing (vi) live running. Some of these stages will proceed in parallel. (i) produces a detailed report on the feasibility of the project with reference to the facilities, manpower, money and time available. It gives its likely savings over a manual system (if any), its development potential and its running costs. (ii) sets out an overall picture of the system to be produced.

This will specify details of files required including their structure, programs needed and operating system requirements. An estimate of storage space needed should now be made.

From this, program specifications can be produced, giving precise details of what the programs are to do with the various files. These are then used by the programmers to develop their flowcharts and from these, the programs.

When coded, the programs can be 'brought live' in sections, each section being tested by suitable data.

Data capture relating to the student and the staff timetable will require suitable forms to obtain the necessary information. The design of these forms will form an important part of the project. When completed, the data on the forms will need to be coded or punched directly into the relevant files. User documentation should be developed in parallel with all the foregoing.

When the system becomes live, debugging will be necessary, followed by testing using 'real data', then the system can be released to the user along with the relevant documentation. The user documentation will contain the systems flowcharts; details of data input needed; how to input this data; approximate processing time; expected output; error message and recovery procedure. Any faults should be reported to the project team immediately.

2 The documentation should include the following:
(i) description of what the program is designed to do
(ii) data required by the program
(iii) how to load the program
(iv) instructions for running the program
(v) error messages and 'what to do next'
(vi) expected running time and time for output
(vii) expected output with sample
(viii) logging-off instructions.

Exercises 9.6

1 A compilation error is one that shows up during compilation time, e.g. a syntax error—LEP A.

An execution error is one that only shows up after successful compilation, during the running (execution) of the program, e.g. a logical error—division by zero.

2 (a)

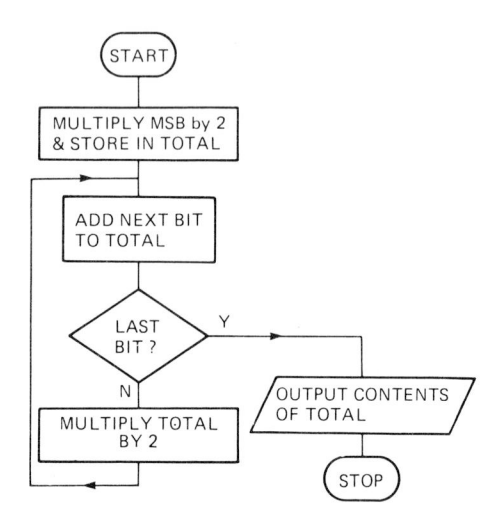

```
          START
            |
    MULTIPLY MSB by 2
    & STORE IN TOTAL
            |
    ┌──────►|
    │       |
    │  ADD NEXT BIT
    │    TO TOTAL
    │       |
    │       |
    │    LAST    Y
    │    BIT? ──────►
    │       |         |
    │       N         |
    │       |         |
    │  MULTIPLY TOTAL │
    │     BY 2        |
    │       |         |
    └───────┘    OUTPUT CONTENTS
                    OF TOTAL
                         |
                       STOP
```

(b)

Input	Next bit	Total	Last?
101110	1	2	
	0	2	
	0	2	No
	0	4	
	1	4	
	1	5	
	1	5	No
	1	10	
	1	11	
	1	11	No
	1	22	
	1	23	No
	1	46	
	0	46	Yes

(c) Change 2 in first and bottom boxes to *n*.

3 (a)

C	T	A	Is A = −1?	Output
0	0	3	N	
1	3	10	N	
2	13	6	N	
3	19	4	N	
4	23	2	N	
5	25	−1	Y	5

(b) A loop.
(c) A rogue value.
(d) The running total of the data.
(e) The count of the number of items of data.
(f) It calculates the mean of the input data.

Exercises 11.1

1 (i) *Punched cards*
A record may consist of more than one card. Each card is sub-divided into fields, e.g. name, address, sex. A field consists of a specified number of characters, which may not all be used on each record.

(ii) *Paper tape*
As one record 'runs into the next' on paper tape, an end of record marker is needed to separate records, usually a control character. The fields are as in punched cards, but it is more usual to have variable length records on tape. If not, the field lengths are usually made up with spaces.

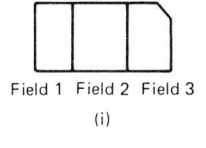

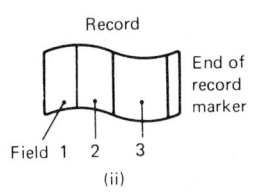

(iii) *Magnetic tape*
There are x fields per record as on paper tape. The shaded area is the interblock gap, necessary to allow starting and stopping of the tape. There may be several records to a block.

(iv) *Magnetic disc*
The records are sub-divided into fields as previously.

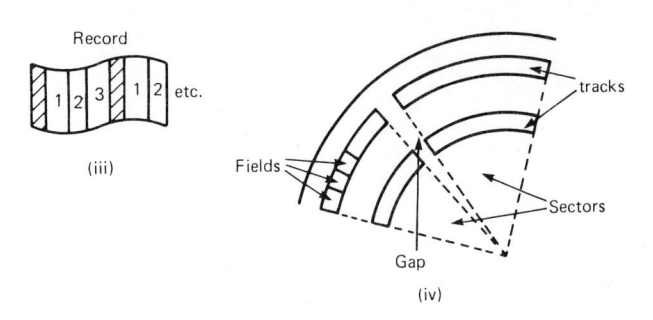

2 (a) Permanent records: name; sex; date of birth; parents name; address; medical history; previous school; date of admission; admission number; exams entered and results.

Temporary records: present form/tutor group; subjects being studied; post fifth form interest; career interest; attendance; subject marks/grades from exams/continuous assessment.

Data that needs to be changed each year: form/tutor group; exam records; subjects being studied; any change in post fifth form or career interest. This is achieved by file up-dating: new entries are added to the file, leavers removed from the pupil file and transferred to a former pupil file. All information relating to up-dating is prepared off-line and an update file created. The old master file is up-dated to a new master file, probably once a year, but more often if necessary.

(b) For a single enquiry, a disc system is preferable. Real time application needs discs. The disc file gives immediate access for single enquiries. A sequentially-organised tape file is useful when producing reports requiring reading of most of the file.

4 (a)

Field name:	Year	Make	Model	Colour	Condition	Price
Type	numeric	alphanumeric	alphanumeric	alpha	alpha	numeric
Size (characters)	4	15?	15?	10?	20?	5
Example	1968	Ford	Zephyr	maroon	moderate	300

4 (*Continued*)

(*b*) Random access, because of its speed and frequency of updating. If the size of field is the maximum needed, all new data will fit into existing blank records.

(*c*) *File creation.* (i) Input from tape/cards from source documents (or direct from terminal or from key to disc). (ii) Validation by program. (iii) File written by program using valid records. (iv) File printout for visual checking.

Interrogation. A standard package such as **FILETAB** or a purpose written program would be used to read the file and look for hit records/field(s). Such 'hits' may then be dumped to a scratch file for subsequent output if required.

Changing data. Use an updating program to delete the record when the car is sold; to change the field(s) in any record to amend data (price); to insert new record for new stock.

5 (*a*) Any suitable form depending on the method of data capture chosen. An example is given below. The form should show pre-defined areas for each field.

(*b*) Each item/product is a record in itself. Each record contains four fields which are item no., item name, manufacturer code, location code.

(*c*) As it is an on-line stock control system, immediate/direct access is required, so therefore magnetic disks/drums are most suitable.

(*d*) Quantity.

(*e*) Price; colours; sizes etc.; stock levels; present; re-order figures etc.

6 (*a*) The 'maximum' birth date could be 31.12.67. The students' sexes can be coded as 1 for male and 0 for female. The form can be coded as a two-digit number e.g. 4K ≡ 18. The date of birth can be considered as a single six-digit number which requires 19 bits for encoding in pure binary. A two-digit denary number requires 8 bits, giving a total of 25 bits.

Examples: 31.12.67 will code as

1 0 0 1 0 1 1 1 1 1 1 1 1 0 0 0 1 1

Male will code as 1
18 will code as 1 0 0 1 0
Giving:

1 0 0 1 0 1 1 1 1 1 1 1 1 0 0 0 1 1 1 1 0 0 1 0

A female in 4K born on the 1st January 1967 will code as:

0 0 0 0 0 1 0 0 1 1 1 1 0 1 1 0 1 1 1 0 1 0 0 1 0

Note that BCD uses 36 bits: 24 for the date; 4 for the sex and 8 for the form.

(*b*) Using Mod 11 check digit, 311267118 ÷ 11 gives a remainder of 8, which becomes the check digit. When 3112671188 is divided by 11, there is no remainder.

8 Most data-processing applications require a *master* file which is the main reference file and is usually updated using a *transaction* file. It is normal to retain three *generations* of file; the most recent version is the *son* file, the *father* file is the previous version of the file and the oldest version is known as the *grandfather* file. The *father* file would be used to produce a new son file should that file become *corrupted*.

Exercises 12.1

1 (i) *Machine tool control.* Data collection: *punched tape prepared in advance* or specially designed chip. Input/output: paper tape reader; servomotors; *mechanism*. Processor: small dedicated mini- or micro-computer, unless multiple control is required (i.e. several machines); real time processing; limited need for storage. Human element: preparation of control tapes direct from drawings; supervision of machines.

(ii) *Weather forecasting.* Data collection: telephone/telex; direct data entry from remote observation stations and from baloons and satellites, Input/output: paper tape/cards; VDU; *lineprinter/plotter*. Processor: large, IAS fast; mathematical modelling application; discs/tapes. Human element: accuracy of captured date and its transmission/encoding.

(iii) *Theatre seat reservation.* Data collection: teletype/*VDU* at point of sale; keypunch. Input/output: as above. Processor: large *multiaccess system* supporting many remote terminals; real-time file interrogation and update application; disc/tapes. Human element: accuracy of input data.

(iv) *Medical Diagnosis.* Data collection: teletype/*VDU*; possibly transducers. Input/output: teletype/*VDU*/lineprinter/plotter. Processor: large filing capacity—discs/tapes; essentially file interrogation (*information retrieval*) application. Human element: skill in interpretation of results; highly *specialised programs* required.

3 In part (*a*), the answer to any category must be more than a simple statement. Examples of answers for part (*a*):
(i) Pupil records; staff records; school accounts; option schemes; timetabling; resource allocation; staff cover (in absences); stock control (text books and consumable items); library cataloguing and referencing.
(ii) Simulation of experiments in biology and physics, particularly where (long) time or danger (e.g. high voltage) are variables; text or word analysis in English; contour drawing from linear cross-sections in Geography.
(iii) Standard tests in any discipline conducted by and for an individual student from the keyboard with automatic up-dating of the student's record; special tests written for a particular topic/purpose/student group: general knowledge tests; IQ testing.
(iv) (Computer based learning); special programs written to teach and test; repetitive testing of simple (arithmetic) concepts.

In part (*b*) marks would be awarded on the following factors: *System* flowchart (not programming flowchart); data capture, or data input or preparation; documentation; computer/terminal use; output.

4 Marks to be awarded under the following categories:
(i) clear explanation of the problem to be investigated
(ii) directions and instructions on loading the program into the computer and running
(iii) test run using small amount of dummy data
(iv) clear description of parameters to be input including any limits to permissable values
(v) description of common error messages—only ones likely to be encountered in running the program
(vi) instruction of what to do when error message received
(vii) flow chart of process (not program)
(viii) indication of time needed to use program (If input/process/output are very different, e.g. long input for statistics, comment to this effect.)
(ix) instructions on how to restart after error or to abort program run
(x) closing down.

5 The actual answer will depend on the type of system chosen, but marks would be awarded under the following headings:
(*a*) Overall description of the system: what it can be used for (teaching, administration, CAL, testing etc). Description of the hardware, commenting on size of IAS, backing store, ease of use, portability and price. Notes on the software availability of packages, ease of use of software, availability of more than BASIC. Processing methods (is batch processing possible?). Data preparation. Use of the facilities.
(*b*) Description of the manual task. Use of a computer to perform the above. Advantages and disadvantages of a computer system compared with the manual system. Input needed and output expected.

One example would be needed for each of the persons named: head teacher (statistics concerning all students), secretary (names and addresses held on file for easy access), librarian (record of book issues), subject teacher (exam and test analysis), tuck shop supervisor (stock control and accounting).

Exercise 12.2
The following factors should be mentioned:
(i) A powerful microcomputer would be used
(ii) The input device would probably be a keyboard; possibly voice.
(iii) There would be a simple output device—a television set with hard copy output.
(iv) A connection to the computer either via Telecom network or via dedicated data network would be unlikely for ordinary home use but could be viable to link, for example, partners in a stockbroking firm.
(v) Computers would be provided on a regional basis with facility to connect through the local 'exchange' to any other computer (different data banks).
(vi) The Open University principle would be extended to allow on-line interrogation.
(vii) Types of jobs would include: education (Open University idea), general calculator, information retrieval, engineering design, news and weather reports (on demand), travel information, timetables, seat reservations (travel, holiday, theatre), medical diagnostics, storage of privately filed information.

Exercises 13.1
1 Obviously, there cannot be one answer to this question. Marks are awarded for reasoned comments based on actual fact for the effects which have taken place and for good ideas about future effects. Do not go into great detail about any single point, try and cover a number of quite different aspects and don't get carried away with science fiction when discussing the future.

2 (*a*) A data bank is a collection of data/data bases independent of any particular application. The data is supplied by different people and from different

sources accessed by different users.

(b) Many applications may be quoted, for example the Police National Computer (including DLV data base), Prestel, health authority, BLAISE, Stock Exchange legal Applications, House of Commons.

(c) Causes for concern:

(i) Data collected for one purpose could be used for another (e.g. mailing lists in commercial exploitation). Use by government for political/personal surveillance, (e.g. access to credit cards/POS terminals records). Unauthorised access to data by individuals for political/commercial/criminal gain.

(ii) Security of data and access by wrong users.

(iii) Integrity of data. Incorrect data may give wrong information on, for example, credit company black lists.

(iv) Security of software.

Remedies could include: a data Protection Agency with wide powers; laws to allow individuals access to data concerning themselves; licensing of 'proprietors' of data bases; use of pass words/terminal blocks, etc; constant visual checks on data.

3 (a) The information will already be held in the company personnel department and should be transcribed for input to the computer by the personnel department on to two separate data preparation forms. The first will hold data items 1–8 (which are not usually considered 'private'), and the second items 9–14. Two separate files to hold this data will be prepared by different data preparation staff, possibly at different times or even using an outside agency to compile one file. The files may be merged to form a master file, or kept separate but used together for any file accessing.

(b) Any employee should be able to see his own record. Only personnel department staff should have access to the master file. Security is improved by keeping the data in two files but if a single file is created it should have at least one password embedded in the file which will prevent unauthorised access.

4 (a) *Car assembly* is repetitious and dirty, and workers have to get into awkward positions. Robots can do the same work more quickly with unvarying accuracy. They are easily re-programmed to do a new job without the need for human re-training.

Cash dispensing is a necessary counter function in banks. The service only available when the bank is open. Cash dispensers provide 24 hour service giving cash and other information relating to the status of customers' account.

Plant control requires many humans to monitor many instruments. Error signals can be ignored or unseen. It is a boring job waiting for an error which might never happen, but a human can do only one job satisfactorily. Computer monitoring is continuous, misreading cannot occur, many more factors can be monitored by one computer. There is automatic print-out of status and errors.

(b) *Teaching*: Computers have very limited ability to interact other than under human control. Other examples from services include waitresses and hairdressers.

(c) (i) Computers can create jobs.

(ii) Many jobs cannot be 'computerised'.

(iii) Computers need software which has to be written by humans.

Answers to revision questions

1 (a) Account number (link to name and address); previous meter reading; present meter reading; tariff code.

(b) See diagram.

(c) (i) Account number; present meter reading.

(ii) Account number; name; address; previous meter reading; tariff code.

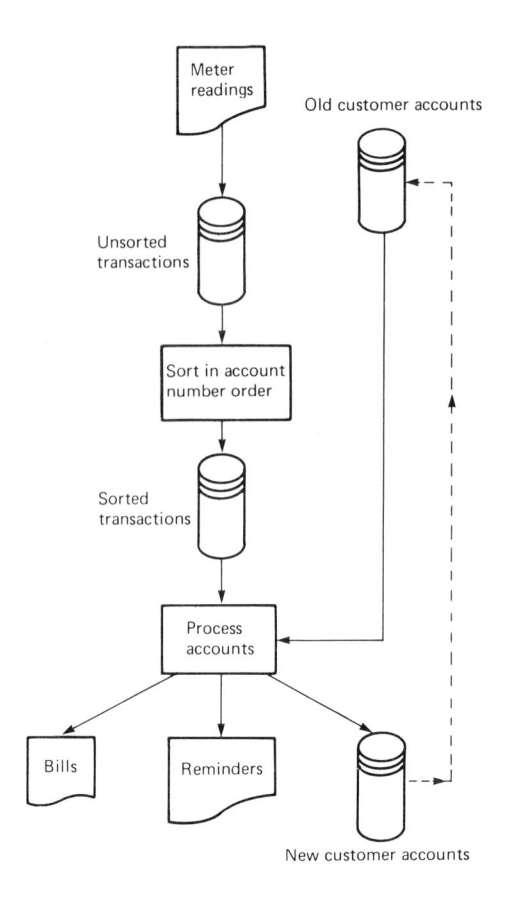

2

Dates*	First 1946–1959(?)	Second 1959(?)–1968(?)	Third 1968(?)–
Names†	Pegasus, Orion, Einac, Madm, Leo	Elliott 803, 903, 4130 IBM 7090; ICL 1900 Atlas	ICL 1900A series IBM 370 series ICL 1900S series
Hardware	*valves*, delay line/cathode ray tube storage	*transistors*, magnetic core store	*integrated circuits*, magnetic core store
Software	*machine code, assemblers,* autocodes	machine code, assemblers, autocodes, *high level languages*	machine codes, assemblers, high level languages, *conversational languages*
Mode of use	*batch* only	*multiprogramming*, some multiaccess, real time	multiprogramming, multiaccess, multiprocessor nets, local intelligent, terminals, *real time*
Operating system	manual	manual and executives	full operating systems
Nature of use	*scientific/ mathematical*	predominantly *commercial*, scientific/ mathematical, some process control	commercial, scientific/ mathematical, *real time process control*
Any special features	addition times in milliseconds	(only Atlas had paged memory), times in microseconds, use of discs	virtual storage (paged memory), times in nanoseconds, use of cassettes, floppy discs
	comparison of relative speeds of arithmetic		

* Dates need only be approximate i.e. ± 2 years
† At least one name or number per generation.

4

	Speed	Power	Reliability
	ms → ns	× 100	Poor to very high
Hardware	Valves → transistors → integrated circuit, more rapid switching, less transmission delay. Faster peripherals for input and output. Faster IAS: delay line to bubble memory. Introduction of disks as fast access backing store.	Closely coupled with speed: as speed capability increased, so amount of data which could be processed in a given time increased.	Valves generated heat and burned-out. Early transistors (germanium) also unreliable. Silicon transistors much more stable. Integrated circuits almost 100% reliable. Fewer inter-connections, less faulty joints. More components formed in solid state. Easier replacement if faulty. Sophisticated testing procedures to identify faulty part.
Software	Machine code → assemblers → mnemonic function codes → autocodes → low-level languages → high-level languages. Paging.	Introduction of supervisor type programs leading to full operating systems, job control languages, multi-programming, multiaccess.	Introduction of techniques for exhaustive testing of software before implementation. Use of disks to update software (cf instructions on paper).

5 (*a*) On-line; real-time. Immediate/changing information; must be passed on at once.
(*b*) Off-line. The tags can be collected and sent for batch processing.
(*c*) On-line; speed of return of results is critical, but real-time not necessary. Recent update is satisfactory.

6
```
10 REM GEOG TEST
20 FOR J=1 TO 5
30 READ A$(J),B$(J)
40 NEXT J
50 DATA "FRANCE","PARIS","WALES","CARDIFF"
,"SPAIN","MADRID","AUSTRALIA","CANBERRA","
JAPAN","TOKYO"
60 PRINT "INFORMATION ABOUT THE TEST AND
SCORING...."
70 FOR J=1 TO 5
80 PRINT "WHAT IS THE CAPITAL CITY OF    "
;A$(J)
90 INPUT C$
100 IF C$=B$(J) THEN 130
110 PRINT"INCORRECT ANSWER"
120 GOTO 150
130 PRINT" CORRECT ANSWER-2 POINTS"
140 T=T+2
150 NEXT J
160 S=T*10
170 PRINT" YOUR SCORE IS";S;"%"
180 END
```

7 (*a*) There are immediate advantages in stock control, invoicing, accounting, payroll. More accurate and up-to-date information will be available, particularly in stock control. The use of terminals in remote distributors enables spares to be located if they are not available at the enquiry point. Agricultural machinery spares suggests some very large parts which could not be held at every depot. There are unlikely to be redundancies as stores and despatch departments employ few staff, mostly in despatch. Sales representatives use terminals (daily) to effect orders and can be updated with new sales information when necessary.

There are probably no disadvantages except possibly education of the staff into the new system and its cost.

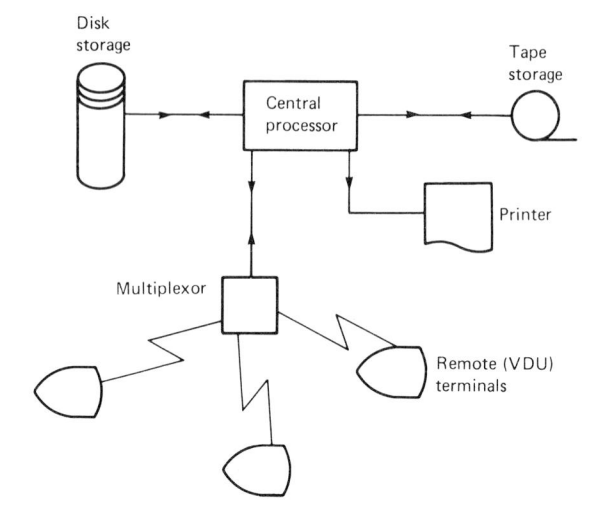

ANSWERS 211

(b) The application suggests: a small central processor with minimum size IAS; disc store; tape store; remote terminal switching unit; remote terminals (teletype or VDU); line printer.

8 (a) (i)

A Bloggs & Co. Vat No:	£ p	VAT £ p
To materials used in construction of extension	975 55	146 33
To labour used in construction of extension	463 12	69 47
To materials supplied by J. Sparks for electrical work	338 23	50 73
To labour, electrical installation	155 92	23 39
To materials supplied by V. Leaky for plumbing work	207 41	31 11
To labour, plumbing	103 03	15 45
	2243 26	336 48
Total (including VAT at 15%)	2579 74	
A. Mugg esq. 15 High St. Anytown.		

(ii) The cost of materials would be calculated from a detailed account prepared by Bloggs or by the subcontractor. The labour cost would have been itemised at so many hours at such-and-such a rate per hour, including allowance for overheads. VAT would have to be calculated.

(b) If this was handled by computer, then each item would have to be put into machine-readable form, including the verbal explanation. VAT and totalling would be performed by computer.

10 (a) *Magnetic tape*: data is stored in frames; Local magnetisation in one of two directions; One character per frame; 7–9 tracks per tape; approximately 600 000 characters per metre; 700 metres per reel; serial access; £1000–£3000 per handler unit.
Floppy Disk: Local magnetisation on sectors on a number of concentric circular tracks; Plastic flexible 13 cm or 20 cm disk coated with metal oxide; retrieval by reference track and position on track; Up to one million characters per disk; read at approximately 1000 characters per second; direct access; cost £300–£1000 per unit; transfer is quick and easy.

Bubble store: magnetic field on level surface; tiny cylinders/bubbles are magnetised in opposite direction to surface material; up to 750 000 bits can be stored in an area 10 mm × 10 mm; immediate access; faster than tapes/disk; less expensive than immediate access store.

(b) *Numbers*: Usually stored using strings (bytes) (words, bits), of binary digits (usually 6), e.g. 000101 = the number 5. However, the size of the maximum number may be limited by the size of byte (or explanation of BCD). Description of floating point.
Characters: These are stored using internal character codes. The number of bits in the code decides how many characters can be coded e.g.

H   E   L   P
101000 / 100101 / 101100 / 110000

(c) Range checks (e.g. marks for examination out of 100 must be in the range 0–100); check digits to ensure that correct account number is being used. Hash totals.

13 (a) 0 0 0 0 0 0 0 0   0 0 0 0 0 0 0 0   1 1 1 1 0 1 1 1
(b) 0 0 1 1 0 0 1 0   0 0 1 1 0 1 0 0   0 0 1 1 0 1 1 1
In (a) the code is pure binary and in (b) the ISO 7 bit code has been used. The eighth (leading) bit has been set to zero.

14

100	I	500
101	I	501
102	I	502
103	B	502
104	S	501
105	C	502
106	K	110
107	C	501
108	D	500
109	B	500
110	J	112
111	P	102
112	T	

Multiple choice answers

1	*a*	2	*d*	3	*c*	4	*b*	5	*b*
6	*a*	7	*d*	8	*a*	9	*b*	10	*b*
11	*d*	12	*d*	13	*b,c*	14	*c*	15	*b*
16	*c*	17	*d*	18	*b*	19	*c*	20	*d*
21	*a*	22	*a*	23	*c*	24	*d*	25	*d*
26	*b*	27	*a*	28	*b*	29	*c*	30	*b*
31	*a*	32	*b*	33	*a*	34	*b*	35	*c*
36	*b*	37	*b*	38	*d*	39	*a, d*	40	*b*
41	*a*	42	*b*	43	*c*	44	*c*	45	*c*
46	*c*	47	*d*	48	*b*	49	*b*	50	*d*

Index

accessing a record, 124
accounting, 152
acoustic coupler, 79
accuracy of representation, 16
adding a record, 138
AEB code, 75
airlines, 157
air traffic control, 164
ALGOL, 77
alpha-numeric data, 1
amending a record, 140
analogue data, 17
analogue representation, 17
analogue to digital conversion, 39
analytical engine, 2
AND gate, 33
annotated listing, 89
application package, 80
application program, 80
applications programmer, 174
arithmetic error, 49
arithmetic unit, 65
ASCII (code), 16
assembly language, 74

Babbage Charles, 2
BABS, 157
backing store, 66
badge reader, 55
banking, 153
Barclaycard, 24
Barclays' Bank, 154
bar code, 56
bar code reader, 160
Basic, 77
batch processing, 78
BCD, 30
binary code, 14
binary coded decimal, 30
binary search, 103
binary subtraction, 44
binary word, 29
Boolean operators, 130
British Airways Booking System, 157
bubble memory, 166, 69

CAD, 37
CAD data bank, 38

card punch, 61
card reader, 56
cash dispensing, 154
cashless society the, 165
catalogue code, 14
CEEFAX, 162
central processor, 62
CESIL, 76
chain printer, 59
character printers, 58
check digit, 27
cheque clearing, 154
chip book, 166
chip technology, 165
circuit designer, 38
clock pulse, 63
CMC7 fount, 54
COBOL, 77
combination check, 26
communications, 166
compiler, 77
compilation error, 77
computer aided design, 37
computer aided learning, 163
computer clinical diagnostics, 161
computer operator, 174
computer staff, 174
control unit, 63
CORAL, 77
core store, 63
course work, 170
CPU, 62
creating a file, 126
cylinder, 128

daisy-wheel printer, 59
data, 1
data bank, 166
data base, 153, 168
data capture, 18
data controller, 174
data processing, 148
data processing manager, 174
data storage, 166
data transcription, 22
data validation, 25
data verification, 25
DC amplifier, 40

214   INDEX

deleting a record, 135
denary to binary conversion, 14
diagnostic aids, 95
dice throwing program, 116
dictaphone, 4
difference engine, 2
digit-sum check, 27
digital data transmission, 166
documentation, 88, 171
document reader, 53
DP staff, 174
drum line printer, 59
dry-run table, 99
dumping, 98
duplex, 80

E13B fount, 54
educational use, 162
effect on employment, 167
effect on freedom, 167
effect on privacy, 168
effect on society, 167
electronic calculator, 7
electronic mail, 4
electronic office, 5
electrosensitive printer, 60
electrostatic printer, 60
EMI body scanner, 69
employment agency, 162
error detection, 94
errors, 93
error messages, 95
error signal, 40
errors in arithmetic, 49
errors in representation, 49
estate agents, 161
even parity, 27
execution error, 94
execute phase, 64
exchange sort, 105
exponent, 47

father file, 133, 148
Ferranti Argus, 164
fetch phase, 64
field, 124
FICO, 158
file creation, 126
file generations, 133, 149
file interrogation, 130
file librarian, 174
file protection, 148
file reading, 127
file security, 147
file storage media, 125
file updating, 133
filing system, 6
finger print files, 158
fixed point number representation, 46
floating point number representation, 47

floppy disk, 68
flowcharting, 82, 171
flowchart symbols, 83
form design, 19
FORTRAN, 77
full adder, 36

garment design, 155
Gerber cutting table, 156
grading rules, 155
grandfather file, 133, 149
graphical display unit, 53
graphics tablet, 57
graph plotter, 61

half-adder, 35
half-duplex, 80
hash total, 28
hexadecimal, 31
high-level languages, 77
hit, 103
Hollerith Herman, 3
holographic store, 69
home-made tracing, 98
home use, 162
hospitals, 160
hybrid computing, 40

IBM 650, 151
ICL 2900, 151
ideas for projects, 170
immediate access store, 62
indexed sequential access, 125
information, 2
ink jet printer, 60
input devices, 52
instruction bits, 30
instruction decoding, 64
intelligent terminal, 25
interactive computing, 78
ISBN code, 14
ISO7 code, App 4
iteration, 111
interpreter, 77
interrogating a file, 130
invoicing, 152

Jacquard Joseph, 3

Key, 103
keyboard, 52
key to disk/tape, 52
Kimbal tag, 56

laser printer, 61
laser scanner, 56, 160
laser store, 69
lay marker, 155
lecture header program, 117
LEO, 151

INDEX

levels of communication, 74
libraries, 8
lightpen, 53
limit check, 26
linear search, 103
logarithms, 2
logical error, 94
longitudinal parity, 27
lottery program, 122

magnetic disk, 127
magnetic disk store, 67
magnetic ink character reader, 54
magnetic tape, 127
magnetic tape store, 67
machine code, 74
mantissa, 47
mark sense card, 24
mark sense document, 24
master file, 123, 148
matrix printer, 60
mechanical calculator, 7
medical use, 160
merge sort, 103
MICR, 154
micro computer, 69, 162
micro film, 8
micro processor, 69
mod 11 check, 28
modem, 78
morse code, 12
multi-access, 78
multi-programming, 78
music synthesis, 62

nand gate, 33
navy flag code, 12
non-intelligent terminal, 25
nor gate, 33
not gate, 33
number guessing program, 122
number of characters check, 26

OCR, 160
octal, 31
on line processing, 78
one's complement, 44
operating system, 78
operation code, 30
operations manager, 174
optical character reader, 53
optical disk store, 69
optical fibre network, 166
optical mark reader, 54
Oracle, 162
or gate, 33
output devices, 58
overflow, 51

papertape, 24

papertape punch, 61
parity check, 26
parity check bit, 26
PASCAL, 77
Pascal Blaise, 3
password, 168
pattern digitiser table, 155
payroll, 151
PERICLES, 153
peripheral devices, 52
personal files, 168
petrol station simulation, 109
photo copier, 4
PLI, 77
point of sale device, 56, 160, 165
police national computer, 158, 165
powers of 2 table, 15
PRESTEL, 162
problem definition, 81
problem specification, 81
process control, 11
programmer, 174
programming flowchart, 84
prompt check, 25
punched card, 24
punched card processing, 7
punched card reader, 24
punched tape reader, 57

Questionnaire design, 19

random access,
random access memory, 63
ranked exam results program, 120
read only memory, 60
real time computing, 164, 10
record, 123
recurring binary fractions, 43
rep. of characters, 16
rep. of fractions, 41
rep. of machine instructions, 29
rep. of negative numbers, 43
remote job entry, 78
restricted value check, 26
rigid disk, 67
robots, 69
rounding error, 51

sampling, 39
school administration, 163
searching, 103
secondary storage, 66
secretarial agencies, 162
semantic error, 94
semiconductor store, 63
sense check, 26
sequential access, 125
serial access, 124
shift register, 65
sign and modulus, 43

sign bit, 47
silicon chip, 38
silicon designer, 38
simplex, 80
simulation, 107
single address system, 30
slide rule, 2
small businesses, 161
software package, 170
solution of polynomials, 112
son file, 133
sorting, 100
sort program, 119
spare part code, 14
square root calculation, 112
stock control, 153
store address bits, 30
symbolic assembly code, 74
syntax error, 94
supermarkets, 159
systems analyst, 174
system builder, 37
systems description, 82
system designer, 38
systems software, 174

tabulator, 3
Teletext, 162
teletypewriter, 57
test data, 172, 101

text editing, 72
three address system, 30
tracing, 95
traffic control, 159
transaction file, 125, 149
trig. curves program, 116
truncation, 51
two address system, 30
two's complement, 44
two state devices, 32
type of data check, 26
typewriter, 4

underflow, 51
universal product code, 56
UPC wand, 160
updating a record, 140
user instructions, 90

verifier, 25
VDU, 24
Viewdata, 162
visual display unit, 52
voice input, 58
voice output, 63, 166
Von Leibniz, 2

wand, 56, 155
weighted mod 11 check, 28
wordprocessor, 4, 71